Future Medicine

Future Medicine

Ethical Dilemmas,
Regulatory Challenges, and
Therapeutic Pathways to
Health Care and Healing in
Human Transformation

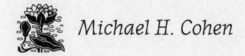 *Michael H. Cohen*

Ann Arbor

The University of Michigan Press

Copyright © by the University of Michigan 2003
All rights reserved
Published in the United States of America by
The University of Michigan Press
Manufactured in the United States of America
⊗ Printed on acid-free paper

2006   2005   2004   2003   4   3   2   1

A CIP catalog record for this book is available from the British Library.

Library of Congress Cataloging-in-Publication Data

Cohen, Michael H.
        Future medicine : ethical dilemmas, regulatory challenges, and
    therapeutic pathways to health care and healing in human
    transformation / Michael H. Cohen.
        p. ; cm.
    Includes index.
    ISBN 0-472-11281-3 (cloth : alk. paper) — ISBN 0-472-08889-0
    (paper : alk. paper)
        1. Alternative medicine.   2. Alternative medicine—Moral and
    ethical aspects.   3. Health planning.   4. Medical care—Law and
    legislation. [DNLM: 1. Delivery of Health Care—trends—Case
    Report.   2. Complementary Therapies—Case Report. 3. Ethics,
    Medical—Case Report. W 84.1 C678f 2002]   I. Title: Ethical
    dilemmas, regulatory challenges, and therapeutic pathways to health
    care and healing in human transformation. II. Title.
    R733 . C646   2002
    610—dc21   2002003606

To Ilana,
And to all the radiant children
With love

Thoughts of Love heal.
Take a thought of the patient
    to God in thought.
Taking will free the sick
Taking will heal the sick
A good idea to give love.
          —Marshall Stewart Ball

The Ocean of Awareness

It is one thing to look at the ocean; quite another to dive in.
The wellspring of ethics
arises from the ocean
of your own awareness.
Therefore, first experience your own inner alchemy; and
    then decide.
Real gold does not fear even the hottest fire.
You are that gold. Now dive
into the crucible
of possibility.
          —Michael H. Cohen

I thank Marshall, who wrote the first poem to
introduce the book.

Contents

Acknowledgments

I thank Karen Adams, M.D., Joseph Finns, M.D., Bridget Guerrera, James Lake, M.D., Deborah Grandinetti, Deborah Holland, Ted Kaptchuk, O.M.D., Kathi Kemper, M.D., Lisa Sjostrom, and Malcolm Riley for reading early drafts of the manuscript and providing insightful and encouraging comments; Maureen Foye, R.N., and Peter Faust, L.Ac., for supportive friendship; David M. Eisenberg, M.D., for being a mentor, colleague, and friend; Christine Carr and Kenneth Mukamal, M.D., for facilitating a process of internal peer review at the Division of General Medicine and Primary Care at Beth Israel Deaconess Medical Center, Boston; Roger Davis, M.D., Kelly Ford, M.D., Mary Beth Hamel, M.D., Russ Phillips, M.D., Christina Wee, M.D., Wendy Weiger, M.D., and other colleagues for providing peer review; my family for an environment that fostered creativity; Barbara Brennan for her gifts as a teacher; Lahila Oppenheimer for life coaching; Elaine Frances Kerry for her special presence in my life; and all my friends, teachers, and companions on the journey. The views in the book are solely my own and not those of any other individual or institution. To all those beings, visible and invisible, whose unwavering support has helped bring this work to fruition, from my heart and with love, I offer acknowledgment and gratitude.

All royalties from sales of this book will go to a not-for-profit foundation dedicated to healing and the exploration of human consciousness.

Introduction

The Growth of Complementary and Alternative Medicine

In the late nineteenth century, the rise of scientific medicine (or bio-medicine) brought ideological and professional coherence to health care; standards for safe, effective, and ethical practice; educational rigor; and recognized parameters for research into the validity of therapies. Biomedicine also provided a clearly articulated framework for understanding health, disease, and mechanisms of remedy in Western, scientific terms and excelled at treating infectious diseases and acute injuries.[1] Biomedical practice followed Newtonian physics and Cartesian dualism in viewing human health largely in a mechanistic and reductionist fashion—for example, understanding the body as a physical system, objectively analyzable in terms of parts, and reducing the complex phenomenon of disease to a standardized set of physical symptoms and cures.[2]

As biomedicine gained political and economic ground in the late-nineteenth-century world of competing medical sects, the biomedical community expelled providers such as homeopaths, naturopaths, and chiropractors from medical societies, prohibited professional association with them, and encouraged prosecution of such providers for unlicensed medical practice.[3] In this way, biomedicine came to dominate not only the delivery of professional health care services in the United States but also legal and regulatory structures governing the delivery of health care.[4]

By the mid–twentieth century, a resurgence of popular interest in therapies such as chiropractic, naturopathy, massage therapy, acupuncture and traditional oriental medicine, nutritional and herbal medicine, folk medicine and spirituality in medicine, and mind-body therapies led to the growth of a recognized movement for "holistic

1

health care" or "alternative medicine."[5] The latter phrase initially was used to define therapies not commonly used in U.S. hospitals or taught in U.S. medical schools.[6] However, as these therapies gained greater footing in U.S. hospitals and in medical school curricula and consumer use of such therapies dramatically expanded, *complementary and alternative medicine* gained recognition as a consensus term for these therapies, which historically had fallen outside of biomedicine.[7] The term *complementary and alternative medical therapies* is also used to describe these modalities.

Complementary and alternative medical therapies have been classified as involving at least seven major fields of practice: (1) mind-body interventions; (2) bioelectromagnetic applications in medicine; (3) alternative systems of medical practice; (4) manual healing methods; (5) pharmacological and biological treatments not yet accepted by mainstream medicine; (6) herbal medicine; and (7) treatments focusing on diet and nutrition in the prevention and treatment of chronic disease.[8] The numerous subfields within these fields have been defined to include, for example, support groups, imagery, hypnosis, biofeedback, yoga, prayer, and mental healing (under "mind-body interventions"); traditional oriental medicine and acupuncture, Ayurveda, homeopathy, naturopathy, and Native American medicine (under "alternative systems of medical practice"); chiropractic and massage therapy (under "manual healing methods"); and European phytomedicine (under "herbal medicine").[9]

By the end of the twentieth century, Congress had funded an Office for Unconventional Medical Practices, which later expanded into the Office of Alternative Medicine and then the National Center for Complementary and Alternative Medicine at the National Institutes of Health (NIH). At the birth of the millennium, the National Center had a $50 million (and growing) budget to stimulate research and enable it to serve as an information clearinghouse for scientists and the public. Congress also had enacted the Dietary Supplements Health Education Act (DSHEA), which allowed manufacturers to distribute dietary supplements without having to prove safety and efficacy, so long as they made no claims linking the supplements to a specific disease. The subsequent market growth of nutraceuticals—for example, the use of dietary supplements, including vitamins, minerals, herbs, and other botanical products—has made some therapies within "complementary and alternative" medicine a widespread part of everyday self-care. The

U.S. nutrition market alone reached $23 billion in 1997, consisting of $12.7 billion in dietary supplements, $7.7 billion in natural foods, and $2.7 billion in personal-care products and representing 31 percent of the $65 billion global nutrition industry.[10] Questions involving potential liability for clinical recommendations of dietary supplements came to the forefront of mainstream practice.

State legislation also increased the visibility and prominence of complementary and alternative medical therapies. By the twentieth century's end, for example, chiropractors had found licensure in every state, acupuncturists and massage therapists in well over half the states, and naturopaths in perhaps a dozen states. Many states mandate insurance benefits for therapies such as chiropractic and massage therapy or require insurance parity where therapeutic services can be provided by complementary and alternative medical providers as well as by physicians and allied health professionals.[11] At least one state, Minnesota, has enacted legislation granting wide latitude to health care providers who provide nonmedical, ancillary modalities but lack health care licensure.[12]

Consumer reliance on complementary and alternative medical therapies has continued to expand dramatically. A 1998 study published in the *Journal of the American Medical Association* revealed a 47 percent increase in total visits to complementary and alternative medical practitioners, from 427 million in 1990 to 629 million in 1997, with total 1997 out-of-pocket expenditures relating to alternative therapies estimated at $27 billion.[13] The study suggests that use of complementary and alternative medicine is likely to continue to increase, particularly as insurance reimbursement for complementary and alternative therapies grows. Further, the study implies that complementary and alternative medical therapies frequently displace biomedicine; are in use alongside biomedical therapies without physician knowledge of or participation in such use; and sometimes are the first route of diagnosis and treatment for patients with chronic disease, back problems, anxiety and depression, and other conditions. Even health maintenance organizations are offering surgical patients guided imagery, spiritual counseling, and other forms of nonbiomedical care.[14]

Increasingly, patients first are searching the Internet rather than approaching health care professionals for health care information. A wide variety of Websites offers information on complementary and alternative medical therapies for many conditions. Patients bring information to their physicians about therapies outside the medical school curriculum. This phenomenon has created opportunities for patients to supplement—or even circumvent—conventional medical care and to pursue or purchase different kinds of health care and health care products on their own. Consumer awareness of risks and benefits relating to complementary and alternative medical therapies also has changed the therapeutic relationship and the kinds of conversations providers and patients can have regarding integration of such therapies into conventional care.

Defining Integrative Medicine

Some segments of the biomedical community react to these developments by denying the growth of a movement away from biomedicine and toward complementary and alternative medical modalities, while others attempt to co-opt and assimilate such modalities.[15] Each approach represents a shift from the strategy of suppression, which was practiced from the late nineteenth century well into the late twentieth century, at which time the court, in *Wilk v. American Medical Association*, declared that the American Medical Association had engaged in a nationwide conspiracy to eliminate the chiropractic profession.[16] The contemporary combination of "burying the head in the sand" and co-opting approaches is expressed by two editorials in leading peer-reviewed medical journals, stating respectively:

> There is no alternative medicine. There is only scientifically proven, evidence-based medicine supported by solid data or unproven medicine.[17]

> There cannot be two kinds of medicine—conventional and alternative. There is only medicine that has been adequately tested . . . [and] if it is found to be reasonably safe and effective, it will be accepted.[18]

These views have been challenged by those observing that the categories, standards, and methods of biomedicine such as randomization, statistical inference, double-blind assessment, and large-scale comparative trials are relatively new in the history of health care and frequently clash with popular desires, autonomy values, and notions of medical pluralism.[19]

Some have used the term *integrative medicine* (or *integrative health care*) to denote some level of clinical integration by physicians of bio-medicine and complementary and alternative medical therapies. Harvard Medical School has created a Division for Research and Education in Complementary and Integrative Medical Therapies. The term *complementary and integrative medical therapies* thus is also emerging to describe the field.

As is described throughout this book, the term *integrative* is complex and expresses a number of different concepts. To date, for example, the clinical parameters of such integration have not been adequately defined or mapped. The problem in part derives from the subjectivity inherent in complementary and alternative medicine itself: in many therapies, there is no generally agreed-upon treatment for a particular diagnosis. For example, one chiropractor will emphasize manipulative techniques, a second nutrition, a third certain therapeutic exercises; one acupuncturist may emphasize herbs, another needling, a third specific meditations. The clinical pathway among providers itself is yet undetermined. Is it better, for example, for a patient with "tennis elbow" to see the chiropractor first or the acupuncturist? Should massage therapy be included in the treatment plan, and where and when is this most therapeutically effective as well as cost-effective?

Further, many physicians insist on an "evidence-based" approach to any such integration, but the evidence—both in favor of and against use of specific complementary and alternative medical therapies—is rapidly changing, and the evidence regarding many possible combinations of conventional and complementary and alternative medical therapies remains unexplored. There may, in addition, be different levels and types of evidence necessary to accept the patient's decision to use certain complementary and alternative medical therapies as opposed to taking an active role in recommending such therapies to the patient.[20] Of course, the argument has been made that for many therapies within biomedicine, there is much less consensus than might be expected or acknowledged; the divergence of opinion with many complementary and alternative medical therapies may be even greater, given the varying streams of medical tradition and varieties of modalities included within the field.

Legal rules governing informed consent also may shed an entirely different light on what must be discussed with or presented to the patient. For example, in states that base the standard for disclosure on what a reasonable *patient* (as opposed to a reasonable *physician*) would consider material to a treatment decision, the physician's perspective on, and comfort with, levels of evidence supporting recommendation of a particular therapy may be less relevant than in states that base disclosure on the reasonable-physician standard.[21] All this suggests that changing terminology does not fully capture the tempest of medical, legal, cultural, and political forces whose collision creates the rich landscape for new models of health care.

I have previously defined integrative medicine (or integrative health care) as the safe, effective, and appropriate integration of conventional medicine with complementary and alternative medical practices, by physicians or allied health providers in conjunction with complementary and alternative medical therapies and providers.[22] By and large, this definition still holds, at least to the extent that the phrase "safe, effective, and appropriate" contains inherent disclaimers that presuppose that clinicians, researchers, and regulators are at the beginning stages of working through the mutually acceptable boundaries of integrative health care. Further, the word "appropriate" lends a qualitative element and sense of balance to the definition. For example, as is discussed in succeeding chapters, "appropriate" suggests that safety and efficacy in this definition are not to be judged solely from the perspective of levels and types of evidence satisfactory to medical consensus but also must be viewed from health care policy perspectives, including those that take into account the value of patient autonomy, the importance of consumer choice, and the concomitant goal of increasing access to complementary and alternative medical therapies.

The working definition proposed is by no means exclusive or definitive. Changing terminology in the field is greatly debated. For example, one definition that is currently circulating views integrative medicine as ongoing efforts to combine the best of conventional and evidence-based complementary therapies while emphasizing the primacy of the patient-provider relationship and the importance of patient participation in health promotion, disease prevention, and medical management. Some have urged that ultimately, modifiers such as "integrative" should be dropped entirely, with everything referred to as "medicine"; other prefer the more generic "health care" to "medicine." Although the terminological landscape may continue to shift, several underlying concepts frame a broader system of health care than conventionally defined.

One current exploration of the definition of integrative medicine is occurring at the Program in Integrative Medicine at the University of Arizona Medical Center. The program presently defines integrative medicine as "a healing-oriented medicine that draws upon all therapeutic systems to form a comprehensive approach to the art and science of medicine."[23] The program articulates several underlying principles of integrative medicine. While these principles may not be universally accepted—and indeed, may describe some aspects of conventional care—they do suggest a commitment to the value of a personal psychotherapeutic process between both provider and patient.

Thus, the principles include the following:

a partnership between patient and practitioner in the healing process; appropriate use of conventional and alternative methods to facilitate the body's innate healing response; consideration of all factors that influence health, wellness and disease, including mind, spirit, and community as well as body; a philosophy that neither rejects conventional medicine nor accepts alternative medicine uncritically; recognition that good medicine should be based in good science, inquiry driven and open to new paradigms; use of natural, less invasive interventions whenever possible; the broader concepts of promotion of health, and the prevention of illness as well as the treatment of disease; practitioners as models of health and healing, committed to the process of self-exploration and self-development.[24]

In one sense, these principles sound like a return to the earlier concept of "holistic" care: the notion that the whole being must receive attention in the process of diagnosis and treatment rather than the symptoms being reduced to a standardized, diagnostic disease category and procedures being prescribed for treatment independent of the mental, emotional, spiritual, nutritional, environmental, and other factors surrounding the origin of illness. Advocates of "integrative medicine" probably would argue, however, that this new movement goes beyond the earlier concepts of holistic care by bringing together biomedicine and complementary and alternative medicine; at the same time, conventional physicians may argue that biomedical care, at its finest, incorporates sensitivity to environmental, emotional, and spiritual factors affecting patient health.

For the present, while the clinical and legal parameters of integrative medicine take shape, the way that one defines integrative medicine can affect the extent to which clinical practice represents a biomedical perspective of integration, or something radically unexpected and new. For example, one contemporary example of an integrative health care practice in biomedicine is treatment of cancer with chemotherapy together with acupuncture to relieve nausea. In this regard, a complementary and alternative medical therapy—acupuncture—that has potential safety and efficacy in biomedical terms is "plugged in" to an accepted biomedical treatment for cancer to aid in symptom management. However, suppose the practitioner is a Tibetan physician, working in a medical culture and language that do not recognize the diagnostic category "cancer." For such a practitioner—treating the patient alone or on a hospital team with, for example, a Western physician, a chiropractor, and a nutritionist—integrative medicine might mean something different.

From this perspective, the shift might represent a potential revolution in medical culture that involves not only new therapies but also new views of the way health care professionals understand health and healing—in other words, a revivification of spiritual and experiential notions of doctor as healer. For example, the literature accompanying the Fellowship for the Program in Integrative Medicine states that Fellows are expected not only to understand the substantive aspects of integrative medicine but also to "transform their own lifestyle and medical practice."[25] In this regard, a potential transformation in personal consciousness becomes an essential part of the purported integration; the program views such personal growth as a prerequisite to any transformation in the larger, collective consciousness of the health care system.

Defining Energy Medicine

As suggested, even the term *integrative medicine* is broad and inclusive; it does not differentiate between combinations of conventional and complementary and alternative medical therapies that can be understood through current Western, scientific models and those that challenge such models to expand or incorporate assumptions of foreign systems of thought (such as traditional Oriental medicine, Tibetan medicine, and Native American medicine). In fact, the major fields of complementary and alternative medicine can further be classified along these lines: some are closer to conventional medicine or purport to operate within the medical model, while others are grounded in vitalistic or "subtle" energies such as the therapeutic transmission of a healing intentionality and consciousness.[26] Thus, the notion of "yin" and "yang" in traditional oriental medicine, the idea of the "innate" in chiropractic, the "spiritual vital essence" (vital force) in homeopathy, and the *"prana"* in Ayurvedic medicine all reflect the unifying notion of vital energy embedded in consciousness.[27] Many practitioners would argue that the attempt to comprehend such therapies through presently accepted physical and biological sciences is fallacious, since these other systems of medicine were neither designed nor defined with biomedical principles in mind.

Hence the paradox: the term *energy medicine* is redolent with esoteric connotations and has not yet been satisfactorily defined or even widely acknowledged in U.S. hospitals and medical schools, yet therapies encompassed by energy medicine (for example, Therapeutic Touch and Reiki, two forms of hands-on healing) are being used in clinical settings, and/or taught during medical and other professional health care education. Thus, I use the term *energy medicine* to define that subset of therapies within the spectrum of complementary and alternative medical therapies that primarily are based on the projection of information, consciousness, and/or intentionality to patients. Salient examples are intuitive medical diagnosis, which uses consciousness and intentionality to gain information about disease and healing, and distance healing, which uses consciousness and intentionality to accelerate patient recovery from symptoms. Aspects of traditional oriental medicine and Tibetan medicine also would come under the rubric of energy medicine—at least to the extent that they emphasize vital energy rather than anatomy and physiology in the Western, scientific sense. Modalities involving laying-on of hands (such as Therapeutic Touch and Reiki) are included: these generally view disease as originating ultimately in consciousness and then translating into correlative symptoms and mechanisms in the physical body.[28]

Parenthetically, practitioners consider the resulting healing in such therapies not as matters of faith, to be accepted under the tenets of a specific religion, but rather as more generalized "spiritual technologies" aimed at human health and healing.[29] As such, energy medicine is not relegated to the realm of superstition or religion but given its own definitional category. Thus, while energy medicine spans medicine and religion, in this context the term refers to therapeutic applications involving mental projection of consciousness and the human energy field (or biofield), which is said to surround and interpenetrate the physical human body and provide a living informational system mediating human physical existence and consciousness. Further, while the word "integrative" has certain connotations and associations, the modifier "energy" in "energy medicine" is somewhat ambiguous, since it refers to spiritual energy, and not to a form of energy (such as electricity or magnetism) that presently can be satisfactorily quantified or physically described. No satisfactory substitute, however, has been proposed. To complicate the matter, the linguistic union of an "energy" based on spiritual principles and "medicine," which is based on material, scientific principles, seems an oxymoron.

Like integrative medicine, energy medicine can be conceptualized in many different ways. One proposed classification involves including at least three different, but somehow linked, kinds of phenomena: (1) potentially explainable transmissions of informational patterns between humans in the form of bioelectromagnetic energy; (2) transmissions of informational patterns that are physically, emotionally, and spiritually mediated between individuals in close proximity—for example, by laying-on of hands—and that presently cannot wholly be accounted for in material or physical terms; and (3) nonlocal phenomena such as distance healing that may or may not be phenomena of body, mind, or spirit (however one defines each of these concepts).[30] For some, such phenomena as hands-on healing, nonlocal phenomena such as distance healing, and prayer ultimately may be understood through an extension of physical principles—in the words of Wayne Jonas, former director of the Office of Alternative Medicine, as "informational biology"; for others, these phenomena fall under the rubric of "spirituality."

In any event, given the contemporary lack of adequate scientific evidence for many claims involving energy healing, this book tackles the most spiritual, and therefore most controversial, form of complementary and alternative medicine. To date, the legal and ethical implications of using or not using energy medicine have remained, for the most part, beyond discussion; yet, as with the human genome project and other novel "technologies," it is important to begin this discussion now so that our health care system may understand the perils and peregrinations involved in use and misuse. Successive chapters elaborate on these paradoxes and the paradigm articulated by the subgroup of energy medicine within complementary and alternative medicine.[31]

Bridging Legal, Regulatory, Ethical, Bioethical, and Spiritual Issues

This book completes a trilogy regarding the legal and ethical implications of the shift in our health care system, from being based almost entirely on conventional or orthodox medicine (or biomedicine)—with complementary and alternative medical practices historically relegated to the fringe of clinical care—to a synthesis, or integration, of biomedicine and complementary and alternative medicine based on principles of safety, efficacy, and an appropriate vision of "integrative" care. The first two books focus on law and regulation, creating a foundation for related ethical issues. *Complementary and Alternative Medicine: Legal Boundaries and Regulatory Perspectives* (Baltimore: Johns Hopkins University Press, 1998) analyzed such issues as credentialing and licensing, scope of practice limitations, provider malpractice and institutional liability, patients' right to receive nonconventional treatments, professional discipline (premised on the use of modalities outside prevailing professional norms), and the availability of third-party reimbursement for complementary and alternative medicine.

These core legal and regulatory issues frame almost any discussion of inclusion of complementary and alternative medicine in mainstream health care. For example, when an insurer or health care institution credentials a complementary and alternative medical provider (for example, an acupuncturist) for inclusion in health care and referral networks, it must address provider licensing and professional credentialing; any legislative, administrative, or judicial limitations on scope of practice boundaries; questions of direct and vicarious liability of the institution for the negligent acts or omissions of the complementary and alternative medical provider; issues surrounding patient right of access to treatments such as herbal medicine; the standard under which medical and other appropriate professional boards can discipline providers who do not conform to conventional standards of care; and issues such as whether the therapy provided is deemed "medically nec-essary," and hence reimbursable, or "experimental," and thus outside the scope of coverage.

Beyond Complementary Medicine: Legal and Ethical Perspectives on Human Evolution (Ann Arbor: University of Michigan Press, 2000) expands the analysis of liability and ethical issues in integrative health care practices. Detailed attention to provider credentialing, evolving malpractice rules, informed-consent disclosure, institutional liability, and legal rules governing physician referrals to complementary and alternative medical providers provide a matrix for preliminary consid-eration of ethical, then bioethical issues.

One of the legal and ethical frontiers explored, for example, is the kind of disclosure physicians must or might make to patients regarding therapies whose risks and benefits cannot easily be described through the lens of Western medicine (for example, those relating to the flow and balance of *chi*—universal life energy—in Chinese medicine). If health care providers adopt a nonbiomedical etiology and treatment of disease for medicine and health care policy, for instance, then legal, regulatory, and ethical perspectives might shift as well. The book also teases out some of the basic implications of considering energy medi-cine as a new paradigm in science and as the basis for a new under-standing of regulation. For example, much of food and drug law is con-cerned with protecting the consumer against personal folly in choices of health care products. The contrast between values such as paternal-ism (the state's prerogative to substitute its judgment for the con-sumer's) and autonomy (the individual's right to make a voluntary, knowing, and informed choice) is enriched by contemplating the role that subjectivity, intuition, and even personal revelation can play in future health care choices. The book proposes, among other things, that energy medicine may yield different clinical, legal, and ethical criteria for delivery than those presently established by state or medical authorities.

Future Medicine synthesizes legal, regulatory, and selected ethical and bioethical considerations to create a new framework for under-standing many of the clinical choices that health care providers, insti-tutions, regulators, and patients face in this field. Drawing on the argu-ment made in *Beyond Complementary Medicine*, this book does not view the regulatory issues and ethical dilemmas solely through the lens of biomedicine but reaches for a more inclusive, pluralistic, and universal framework that includes different sociological, philosophical, and religious viewpoints than those embedded in biomedicine. As such, the book admits that prevailing scientific evidence may or may not support many of the systems and claims proposed by much of integrative and energy medicine. Yet this book proposes that such systems and claims nonetheless deserve a focused review, in part because of their affinity with and implications for such aspects of health as intensive care (and death and dying), mental health care, medical ethics, and spirituality. Moreover, integrative and energy medicine bear on the awareness of health and human healing in human transformation and thereby present us with reflections on *future medicine,* in the sense of health care as most broadly defined.

Organizational Strategy

Future Medicine addresses legal, ethical, clinical (and spiritual) concerns of interest to at least four groups within the health care arena: (1) physicians and allied health care providers (such as nurses, optometrists, and physical therapists); (2) complementary and alternative medical providers (such as chiropractors, acupuncturists, naturopaths, massage therapists, and spiritual healers); (3) mental health care professionals; and (4) attorneys, regulators, policymakers, ethicists, patients who use complementary and alternative medicine (and their families), and graduate and undergraduate students (and faculty) in many different programs (such as psychology, religion, and sociology). The phenomenon of complementary and alternative medicine unifies these four audiences, who share an underlying interest in the clinical, legal, and ethical parameters of health care practices beyond biomedicine. Yet each audience has a slightly different orientation to these issues.

First, *physicians and allied health care providers* face legal and ethical dilemmas applicable to their delivery of, and referral of patients for, complementary and alternative medical therapies. From a regulatory perspective, physicians have an unlimited scope of practice, which means they can use almost any medically responsible method of diagnosing and treating disease. Nonetheless, physicians have genuine concerns with malpractice liability and the prospect of professional discipline when practicing beyond the bounds of conventionally accepted standards. Further, physicians often face a conflict when patients demand therapies lacking satisfactory proof within contemporary scientific methods. Of particular interest to physicians are the areas within clinical practice in which the physician lacks clear scientific or medical guidance regarding the safety or efficacy of the therapy in question or in which professionally adopted ethical norms for complementary and alternative medical therapies either are lacking or present unusually compelling scenarios at the intersection of ethical and malpractice rules.

Complementary and alternative medical providers do not always share the methods and materia medica of their physician counterparts. They also are confined to a legislatively authorized scope of practice, however (for example, in the case of chiropractors in some states, spinal manipulation and its ancillary therapies), and are prohibited from the unauthorized practice of medicine.[32] Such providers typically face legal and ethical dilemmas relevant to the intersection of their diagnostic and therapeutic armamentarium with that of physicians. The borderland between biomedicine and the complementary and alternative medical profession in question thus becomes an interesting "gray zone." How, for example, can an acupuncturist address the "imbalance underlying" the disease yet not be understood to treat the disease itself? How can an herb be understood as "supporting wellness" (and thus included in the protected legal definition of a dietary supplement) yet not be viewed as a medicinal drug? Of particular interest is the changing role of touch in these therapies. Over a century or more of regulation, the profession of massage therapy has managed to find ways to distinguish caring or healing touch from sexual touch, yet touch remains largely anathema to the mental health professions. As biomedical and complementary and alternative medical providers increasingly become collaborative partners, responding to patients in physical, mental, emotional, and spiritual distress, the dividing lines between the professions will continue to blur, along with the legal and ethical boundaries separating nonphysician providers from their physician counterparts.

Mental health care professionals face particular legal and ethical concerns when using therapies that integrate mind, body, and spirit in such a way that traditional notions of patient boundaries begin to crumble. A mental health care provider who pushes these boundaries may be challenged by liability or judged incompetent or otherwise guilty of misconduct by the relevant professional board. For example, as suggested, the professions of psychotherapy and psychiatry for the most part have repudiated the role of touch in mental health care, owing to the twin fears of excessive transference and of liability. Yet some areas within these professions—such as bioenergetics, which incorporates therapy with bodywork—bridge the "mental health" professions with "complementary and alternative" modalities such as massage therapy. Mental health care providers face professional and regulatory ambiguity, at best, regarding therapies such as prayer, non-local healing, and hands-on energetic approaches to health. In another arena of complementary and alternative medicine, many mental health care providers are concerned with the liability and ethical implications of recommending herbs—such as St. John's wort, kava kava, and valerian—to affect relaxation and mood and sometimes as a substitute for prescription drugs.

Similar questions about the borderland between biochemical and consciousness-based approaches to emotional well-being arise with therapies such as hypnotherapy and neuro-linguistic programming (NLP) and even homeopathy and aromatherapy. A salient question is the extent to which the mental health professions will find synthesis and reconciliation as boundaries between mind, body, and spirit further dissolve and as historically sensitive areas within these professions face new challenges.

Finally, *regulators and medical ethicists* face particular legal and ethical concerns when encountering therapies that bridge medicine and spirituality. Although there are many different traditions and perspectives within bioethics, rational principles tend to dominate the analysis of any specific bioethical dilemma. Arguably, however, the rational tools of prevailing legal and ethical rules anchor bioethics in its biomedical orientation, whereas the distinctively emotional, spiritual, or other perspectives of different complementary and alternative medical therapies can propel the discussion into disorienting realms in which heart, mind, and spirit claim different roles. One question is whether the gap between conventional and complementary and alternative medicine, which scientific research is purporting to bridge, finds any analogous or dissimilar resolution in the field of bioethics. Of crucial import is the way clinical dilemmas involving spiritual therapies can lead to new understandings of consciousness, the body, and what it means to be fully human.

Future Medicine provides overlapping considerations of interest to all four groups of readers. While the book's organization reflects a progression from implications of integrative and energy medicine for conventional medical care to implications for mental and spiritual health care to implications for frontier issues in bioethics, the content is arranged thematically rather than by professional discipline. The discussion thus proceeds from the most basic and readily accessible (for example, concerns of safety and efficacy) to the more subtle or sublime (for example, energy medicine perspectives on death and reproductive and other technologies). Moreover, the tone of the book deliberately ranges from academic to lyrical and figurative. This is integration, rather than an exhaustive compendium, and therefore the content and style mirror attempts to integrate scholarly, professional, and other forms of knowledge, information, and perspective. Ideally, even within this integrative approach, each group of readers will find the range of discussion of practical interest. For example, conventional physicians deal with mental and spiritual care as well as bioethical issues, psychologists and counselors refer cases to physicians as well as ethicists, and the development of complementary and alternative medicine and bioethics in turn reflects on evolving legal and ethical considerations in integrating complementary and alternative medical therapies into conventional medicine.

Guideposts

The book increasingly proceeds toward a synthesis of clinical, legal, ethical, and spiritual considerations. In Part 1, chapter 1 begins the exploration with the broad question of when it is ethical for physicians to provide (or refuse to provide) a complementary and alternative medical therapy to patients who either request such a therapy or, in the physician's best medical judgment, might benefit from such a therapy. This chapter evaluates the application of nonmaleficence as a central guiding principle. The traditional understanding of the maxim "do no harm," then, is evaluated in the light of premises common to complementary and alternative medical therapies.

Chapter 2 addresses the question of whether or not it is ethical for a physician to refer a patient to a complementary and alternative medical provider if the physician has insufficient scientific evidence regarding, or personal belief in, the safety and efficacy of the therapies offered by the provider. This chapter analyzes legal rules surrounding liability for referrals, the possible liability and ethical implications for failure to refer, and physician interaction generally with nonbiomedical healing professionals. Chapter 2 also describes the general ethical duties as defined in major professional ethical codes of chiropractors, acupuncturists, naturopaths, massage therapists, and homeopaths, such as rules surrounding claims, advertisements, and representations.

Chapter 3 draws on transpersonal psychology to suggest a hierarchy of regulatory values that might govern legal, policy, and ethical analyses of integrative and energy medicine. Transpersonal psychology addresses experiences in which "the sense of identity of self extends beyond (trans) the individual or personal to encompass wider aspects of humankind, life, psyche or cosmos."[33] This chapter also focuses on emerging mind-body therapies for which scientific evidence, or even explanation, largely is lacking—such as therapies involving spirituality and projection of mental energy. One question of interest is that of how to guide the physician desiring to offer patients therapies that cross the line into religious belief (for example, yoga, meditation, and prayer) and thus present unusual ethical challenges.

Turning in Part 2 to implications for mental and spiritual health care in medicine, chapter 4 opens with a discussion of energy healing, a therapy based on the projection of spiritual or mental energy through intentionality and consciousness.[34] The physiological mechanism and parameters of energy healing have not, to date, been adequately scientifically defined or resolved. A major premise of energy healing is the existence of a human energy field (or aura) surrounding and interpenetrating the physical human body and containing information, in the form of consciousness, relevant to disease and healing. This chapter does not attempt to resolve the debates regarding the truth or nontruth of the latter proposition. Rather, the chapter investigates whether the notion of "energetic" interpersonal boundaries could change the way mental health professionals (as well as physicians, allied health providers, and complementary and alternative medical professionals) view their clinical, legal, and ethical obligations to patients.

Chapter 5 continues this analysis by evaluating new ideas about touch, privacy, and confidentiality in the application of energy healing modalities (such as Reiki) within psychotherapy and other mental health disciplines. This chapter also describes ethical duties applicable to energy healers and emerging mind-body professionals, where such providers are by and large unlicensed or are licensed under other professions such as massage therapy or psychology. The potential role of intuitive medical diagnosis in changing notions of touch, privacy, confidentiality, and other boundary issues between provider and patient also receives consideration.[35]

Chapter 6 focuses on issues of fraud, abuse, and heightened patient vulnerability where "spiritual technologies" are concerned. This chapter summarizes some of the ethical implications of incorporating the human energy field (or biofield) into the mental health care paradigm. Both the potentially beneficent as well as the shadow aspects of manipulating the biofield are presented. This chapter also explores the extent to which analogies can be drawn between ethics in medicine and the allied health professions and ethics in complementary and alternative medical therapies based on energy healing concepts. The notion is that, whether or not they are satisfactorily scientifically validated in the near future, the concepts asserted by energy healing may stretch the way health care providers address emotional and spiritual boundaries with patients.

Turning in Part 3 more specifically to bioethics, chapter 7 describes the potential foundational contribution of energy medicine. Parenthetically, some 90 percent of Americans believe in God or a universal spirit, and a good number of these believe that prayer works.[36] Studies have purported to show the beneficial effects of spiritual practices.[37] These trends suggest that consciousness and intentionality should be taken seriously as factors in bioethical considerations. The suggestion is made that if a human being is understood in terms that transcend the body but do not necessarily derive from principles one might consider "religious" or "faith-based," then the field of medical ethics must find ways to integrate dimensions of human health and existence beyond the biomedical or physiological. Chapter 7 applies this framework to changing definitions of death, exploring the notion of the "peaceful death" in bioethics as a basis for new perspectives on ethical dilemmas in death and dying drawn from complementary and alternative medical therapies.[38]

Finally, chapter 8 describes how understandings from energy healing might shape the controversial ethical debates surrounding reproductive and other technologies. This chapter attempts to describe phenomena and experiences that do not fit dominant scientific or medical models and to explore the further reaches of potential bioethical implications. Again, this chapter continues the theme of exploring issues from perspectives outside the biomedical model, using a variety of tools to help bridge the gap.

Paradigm Shift as Appropriate Metaphor

This book does not aim to present a comprehensive synthesis of Western and Eastern medicine or medical ethics nor to guess at what guidelines for integrative and energy medicine ultimately will emerge in a clinical sense.[39] Rather, *Future Medicine* attempts to provide some foundational approaches to integrative and energy medicine by applying familiar legal, ethical, and bioethical rules to some radically novel clinical situations and experiences of health and disease.

"Foundational" means that this book explores a different intellectual, emotional, and creative platform for the analysis of complementary and alternative medical therapies than one that would be constructed from the usual perspective. Ethical analysis of complementary and alternative medicine to date is sparse; like much contemporary medical and legal analysis, it often rests on and builds in the assumptions, premises, and judgments of biomedicine.[40] These include, for example, the following: an inherent skepticism or antipathy toward therapies outside the paradigm of biomedicine, particularly where levels of scientific evidence for safety and/or efficacy are unsatisfactory; the assumption that prevailing scientific models are the ultimate arbiter of evidence relating to health; the notion that regulation of complementary and alternative medical providers by and large is nonexistent or is less rigorous than regulation of comparable allied health professionals (such as nurses, optometrists, and physical therapists); the reliance on the material and physically demonstrable and the concomitant decision to decline to integrate the nonphysical (for example, the dismissal of dying patients' experiences of their departed relatives as "hallucinations"); and the tendency, criticized even within biomedicine, to view medical events in isolation from sociological, psychological, and religious ones.

Since biomedicine has dominated the political landscape for health care and its legal and regulatory framework from the late nineteenth century to the present, it is natural that biomedicine would imbue the field of ethics with its own understanding of the human condition.[41]

The aim is not to challenge or attempt to replace one bias with another but rather to supplement and enrich the language and parameters of existing discussion. As we know, paradigm shifts occur by revolution rather than accretion.[42] Further, biomedicine has been antagonistic to its competitors, to the point of attempting to extinguish rivals. Thus, the exploratory enterprise this book presents inevitably may resound to some, at times, with an undercurrent of the revolutionary call that inclusion of these therapies represents. This in no way represents a denigration of scientific method or of the importance of using conventional therapies where necessary and appropriate; to the contrary, the notion of integration implies building on existing models, discarding what is conclusively shown to be dangerous and ineffective, yet evolving new ideas based on emerging information and perception.

Reflecting the Future and Nature of Medicine

The terms *integrative medicine* and *energy medicine* ideally evoke a contemplation not only of the future of medicine but also of the nature of medicine. To date, biomedicine largely has focused on the contemporary Western, scientific understanding of physical reality—for example, on health and disease as understood through disciplines such as pharmacology, biochemistry, physical anatomy, and physiology. The focus of many complementary and alternative medical therapies on emotional and spiritual models to find correlative factors in human health and healing challenges Western scientific models and stretches attempts to measure or map the numinous in physical terms or efforts to define in these terms the meaning of being fully human.

In part, conventional medicine's response to complementary and alternative medicine has been to recognize its shortcomings and then strive toward a whole-being approach to health care—in other words, the cultural revolution has stimulated a partial reformation of medicine. Examples of such "holistic" thinking in conventional medicine include incorporating nutritional approaches to cancer care; partial recognition of the importance of psychospiritual realities during end-of-life care (at least proposing the importance of a "peaceful death"); softening of official positions toward use of opiates for control of unbearable physical pain toward the end of life; use of hypnotherapy and guided imagery as part of dental care, presurgical care, and other forms of conventional care; and the notion that good medical doctors ideally are empathetic, compassionate, and attentive to patients' emotional and spiritual as well as physiological needs.[43] Energy medicine goes further, however, and makes the ultimate assertion that disease, medicine, and healing are biopsychical and spiritual as well as biophysical phenomena. Further, some complementary and alternative medical therapies within the realm of energy medicine strive not only toward integration of body, emotions, mind, and spirit but also toward larger, transcendental goals such as self-actualization. Such therapies aim toward bringing the patient higher planes of consciousness. In this sense, the fragmentation that integrative and particularly energy medicine purport to heal is even larger than the Cartesian split, embodied in conventional medicine, between body and mind. These disciplines also address the splits between thinking and feeling, between understanding and knowing, and even between doing and being. In this light, existing definitions and structures (for example, conventional understandings of ethical values such as nonmaleficence and beneficence) may require new parameters. Again, this broad theme is played out in subsequent chapters.

Yet another challenge energy medicine poses to conventional care is the assertion that measurement and validation in some instances are not only impossible but even unnecessary or counterproductive, since healing, a broader concept than curing, involves the reclaiming of wholeness on all levels: physical, mental, emotional, and spiritual. The spiritual, according to these therapies, cannot always be measured; as Pascal observed, the heart has its reasons that reason cannot know. While a patient's improvement in physical health, for example, might be measured after acupuncture, tai chi, or *qigong*, and changes in mood might be monitored through psychological testing, changes in the relative balance of yin and yang, increases in subtle or vital energy, and increases in accelerated portals of human consciousness (such as, for example, an expanded ability to communicate with subtle forces and presences within nature) lack measurement, or at least resist measurement in terms acceptable to present Western scientific models. The latter tend to relegate such phenomena to the mystical, the improbable, the fantastic, the delusional, or the frankly religious and thus to the unprovable and marginally meaningful to standardized therapeutic protocols; yet, as these therapies suggest, subjective experiences may have a larger place in medicine and health care than currently assigned by the category of "anecdotal evidence." Further, such experiences may contain larger implications for psychosocial dimensions of healing, a sense of human connectedness in the cosmos, environmental issues, notions of harmony, issues of social support, and different understandings of wholeness and well-being than those strictly defined by models of biomedical pathology.

Integrative and energy medicine thus suggest the need for reexamination of some of the most foundational assumptions of conventional medicine regarding the meaning of disease, health, and what it means to have wholeness of being. This will also challenge legal, ethical, and regulatory models to assimilate various principles of integrative and energy medicine and thus produce rules through which biomedical, bioenergetic, and environmental models of health care are integrated in novel ways so as to maximize patient well-being.[44] More specifically, biomedical concepts—such as, for example, reliance on "evidence-based" scientific standards—may control some legal requirements (such as the reasonable-physician standard in informed consent) but not others (such as the reasonable-patient standard).[45] The palpable links to subjective spiritual realities suggest that integrative and energy medicine will be analyzed in ways that incorporate "evidence-based" concerns but are not limited to, or defined exclusively through, such concerns.

Rachel Naomi Remen, describes an experience of shifting to other levels of understanding the healing process. She attended an Easter service on a reservation that was delivered entirely in the Navajo language. At the conclusion of the service, the priest labored to translate the resurrection of Jesus into English for the benefit of Dr. Remen and her friend, neither of whom spoke Navajo. But the priest indicated that his broken English was inadequate to the task. Finally, the priest gave up and summarized the resurrection story as follows: "That man Jesus . . . *he is good medicine.*"[46] Dr. Remen remarked that this comment— rather than the literal story—precipitated a shift in consciousness, and on a cognitive level, made her realize that in many situations, *being is medicine.*

The term *traditional medicine* also stimulates contemplation of the nature and future of medicine if premises of energy healing find sufficient validation and/or correlation with observed phenomena in related disciplines such as psychology and in the social sciences. Two individuals at the same conference presented their views on complementary and alternative medical therapies. One was an oncologist, the other a Native American healer. Each described himself as practicing "traditional" medicine. Attending providers asked: Are we exploring the future of medicine? Is this a corner of medicine? Is it simply good medicine? Or is integrative medicine a euphemism for human caring? Similarly, when looking to aspects of complementary and alternative medicine such as the explosion of botanical (or herbal) medicine in health care, is complementary and alternative medicine to be understood through the lens of medicine or through other cultural lenses?

The present debate about herbs exemplifies the effect of divergent clinical and spiritual paradigms on regulatory perspectives. For physicians and pharmacists (concerned with practical issues in counseling patients), hospital executives (concerned with potential liability for care outside conventional standards), and regulators such as the Food and Drug Administration (FDA) (concerned with protecting patients from unwise choices as well as those mediated by fraud), use of botanical medicine requires above all a detailed understanding of pharmacology and potentially adverse herb-drug interactions. One recent report alone describes one hundred cases of extensive interstitial fibrosis of the kidney in Belgian women who took a misformulated Chinese herb.[47] Based on such reports, one could argue that herbs, botanicals, and other substances that are dispensed as similar to conventional medications should be subjected to standards of safety and efficacy similar to those for Western drugs and regulated as such. Yet, many herbal traditions are not based in Western science.

In Native American tradition, for example, medicine men speak to the plants and purport to glean wisdom from them prior to harvesting. For such practitioners, there is a relationship between botanicals and environment, Earth, nature, and universal values such as harmony, respect for creation, and peace. In biblical Hebrew, the connection is etymologically apparent: the word *shalom*, peace, also means wholeness. Healing is also about relationship, and relationship affects healing. The ways plants are harvested, manufactured, distributed, sold, and regulated all affect transmission of these values. From the perspective of a medicine man, when botanicals are mass-produced in ways that separate the consumer from the soil from which they are derived and are prescribed to be used as "magical pills" like drugs, the culture itself distorts the healing process, disturbs the healing relationship between human and herb, and depreciates the healing gift of the plant.

In short, the way we use complementary and alternative medicine shapes our understanding of complementary and alternative medicine and in turn of health and health care generally.

Such larger themes form leitmotifs for this book. As such, the material examines the frontiers of law, regulation, public policy, ethics, and medical ethics, as integrative and energy medicine assume increasing importance in global paradigms for human health and healing. *Future Medicine* thus presents the idea that as the biomedical community and its structures of thought adjust to the inclusion of complementary and alternative medical providers and therapies in a way that has balance, harmony, and wisdom, legal and ethical paradigms also shift. With daring reflection, new understandings can emerge. May this book serve as a bridge to new ways of thinking, feeling, doing, and being, as notions of health, existence, and medicine continue to evolve.

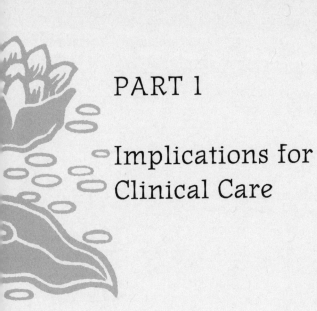

PART 1

Implications for Clinical Care

1

A New View of Nonmaleficence

Case lA   The Patient Who Chooses Yoga, Colonics, and
Reiki over Surgery

 A fifty-two-year-old woman is referred by her naturopath to a medical doctor for evaluation of an abnormal pap smear. Cervical biopsies reveal a premalignant condition, which, if left untreated, can progress and create lesions. The physician's recommendation is a hysterectomy, to be sure all the abnormality is removed.

The patient tells her physician that she plans to pursue yoga, colonics, and Reiki for three months, rather than surgery, and then have her condition evaluated. She does, however, want the physician to continue monitoring her care. The physician is reluctant to do so and is concerned about legal and ethical implications of remaining in the therapeutic relationship.[1]

Case lB   The Parents Who Seek a Non-FDA-Approved
Cancer Therapy

 A four-year old child is diagnosed with inoperable brain cancer. The child's parents wish him to receive a controversial therapy derived from human urine, but the therapy lacks FDA approval, and the child has not been approved for any clinical trials that might offer hope for receiving other relevant, experimental treatment. The FDA therefore insists that the child undergo standard radiation and chemotherapy; the parents, however, are reluctant to subject their child to the "harsh effects of these treatments." Further, the parents have met other parents whose children have successfully received and benefited from the controversial therapy, without experi-

27

encing toxicities or adverse side effects. The parents insist the decision belongs to the family, while the FDA insists it is merely following its congressional mandate to protect the public from interstate distribution of drugs not proven safe and effective.

The family physician feels it is her ethical obligation to treat the child with chemotherapy and considers seeking a court order to do so. Meanwhile, the state welfare agency initiates proceedings to declare the parents guilty of abuse and neglect and unfit for custody. The physician is called as a witness in the proceedings and has mixed feelings about the testimony she plans to present.[2]

Preliminary Ethical Concerns about Using Complementary and Alternative Medical Therapies

With the changing face of medicine and the burgeoning integration of complementary and alternative medical therapies into mainstream clinical practice, there is increasing interest in the ethical implications of providing, or *not* providing, such therapies, as well as in the ethical parameters and principles that might guide the choices of physicians and other health care providers in the delivery of, or referral for, such therapies. For example, is it ethical for a physician to recommend specific herbs and other dietary supplements, special nutritional regimens, Chinese longevity exercises, and other therapies that are not proven safe and efficacious to the physician's satisfaction or are not sufficiently proven to receive general medical acceptance? Similarly, should the physician provide, or refer patients to other practitioners for, therapies such as chiropractic, acupuncture, naturopathy, massage therapy, homeopathy, nutritional care and herbal medicine, and various mind-body interventions when the physician has insufficient scientific evidence regarding the safety and efficacy of such therapies? On the flip side, when is it unethical to fail to recommend, deliver, or refer for therapies when there is some level of evidence for safety and efficacy?

Likewise, what should the clinician in mainstream practice say to a patient who insists on receiving such therapies? Is there a meaningful ethical distinction between recommending therapies and approving the patient's autonomous pursuit of such therapies (as opposed to discouraging the patient from using such treatments)? These questions become even more difficult with therapies when there are discrepancies between the belief systems of provider and patient. For example, should health care providers who are atheists pray with their patients—assuming scientific investigation suggests that prayer has some level of efficacy—and what kinds of conversations should providers have with patients regarding the efficacy, appropriateness, and medical understanding of prayer and other practices involving spiritual preferences? If evidence suggests that failing to pray (or provide other spiritual therapies) may diminish the therapeutic impact of the provider-patient relationship, what should the provider do?

For instance, what should the physician in case 1A say to her patient about the initial choice of yoga, colonics, and Reiki for several months instead of a hysterectomy? Should the physician in case 1B accede to the parents' wishes, terminate conventional treatment, and encourage the parents to pursue the option they deem most beneficial for their child? Or should the provider declare the parents unfit and face the possibility of separating a terminally ill child from his or her parents? How far does the state's role extend in intruding into family choices regarding different systems of medicine?

What kinds of conversations will satisfy informed consent? Which conversations will satisfy the conscience? Which, by enhancing the provider-patient dialogue and increasing communication, will reduce the risk of later malpractice exposure if the patient claims injury from insufficient disclosure? How does the provider handle paradigm shifts that challenge existing models, not only within the culture and the profession but also within his or her own being?

These questions begin to frame the broad question: When is it ethical for a physician to provide (or refuse to provide) a complementary and alternative medical therapy to a patient who either requests or demands a therapy that does not comport with the physician's best medical judgment for that patient? Again, on the other hand, when is it ethical for providers to refrain from even discussing therapies either desired by patients and their families or for which there is preliminary scientific evidence, when neither the provider nor the profession generally has accepted the safety, efficacy, clinical relevance, or even plausibility of such therapies (for example, homeopathy)? The exploration is grounded in larger questions, such as those of the role of safety and efficacy in provider decision making, the future parameters of clinical practice, and the health care provider's guiding role for the patient as such practices are more deeply integrated into mainstream health care and as such integration (in varying degrees) comports with or diverges from medical evidence and comfort.

These are, by and large, unanswerable questions—or at the least, questions requiring deeper investigation as the social order integrates the phenomena known, for the moment, as therapies encompassed by integrative and energy medicine. Moreover, the question of what is ethical can be used as a surrogate for a range of questions, including those that are legal, professional, moral, cultural, clinical, and personal.

Ethics is a broad field, encompassing theories, virtues, principles, and rules. Integrative and energy medicine, as previously defined, do not necessarily implicate new ways of conceptualizing the entire field of ethics. Therefore, the approach here is not systematic. In many cases, ethical considerations applicable to conventional and complementary and alternative medical therapies overlap. For example, health care providers have an ethical obligation to keep patient records and medical history confidential, whether the record involves prescription drugs or a history of specific dietary supplements. Similarly, both conventional and complementary and alternative medical providers have an obligation to refrain from invading the patient's physical body and personal boundaries in an assaulting manner, or their actions could be construed as battery. In this limited sense, complementary and alternative medicine covers no new ethical ground.

In some cases, the ethical conflicts arising within conventional medicine are heightened with complementary and alternative medical therapies. Specifically, complementary and alternative medicine often presents the clash between medical paternalism (the desire to protect patients' voluntary choices and to protect patients from foolish or ill-informed decisions) and patient autonomy. This conflict can be accentuated by patients' selection of therapies that lack medical acceptance (for example, colonics and Reiki) or that some consider medically dubious (for instance, the non-FDA-approved therapy in case 1B).

In still other cases, ethical considerations in integrative and energy medicine involve a logical extension of ethical principles in conventional care. For example, in conventional care, the obligation to obtain adequate informed consent from the patient requires disclosing the material risks and benefits of a particular modality and making note of risks and benefits that are speculative or unknown. "Material" refers to whether disclosure of the risks, benefits, and existence of a particular therapy would make a difference to the patient's decision to undertake or forgo a specific treatment plan. Presumably, no different duty applies with complementary and alternative medical therapies.[3] In other words, the materiality standard also should govern the nature and scope of such disclosure in complementary and alternative medicine.[4] If, for instance, gingko biloba improves dementia due to circulation problems and possibly Alzheimer's, then its risks and benefits should be disclosed for treatment of these conditions.[5]

Finally, complementary and alternative medical modalities can raise ethical problems that challenge the provider's personal belief system in greater force than many conventional therapies. This is especially true when complementary and alternative medicine incorporates spiritual systems or operates along principles neither accepted nor proven in conventional scientific terms (such as the notion of energetic acupuncture meridians, involving neither a "placebo" effect nor a physiological one). For example, the physician in case 1A faces a patient who insists on delaying conventional care in favor of modalities with which the physician is not personally familiar and that have not or cannot be evaluated in terms with which the physician is familiar. On one hand, the patient's request creates an immediate moral and legal dilemma. The provider must assess liability exposure, as well as the possibility of unwittingly causing the patient injury. Viewed in other ways, however, the request creates the possibility for a transcultural dialogue, in which the patient's mental, emotional, and spiritual realities are tested against the provider's *perception* of the obligation to safeguard the patient's welfare. This creates a larger conflict than the one between paternalism and autonomy. Specifically, the conflict may be not so much about whose choice should control as about what criteria should govern clinical evaluation of therapies foreign, and even repugnant, to prevailing biomedical models and/or governmental sensibilities.

Case 1B presents a similar conflict between professional standards and private ideals. Here, the provider faces a family that ardently and sincerely believes in reports of efficacy for a therapy the FDA considers not only untested but also possibly worthless and even dangerous. Not only the medical profession and a federal agency but also the machinery of the state have been brought to bear against the parents. The physician's own belief systems may preclude standing by the parents and defending their choice against these external forces. This conflict, again, may be framed as a choice not so much between a proven and an unproven therapy as between therapies accepted by majoritarian consensus within medicine and those accepted in the minds and hearts of patients. The choice thus can be framed as cultural as well as ethical. It is a power struggle.

One common ground in both case 1A and case 1B is that the patients' choices have spiritual and emotional components—for example, the decision to try yoga and Reiki or the choice to abandon chemotherapy in favor of a therapy whose mechanism is unknown but that seems to have helped other families. The provider is pitted against his or her own scientific principles, conscience, ethical obligations, and personal proclivities; the patient's wishes; the uncertainty inherent in pursuing the unknown; and the desire to help the patient avert unnecessary suffering and find the least harmful path back to health. Case 1B involves a patient with an incurable condition, but the scenario could be generalized, making decision making more variable.

The Effect of Overlapping and Competing Legal Concerns on Ethical Duties

The ethical dilemma is complicated by overlapping and sometimes competing legal and liability considerations. This presents variations on the ways in which these obligations intersect in health care more generally.[6] For instance, licensing and credentialing issues overlap with ethical concerns when physicians find their patients visiting providers who lack independent state licensure. The current list of non-licensed providers (in some states) includes lay homeopaths, counselors, herbalists, and spiritual healers. The extent to which lack of licensure makes the modality and the provider in question more or less acceptable receives further consideration elsewhere.[7] Among other things, while the physician is on safer legal ground referring only to licensed complementary and alternative medical providers and using modalities that commonly are accepted among such providers, the need for (and scope of) licensure, certification, and other forms of credentialing vary by state and by profession.[8]

For example, in many states (such as California and Massachusetts), there presently is no state licensure for massage therapists; yet the practice of massage therapy is not prohibited or is regulated by individual town ordinance. In many such cases, the practice of massage therapy is neither legal nor illegal—rather, it lies in the shadowy world of the unregulated (or under-regulated). The physician may feel such a provider might be helpful to the patient (for example, particularly for stress reduction) even though there are no state mandates regarding required training and education for the practitioner. In this situation, one might consider it ethical (in the sense of beneficence) to send the patient to the massage therapist, although the massage therapist's legal status may be unclear. By analogy, in case 1B, the physician may consider it ethical (in other words, beneficial) to help the patient obtain a nontoxic therapy other families have found effective for treatment of a child's inoperable brain tumor, but the treatment itself may be illegal.

In a converse situation, a practice involving complementary and alternative medicine may be legal but unethical. For example, many states do not license acupuncturists—or they allow physicians to practice acupuncture with a modicum of training. The physician may learn a smattering about needle placement in a weekend training course. This training, however, would be insufficient to qualify the provider as an expert in traditional oriental medicine. Therefore it may be legal but not ethical for the physician to purport to provide the patient with comprehensive acupuncture treatment. Parenthetically, the notion that physicians offering complementary and alternative medicine should have training on parity with that received by complementary and alternative medical providers offering the same treatment recently has received greater impetus from a report by the Select Committee on Science and Technology in the United Kingdom's House of Lords.[9]

Liability issues also can raise situations in which legal and ethical obligations diverge. For example, in case 1A, one might consider it ethical for the physician to condone yoga, colonics, and Reiki for a period of three months rather than surgery. Indeed, to the extent that this, or some analogous scenario, is clinically tolerable, the physician's tolerance expresses respect for the patient's wishes, together with a "wait-and-see" attitude in which the physician continues to monitor the patient conventionally. But if the patient's condition deteriorates and the patient sues (arguing negligent care in the choice of treatment), the physician's tolerance of the patient's choice might lead to liability. If, on the other hand, the patient's condition improves, the physician would be free from liability (since malpractice liability requires a negligent action that causes the patient injury). But even if the patient's condition improves, the decision to tolerate yoga, colonics, and Reiki (or to provide, for example, nutritional supplements or homeopathic remedies) might be considered unethical by medical peers and lead to professional disciplinary proceedings by the state medical board.[10] In short, the very newness of integrative practice and the uncertainty inherent in creating clinical pathways to integration suggest the possibility that any given course of action (or its opposite) will lead to liability, discipline, ethical wrongdoing, or a combination of these three. In this sense, integrative medicine can present a "no-win" situation.

A recent version of the *Ethics Manual* for the American College of Physicians devotes only two paragraphs to complementary and alternative medical therapies. This brevity perhaps expresses the profession's thoughtful approach but present inability to guide physicians fully as they map the frontiers of integrative care in daily clinical practice. The *Manual* first notes that the physician "should not abandon the patient who elects to try an alternative treatment."[11] This suggests that the patient's mere request for complementary and alternative medicine should not lead the physician to terminate treatment. Further, the *Manual*'s recommendation accords with the legal and ethical principle that the physician not abandon the patient but rather refer him or her, where appropriate, to a provider that can offer the necessary care. For example, if the physician feels he or she in good conscience can no longer treat a family that declines recommended immunizations, the physician should document his or her recommendation and the patient's refusal in the chart and refer the family to a provider than can offer care under such circumstances.

Next, the *Manual* states obliquely that patient requests for complementary and alternative medical therapies "require balancing the medical standard of care with a patient's right to choose care on the basis of his or her values and preferences."[12] This statement accords respect to the balance between medical paternalism and the patient's autonomous choice. The *Manual* then recommends ascertaining the reason for the request—for example, determining whether it stems from dissatisfaction with current care—and ensuring that the patient understands his or her condition, standard medical treatment options, and expected outcomes.[13] The *Manual* counsels the physician to coach the patient through the decision to choose such a therapy. This suggestion provides some legal protection: the patient's choice conceivably could lead to heightened liability for the physician if the therapy is outside conventional standards of care.

Finally, the *Manual* suggests that the patient "be clearly informed if the option under consideration is likely to delay access to effective treatment or is known to be harmful."[14] According to the *Manual*, the physician need not participate in the monitoring or delivery of the particular complementary and alternative medical therapy.[15] This final recommendation addresses the risk of indirect toxicity—the possibility that the patient will suffer from delay of conventional care. This risk presents liability concern and suggests the need to have clear communication with the patient regarding the choices presented and to document this discussion in the medical record.

Applying this principle to case 1A, the physician faced with this clinical situation should ask whether *necessary* conventional care would be *inappropriately* delayed by the patient's choice of complementary and alternative medicine. If so, then the physician's prospect of liability, as well as his or her ethical responsibility to the patient, may conflict with the patient's choice. If not, it may remain unclear which clinical path is most appropriate for the patient and yields the least harm.

This represents a preliminary view of sometimes overlapping and sometimes competing considerations involving ethical analysis of complementary and alternative medicine. Again, the discussion suggests that it would be premature to carve out an entirely new set of principles, rules, and theories for ethics in complementary and alternative medicine; further, the dichotomy of "ethical/unethical" may be too simplistic for these emerging aspects of clinical practice. On the other hand, some unusual features of complementary and alternative medicine—for example, its frequent reliance on vitalistic understandings of illness; its unfamiliarity, or partial inaccessibility, to Western thought and methods of validation; and its synthetic approach to physical, emotional, mental, and spiritual aspects of disease—suggest the need for subtler, case-by-case evaluations that incorporate changing information regarding patient needs, medical literature, and liability concerns.

Today, physician education and clinical practice focus on evidence-based medicine as a model for recommending, discussing, or accepting therapies. A working definition of evidence-based medicine is "the integration of best research evidence with clinical expertise and patient values."[16] On the one hand, an evidence base associated with complementary and alternative medical therapies is beginning to emerge.[17] Certainly, physicians will not want to make clinical recommendations that are unsupported by evidence; yet their personal experience with modalities such as massage and acupuncture may influence their views of the evidence. Further, this definition does not resolve to what extent *clinical experience* as well as *patient values* will modify and moderate reliance on existing research results, if complementary and alternative medical therapies gain credibility. It may be difficult to "interpret realistically" results of clinical trials and predict effectiveness or benefits in the context of the therapeutic relationship, especially given psychological and spiritual aspects of complementary and alternative medical therapies.[18] Among other things, complementary and alternative medical therapies have a number of cross-cultural aspects, including disease and treatment models that vary from conventional ones or that are not supported by conventionally recognized mechanistic explanations.[19] Presently, clinical pathways for, and parameters of, integrative medicine are emerging and thus present multiple and converging medical, social, legal, and ethical considerations.

Applying Moral Principles to Complementary and Alternative Medical Therapies

Four ethical principles provide one commonly accepted starting group for evaluating the ethical obligation to provide or not provide a complementary and alternative medical therapy. The first is the physician's pledge: "Above all [or first] do no harm."[20] Sometimes expressed as the Hippocratic oath, this ideal of nonmaleficence governs all physician-patient conversations and interactions. In an approach to medical ethics based on moral principles, nonmaleficence (avoiding the causation of harm) is viewed as a central moral principle for decisions involving conventional medicine and, by extension, can be applied to complementary and alternative medical therapies. The other three principles are respect for patient autonomy; beneficence (providing benefits and balancing benefits against risks and costs); and justice (distributing benefits, risks, and costs fairly).[21]

When applied to therapeutic decisions by the provider involving complementary and alternative medicine, nonmaleficence could be understood in three fundamental respects: (1) shielding patients from direct and indirect toxicity associated with complementary and alternative medical therapies; (2) discussing risks and benefits neutrally and dispassionately, not disparaging a patient's cultural and spiritual beliefs regarding complementary and alternative medicine (for example, not undermining the patient's self-esteem and cultural identity); and (3) remaining open to the possibility of offering therapies—even with mixed evidence regarding efficacy—that are less costly, invasive, or toxic than the conventional alternatives and that may result in overall benefit.[22]

With regard to shielding patients from direct toxicity, such toxicity arises when the patient is injured directly by a complementary and alternative medical therapy—for example, by an herb known to be toxic that carries FDA warnings as a result of documented case reports or clinical studies. Indirect toxicity may result, as noted, from harm due to delay in implementing a proven conventional treatment in favor of pursuing an unproven complementary and alternative medical therapy.[23] With regard to discussing risks and benefits neutrally, this involves shielding the patient from personal bias and communicating the evidence and the provider's perspective, without denying the emotional validity (and potential truth) of the patient's perspective, even if culturally and logically opposed to the provider's. With regard to remaining open, acknowledging issues of toxicity, invasiveness, and harshness of conventional therapies on the physical body (for example, chemotherapy) also are part of the principle of doing the least harm possible.

The next principle, autonomy, means acknowledging the person's right to make knowing, voluntary, and intelligent health care choices—in this case, choices concerning use of complementary and alternative medical therapies. Disrespecting autonomy means ignoring, insulting, or demeaning those choices by substituting conventional medical standards and practices for patient decisions and preferences.[24] The duty to respect patient autonomy parallels the obligation to refrain from demeaning or insulting the patient due to personal or cultural bias, even if the culture is defined in terms of prevailing scientific and medical norms.

Next, beneficence in complementary and alternative medicine includes encouraging strategies for health promotion and disease prevention, helping patients utilize self-care and complementary and alternative medical therapies that relieve pain and suffering, and providing therapies that complement conventional medical tools by emphasizing emotional and spiritual care.[25] Beneficence is the reverse of nonmaleficence: it implies actively benefiting the patient.

Finally, the principle of justice entails ensuring access to complementary and alternative medical therapies that are known to be safe, effective, and appropriate for the condition in question.[26] "Access" implies autonomy on a collective, social scale. Indeed, this value has been noted during testimony for the federal White House Commission on Complementary and Alternative Medicine Policy regarding such issues as licensing and credentialing complementary and alternative medical providers.[27]

While the four principles represent one consensus statement for assessing the ethical appropriateness of a given clinical decision, many have argued that medical ethics places too much emphasis on these principles and that other perspectives should be brought to bear. One such perspective, "casuistry," is a model of bioethical reasoning that eschews an approach based entirely on principles and instead relies on the evaluation of practical decisions in specific cases.[28]

Casuistry may be particularly appealing to ethical analysis of complementary and alternative medical therapies for several reasons. First, like casuistry, some complementary and alternative medical therapies question over-reliance on generalized, universal principles. Second, it could be argued that the moral principles in bioethics are derived from a biomedical perspective on health care, and not from the perspective of such therapies as traditional oriental medicine, chiropractic, and naturopathy. In other words, these disciplines may contain parallel, but not identical, starting points for ethical analysis. For example, in ancient China, the doctor did not receive payment unless and until the patient was cured. Third, casuistry's modification of the "principles" approach represents a rough analogue to the role of evidence-based medicine suggesting, in delivery of complementary and alternative medicine, a willingness to base innovative clinical decisions on accumulated information and analysis of past experience. Thus, a more case-based ethical approach offers hope for softening the desire to ground decisions involving complementary and alternative medicine strictly on notions of what is definitively "proven" or "validated."

Further, even with the basic guiding principles, proponents of principlism acknowledge that in some contexts, patient rights, specific virtues, and emotional considerations outweigh any balancing of the four clusters of moral principles.[29] In any event, while casuistry and other perspectives are helpful and deserve their own comprehensive

A New View of Nonmaleficence • 39
analysis in complementary and alternative medicine, the principle of nonmaleficence furnishes one starting point for ethical analysis to evaluate inclusion of complementary and alternative medical therapies in clinical care.

Balancing Paternalism and Autonomy

When evaluating nonmaleficence in provision of complementary and alternative medical therapies, physicians frequently face the issue of how to balance paternalism against other principles, particularly autonomy. Opponents of complementary and alternative medicine sometimes critique the autonomy value as unbridled consumerism. They assert, for example, that consumer demand for complementary and alternative medical therapies provides no justification for either clinical decisions involving complementary and alternative medicine or public policy and regulatory perspectives on access to complementary and alternative medicine. This perspective undervalues the role of informed patient choice and misstates the value of autonomy as a guiding principle. Autonomy does not reflect a blind obeisance to market forces but rather represents deep respect for the person and his or her own free choices. Thus, when paternalistic and autonomy perspectives conflict, the question is whether the two are equally weighted—in other terms, which should control. For example, which principle should trump in cases 1A and 1B?

Physicians should be able to help educate and guide their patients without making choices for their patients. A more extreme paternalistic perspective holds that patients should be protected from their own ignorant or foolish choices, particularly when making health care choices outside biomedical orthodoxy. This authoritarian model— sometimes summarized as "doctor knows best"—has dominated biomedicine. Jay Katz has argued that against the coercive, historical force of medical paternalism, even such legal and ethical principles as informed consent represent breakthroughs that still engender reluctant and partial compliance.[30] In general, bioethicists have held that overriding patients' known, voluntary, and intelligent choices is unjustified, absent compelling reasons such as: (1) the patient being at risk of a significant, preventable harm; (2) the paternalistic action being able to prevent the harm; (3) the projected benefits of the paternalistic action outweighing its risks to the patient; and (4) the least autonomy-restrictive alternative being adopted.[31]

Such criteria are not met merely because the patient has chosen a complementary and alternative medical therapy.[32] Yet by and large, paternalism has dominated regulatory analysis of patient access to complementary and alternative medicine. This perspective has pervaded medical board hearings, judicial decisions, and ethical discussions surrounding complementary and alternative medicine, without a rigorous analysis of the necessary preconditions to imposing such paternalism. More specifically, medical boards, for example, not only have stripped physicians of their licenses for using complementary and alternative medical therapies, even where no patient harm was shown, but also have excluded patients from testifying on the basis that patients lack competence to testify about their own medical care.[33] This reflects not only denigration but also a lack of respect for patient perspectives regarding their own health and health care choices. In a similar vein, various courts have asserted that a "reasonable patient would not even consider" alternatives to chemotherapy; that the testimony of the "lay sufferer" of cancer is "entitled to no weight"; and that patients must be protected from their own therapeutic choices when such choices are not FDA-approved under federal law, even if such patients will "die of cancer nonetheless."[34]

This conflict between paternalism and autonomy, played out in litigation involving therapeutic use of complementary and alternative medicine, suggests that nonmaleficence has been conceptualized almost exclusively in terms of being satisfied by either (1) withholding a complementary and alternative medical therapy of dubious efficacy from a patient or (2) dissuading the patient from using such a therapy. Yet the principle of nonmaleficence conceivably could mean something entirely different. For example, the principle of nonmaleficence might be satisfied by *providing* (rather than withholding) a complementary and alternative medical therapy—for example, when the patient requests such a therapy and there is some minimal or reasonable therapeutic support for the request (see chart 1).

Although the exact threshold for evidence may change over time or may vary by institution and practitioner, at the very least, this reconceptualization of nonmaleficence shifts the burden of persuasion from the patient seeking to use complementary and alternative medicine to

CHART 1. Moral Value in Complementary and
Alternative Medicine: Conceptualizing Nonmaleficence

Value	Traditional Meaning	New Conceptualization
Nonmale-ficence	"Do no harm"	Shield patients from direct and indirect toxicity
		Discuss risks and benefits neutrally and dispassionately
		Respect patient perspectives through nondisparagement
		Account for issues of cost and toxicity with clinically relevant conventional therapies
	Withhold therapy of dubious efficacy	Provide therapy with reasonable therapeutic support if patient so requests and is informed regarding physician's view of safety, effectiveness, and potential lack of cost-effectiveness.

the provider (or institution or regulatory body) seeking to deny the patient access to complementary and alternative medicine. For example, even if the therapy's benefit is questionable from the perspective of the physician, consensus medical standards, or testing to the satisfaction of a government agency, withholding the complementary and alternative medical therapy in question could still be considered ethically problematic if the patient finds the therapy is working and the alternative is death, further deterioration, or severe side effects of a conventional treatment.

In other words, the decision to *withhold* from the patient complementary and alternative medical therapies that potentially may be of benefit in fact may violate the requirements for nonmaleficence articulated earlier.[35] For instance, in cases 1A and 1B, withholding the complementary and alternative medical therapy or information regarding the complementary and alternative medical therapy in effect forces the patient to undergo surgery and chemotherapy, respectively. These therapies impose a minimum threshold of violence. The issue of whether this level of violence is justified necessarily implicates cultural as well as medical norms. A judge may have opined that there *is* no reasonable alternative to chemotherapy; yet chemotherapy engenders violence nonetheless, and the judge quoted does not take into account the *felt needs* of the person inhabiting the body that is subjected to that violence. The attending physician will have to navigate between the competing emotional tugs, as well as principles, of paternalism and autonomy.

Case 1B presents a particularly compelling scenario, as it involves a real family in a plea to allow a four-year-old boy to forgo costly and painful radiation and chemotherapy (which have high likelihood of permanent damage) and choose to receive an investigational new treatment for his brain tumor (which has unknown likelihood of success and is said to have low toxicity).[36] The struggle pits fully informed, intelligent patients seeking treatments for a brain tumor against the U.S. government, because the FDA did not approve the treatment as safe and effective.[37] This conflict between patients and families and the FDA gives concrete dimensions to the claimed ideal of "patient protection."

In the congressional hearings relating to case 1B, the family in fact appeared at the proceedings, with one child who had been successfully treated with the unapproved drug and with another child "visibly suffering the toxic effects of radiation and chemotherapy."[38] During the testimony, the FDA continued to deny the family access to the requested therapy yet continued to assert that it was protecting the family. Hence, "patient protection" was used to justify a paternalistic approach. Later, the FDA spokesperson was quoted as stating that "there is no scientific and ethical justification for using a child in research when a proven, effective treatment is available."[39]

Such language is significant, since it indicates some hidden assumptions behind the paternalistic vantage—for example, the notion that the child would be "used" in "research" rather than making a voluntary and informed choice for a drug the government has not approved; the assumption (without fuller explanation) that chemotherapy is "effective" and the failure to include side effects, especially through the lens of the patient; the use of the word "proven" and the bypassing of the question of *who decides what works (and how well it "works"*)—the government bureaucracy or the individual with the brain tumor and his or her family. The statement also exemplifies a pervasive view of patients as helpless, gullible, and in need of government protection, despite the fact that this level of protection is one the patients themselves have rejected. In this case, the federal government imposed a paternalistic view of nonmaleficence in a successful attempt to trump the autonomy value, but one may question whether this legal success in fact was ethical. This situation suggests that nonmaleficence in complementary and alternative medicine requires not only potential reconceptualization but also rethinking of its weight relative to the value of paternalism.

Bridging Autonomy Interests

Medical paternalism is not a necessary component of a public health approach to complementary and alternative medicine. Rather, paternalism results partly from history: in the process of translating philosophical and economic rivalries among competing medical sects into law, legal and medical authority historically marginalized, dismissed, or condemned complementary and alternative medical systems as undeniably deviant or dangerous.[40] Thus, the notion of viewing complementary and alternative medical therapies through the lens of nonmaleficence itself has reflected embedded biomedical bias. The seeds of new thinking are found in existing legal developments.

For example, in a recent decision involving labeling of dietary supplements, *Pearson v. Shalala*, the D.C. Court of Appeals rejected the emphasis on paternalism that to date has dominated the case law in the area of food and drug law.[41] Specifically, the court upheld a challenge to the FDA's rejection of four health claims for dietary supplements; the challenge was based on the FDA's failure to define adequately the standard of "significant scientific agreement" for such health claims. The court stated: "[The FDA's position is] as if the consumers were asked to buy something while hypnotized, and therefore . . . are bound to be misled."[42] The court characterized the FDA viewpoint as "almost frivolous," drawing an analogy to a case in which the Supreme Court rejected the "paternalistic assumption that the recipients . . . are 'no more discriminating than the audience for children's television.'"[43] Among other things, by placing autonomy ahead of paternalism, the opinion suggests a possible opening to an ethics of care, in which fidelity to patient needs, sensitivity, and trust becomes a central value in a healing relationship between patient and caregiver, replacing dominance and dependence with collaboration, mutual respect, and equal exchange.[44]

The preference for paternalism over autonomy interests in defining nonmaleficence in complementary and alternative medicine has persisted for several additional reasons. First, this perspective perhaps suggests the unfamiliarity and paradigmatic challenges much of complementary and alternative medicine presents to biomedical models. "Do no harm" in fact may be a truism articulated as a cover for fear. What exactly, for example, would it mean for the conventional medical zeitgeist if homeopathy "worked" or if persons in fact were surrounded by living matrixes of information, known as bioenergy fields?[45] Drawing on Thomas Kuhn's work, such a view might be liberating or destabilizing, depending on how tightly one wanted to hold on to the existing order.

Whatever the patient's autonomous desire, the present main moral objection appears to be the possibility of harm from a therapy that lacks conclusive scientific evidence of safety and/or efficacy. The continuing emphasis on the need for "proof" to prevent harm has recurred in references by groups such as the Federation of State Medical Boards and the American Medical Association to many complementary and alternative medical therapies as "unproven" and "quackery."[46] These pejorative terms (which are rapidly disappearing from the consensus vocabulary) have done little to advance the debate. At best, they merely reflect a desire to understand what is effective.

Second, the requirement that the physician above all refrain from harming the patient does not vary depending on the therapy. Therefore, the principle of nonmaleficence ought to apply equally whether the therapy involved is biomedical (for example, radiation or surgery) or complementary and alternative (for example, acupuncture or homeopathy). Paternalistic attitudes in one realm will translate into the other. So will autonomy interests. Thus it is interesting that nonmaleficence has played such a disproportionate role as an objection to complementary and alternative medical therapies.

Third, the ethical principle of nonmaleficence in part coincides with the legal principle of due care. Physicians ordinarily satisfy nonmaleficence when their conduct meets the standard of due care; in such cases, they are deemed to be acting reasonably under the circumstances and not to be liable for medical malpractice.[47] Hence physicians are likely to view therapies outside general medical acceptance with fear of liability as well as clinical skepticism. To address this latter concern, the next section investigates the relationship among views of nonmalefi-cence, legal definitions of physician malpractice, and use of safety and efficacy to measure nonmaleficence.

Using Safety and Efficacy to Measure Nonmaleficence

Negligence (medical malpractice) classically has been thought of as incorporating a risk/benefit calculus. An individual acts as a reasonably prudent person under the circumstances when he or she takes an action in which the benefits outweigh the risks. The professional standard of care generally coincides with this implied calculus: health care professionals approve of procedures in which benefits to patients outweigh the risks.

The question of nonmaleficence thus initially may be analyzed by classifying complementary and alternative medical therapies in the following general categories: low risk/high benefit; high risk/low benefit; low risk/low benefit; high risk/high benefit (see chart 2).[48] The caveat is given that this presents a preliminary analysis that can be refined over time as data accumulates regarding benefits and risks and as judges and legislatures incorporate other variables into the framework. Further, ethical/unethical dichotomies can only summarize a subtler, shifting evaluation of how to approach patient care beyond the limits of conventional treatments.

In this preliminary analysis, *low risk* and *high risk* mean that the therapy is relatively safe or dangerous, respectively, while *high benefit* and *low benefit* mean that the therapy is relatively effective or ineffective, respectively. Again, the question of what kind and level of scientific studies will satisfy these categories remains to be elaborated; further, one could argue that a risk/benefit analysis does not entirely coincide with a safety/effectiveness analysis. One also could add other dimensions to the chart—that of cost-effectiveness and that of the ability of the consumer to access such therapies (for example, if the therapy is not reimbursed or if the patient lacks financial resources to obtain the therapy). Last, all charts present generalizations. Thus, the present analysis merely offers a thumbnail sketch to help deepen present discussion of the value of "doing no harm." It suggests that asking whether providing the therapy satisfies nonmaleficence can in part be evaluated by assessing the relative combination of risk and benefit.

1. Low Risk and High Benefit/Safe and Effective—Ethical to Provide. If the complementary and alternative medical therapy is both safe and effective, it is presumptively both non-negligent and *ethical* for the physician to offer the therapy.

Note that the word "effective" can have many meanings and requires further definition. There is much debate, for example, as to whether the fact that some complementary and alternative medical therapies have been used for centuries—or whether patients are satisfied with these therapies—itself constitutes efficacy.[49] This chapter merely offers a generalized guide for purposes of analyzing one's ethical position. For example, the meaning of "effective" for the purpose of a new drug to be approved by the FDA rests on a legal definition that requires a high level of clinical proof. Some have attempted to delineate specific and narrow definitions of efficacy that must be met before a complementary and alternative medical therapy can be recommended to a patient.[50]

A lower standard could consider a therapy "effective" if it relieves certain symptoms. Using the term even more loosely, a complementary and alternative medical provider might consider a therapy "effective" if it clears the organism of unresolved emotional and spiritual residue that is claimed to be a precursor or companion to medically diagnosed disease. One could argue that in integrative care, the ultimate determi-

CHART 2. Safety, Effectiveness, and Ethical Presumption

Risk	Benefit	Safety	Effectiveness	Nonmaleficence
Low	High	Safe	Effective	Presumptively *ethical*
High	Low	Unsafe	Ineffective	Presumptively *unethical*
Low	Low	Safe	Probably ineffective	*Possibly* unethical
High	High	Probably unsafe	Effective	*Probably* unethical

nation of "effectiveness" may depend on whether the therapy is being used to treat the disease itself (as in chemotherapy to treat a malignant cancer), adjunctive to other treatments (as in support groups to treat breast cancer), or to treat specific conditions (for example, chiropractic and massage therapy for relief of acute low-back pain or the Ornish program for reversal of coronary artery disease); or it may depend on who is defining the term and for what purpose.

Using the term "effective" under standards most generally acceptable in medicine, a physician's obligation of nonmaleficence arguably is satisfied when providing complementary and alternative medical therapies proven safe and effective under the most rigorous criteria.

2. High Risk and Low Benefit/Unsafe and Ineffective—Unethical to Provide. If the complementary and alternative medical therapy has high risk and low benefit and thus is both likely unsafe and ineffective, it is presumptively both negligent and *unethical* for the physician to offer the therapy. If conventional alternatives of known safety and efficacy are available, the physician should use them instead. A physician's obligation of nonmaleficence presumably is violated when providing complementary and alternative medical therapies in the unsafe/ineffective category.

3. Low Risk and Low Benefit/Safe yet Probably Ineffective—Possibly Unethical. Therapies that have low risk and low benefit present a "gray zone" in which legal conclusions and ethical questions are more complex. From the perspective of many clinicians, safety trumps efficacy. In other words, if safety is assured, yet efficacy dubious, the possibility of direct toxicity is diminished, and the patient may well benefit at least from a placebo effect. On the other hand, the possibility of indirect toxicity arises when the patient is led to an ineffective substitute for necessary conventional care. Therefore, a physician's obligation of nonmaleficence is *possibly violated* when providing complementary and alternative medical therapies in this category.

4. High Risk and High Benefit/Probably Unsafe yet Effective—Probably Unethical. Theoretically, if safety trumps efficacy, then providing a therapy that probably is unsafe yet is effective could lead to malpractice liability if the patient is thereby injured. Although this might not be true in conventional care, in complementary and alternative medicine, safety concerns are likely to be heightened, the so-called double standard being a function of the culture's general level of acceptance for the complementary and alternative medical therapy in ques-

tion. One could quibble as to whether *possibly* unethical or *probably* unethical is the correct conclusion. For the present, to match the liability assessment, this chart concludes that the physician's obligation of nonmaleficence is *probably violated* in this category.

Evaluating Safety and Efficacy in Complementary and Alternative Medicine

Chart 2 provides a framework for the physician in clinical practice to evaluate complementary and alternative medical therapies and make a determination as to whether the obligation of nonmaleficence is satisfied by a given patient request. As noted, however, "safety" and "efficacy" are controversial terms and depend on the defining criteria for each term.

For example, peer-reviewed medical journals, medical associations, and educational and government institutions may use consensus scientific tools to determine safety and efficacy and be able thus to classify a particular complementary and alternative medical therapy—for example, chiropractic for acute low-back pain—into one of the four listed categories. Such an effort can yield general guidelines for anticipating malpractice liability and for resolving the question of nonmaleficence in accordance with the framework detailed earlier. Some therapies unambiguously present proven dangers, while others conceptually present a variety of concerns. For example, safety issues associated with herbs in connection with surgery include a potential increase in bleeding time, skin reactions, and herb-drug interactions.[51] But the notion of creating a definitive matrix is deceptively simple and may fail to capture the complexity and uniqueness offered by the many fields and subfields within complementary and alternative medicine.

For example, at present, data does not exist to classify definitively most complementary and alternative medical therapies within the categories listed earlier. This leaves the categorization subject to rhetoric on both sides. For instance, many complementary and alternative medical providers claim that herbs are "more natural" or "less toxic" than drugs. When stated as gross generalizations, these assertions lack scientific foundation, delude the health care consumer, and justify appropriate sanctions. Public policy asserts a particular concern when providers or manufacturers make specific claims regarding safety, efficacy, or other aspects of a complementary and alternative medical therapy.[52] At the very least, such concern underlies many federal regulations concerning the prohibition against making "disease" claims for dietary supplements.[53]

On the other hand, many invoke the principle of nonmaleficence to suggest that it is unethical to provide the patient access to complementary and alternative medical therapies since most such therapies lack an evidentiary basis comparable to that of pharmaceuticals and medical procedures.[54] In other words, since most complementary and alternative medical therapies fall within category two (presumably unsafe and ineffective until proven otherwise), a few within category one, and the rest within the gray zones of categories three and four, it is both unethical and a high liability risk to offer most complementary and alternative medical therapies. In fairness to clinicians, the evidentiary ambiguity leaves them in a difficult situation: if they recommend therapies that lack satisfactory evidence, they err on the side of increased liability risk; yet if they deny the patient information concerning these same therapies, they err on the side of excessive paternalism.

In any event, the terminology physicians use with their patients carries implications for the therapeutic relationship and communication with integrity. The words "proven" and "unproven," "untested" and "unregulated," for example, can become conclusory labels, much like traditional legal conclusions such as the application of the terms "fraud" and "quackery" to therapies outside biomedicine.[55] When phrased this way, the question of nonmaleficence itself presupposes the answer: since complementary and alternative medical therapies are dangerous and ineffective and patients are poorly informed, it must be unethical to provide these therapies.[56] Such analysis also assumes away the question as to *how much* and *what kind of* evidence is satisfactory for the given therapy and *who decides* what kind and level of evidence suffices for a given therapy to be "tested," "proven," or made available to patients. Researchers describe a hierarchy of evidence—ranging, for example, from levels one (randomized controlled trials) and two (cohort studies and outcomes research) through three (case-control studies) and four (case-series and expert opinion without explicit critical appraisal).[57]

Of course, if the best contemporary scientific tools definitively and conclusively prove a therapy unsafe and ineffective, it is presumably unethical to provide such a therapy, and in addition, doing so probably would lead to liability. This assumes that such tools have a sufficient degree of reliability as to be conclusive indicators of validity, even for therapies whose mechanisms defy conventional models.[58] Doubtless, many complementary and alternative medical therapies touted as safe may in fact be dangerous; for example, numerous case reports exist suggesting that herbal remedies and even therapies such as homeopathy may have adverse effects.[59] Yet it may be difficult to generalize concerning the safety and efficacy of complementary and alternative medical therapies where such therapies encompass complete medical systems—such as Ayurvedic medicine or Tibetan medicine—that are embedded in coherent systems of thought foreign to biomedicine.[60] Such systems include not only models of health but also unique theologies, ontologies, and even eschatologies. Many practitioners claim that these whole systems of medicine cannot—and should not—be presented out of context and captured within a mechanistic, reductionist, and biopharmacological model of health. For example, although "sham" acupuncture needles can be used to test research hypotheses, the relationship between traditional oriental medicine and the concept of the Tao (sometimes translated as "the Way") cannot be captured by a clinical trial; similarly, the Tibetan Book of the Dead, which purports to guide the newly dead patient on subsequent astral journeys, is not amenable to randomized, controlled, double-blind studies, and some therapies (such as yoga) aim at models of physical, emotional, and spiritual health that may or may not have analogues in Western medicine.

Other complementary and alternative medical therapies involve beliefs and traditions that again do not easily lend themselves to Western, scientific scrutiny. The Native American sweat lodge is one example: since the gods are said to be performing the purification and healing, it is difficult to conceive of a trial, in which these same gods are asked *not* to occupy the "control group" tent. Health practices, spiritual beliefs, cultural traditions, and disease models intermingle. Still other practices—such as energy healing—place such an emphasis on intentionality and consciousness that physiological results in some cases become a secondary objective. The adage that holistic health emphasizes healing and harmony, as well as symptom management and curing, arguably precludes complete reduction of complementary and alternative medical therapies to comprehensive testing, validation, and comprehension via Western notions of safety and efficacy.

Moreover, there are at least three broad objections to placing pri-

mary emphasis on safety and efficacy—as interpreted by the norms
and evaluative models of biomedicine—as criteria for nonmaleficence
in complementary and alternative medicine. First, the notion of safety
and efficacy is inherently paternalistic, in the sense that it represents
consensus medical opinion regarding justification for patient access to
a therapy, not the patient's perspective. While the patient does care
whether the therapies he or she receives are both safe and effective, traditionally the physician has been the authority figure from the dominant culture. It is the physician—or the medical profession or the government—and not the patient that ultimately makes the determination
of safety and efficacy. The patient has a minimal role in the process and
is subject to a remote and impersonal determination following medical
and political principles in which the layperson is presumed to lack
competence. In this respect, the patient lacks equal power, particularly
if within an ethnic or religious minority. While some patients may prefer a more hierarchical relationship, for others even the hierarchy of
evidence will be seen to operate as an unwelcome imposition on their
preferences. The patient usually is far more willing to try therapies at
the borderland of safety and efficacy, whereas medical and political
authorities are far more willing to prejudge the matter and deprive the
patient of these possibilities.

This is the scenario presented in case 1B. From the patient's stand-
point, safety and efficacy—and the doctor's good judgment—are
meaningful, but not necessarily the most central concerns; from the
perspective of medical paternalism, what the government or the medical profession has to say about the safety and efficacy of a particular
therapy determines whether the patient should, and will, receive it. In
addition, pharmaceutical companies and manufacturers of medical
devices, have enormous financial and political power and great invest-
ment in determinations of safety and efficacy. While couched in terms
of patient protection, social, economic, and political concerns in fact
dominate or at least overshadow issues of safety and efficacy.

Second, the reliance on safety and efficacy reflects biomedical
dominance and a biological orientation to health, disease, and the
meaning of being human. When we speak of "safety," we mean safe for
the patient's body; when we speak of "efficacy," we mean pharmaco-
logically or physiologically efficacious. Yet if the patient is ultimately
responsible for his or her body, then the conclusions of the medical profession or the FDA or other persons and institutions are relevant, but

not authoritative. Such institutions ultimately may become certifying, but not authoritative, bodies, giving the patient greater latitude to ignore medical authority in favor of personal authority.[61] Further, physical care implicates emotional and spiritual care; many patients choose therapies on the basis of intuition and a personal, cultural, or spiritual sense of health that may or may not coincide with medical information and advice.

Third, the requirement of safety and efficacy is ethnocentric and fails to account for potential uses of complementary and alternative medical therapies outside a narrow range of acceptance. For example, the consensus panel convened by the NIH recently concluded that there is clear evidence that acupuncture is effective for only a few conditions, such as pain and chemotherapy-induced nausea and vomiting.[62] But the acupuncture tradition does not limit its therapeutic value in this fashion. Nor do patients. "Unproven" uses standards of proof and evidence approved by orthodoxies and traditions other than those accepted by the patient. Such labels often violate the second definition of nonmaleficence—nondisparagement of patient perspectives (in which "anectodal" evidence—the experience of one—may count). Yet for the physician, this also creates a double-edged sword: if the patient makes a decision based on what the physician considers to be inappropriate anecdotal evidence and is thereby injured, the physician could find himself or herself the target of a malpractice lawsuit.

Historically, biomedicine has used its own internal criteria to ensure that its definitions of reality control the rate, level, and interpretation of therapies such as acupuncture and chiropractic.[63] Hence the attempts to Westernize acupuncture; separate the therapy from its cultural, philosophical, and spiritual context; dismiss its underlying tenets as "'Oriental hocus-pocus'"; and begin "subjugating it under a biomedical interpretive framework."[64] Even if safety remains one litmus test for complementary and alternative medical therapies, such criteria leave many ethical questions, alongside issues of liability, unanswered.

Dimensions of Health

One way to interpret conventional notions of safety and efficacy in terms more indigenous to complementary and alternative medicine is to return to the notion of holism. As noted, the term *complementary and alternative* gradually has replaced the term *holistic*, partly because of its greater political resonance and social acceptance. Nonetheless, holistic ideals permeate complementary and alternative therapies.[65] Essentially, holism asserts that nature in general and individuals in particular express themselves in irreducible, multidimensional wholes. Holistic theory views health as the conflux of at least five dimensions of being—physical, mental, emotional, social, and spiritual. This suggests that the principle of nonmaleficence must address each level of health, not only the physical (see chart 3).[66]

Biomedicine often views the goals listed in chart 3 as hierarchically descending from the goal of cure, but this has not necessarily been true for all medical systems at all times. Even on the physical level, the admonition to "do no harm" could include theories and conceptualizations of physical health that differ from those in conventional care. One such example is the movement toward "holistic dentistry," which carries controversial ideas about how conventional dentistry sometimes creates toxicities in the body. Another is "functional medicine," which is grounded in biochemistry yet asserts theories of toxicity and detoxification that are not widely accepted in the conventional medical community.[67] Toxicity and detoxification were prominent ideas in the history of medicine (for example, purging and emetics) and remain a controversial component of many complementary and alternative medical therapies.

On the mental level, physiological safety and efficacy alone do not account for such concepts as lucidity of mind, clarity, gentleness of mind, or pure Presence. Again, the medical model might look to how well a pharmacological agent, for example, reduces symptoms of anxi-

---

CHART 3. Nonmaleficence in Varying Dimensions of Health

Dimension of Health	Representative Care Goals
Physical	Detoxification; cleansing
Mental	Lucidity; clarity of mind
Emotional	Emotional safety; emotional efficacy (healing balm)
Social	Respecting cultural beliefs
Spiritual	Enhancing welfare of the soul; presence

ety or even psychosis. Yet such a model probably lacks the different theories of mind presented by, say, Eastern philosophies. For example, what biomedicine means by a "clear mind" and what a spiritual healer, Reiki practitioner, or Tibetan physician (who follows the teachings of the Medicine Buddha) means by a "clear mind" presumably are different. At the very least, one might say that the Buddha's concept of a clear mind must be entered into experientially, since an attempt to define such a concept through diagnostic and statistical categories familiar to Western psychiatry evaluates the Buddha mind *from* a mind that lacks diamond clarity. The very insistence on the subjective world, with its fuzzy, imprecise borders, its psychic landscapes, its open defiance of conventional measurement and rational investigation, defines much of complementary and alternative medicine and challenges present clinical, legal, and ethical models.

On the emotional level, "safety" takes on an entirely differently meaning and has subtle dimensions according to individual variability. The subjective component becomes more important and thus less amenable to the objective framework and mass scale implicit in evidentiary hierarchies. For example, one patient may feel safe with a physician who discusses strictly conventional medical possibilities and feel invaded if the physician raises complementary and alternative medical therapies that are more esoteric. Another patient may feel safest with an intimate bedside manner; yet another may find this invasive. One patient may feel safe with a physician who leaves space for emotional disclosure, as the emotional unweaving may provide hidden cues to the underlying etiology and constitute the beginning of healing; yet another may find safety in continuing denial of the emotional factors underlying the disease process.

Similarly, on the emotional level "efficacy" may yield different meanings than when analyzed solely on the physical level. A pharmaceutical agent may be physically efficacious yet emotionally (or culturally) void of any meaning for the patient's understanding of the meaning of the disease and his or her personal healing process—for example, the drug that cures but does not heal. Similarly, an herb may be physically efficacious yet, if used like a drug, have no emotional impact. On the other hand, an herb used specifically to address an emotional or spiritual imbalance may be efficacious in terms of correcting an underlying disturbance and have meaning for the patient within the framework of a certain herbal tradition (for example, a Chinese herb to help the lung meridian, associated with grief). The sacred dimensions of the therapeutic encounter then assume front stage.

The therapeutic relationship also becomes central in the social dimension. "Doing no harm" may mean respecting cultural beliefs and the patient's reintegration into social structures preexisting the illness. Safety and efficacy may be measured by the delicate refitting of the individual into social patterns and restoring the person's mood and social function, even as the body and being heal on all levels.

On the spiritual level, safety and efficacy are the most subtle and complex. What is safe and efficacious for an individual with one belief system is not so for another. For example, is it spiritually safe for the Jehovah's Witness to accept a blood transfusion, which will save the physical life but wreak havoc, in the view of the patient and the patient's family, on the spiritual life? Similarly, the patient in case 1A may prefer to make a spiritual choice to try Reiki, colonics, and yoga for a period—healing the body energetically and hoping the physiology aligns—rather than subject her physical body to what she views as an invasive, cutting procedure that could be ultimately unnecessary.

In a system of medical ethics that measures nonmaleficence solely in physical terms, the answer is straightforward: we can measure the life of the body and not the life of the soul; hence, by and large, where the continuation of physical existence is pitted against the welfare of the soul, physical existence trumps. Although some exceptions might be made out of respect for the religious beliefs of *others*, such deference does not accord respect to the content of such beliefs but only to the principle of respect for others' autonomous choices based on religious belief. Thus, the exceptions do not respect the spiritual dimension or the soul per se—rather, they respect the person's *choice* of a spiritual decision.

Applying Safety and Efficacy to Spiritually Based Therapies

Because they implicitly incorporate or expressly rely on spiritual principles, many complementary and alternative medical therapies challenge governing scientific paradigms or by their terms purport to operate on different principles. As one example, the understanding of *chi* in acupuncture and traditional oriental medicine derives from philosophical systems and beliefs different than those that undergird modern,

Western science. *Chi*, practitioners assert, does not reduce to physio-logical and anatomical principles. The same is true of *prana* in Ayurvedic medicine. Similarly, Chinese herbs are not dispensed according to pharmacological principles but rather are said to affect different aspects of the patient's "vital energy."

Similarly, in energy healing, the patient's bioenergy field (the energy body or subtle body) is more easily detected by human faculties than by contemporary scientific instrumentation. By and large, con-sciousness defies objective measurement. As is true for other comple-mentary and alternative medical therapies that challenge prevailing scientific and medical models, more "proof" may not necessarily increase acceptance. As Ted Kaptchuk suggests, issues of belief perme-ate even scientific inquiry into such topics. Kaptchuk expresses doubt that more trials, with greater methodological rigor, will be persuasive to the medical community:

> The situation resembles the predicament with homeopathy trials, another seemingly implausible intervention, where the evidence of multiple positive, randomized controlled trials . . . will not con-vince the medical community of its validity. . . . It seems that the decision concerning acceptance of evidence . . . ultimately reflects the beliefs of the person that exist before all arguments and obser-vation.[68]

Even in the field of massage, notions of efficacy may require rein-terpretation to incorporate the importance of underlying spiritual real-ities in the therapeutic process. Not all the purported benefits of mas-sage therapy translate into the way efficacy is usually conceptualized. For instance, one study suggested that when workers were given fif-teen minutes of massage therapy a week, math problems were com-pleted in approximately half the time required without massage, with approximately 50 percent fewer errors.[69] If disease is conceptualized in its narrow sense, then the scientific notion of efficacy corresponds; on the other hand, if disease is given a broader definition—to include, for example, losses in satisfaction and productivity due to muscle ten-sion—then efficacy, too, gains a broader and more inclusive meaning.

Wilhelm Reich theorized that such a broader understanding of dis-ease accounted for social problems whose solutions could only be found at the level of body musculature. He believed that individuals accumulate muscular tension through the suppression of basic orgiastic impulses, ultimately developing a psychological shield consisting of "body armor," preventing the possibility of deep emotional contact and true spiritual intimacy.[70] Reich's ideas found further expression in the work of Alexander Lowen, who developed bioenergetic therapy, and of others who carried the techniques into psychotherapy and energy healing.[71] Such theorists found therapies such as massage to operate on several levels, the physical being perhaps the least important or the most "gross" and least "subtle." The true purpose of bodywork, according to these individuals, is emotional release and the accompanying shift in spiritual energies, resulting in a change in the person's spiritual consciousness. Thus, for example, bodywork is said to enhance the flow of the life-force—a person's vital energy—and thereby affect "the systemic implications of an illness, whether the primary symptoms surface in physical disabilities, emotional imbalances, or warped thinking."[72] If complementary and alternative medical modalities such as massage therapy and body-oriented psychotherapy (for example, bioenergetics) purport to release emotional and spiritual, as well as physical, toxins, then analysis of nonmaleficence touches the uncomfortable ethical borderland between medicine and spirituality.

In this context, prayer introduces particularly controversial applications. Larry Dossey has made the provocative suggestion that— if studies suggest prayer is efficacious—it could be malpractice (or unethical) for physicians in the future *not* to pray with/for their patients.[73] Questions of safety and efficacy bear new meanings in the world of prayer.[74] If prayer is, on some level, equated with nonlocal healing and if thoughts—both positive and negative—along with provider expectations regarding patient health can impact the patient's well-being from a distance, then the provider's religious disposition or absence of religious disposition may play a role in the evaluation of safety and efficacy.[75]

Conclusion

Many of the paradigmatic and philosophical differences between biomedicine and some complementary and alternative medical therapies suggest changes in the criteria typically used to assess whether given therapies are efficacious or appropriate in specific clinical situations.

For example, even if safety and efficacy continue to serve as indicia of nonmaleficence, integrative health care strategies suggest such criteria no longer can be measured solely in the realm of the physical. Such measurement limits clinical possibilities to the internal logic and rules of biomedicine. As further articulated in subsequent chapters, robust understanding of safety and efficacy must transcend historical paternalism, biomedical dominance, and ethnocentric notions of health and disease and begin to incorporate the mental, emotional, social, and spiritual aspects of human life from the new and startling perspectives of other health care disciplines.

Referral Strategy and the Ethics of Integration

Case 2A Referral to an Acupuncturist Who Turns out to
Be Negligent

 A physician is treating a patient for cervical cancer with
chemotherapy, radiation, and other conventional therapies.
The patient requests a referral to a licensed acupuncturist,
as she has read an article in a popular health magazine noting that
acupuncture is effective in reducing nausea and other symptoms of
chemotherapy. The physician refers the patient to an acupuncturist
who is covered by the same health maintenance organization that covers the physician's services to the patient.

The physician speaks to the acupuncturist once prior to making
the referral and learns that the acupuncturist uses needling, together
with standard herbal formulas, to relieve nausea and other side effects
of chemotherapy. As it turns out, however, the acupuncturist is negligent in three ways: he or she (1) fails to follow clean needle technique;
(2) uses a Chinese herb not tested by Western scientific standards for
this patient or condition that has toxic side effects; and (3) uses Western
herbal medicine even though the applicable state licensing statute only
authorizes use of traditional oriental herbal medicine. The patient suffers an adverse reaction and sues the physician.

Meanwhile, the state medical board brings charges against the
physician for unprofessional conduct, alleging that the physician negligently as well as unethically referred a patient to an acupuncturist during the cancer treatment and negligently failed to supervise the
acupuncturist's use of both Chinese and Western herbal medicine.

Case 2B   Failure to Refer to a Competent Acupuncturist

 The same physician is treating another patient for cervical cancer with chemotherapy, radiation, and other conventional therapies. The physician reads in medical literature that acupuncture is effective in reducing nausea and other symptoms of chemotherapy. The physician, who still is defending the earlier lawsuit, declines to refer the patient to a licensed acupuncturist, even though the acupuncturist is reimbursed by the same health maintenance organization that covers the physician's services to the patient.

The patient later reads an article on the Internet from a prestigious, peer-reviewed medical journal suggesting that acupuncture and Chinese herbal medicine would have reduced side effects of chemotherapy, including nausea and various gastrointestinal complications resulting from chronic malnutrition. The patient sues the physician for malpractice, based on failure to obtain adequate informed consent, and for intentional (reckless) infliction of emotional distress, based on physical injuries accompanying failure to disclose a therapeutic option whose effectiveness in relieving suffering was medically proven.

Case 2C   Referral of a Heart Patient for Yoga Therapy

 A cardiac patient has read on the Internet that the Ornish program, consisting of lifestyle and dietary changes, meditation, and yoga, can reverse heart disease. The patient asks the physician for an opinion regarding the risks and benefits of yoga therapy. The patient's yoga instructor has reported that ancient yogis discovered yoga postures in meditation.

The physician never has practiced yoga, does not believe in its precepts and claims, and considers the philosophy of yoga to be religious rather than descriptive—a set of beliefs adopted in faith. Further, the physician feels the yoga teacher who tries to help a cardiac patient is practicing medicine—aimed at ameliorating or curing disease—and therefore must show that yoga has the same evidence base for safety and efficacy in treatment of cardiac disease as conventional medicine.

The patient's accountant has informed the patient that she can only take yoga therapy as a tax deduction if prescribed by a physician. The patient insists on a referral and threatens to sue if the physician declines. The physician is particularly concerned about risks to heart patients from headstands and other inverted postures and wonders about the legal and ethical implications of writing out "yoga therapy" on a prescription or referral slip.

Liability and Ethical Rules Surrounding Referrals for Complementary and Alternative Medical Therapies

Cases 2A through 2C help frame the question of whether it is legal and/or ethical for a physician to *refer* a patient to a complementary and alternative medical provider if the physician has insufficient scientific evidence regarding, or personal belief in, the safety and efficacy of the therapies offered by the provider. Further, is it legal and/or ethical *not* to refer? Areas of particular relevance to this question are those within clinical practice in which professionally adopted ethical norms and standards for complementary and alternative medical therapies are either lacking or recently developed or present unusually compelling scenarios at the intersection of ethical and malpractice rules. Such therapies include guided imagery and hypnotherapy, certain forms of spiritual healing, and mind-body-spirit therapies such as yoga.

The general legal rule is that a physician bears no malpractice liability merely for referring the patient to another health care practitioner. No published opinions yet have arisen involving referral for complementary and alternative medical therapies, but such cases are likely forthcoming as integrative care becomes increasingly mainstream. Moreover, since malpractice liability principles arise from state law, courts are likely to emerge with different opinions, based on specific factual scenarios, on whether liability attaches in any given situation. Thus, at best it is possible to predict and/or guide clinicians (and judges) based on cases and principles that have emerged in conventional care. Notably, there are several prominent exceptions to the general rule, each of which conceivably could generate malpractice liability.[1]

First, direct liability attaches to the referring physician if the decision to refer itself reflects a lack of due care, resulting in patient injury. This could happen if, for example, the physician refers to a practitioner of acupuncture and traditional oriental medicine and the referral creates unnecessary delay or induces the patient to forgo necessary conventional treatment.

This argument for direct liability likely would fail in case 2A, since the physician continued conventional monitoring and treatment. If, however, the physician in case 2A also was negligent in making the referral, the physician could be directly liable for the referral. This could occur if, for example, the acupuncturist had a documented history of professional discipline and/or malpractice liability for failing to follow clean needle technique or for using herbal medicine inappropriately. One could argue that the referring physician's duty of due care would include checking with the state acupuncture board regarding the acupuncturist's history of professional discipline and checking public records for a history of malpractice claims. These simple acts would at least constitute some reasonable diligence in investigating the acupuncturist's competence. In cases where the physician knew or should have known of such history, referral to the acupuncturist not only could trigger liability on the physician's part but also could be considered unethical, as it would violate the physician's obligation to do no harm.

The same argument for direct liability also might succeed in case 1A (discussed in chap. 1) if the physician referred the cancer patient to a naturopath, for example, for colonics, yoga, and Reiki in lieu of (rather than as a possible prelude to) surgery. This scenario is possible given the confusion and debate, in states licensing naturopaths, regarding the extent to which naturopathic physicians have sufficient clinical training, skill, and legal authority to render primary care. If the patient's condition deteriorated, then the patient could argue that the referral itself—even though requested by the patient—was inappropriate or negligent, in that it delayed or deferred necessary conventional care (the surgery).

In such a scenario, the physician might have available as a defense the argument that the patient assumed the risk of injury; many courts, however, would reject the argument.[2] Courts sometimes strike down assumption of risk defenses in favor of "public policy" considerations, such as the physician's fiduciary obligation to not abandon the patient and to continue providing necessary medical care, even when the patient requests otherwise.[3]

The next series of exceptions to the general rule involves vicarious liability. This means that although the referring physician is not directly negligent, courts will impute the negligence of the treating practitioner to the referring physician. The first scenario for vicarious liability arises when the treating practitioner is regarded as an *agent* of the referring physician. This could arise if, for example, the physician refers to an acupuncturist and the law in that state requires physician supervision of acupuncturists for the treatment of the condition in question. In other words, physician supervision potentially makes the acupuncturist the physician's agent for liability purposes.

A second likely scenario for agency involves coordinated care between the referring physician and the treating practitioner, who both are operating within a common insurance network. That the physician and acupuncturist in case 2A are covered by the same health maintenance organization and have spoken at least once regarding the patient's care could augur shared liability between physician and acupuncturist. Even though the acupuncturist has provided services that are nonmedical and that remain distinct from the conventional care offered by the physician, some courts liberally construe "joint treatment" and agency principles, so as to extend liability along the chain of treatment.[4]

A third variation on vicarious liability involves referral to a provider that the referring physician knows or has reason to know is incompetent. If, for instance, the physician refers the patient to a practitioner who is nonlicensed and lacks even the minimum professional training and skills to satisfy standards of competence within the practitioner's professional peer group, such a referral might be deemed one to a "known incompetent" and thus fit principles of vicarious liability. (Conceptually, referral to a "known incompetent" also can be viewed as a variation on direct liability.)

To give an example, in case 2C, if the physician refers the patient to a yoga instructor who lacks minimal competence and whose therapeutic techniques aggravate the patient's condition, the referring physician theoretically could be held liable for referral to a "known incompetent." Like homeopaths, naturopaths, herbalists, and energy healers in many states, yoga instructors presently lack licensure. This raises the possibility that the "known incompetent" category could be triggered by a court philosophically predisposed against such nonlicensed complementary and alternative medical modalities.

Parenthetically, as in other professions, leaders within yoga recently have explored development of minimum educational standards for the profession.[5] Among other objectives, this represents an attempt to enhance professional status, preempt government regulation and insurance standards, and perhaps avert excessive liability. Arguably, the development of internal professional standards for competence, as well as sufficient intraprofessional coherence and agreement to create the beginnings of professional self-regulation, suffices to preclude application of the "known incompetent" category. Yet another issue arises, however, concerning the boundaries between the nonlicensed profession and the practice of medicine. Yoga masters (such as B. K. S. Iyengar) recommend specific asanas (postures) and combinations of asanas for particular medical conditions (for example, for high blood pressure, bronchitis, colitis, diabetes, epilepsy, migraines, and ulcers).[6] Yet leading yoga teachers in the United States advise refraining from "prescribing" postures for specific conditions, as this could be viewed as unlicensed medical practice.[7]

The boundaries between yoga therapy to achieve harmony and balance, physical as well as mental, and advising the patient regarding treatment of a medical condition can be blurred and ambiguous—just as lines between Western medicine and other professions such as chiropractic, acupuncture, and even massage therapy can blur when human health is addressed in a holistic fashion.[8] While asanas, and modalities such as spinal manipulation or massage of muscles, are distinct from high-technology medical modalities such as CAT scans and ultrasounds, many complementary and alternative medical therapies claim some relationship to the imbalance underlying disease. Thus, referring to a provider who crosses the line—even unwittingly—into unlicensed medical practice conceivably could trigger application of agency principles, rendering the referring physician vicariously liable for a treating complementary and alternative medical practitioner's negligence.

The various rules of liability create both a legal catch-22 and a liability paradox. The legal catch-22 involves conflicting notions of how to protect one's professional practice from unwarranted liability. In the Greek epic *The Odyssey*, the seafaring hero Ulysses is trapped at one point between two monsters, Scylla and Charybdis. Whichever way Ulysses steers his ship, he faces one deadly adversary or another. In the same way, the physician is caught between the Scylla of liability for excessive supervision and the Charybdis of liability for inadequate supervision.[9] In other words, the more the physician supervises and controls the treating practitioner, the greater the risk of vicarious liability; the less the physician supervises and controls the treating practitioner, the greater the risk of direct liability if the treating practitioner acts negligently. Current law provides no satisfactory resolution to the dilemma.

The liability paradox involves the prospect of shared liability up and down the chain of providers. In integrative care, the model includes a team approach to patient management, in which various providers engage in "cross-cultural" discussions of their various approaches to helping the patient. In other words, "joint treatment" is almost an inherent part of care. Thus, the more providers share information, knowledge, and coordination of approaches, the greater the risk of shared liability among them. Information sharing may expand liability but ultimately reduce risk to the patient; yet maintaining sharp boundaries between providers may decrease risk of shared liability but ultimately increase risk to the patient. The liability paradox involves trading potentially shared liability against reduction in potential harm to the patient; thus, nonmaleficence may entail sharing liability risk in an integrative setting.

Legal Implications of Declining to Refer

As noted, the arms-length referral between a physician and a specialist in conventional care must be modified in the integrative model, which requires a high degree of coordination among physicians and allied as well as complementary and alternative medical providers. Integration implies a team approach to the various sources and levels of the patient's affliction. As shared liability increasingly is likely, attempts to create clear lines of separation become increasingly artificial. Presumably, as well, the referring physician wants to be informed about the nature and scope of complementary and alternative medical treatments being furnished to his or her patient. The need for information is especially compelling when the complementary and alternative medical therapy has strong, potential adverse effects—such as the possibility for adverse herb-drug interactions.

The legal catch-22 also means that the physician can be caught between potential liability for referring the patient to a complementary and alternative medical provider who is negligent and potential liability for *failure* to refer for a beneficial complementary and alternative medical therapy. To date, no court has held a physician liable for failing to provide the patient with, or refer for, complementary and alternative medical therapies. Litigation over use or omission of complementary and alternative medical therapies, however, is just beginning, and future cases may hold a physician liable on an informed-consent theory for failing to direct the patient to an appropriate complementary and alternative medical therapy that has significant medical acceptance. Further, liability attaches when the physician deviates from the standard of care and such deviation results in patient injury. Therefore, as research increasingly uncovers complementary and alternative medical therapies of demonstrated benefit to the patient, such therapies increasingly become incorporated into "conventional" care and must be considered part of the required standard of care. For example, if gingko biloba is found useful in treatment of dementia, then the physician presumably has a legal obligation to make such a therapy part of the therapeutic armamentarium, even though it is herbal rather than pharmaceutical. Similarly, there may be therapies once considered philosophically objectionable that, when incorporated into conventional standards of care, become effectively mandated by legal rules governing malpractice. This could be the case if, for example, a therapy such as homeopathic treatment becomes indicated for a condition such as recurrent childhood ear infections. Once sufficient medical acceptance brings a complementary and alternative medical therapy within the standard of care, then failing to provide, or refer for, such a therapy satisfies the first element of malpractice.

Thus, in case 2B, the physician who fails to refer the patient to a competent acupuncturist when peer-reviewed medical literature indicates acupuncture for treatment of the patient's condition conceivably could be liable for failure to provide the patient with adequate informed consent. At least one court, in *Moore v. Baker*, has stated that if the patient could show that reasonably prudent physicians generally recognize and accept a complementary and alternative medical treatment for coronary blockages, the patient who fails to receive the requisite information could have a valid informed-consent claim.[10]

A more complicated scenario than case 2B is case 1A, in which the physician is asked to refer to complementary and alternative medical providers for therapies the patient wishes to explore in an attempt to stave off surgery. Here, legal issues surrounding the referral and the informed-consent obligation involve displacing conventional treat-ment with complementary and alternative medical therapies for a time—for example, delaying surgery for two months while the patient uses yoga, colonics, and Reiki. The more subtle clinical decision that the case illustrates is not whether to provide, refer, or discuss but whether to provide, refer, or discuss complementary and alternative medicine with appropriate disclosure of risks and benefits, while continuing to monitor conventionally.

When framed this way, the choice is apparent: the physician can allow patients to make their own health care choices without necessar-ily abandoning the obligation to do no harm. The caveat is given that conventional monitoring would help the provider know when to inter-vene conventionally, should the complementary and alternative med-ical therapy prove unavailing and the patient's condition dangerously deteriorate; this can help protect the patient against unwarranted injury and the provider against resultant liability. Further, if either severe direct or indirect toxicity results, the provider probably should recommend discontinuing the complementary and alternative medical therapy and revert to necessary conventional care.

Ethical Implications of Declining to Refer

The decision *not* to refer carries ethical as well as legal implications. As suggested, at the least failing to inform could, in an appropriate situa-tion, result in liability. Legislative developments probably will support increased pressure to refer to complementary and alternative medical providers, where appropriate. As suggested, these developments fol-low political and social changes, rather than solely changes in medical evidence.

For example, the National Center for Complementary and Alter-native Medicine at the NIH was not created following proof of efficacy of any given therapy but rather because of the anecdotal experience of two patients who happened to be members of the U.S. Congress. The first, Representative Berkeley Bedell, reportedly found an effective treatment for his lyme disease in a product that could not be obtained in the United States because it was not FDA-approved. The second, Senator Tom Harkin, reportedly found his allergies cured by bee pollen. Neither therapy had compelling proof in the scientific or medical literature, but each had proof in the minds of these two individuals. Their creation of an office within the NIH to study complementary and alternative medical therapies could be dismissed as a bow to consumerism or could be regarded as respect for therapeutic potential outside conventional orthodoxy. In any event, the creation of such an office prior to any significant evidence of efficacy for most complementary and alternative medical therapies suggests that to some extent, "legislative recognition trumps medical recognition."[11]

In short, public policy concerns differ from scientific concerns such as safety and efficacy; policy concerns encompass consumer desires, autonomy interests, access to varying therapies, innovation in clinical care, and other values. Similarly, once a state legislature decides to license a specific category of complementary and alternative medical providers (for example, naturopaths), a duly licensed provider is legally authorized to deliver therapies within his or her education, training, and skill, as opposed to those accepted by conventional medical communities. Whether the medical profession embraces chiropractic or dismisses it as quackery, values massage therapy or reduces it to a "relaxation response," investigates traditional oriental medicine on its own terms or regards acupuncture as a "placebo effect," the profession's philosophical and economic rivals have legislative sanction to ply their craft.

While legislative developments may be at odds with medical and scientific acceptance, both changing medical evidence and legislative changes will sharpen decisions to recommend or deliver complementary and alternative medical therapies (or not) and/or refer or decline to refer for such therapies. For example, assuming the medical literature continues to support the conclusion that yoga is beneficial overall for the patient's heart condition, then in case 2C it might be considered unethical for the physician not to refer the patient for yoga.[12] The fact that yoga has emotional and spiritual dimensions that the physician does not feel competent to evaluate does not make referral inappropriate. So long as the yoga instructor is appropriately certified (if applicable), does not make claims that induce reliance on yoga in lieu of conventional medical therapy, and does not use postures that are contraindicated for the patient's condition (for example, inverted poses are contraindicated for individuals with high blood pressure, women in the first few days of their menstrual cycle, individuals with eye disorders such as detached retina, persons with neck pain or irregular configurations of the neck vertebrae, and persons with lower-back pain or injury), referral is not inappropriate.[13] Rather, failure to refer would violate beneficence and deprive the patient of the potential benefits yoga may offer in reversing heart disease.

Ideally, leading medical academics, societies, journals, and institutions will create clinical guidelines both for the practice of integrative care and also for when it makes sense to refer the patient to (or co-manage the patient with) complementary and alternative medical providers. In the initial phases of clinical exploration, such guidelines are likely to err on the conservative side and not account for the full panoply of available therapies within a given modality. For example, a Consensus Panel convened by the NIH indicated that acupuncture is effective for relief of nausea following chemotherapy and for certain other conditions.[14] These conclusions, while hailed by some members of the acupuncture community as validating acupuncture treatment, also reduce the corpus of traditional oriental medicine to a handful of specific uses. At least, however, given the Consensus Panel's conclusion, the physician who fails to refer the patient for acupuncture in conjunction with chemotherapy may be violating the obligation of nonmaleficence. One unanswered but important question is that of whether the physician violates the obligation by failing to refer for acupuncture for other conditions, when referral has some justification in the medical literature but not the same level of "proof" (or acceptance) as a statement by an NIH Consensus Panel.

The Reverse Duty to Refer

Complementary and alternative medical providers such as chiropractors have a duty to refer their patients to a licensed medical doctor when the patient's condition exceeds the scope of the complementary and alternative medical provider's competence. Failure to refer in such cases is grounds for malpractice liability.[15] For example, when a chiropractor finds a possible herniated disk or takes an X ray and finds a fracture, referral to a physician for medical treatment is indicated.[16]

No court yet has indicated a *reverse* duty to refer on the part of the physician when the patient's condition exceeds the physician's scope of competence and requires care by a complementary and alternative medical provider. In large part, this reflects biomedical dominance of health care law and regulation: health care licensing statutes assign primacy to medical doctors, who have statutory authority to diagnose and treat disease, while all other providers are allocated a more limited scope of practice within which they can provide health care services. In part, the clinical competence of a medical doctor is presumed (by many) broader than that of other providers, because the clinical training is more scientifically comprehensive. In any event, the notion that other providers have a "limited" scope of practice has resulted in many courts interpreting the legislatively authorized range of practice narrowly. In many states, for example, courts interpret chiropractic licensing statutes to limit chiropractors strictly to spinal manipulation and certain ancillary services; even recommending nutritional supplements has been held to cross the line into "prescribing drugs" and thus to constitute the unlawful practice of medicine.[17] Given such interpretation, many physicians may not find referral either legally or ethically compelling; clinically, they will likely err against referrals to chiropractors.

Yet as integrative health care gains ground, it is not inconceivable that courts may establish a reverse duty to refer. Integrative care views the patient as a whole being, potentially amenable to interventions on multiple levels in a coordinated team approach—for example, chiropractor, massage therapist, medical doctor, pastoral counselor, nutritionist, exercise physiologist, nurse, herbalist, and healer working together to bring the patient back into balance on all levels. While clinical training in medicine is broad, it does not encompass many areas within the training of complementary and alternative medical providers, such as chiropractors and acupuncturists; hence medical competence does not embrace many aspects of these professions. This suggests that there may be arenas in which referral to complementary and alternative medical providers is necessary and appropriate—for the present, at least in cases in which (1) conventional care has failed to produce satisfactory results for the patient; and (2) complementary and alternative medical therapies can help adjunctively to reduce symptoms, provide relaxation, or otherwise relieve suffering.

Moreover, while physicians are said to have unlimited licensure, malpractice rules constrain physicians' inclusion of complementary and alternative medical therapies.[18] The way state medical boards investigate and sanction professional discipline for "unprofessional conduct," as applied to such practices, also constrains the scope of medical authority.[19] Thus, as a practical matter, physician authority is not unlimited; physicians have a scope of practice, though not defined by statute or regulation. In the integrative care model, one could argue that physicians would have a duty to refer the patient to an appropriate complementary and alternative medical provider whenever the patient's condition exceeds the physician's scope of competence.

This "reverse duty to refer" has legal implications: failure to honor the duty would result in malpractice liability if the patient is injured by the failure to refer. Aggravation of an existing condition or the lost opportunity to ameliorate suffering through use of a complementary and alternative medical modality could constitute the requisite injury. Thus, if the physician in case 2B fails to recommend acupuncture to relieve nausea following chemotherapy, the physician could be liable for the consequent physical and emotional distress. Such a duty, while controversial, can be justified, as it "respects patients' interest in the most complete, comprehensive, balanced and effective approach to health care, whether within the biomedical or holistic healing paradigm."[20] A secondary result of such a reverse duty to refer is that it would change the balance of power between medical doctors and complementary and alternative medical providers and thus, by introducing more equal responsibility for patient health, alter the social landscape for integrative care.

Referral to a Complementary and Alternative Medical Provider
Who Exceeds Scope of Practice

The authority of complementary and alternative medical providers is defined in their licensing statutes or in regulations issued by their professional boards pursuant to such statutes. The narrower authority afforded to complementary and alternative medical providers thus creates potential liability for the physician who refers to a complementary and alternative medical provider who exceeds the legislatively authorized scope of practice. For example, in case 2A, the physician refers to an acupuncturist who uses Western herbal medicine even though the applicable state licensing statute only authorizes the acupuncturist to use traditional oriental herbal medicine. If the court applies agency principles broadly, the physician conceivably could be liable for the acupuncturist's negligence. The physician also runs the risk of prosecution for aiding and abetting the unlicensed practice of medicine.[21] In practice, it may be difficult for physicians to understand exactly what a complementary and alternative medical provider's legislatively authorized scope of practice is and whether a particular complementary and alternative medical provider tends to stay within it.

Scope of practice usually is expressed in the licensing statute—for example, Colorado defines acupuncture as "a system of health care based upon traditional oriental medicine concepts that employs oriental methods of diagnosis, treatment, and adjunctive therapies."[22] Some statutes expressly include specific modalities—for example, New Mexico expressly includes nutritional counseling, and Vermont expressly includes nutritional and herbal therapies in the licensing statute for acupuncturists.[23] Interpretation is more difficult when the statute is silent regarding nutritional and herbal therapies and other modalities. The statute may be amplified by regulations from the relevant professional board, as well as by case law. On the other hand, there may be no clarifying regulations and no interpretive case law. The regulatory fuzziness around scope of practice puts a burden on the physician, for whom it may be expensive or impractical to read statutes or seek legal counsel prior to making a simple referral.

Ideally, professional organizations can help simplify such issues by creating guidelines for physicians in each state. Absent such groundwork, physicians must make their own assessments. As a broad proposition, unless more carefully circumscribed by specific language in licensing statutes (for example, language prohibiting use of particular modalities), health care professionals have the legal authority to offer modalities within the scope of their professional training. Scope of competence provides a useful concept, in that it determines scope of practice. In other words, ideally, the scope of practice allocated to a provider by the licensing statute is no broader than the scope of competence, as measured by professional training. Referring physicians should make an assessment of the complementary and alternative medical provider's scope of competence and the kind of modalities the provider will use pursuant to the referral.

Physician Referrals and Ethical Duties of Complementary and Alternative Medical Providers

When physicians refer to complementary and alternative medical providers, they should be aware that complementary and alternative medical providers are held to a medical standard of care in cases in which complementary and alternative medical therapies and conventional medical treatment overlap.[24] This could occur if, for example, a chiropractor takes X rays, performs urinalysis, orders blood and other routine laboratory tests, or performs physical examinations.[25] The medical standard of care also applies if the complementary and alternative medical provider makes claims exceeding the scope of competence—for example, if a chiropractor purports to cure a disease such as diabetes through the practice of chiropractic.[26] The chiropractor additionally risks liability for misrepresentation, professional discipline, and possible loss of licensure for making such a claim.

Under agency principles, physicians conceivably could be held vicariously accountable for such gross lapses in judgment by a complementary and alternative medical provider, which lapses result in patient injury. The risk of physician liability becomes more acute the more severe and consistent the complementary and alternative medical provider's ethical violation, as the court could construe such a case, again, as a referral to a "known incompetent." Therefore, it behooves referring physicians to be aware of ethical obligations accruing to complementary and alternative medical providers generally.

The ethical obligations of complementary and alternative medical providers are similar to those of physicians and typically are stated in codes adopted by membership organizations within each profession. For example, the *Code of Ethics* of the American Chiropractic Association includes duties of confidentiality, privacy, and loyalty; obligations not to neglect or abandon the patient; duties of honesty and competency; and the obligation to use modalities that are in the patient's best interest and not in conflict with applicable statutory or administrative rules.[27] Duties of confidentiality, nonabandonment, and competency also are reflected in ethical codes and manuals for physicians.[28]

Similarly, the *Model Code of Ethics* for the Acupuncture and Oriental Medicine Commission provides, among other things, that practitioners should be competent, maintain patient confidences and records, not abandon patients, provide a clear treatment plan, charge fees that are not excessive, inform the patient regarding contraindications, maintain appropriate therapeutic boundaries, and refrain from false or misleading advertising.[29] Likewise, the *Naturopathic Code of Ethics* for the American Association of Naturopathic Physicians includes nonmaleficence among its guiding principles—*primum non nocere* ("first, do no harm"; "provide the most effective health care available with the least risk to his/her patients at all times")—and requires that naturopathic physicians maintain competence and honesty.[30]

Such ethical standards are similar to those in conventional medicine. The ethical standards also contain obligations that herald the unique philosophy of the particular complementary and alternative medical profession. For example, acupuncturists are encouraged to recognize "the energetic basis and respect the dynamic, evolving nature of Acupuncture and Oriental Medicine," as well as "the need for continual expansion of human understanding through research, analysis and practical experience focused on the interactions among body, mind, spirit, emotions and faith of the individual, society and nature as a whole."[31] Similarly, naturopaths are urged to follow principles such as *vis medicatrix naturae* ("recognize, respect and promote the self-healing power of nature inherent in each individual human being") and *tolle causum* ("strive to identify and remove the causes of illness, rather than to merely eliminate or suppress symptoms").[32] In this respect, portions of such ethical systems are likely to clash with principles taken as foundational in conventional care. They also suggest different perspectives on health and disease that may, in clinical practice, result in conflicting recommendations as these modalities are integrated with biomedical care. The naturopathic principle of *tolle causum*, for example, harkens back to the historic conflict between homeopathy and biomedicine: Samuel Hahnemann, the founder of homeopathy, named his system of medicine based on the idea that unlike allopathic medicine ("allo" meaning "different"), homeopathic medicines attempt to encourage the body's self-healing response to illness, rather than to eliminate or suppress symptoms. Differences in clinical philosophy likely will complicate referral issues, including liability considerations.

The ethical principles announced by more established complementary and alternative medical providers—such as chiropractors, acupuncturists and practitioners of traditional oriental medicine, and naturopaths—also provide models for ethical codes by less recognized complementary and alternative medical providers, such as practitioners of energy healing modalities like Reiki and Healing Touch (see chap. 4). For instance, the code of ethics for one organization of Reiki practitioners has a standard obligation of maintaining client confidentiality.[33] Other provisions are geared toward minimizing liability: a Reiki practitioner "refers the client to an appropriately licensed professional when necessary"; "refrains from commenting about or interfering in any way with the treatment program prescribed by the client's licensed health care provider"; and "does not diagnose, counsel or prescribe except within the specific guidelines of his/her licensed professional practice specialty, and advises the client that Reiki is not a substitute for medical care."[34] These provisions presumably aim to help ensure that the Reiki practitioner remains free from civil liability as well as criminal prosecution for unlicensed medical practice.

Still other provisions in the Reiki ethical code reflect ecological concerns. While the ethical codes for physicians and allied health providers share some of these concerns, the Reiki code states such concerns in unusual ways. For example, the Reiki practitioner "provides a safe, welcoming, supportive, and comfortable atmosphere for clients."[35] The practitioner "recognizes that we all share the same Reiki energy" and "contributes to peace, harmony, and cooperation . . . by courteous and respectful speech, thoughts, and actions."[36] The code refers to kind *thoughts* as well as speech and actions, emphasizing the notion within energy medicine that thoughts and feelings translate into effects in subtle realms that, by affecting consciousness, can affect physical health (see chap. 4).

To safeguard concerns about intimacy and personal space, the same code emphasizes that a practitioner "respects each client's particular boundary needs, . . . maintains appropriate boundaries between self and client," and "uses appropriate touch at all times."[37] Further, if "the breasts or genital areas need Reiki, the practitioner works off the body and above these areas" (in other words, on the biofield rather than on the skin).[38] Certainly, one would not expect to see a provision for working above the body, in the human energy field, in any ethical code currently approved by the American Medical Association.

Such ecological and spiritual concerns also are found in the *International Code of Ethics* for Healing Touch. Healing Touch is a biofield modality taught by the American Holistic Nurses Association, typically in a series of weekend workshops for nurses and other health care professionals. The code begins by stating that Healing Touch "provides care and comfort to an individual through balancing the Energy System, thereby helping the client to self heal."[39] Healing Touch is "based on a heart-centered caring relationship." Again, while one might find words such as "empathy" and "compassion" in relation to a good bedside manner, the language of Healing Touch alludes to the possibility of something more than a heartfelt exchange, which may implicate new aspects to the therapeutic relationship (see chap. 4).

Referral for Spiritually Oriented Therapies

These sample ethical codes suggest that while some aspects of complementary and alternative medical modalities may be familiar to physicians, others are expressed in language, paradigm, and practice that are foreign or challenging, in the sense of proposing encounters beyond the biochemical and physiological. While in some ways such therapies comport with the "ethics of care"—which accounts for feelings and relationships as much as obligations and rights—in other respects the ethical language of these therapies may appear to some physicians to be pseudoreligious, as with the discussion of yoga in case 2C.[40]

Yet the language of such codes is internally consistent with other principles within these professions. Many complementary and alternative medical therapies—such as yoga—have their own internal ethical codes, arising from a particular discipline itself, and not superimposed by a contemporary professional organization. In yoga, for example, such codes are built in from the ancient philosophical and textual roots of a long-standing tradition. The main principles of yoga were codified by a sage named Patanjali between the fourth century B.C. and the fourth century A.D. In his *Yoga Sutras* (yoga aphorisms), Patanjali describes eight limbs of yoga, as follows: various forms of abstention from wrongdoing (*yama*), observances (*niyamas*), posture (asana), control of the life-force (*pranayama*), withdrawal of the mind from sense objects (*pratyahara*), concentration (*dharana*), meditation (*dhyana*), and absorption in God (*samahdi*).[41] The tradition thus is broader than the physical practice many conceptualize as yoga and suggests that health care providers cannot reduce yoga to flexibility and stretching or to a mere variation on physical therapy. Rather, yoga encompasses mental, emotional, spiritual, and potentially dietary and environmental discipline as well.

Patanjali defines yoga as stilling of the modifications (thought-waves) of the mind and the eight limbs of yoga—including but not limited to the postures—as spiritual disciplines by which the individual's consciousness might be purified.[42] He defines *yama* as "abstention from harming others, from falsehood, from theft, from incontinence, and from greed."[43] The first part of the definition—abstention from harming others—is a statement of nonmaleficence. In Sanskrit, the term is *ahimsa*, also translated as "nonviolence."[44] According to one commentary on the text, this means that "we are to live so that no harm or pain is caused by our thoughts, words or deeds to any other being."[45] The abstention from harm includes *thoughts*, as in the Reiki code. The reference is not merely to patients nor even to human beings generally, but rather to all beings. Thus, ahimsa is not merely the negative command to avoid violence but also a positive ethical obligation to love.[46] It means that "we must cultivate love for all."[47]

The obligation of ahimsa is an integral part of yoga practice, whether embodied in a formal, institutional code; taught as an ethics portion of an institutional curriculum; or reviewed as part of the literary corpus of the yoga tradition.[48] Thus, the ethical obligations outlined by Patanjali are more than ethical injunctions governing the delivery of yoga teachings as a "complementary and alternative medical therapy." Rather, they are "rules . . . which if not obeyed bring chaos, violence, untruth, stealing, and covetousness . . . [and the corresponding] emotions of greed, desire and attachment. . . . pain and ignorance."[49] Since yoga is defined as control of the thought-waves in the mind, yoga allows the practitioner to "abide in his real nature"; when not in the state of yoga, a human being "remains identified with the thought-waves in the mind" and thus lives in delusion.[50] To violate the obligation of ahimsa therefore is not only to violate an ethical rule of nonmaleficence but also to contravene the very essence and purpose of yoga.

When physicians refer for therapies such as yoga, it is helpful to understand not only the profession's formal, institutionalized, ethical codes—as well as the legal risks, articulated earlier, relating to unlicensed medical practice—but also some of the tradition's root principles, such as the obligation of ahimsa in yoga. If the treating practitioner is practicing responsibly, within the scope of practice established by the relevant state licensing statute (if licensure is applicable) and within the scope of competence established by the profession (in other words, within the education, training, and skill of the provider within that profession), then certain internal ethical obligations may accrue by virtue of maintaining the traditions of that practice. And liability risks correspondingly are reduced.

Of course, receiving certification in yoga, Reiki, or Healing Touch is no guarantee that the practitioner is ethically responsible or free from potential liability. Concern for clinical contraindications also will remain. Yet basic familiarity with the applicable traditions can help alleviate the confusion and indeterminacy associated with requests for referrals such as in case 2C.

Conclusion

As the applicable therapy moves further away from the biophysical and more into the biopsychic, energetic, and spiritual, the physician is likely to find less familiar clinical ground and thereby to feel less comfort in including the provider within a team approach that is "integrative medicine." Referral is likely to trigger legal and ethical concerns that remain largely unanswered or that cannot, at present, be satisfactorily answered by hospital administration or legal counsel.

Complementary and alternative medical therapies with a spiritual origin or focus offer significant challenges to prevailing notions of what is legally and ethically appropriate in a given clinical situation. For example, prayer is within the field of "mind-body interventions" catalogued by the Chantilly Report (see introduction), together with yoga, mental healing, imagery, hypnosis, and other complementary and alternative medical modalities. One's perspective on prayer also is culturally, socially, religiously, and historically determined. Any legal and ethical analysis of prayer as a "complementary and alternative medical modality" that purports to operate solely on principles that are neutral, objective, or scientific overlooks the presence of highly idiosyncratic preferences, personal proclivities, and psychological predilections of the caregiver facing the question of prayer. Indeed, to the extent caregivers ignore the issue of prayer—focusing solely on scientific data—it has been argued that science itself is based on human values and therefore is a value system or faith culture.[51] This argument suggests that prayer as therapy may require deeper consideration of values outside the medical arena. For example, what kinds of conversations should such providers have with their patients regarding the efficacy, appropriateness, and medical understanding of spiritual practices such as prayer, visualization, spiritual healing, and projection of mental energy? What should the clinician in mainstream practice, who has no training in pastoral counseling, say to a patient regarding these therapies? Should the American Medical Association and other professional health care organizations issue draft language regarding the efficacy of prayer? Would it be phrased in generally acceptable, neutral, and humanistic terms—and if so, would various religious bodies object to such a "watered-down" treatment of a subject as important as prayer? Would providers who identify themselves as atheists be forced by malpractice standards to pray with their patients if scientific investigation shows that prayer is efficacious? Would any such implication raise First Amendment concerns?

Harold Keonig, at Duke University, investigated the impact of traditional religious faith and practice on physical health and emotional well-being. Among other things, he found that people who regularly attend church or pray have significantly lower diastolic blood pressure than the less religious and are hospitalized less often than those who never or rarely participate in religious services; further, people with strong religious faith are less likely to suffer depression from stressful life events, tend to have healthier lifestyles, have significantly better health outcomes in recovering from physical illness, live longer, and have healthier immune systems.[52] Koenig also cites studies observing that religious involvement helps protect health and that this protection can be quantified like other health variables such as diet, exercise, smoking, or alcohol use.[53]

Koenig does not conclude from these data that doctors should pray with patients or prescribe belief in God, regular attendance in religious worship, or daily reading of spiritual literature. Nor does he study whether the physician's belief or disbelief in the efficacy of prayer affects the outcome. Rather, he suggests that physicians take a "religious history" of their patients and ask them, in stressful situations, if prayer would be helpful. He further suggests that the physician might participate by letting the patient pray and then saying "amen" or by leading a short prayer if the patients so wishes. Finally, Koenig recommends that health care institutions include a chaplain on the patient-care team in the hospital.[54]

This is not the final word on prayer as therapy, but it does suggest some ways to include spiritual therapies in a fashion that does not overly intrude on personal beliefs in the clinical setting. This has been a controversial subject in a community founded on humanistic ideals but grounded in material reality. The interplay between the coercive effect of malpractice law on inclusion of complementary and alternative medical therapies such as yoga and prayer, the obligations of informed consent, the First Amendment's protection of the *free exercise of religion,* the First Amendment's prohibition on the state *establishment of religion,* and the role of spiritually oriented therapies in a secular, integrative clinical practice remain to be more fully developed. In the meantime, the prospect of deeper inclusion of spiritual therapies in future health care challenges regulatory values as well as present patterns of legal and ethical decision making surrounding such therapies.

Ascending the Hierarchy of Regulatory Needs

Case 3A   The Terminally Ill Patient Who
Seeks Supplements

 A terminally ill patient seeks access to nutritional supplements that claim to reverse his disease. Because the label on these supplements has made an unapproved "disease claim"—linking the supplement to cure of a specific disease—the federal FDA has declared the supplements to be "new drugs" that cannot be distributed in interstate commerce without FDA approval. Pending resolution of the disease claim, the FDA has neither made any arrangements for expedited approval of access to the supplements nor authorized any regulatory exception allowing the patient access to the supplements. The FDA further has ordered the manufacturer to stop marketing the product and has required distributors to remove the product from the market.

The patient claims that he has a constitutional right of freedom of access to the medication of his choice and, further, that the FDA is acting unethically in depriving him of such choice. The patient further argues that as his condition is terminal, the FDA is overstepping its role as a guardian of public health and has no right to interfere in his medical affairs.

Case 3B   The "Incompetent" Patient Who Subtly
Evidences His Wishes

 An elderly patient on life support has been declared legally incompetent. The family is debating whether and when to disconnect the patient's life support systems. The patient's sister whispers in the patient's ears that "it is okay" for him to "let go and move on into the Light." She then asks if this is what he wants. The patient's pinkie visibly lifts an eighth of an inch. She asks again and receives the same signal. The sister asks that this tiny ideomotoric signal be accepted as "clear and convincing" evidence of the patient's wishes, when there is no other evidence from prior written authorizations or verbal conversations. The sister then enters meditation in order to connect with the "spirit and life-force" of her brother and ascertain his wishes.

She sees him clearly in meditation and reports receiving instruction from him that life support should be disconnected and that his body should remain in the hospital bed for three days following the disconnect, during which time she is to recite to him instructions from the Tibetan Book of the Dead, as he will be traveling through different realms en route to higher consciousness.[1] She also states that if his body is prematurely moved, his consciousness will experience a great disturbance, which could ultimately result in less than satisfactory rebirth.[2] She produces personal letters confirming that although her brother did not express clear preferences regarding his body and burial, he was profoundly influenced by Tibetan Buddhist teachings.

The hospital ethics committee does not accept the ideomotoric signals or the information from her meditation as evidence regarding her brother's wishes. The committee concludes that it is unethical to disconnect the life support and, further, that hospital policy is to have an undertaker remove a body within three hours after death is ascertained.

Case 3C   The Professor Who Receives Dictation
         from "Jesus"

 A medical school professor goes home one night and begins hearing a disembodied voice tell her to write notes for a new course. The physician by birth and childhood education is Jewish but professes to be an atheist. She consults her physician and is told that she has been hyperventilating as a result of stress from work and that the imbalance of oxygen and carbon dioxide could be resulting in hallucinations. She also is told that she is experiencing a mild mood disorder and that as her sleeping habits are irregular, her sense of reality has become more precarious. Her physician prescribes regular exercise, relaxation, a temporary muscle relaxant, and sleep medication.

When the voice persists despite her best efforts to follow the therapeutic recommendations, the professor consults her psychiatrist. The psychiatrist prescribes one antidepressant and a second medication to control hallucinations. Yet the voice persists. Different kinds of medication are prescribed, to no avail.

The professor consults her best friend, an intuitive healer, who advises her to discontinue the medications and pay attention to the voice. The voice continues to visit and insists that she take notes for a course to be entitled "A Course on Miracles." The professor listens, asks the voice to identify itself, and is told the narrator is Jesus Christ.

After taking dictation for some days, the professor asks the voice, "Why aren't you dictating your course to some pious nun?" The voice replies, "Because you are listening and you are a good note-taker." Over a period of several years, the professor—while keeping her sanity, her job, her family duties, and much of her earlier belief system—"receives" (or "channels") thousands of pages of notes; the course becomes an inspirational series of lessons. The lessons are avidly studied, followed, and praised for their psychological clarity by millions of people across the globe, of varying Christian and non-Christian denominations.[3]

The Antifraud Rationale in Legal Decision Making Governing Complementary and Alternative Medicine

Historically, the biomedical perspective on health and disease has dominated legislative, administrative, and judicial drafting, administration, and interpretation of health care law.[4] For example, courts typically have deferred to biomedical authority in cases involving complementary and alternative medicine and physician malpractice, informed consent, professional discipline, health care fraud, and insurance coverage for "medically necessary" and "experimental" treatments.[5] The question is whether legislatures will continue to follow this perspective of disease and health and whether administrative agencies will enforce, and courts continue to interpret, legal rules that emerge from this same paradigm. Cases 3A through 3C frame the larger question regarding which regulatory values currently govern or ought to govern legal and ethical decision making and whether integrative and energy medicine potentially expand such values.

Historically, when discussing health care modalities outside of biomedicine, most legislatures and courts have emphasized as a dominant, if not exclusive, regulatory value the need to protect the public against charlatans and fraud. In 1760, for example, one of the first statutes licensing physicians in the United States was enacted in order to prevent "ignorant and unskilful persons" from "persuad[ing]" unsuspecting individuals to become their patients.[6] In 1888, in *Dent v. West Virginia*, when an individual who attended an eclectic medical college challenged the state health board's denial of his license, the U.S. Supreme Court held that he had no constitutional right to practice medicine. The Court justified its decision by stating that the state's police power included the power to "prescribe all such regulations as, in its judgment, will secure or tend to secure . . . [the public] against the consequences of ignorance and incapacity as well as deception and fraud."[7]

Since then, the antifraud rationale has pervaded health care law and regulation governing access to complementary and alternative medical therapies. For example, in 1947, a New York decision (*People v. Steinberg*) upholding the conviction of a hands-on healer emphasized the government's role in protecting the public against "the menace of the ignorant, the unprepared, the quacks and the fakers."[8] Similarly, in *Stetina v. State* (1987), an Indiana appellate court, upholding the conviction of an iridologist for the unlicensed practice of medicine, emphasized its role in "protect[ing] people against their own credulity" in medical choices.[9]

The theme of public ignorance, gullibility, and vulnerability to deception is woven in to the antifraud rationale. For example, a medical board in Florida refused to allow patients to testify on behalf on a physician in disciplinary proceedings involving the use of complementary and alternative medicine; the board justified its decision by asserting patients' lack of competence regarding their own medical care.[10] The Fifth Circuit Court of Appeals employed a similar rationale in stating that the testimony "of the lay sufferer [with cancer] is entitled to no weight."[11] Similarly a Texas federal court responded to patients seeking a non-FDA-approved drug as follows: "The State of Texas . . . protects these patients from exploitation. . . . We will not allow our sympathy for the terminally ill to hinder our duty to uphold the law."[12]

The seminal case denying patients access to complementary and alternative medical therapies is *U.S. v. Rutherford*.[13] As in case 3A, this case involved a group of terminally ill patients who argued for a constitutional right to the treatment of their choice, even though the treatment lacked FDA approval. The U.S. Supreme Court denied such a right and affirmed the rationale that Congress intended to protect patients from their own desperation, gullibility, and unwise medical choices—the temptations offered to patients by "resourceful entrepreneurs."[14] The result in *Rutherford* was based on an interpretation of the federal Food, Drug, and Cosmetic Act: the Supreme Court declared that it was merely interpreting congressional intent and that if Congress wanted to change the law, it could do so. Yet Congress did not change the statute, and *Rutherford* exemplifies judicial reliance on the antifraud rationale to invoke extreme medical paternalism.

Applying the Court's rationale in *Rutherford*, the patient in 3A not only would have no right, constitutional or otherwise, to access the supplements once they were labeled unlawful "new drugs" by the FDA but also would have no judicially sanctioned autonomy interest in his or her own health care choices involving the supplements. In short, the antifraud rationale has served as the regulatory correlative to paternalism in biomedicine and the ethical principle of nonmaleficence as traditionally understood when applied to complementary and alternative medicine. In each case, the state and physician are viewed as benevolent parents helping to correct the patient who, when left to his or her own intelligence, will make choices contrary to his or her physical well-being.

A Richer Web of Regulatory Values

Although the antifraud rationale expresses a legitimate concern for public health, safety, and welfare, it is not the only concern. In fact, the single emphasis on fraud has had disproportionate influence on judicial decision making and regulatory policymaking regarding complementary and alternative medicine. This disproportionate emphasis has historical roots: regulation of complementary and alternative medical therapies was born of the late-nineteenth- and early-twentieth-century rivalries between "regular physicians" (the precursors to modern, scientific medical doctors) and "irregular physicians" (as they were dubbed by the "regular physicians"), who practiced modalities such as naturopathy, herbal medicine, and manual healing methods (such as chiropractic).[15] Ideological, economic, and social rivalries created a war of epithets among groups battling for dominance in a fragmented health care market.

An increasingly pluralistic medical system suggests the need for new regulatory and intellectual structures. A predominant focus on fraud prevents legislators, administrators, and judges from applying other public policy concerns and values to the use of complementary and alternative medical therapies in conventional and other health care settings. For example, an exclusive focus on fraud control precludes attention to consumer interests and concerns. Such a focus also may be economically unwise, as it prevents the emergence of innovative approaches to health care that do not rely on technologically sophisticated diagnostic and therapeutic techniques.[16]

A broader perspective on public policy can bring in additional goals of interest and concern to health care consumers, which together with the antifraud rationale create a richer web of regulatory values. In addition to (1) fraud control, regulators should consider at least the following additional four policy goals: (2) quality assurance, (3) health care freedom, (4) functional integration, and (5) human transformation. Following, each of these five policy goals is defined more carefully, with examples of historical as well as modern attempts to satisfy such regulatory values.

1. Fraud Control. This regulatory value refers to preventing dangerous and deceptive practices by complementary and alternative medical practitioners or physicians and allied health providers delivering complementary and alternative medical modalities. The goal of fraud control encompasses concern for protecting the public against the "quacks and the fakers," "resourceful entrepreneurs," and others who would take advantage of vulnerability created by disease to deceive patients.

Legislation, administrative rules, and enforcement activities by government entities (such as the Federal Trade Commission) that aim to prevent false and misleading advertising by entities offering complementary and alternative medical services and products help satisfy the regulatory goal of fraud control. Such agencies help ensure that consumers are not deceived by exaggerated marketing material and claims relating to complementary and alternative medical therapies. Yet another aspect of fraud control concerns food and drug regulation that ensures that dietary supplements are adequately and appropriately labeled, do not make misleading claims, and do not contain adulterants.[17] Similarly, although the DSHEA widely has been regarded as a consumer-driven statute, divesting the FDA of significant authority regarding dietary supplements, this legislation also has aspects of fraud control. Specifically, the DSHEA provides that supplements are classified as new drugs, requiring FDA approval, when they purport to diagnose or treat disease. This helps ensure that patients are not defrauded or deluded into mistaking vitamins, for example, for cures for disease.

Parenthetically, it should be noted that under the common law, fraud requires intent to deceive as well as deception; hence the label of fraud is not applicable per se simply because the patient has been deceived.[18] The regulatory value of fraud control thus aims at deterring and punishing intentional deception by purveyors of health care services.

2. Quality Assurance. This regulatory value refers to promoting professional standards so that products and therapies are relatively safe for public use and consumption. Federal regulatory requirements for good manufacturing practices for drugs, for example, help create quality assurance. On the state level, licensing laws also promote the value of quality assurance by mandating that practitioners receive minimum amounts of training and sufficient testing to ensure competence.[19] Similarly, scope of practice rules ensure that providers practice only within the parameters of their education and knowledge.[20]

Concern for credentialing, whether among legislatures, hospital administrators, or professional organizations, also expresses the value of quality assurance. Institutions can help ensure that complementary and alternative medical therapies are provided in a clinically responsible fashion by including within their networks only providers who have been sufficiently vetted, according to rigorous criteria reflecting sufficient education, training, skill, and adherence to requisite ethical codes.[21] Again, institutional actors across the spectrum of players in complementary and alternative medical regulation share an interest in ensuring that providers meet high standards of professional competence and that consumers can rely upon standards set by individual complementary and alternative medical professions.[22]

3. Health Care Freedom. The regulatory value of health care freedom entails safeguarding the flow of information so that consumers

can feel that they belong to a system in which they are allowed to make intelligent, autonomous health care choices. The ethical value of autonomy is expressed through the value of health care freedom, since autonomy entails personal responsibility for making decisions. Thus, health care freedom often serves as a counterweight to the value of fraud control, which tends to express paternalism. Curiously, courts have adopted the value of health care freedom for medical matters not involving complementary and alternative medical therapies, such as contraception, abortion, and the right to be disconnected from artificial life support.[23] But most courts, following *Rutherford*, have denied patients a constitutional right to non-FDA-approved therapies. In other words, the principle by and large has not been extended into the arena of choices involving access to complementary and alternative medical therapies.

Some judges have emphasized the value of health care freedom in complementary and alternative medicine despite the paternalistic overtones of *Rutherford*. In one dissent, for example, former chief justice Rose Bird of the California Supreme Court affirmed the patient's right to choose an unapproved cancer therapy, despite the state's judgment that the treatment was "ineffective."[24] Similarly, in one decision, the New Jersey Superior Court upheld a terminally ill cancer patient's right to choose laetrile as a last resort, noting that "the public harm is considerably reduced" under these circumstances.[25] In these cases, the value of health care freedom trumped the desire for fraud control. But terminal cancer represents an extreme case; more generally, the question remains as to how these values may be reconciled.

In one attempt to do so, the executive director for the Medical Board of California acknowledged, "There is a subtle tension which arises from the state's obligation to protect the public from harm and the public's right to freedom of choice."[26] The acknowledgment of this tension has a different tone than earlier regulatory descriptions of patient interest in access to complementary and alternative medical therapies. For example, the Federation of State Medical Boards historically had a Committee on Questionable and Deceptive Health Care Practices, charged (among other things) with addressing the "proliferation of unconventional and unproven medical practices and promotions."[27] The phrase "questionable and deceptive health care practices" included the organization's denotation for complementary and alternative medicine; such terminology clearly expresses the goal of fraud control and, together with the call to checking the "unprofessional, improper, incompetent, unlawful, fraudulent and deceptive practice of medicine," brooks no tolerance for the value of health care freedom.[28] The regulatory language, in other words, reflects the collision of paradigms: an either/or scenario in which fraud control and health care freedom can not coexist. One could argue that the language of the officer of California's medical board reflects an evolution in thinking—or at least a broader perspective—regarding policy goals in the protection and promotion of public health. Certainly, such language expresses greater respect for balancing regulatory values.

4. Functional Integration. The regulatory value of functional integration refers to advancing the safe, effective, and appropriate clinical integration of all world systems of knowledge about healing. Such a system arguably helps restore patients' participation in healing and care for the self. The value of functional integration broadens the inquiry beyond complementary and alternative medical therapies in the United States and envisions a global process of testing, synthesis, and reconciliation among different systems and cultures of health care. At least in the United States, the value of functional integration has not been cogently expressed in the regulatory system.

The rudiment of this value is expressed in increased use of the term *integrative medicine*. The legal framework for complementary and alternative medicine, however, has barely been given recognition as a distinct field of study in the United States, let alone a comparative, international analysis.[29] On a clinical level, it is difficult to conceptualize how integrative medicine might appear in hospitals in the future. Some overseas hospitals may combine ancient herbs, modern technology, and the sweep of the *chi-gong* master's hand. Yet these models may or may not provide a clinically sound forecast of what patient care may resemble in the near future.

As is suggested in the introduction, the question remains as to the potential scope of what may be "integrated" into conventional care— and on whose terms. The definition of "integrative" medicine is an evolving one, whose scope and contours depend as much on the consciousness of those advancing the field—and of the medical, scientific, regulatory, and other personnel they hope to influence—as on outcomes of clinical care and research. Thus, a narrow definition would include only modalities specifically tested and validated according to certain prescribed and rigorous criteria, following, perhaps, the hierarchy of scientific evidence. A broader definition might include a blending of such diverse forms of knowledge as scientific information and medical knowledge; knowledge of human health, healing, and being gleaned through myth, music, and art; and knowledge of inner worlds gained through prayer and meditation. Under this definition, "it is surely time to foster discourse and incorporate different points of view and to abandon the forced choice between different, global systems . . . and to start embracing pluralism."[30]

This tension between the narrowly scientific and the broadly humanistic is a leitmotif throughout this book. It suggests the need for a multidisciplinary approach—one broad enough to encompass views theologically foreign to principles of scientific medicine; therefore, different audiences may have different responses to the material in this book. Provocatively, case 3A suggests that focusing on values such as fraud control and quality assurance to the exclusion of other regulatory values may overly intellectualize the problem and thus immunize regulators from a compassionate view of the person's search for appropriate health care. The regulatory perspective regarding complementary and alternative medical therapies in this case means something to real human beings who are suffering, seeking choices, and making life-and-death decisions. Functional integration respects the commitment to the actual process of testing and validating therapies—and yet it also suggests that there is value in incorporating and applying the entire corpus of human knowledge over history to the field of health care. It moves beyond the scientific theories and methods of a specific culture during a specific period in that culture.

On a practical level, the value of functional integration may partly define the notion of integration. For example, the fact that Tibetan medicine claims to have ways to treat certain kinds of cancer yet does not recognize the diagnostic category of "cancer," or have such a term in its lexicon, would have to be confronted as Western and Tibetan physicians engage in joint diagnostic and therapeutic teams. Although statutory prohibitions on the unlicensed practice of medicine may, for the present, theoretically constrain clinical collaboration, physicians to the Dalai Lama have collaborated with physicians at major academic medical centers to compare systems of diagnosis and treatment for cancer.[31]

On the regulatory front, at least one medical board (in Texas) has gone beyond traditional professional disciplinary rules to acknowledge what it calls "integrative and complementary medicine." This board recognizes "that patients have a right to seek integrative and complementary therapies," thus acknowledging the value of health care freedom. The Texas board defines such therapies as interventions beyond biomedicine "that provide a reasonable potential for therapeutic gain in a patient's medical condition and that are not reasonably outweighed by the risk of such methods."[32] The rules permit the individual physician to make a clinical judgment concerning potential risks and therapeutic gains. At least in this respect, the rules move toward functional integration by allowing clinicians in everyday practice to make what they consider to be reasonable judgments concerning what is best for the patient.

5. Human Transformation. More than curing, the regulatory value of transformation involves promoting healing of mind-body-spirit, igniting individuation, advancing human wholeness, and moving toward individual and collective enlightenment on the scale of planetary evolution. This broad definition of transformation is striking, in that it explicitly adds a spiritual component to regulatory definitions. It thus ensures that regulatory criteria will take the broadest possible views of the ultimate purposes of future medicine.

Adding this value suggests that the goal of regulating complementary and integrative medical therapies is not merely safeguarding the public from charlatans, promoting standards in health care products and services, protecting autonomous individual choices, or serving globalization of information and responsible clinical integration; rather, the goal includes the highest of which human beings—on a planetary level—are capable. Thus, as health ultimately has biopsychical, environmental, social, and spiritual as well as biophysical dimensions, the value of transformation describes the regulatory system's role in protecting all aspects of human health and psychospiritual evolution.

No judicial decision, administrative rule, or legislation to date has expressly acknowledged transformation as an important regulatory objective governing the integration of complementary and alternative medical therapies into conventional care. In one sense, this omission reflects the conservative nature of law, which builds by accretion, based on precedent; there has been insufficient precedent in the biomedical, as well as legal and ethical, communities, to support overt acknowledgment of the importance of human transformation in human health care. In other words, the field of complementary and

integrative medicine (like hospice and palliative care once were) is edg-
ing forward from a shadowy outpost at the wild frontier. Because
many complementary and alternative medical therapies make patients
and providers alike confront emotional, environmental, social, and
spiritual aspects of illness, transformational aspects are sometimes
indicated, but more often relegated to palliative care or regarded as
treatment of last resort; frequently these aspects are pushed aside,
ignored, or widely feared.

In another sense, the failure to adopt, as yet, the transformative
and spiritual vision of integrative and energy medicine reflects a lag
between developments in health care and evolution in regulatory
structures. Transformation also must occur on the personal as well as
social level. As the Fellows enrolled in the Program in Integrative Medicine at the University of Arizona School of Medicine are expected not
only to understand the substantive aspects of integrative medicine but
also to "transform their own lifestyle and medical practice" (see chap.
1), so regulators similarly must understand transformation from the
inside before implementing it as a regulatory goal. Again, a potential
transformation in personal consciousness becomes an essential part of
the integration. Such a transformation must necessarily be individualized, or there is no wisdom for the collective.

Recently, for example, during a conference on integrative medicine in Hawaii, the program opened with a sacred dance invoking the
spiritual energies of the island for healing. The kahuna (shaman) leading the ceremony observed that *Hawaii* means the following: *Ha*, healing through breath, hands, power of prayer, and other forms of consciousness; *Va*, breath; and *I*, spirit. Healing, he told the audience, is
inherited from the gods; hula dance is a prayer with the body. Many
souls, he said, are waiting for this field to get sorted out so they can
come in; many are in attendance at this conference and watching what
we say and do. As the kahuna spoke, sang, and danced, his trance was
a direct conversation with God. Many in the audience appeared to be
moved by the power of the sound/dance to infuse their work with new
light, but reportedly one participant—a regulator—was playing soli-
taire on a laptop computer during the ritual.

The choice of the word "transformation" reflects the notion that
ultimately the shift is one in consciousness , and not merely the substi-
tution of one statute or judicial precedent for another. Whatever the
regulatory structure ultimately ensures, it will have to reflect goals

additional to fraud control, quality assurance, health care freedom, or even functional integration. It will have to focus on supporting and nurturing the spiritual evolution of the collective consciousness of the human race.

The Relevance of Abraham Maslow

In analyzing regulatory values in terms of a complex of needs, concerns, and public health objectives, one building block is the work developed by psychologist Abraham Maslow in the notion of a hierarchy of personal needs. Maslow's work evolved in part out of frustration with the two existing, dominant psychological theories—the experimental, behaviorist approach and the clinical, psychological approach. Maslow felt that each was couched in cold, mechanistic terms that failed adequately to account for the full range of human potential. By way of contrast, he developed a "humanistic, Third Force Psychology," which consciously emphasized the highest possibilities of human nature.[33]

This setting for the development of Maslow's work is analogous to the emergence of complementary and alternative medical therapies, in that health care providers and regulators today appear to oscillate between two poles. The first is a view of health care that excludes, dismisses, or marginalizes many complementary and alternative medical modalities that do not meet its criteria for safety and efficacy or have unknown or "implausible" mechanisms of action. This view is expressed, for example, in the comment quoted earlier about there being "only scientifically proven, evidence-based medicine supported by solid data or unproven medicine." The opposite response is an overly expansive view of complementary and alternative medicine that exaggerates claims, overpromises curative value, or abandons scientific principles in an unfounded and delusional optimism. This view is reflected in many promotional materials offered by a variety of complementary and alternative medical providers and organizations and gives rise to the need to regulate deceptive conduct and practices.

A "Third Force," or mediating, approach would reflect neither extreme but rather incorporate, synthesize, and transcend the limitations of both biomedical and complementary and alternative medical approaches. Science and mysticism ideally would find common ground in such a dialogue. Indeed, the way Maslow defines science suggests such common ground: it is "the organization of, the systematic pursuit of, and the enjoyment of wonder, awe, and mystery."[34] Science, Maslow concludes, "can be the religion of the nonreligious, a source of deeply rewarding religious experience."[35]

It has been argued that some complementary and alternative medical therapies reflect a broader epistemology of science and that therapies within energy medicine, particularly, require a "reappraisal of fundamental assumptions underlying contemporary scientific understandings of principles inherent in basic concepts of 'disease' and 'healing.'"[36] Maslow consciously tried "to make science consider all the problems that nonscientists have been handling—religion, poetry, values, philosophy, art"—and thus create in the field of psychology "new ways of perceiving and thinking, new images of [the human] and of society, new conceptions of ethics and of values, new directions in which to move."[37]

One aim of integrative medicine is to broaden biomedicine's perspective on disease and health and to bring in religion, literature, philosophy, anthropology, art, and the other humanistic disciplines as containing valid understandings of health and the disease process that can feed into everyday clinical experience. For example, while the notion of "human energy fields" might be foreign to some, the halo is an integral part of the artistic vision of saints. There is a transformative potential in the notion that the halo is more than imagination, religious whimsy, speculation, delusion, or fantasy, even though conventional care presently leaves the halo out of its formal account of the human anatomical structure. In short, energy medicine contemplates inclusion in health care of perceptions from religion, poetry, art, and other disciplines and the notion that some contributions from these fields be taken as more than metaphors for the human condition.

Maslow suggested that he considered his humanistic psychology only "transitional, a preparation for a still 'higher' Fourth Psychology, transpersonal, transhuman, centered in the cosmos rather than in human needs and interest."[38] Maslow inaugurated the field of transpersonal psychology, which sought to bridge humanistic psychology and spirituality. Transpersonal psychology provides both an analogue for and a bridge to certain aspects of future medicine. Like "Third Force" psychology, the aspects of complementary and alternative medicine that are most readily accepted by biomedicine may be transitional. Such fields may be preparing humanity for still "higher" systems of health care that integrate global healing modalities; accelerate the collective human consciousness; and, like the myth of the Grail, lead humanity through the inner personal journey and to the transpersonal, transhuman Grail King (see chart 4).

As psychology moved from Freudian theory to behaviorism to humanistic psychology and into transpersonal and still other forms of psychology, medicine may be moving from a purely biophysical model to models that integrate indigenous and other traditions of health care to models that operate purely in the realms of "subtle energies," such as the nonlocal phenomena observed in distance healing. For example, future medicine may move from including Western herbal medicine in conventional care to integrating acupuncture following chemotherapy to including prayer and meditative techniques in the healer's therapeutic regimen. In the process, health care will evolve beyond the biomedical perspective yet must remain grounded in sound clinical concerns. Hence, "human transformation" is not an exclusive and overarching value, but one of five. This value suggests that legislators, administrators, medical boards, and other policymakers should consider the extent to which law and complementary and alternative medicine regulation serve a transhuman, as well as a human, perspective—however these notions might further evolve.

CHART 4. Parallel Movements in Psychology and Medicine

Force	Movement in Psychology	Movement in Medicine	Examples
First	Freudian theory	Biomedicine	Surgery
Second	Behaviorism	Complementary and alternative medicine	Western herbs
Third	Humanistic psychology	Integrative medicine	Chemotherapy plus Chinese medicine
Fourth	Transpersonal psychology	Energy medicine	Long-distance healing

Maslow's Ascending Hierarchy of Personal Needs

Maslow argues that basic human needs are organized into a hierarchy of relative prepotency. When one set of needs is frustrated, other sets of needs cannot emerge; once one set of needs is relatively well gratified, then the next set of needs emerges.[39] If, for example, a human being is dominated by physiological needs (such as hunger), then all other needs are pushed into the background until the hunger is satisfied. This point is illustrated in the film *Joe Gould's Secret.* Joe Gould, a homeless bohemian, pours an entire bottle of ketchup onto his meal at a local diner. When the waitress asks why he does not have more self-respect than that, Joe Gould snaps, "I have no self-respect when I'm hungry."

On the other hand, once the primal need of hunger is satisfied, then a person is freed to think about such loftier matters as love, community feeling, and philosophy. Thus, once Joe Gould's work becomes visible and he finds a patron, he is freed from concern over a bottle of ketchup to work on his magnum opus, which is purported to be an oral history of contemporary civilization.

Of course, the needs listed in Maslow's hierarchy are not invariably and inevitably mutually exclusive. For example, many saints have used physical deprivation (such as fasting) to accelerate spiritual achievement. Similarly, in Freudian psychology, sublimating libidinal urges may provide one way of redirecting needs toward creative development. Indeed, Maslow softens his hypothesis about emerging needs by suggesting that most humans have varying degrees of satisfaction for any particular set of needs at one time; thus, the extent to which specific needs are pushed to the foreground or background is highly variable, and the different sets of needs often appear in the human psyche in varying combinations.[40] With this caveat, Maslow describes five sets of basic needs in the following ascending hierarchy:

1. *Physiological:* These include the needs for food; sleep; and various sensory pleasures (such as tastes, smells, and stroking).
2. *Safety:* These include the needs for security; stability; dependency; protection; freedom from fear, anxiety, and chaos; structure, order, law, and limits; and strength in the protector.
3. *Belongingness and love:* These include the needs for relationships and for giving and receiving affection.
4. *Esteem:* These include the desires for achievement, adequacy,

mastery and competence, and independence and freedom, as well as for reputation, status, recognition, dignity, and appreciation.

5. *Self- actualization:* This involves the need to do what the individual is fitted for; being true to one's nature; and being self-fulfilled, or actualized in what the person is potentially.[41]

Maslow argues that a complete human is one who satisfies all five sets of needs; further, he argues that a person who is thwarted in *any* of the basic needs "may fairly be envisaged simply as sick or at least less than fully human."[42] Rhetorically, Maslow asks, "Who will say that a lack of love is less important than a lack of vitamins?"[43] Further, Maslow argues that since "a person is to be called sick who is basically thwarted" and since such basic thwarting "is made possibly ultimately only by forces outside the individual," then sickness in the individual ultimately emanates from a sickness in the society. Maslow thus traces individual illness to social illness, to a stunting of human needs by that cultural container. Maslow's position resembles the Buddhist notion that "there is no liberation absent collective liberation"—that health and sickness ultimately are societal, and not individual, issues.[44] Maslow defines a "good or healthy society" as "one that permit[s] people's highest purposes to emerge by satisfying all their basic needs."[45]

The Ascending Hierarchy of Regulatory Needs

Maslow's definition of a healthy society provides an implicit critique of relying on the antifraud rationale as the controlling motivation in health care regulation involving complementary and alternative medicine. This is akin to committing the government's resources to ensuring satisfaction of only one set of human needs—for example, the physiological. If a healthy society is one that promotes individual satisfaction of all basic needs, then the range of regulatory values in complementary and alternative medicine and medical regulation should account for the full range of human health needs, from the physiological through the needs for safety, belongingness and love, esteem, and self-actualization. Indeed, feelings of safety, social support and community, and a healthy interior life have been recognized not only as aspects of health but also as helpful in maintaining health; notably, their absence can create risk factors for heart disease and other conditions.[46] To focus on only one regulatory concern—such as prevention of fraud—is inherently unhealthy.

Further, a narrowness of regulatory focus arguably constricts the flow of healing modalities to health care consumers, thwarts choice, and bases health care policy in complementary and alternative medicine on worst-case scenarios. As Maslow argues:

> The motivational life of neurotic sufferers should, even in principle, be rejected as a paradigm for healthy motivation. Health is not simply the absence of disease or even the opposite of it. Any theory of motivation that is worthy of attention must deal with the highest capacities of the healthy and strong person as well as with the defensive maneuvers of crippled spirits.[47]

In other words, basing complementary and alternative medicine regulation entirely on the motivational life of frauds and charlatans should be rejected as a paradigm for regulation of health. Rather, regulatory values should encompass the highest capacities of healers in our culture, whether such healers are biomedically skilled and trained or have intuitive abilities and sensitivities; whether such healers perform therapies within the medical model or use other modalities which—while admittedly capable of abuse (see chap. 6)—also potentially expand present biomedical frontiers.

That complementary and alternative medicine regulation to date has focused on the neurotic, the sick, and the despotic, rather than on the positive potential for human transformation, reflects, in Maslow's terms, the psychological predisposition and collective consciousness of those creating the regulatory structure. Maslow notes that

> in any judging of the motivations for a person's behavior, the character of the judge also has to be taken into account. He *chooses* the motivations to which he will attribute the behavior, for instance, in accord with his generalized optimism or pessimism. . . . It is a kind of paranoid-like suspicion, a form of devaluation of human nature.[48]

Such pessimistic views of the motivations of health care providers outside of biomedicine accord with the economic, philosophical, and political rivalries between the various "sects" of practitioners during the late nineteenth and early twentieth centuries.[49] During this time period, legal authority, in conjunction with biomedical authority, chose to attribute fraudulent motivations to institutions outside the biomedical paradigm. This viewpoint embodied a kind of "devaluation of human nature."

In Jungian terms, the tendency to ascribe fraudulence to therapies outside biomedicine could be understood as projecting one's "shadow" onto *other* health care providers rather than confronting one's own darker nature (see chap. 6). As Jung puts it, "whoever looks into the mirror of the water will see first of all his own face."[50] In the words of Roberto Assagioli, the "pathological approach" produces a "rather dreary and pessimistic picture of human nature" and places "an exaggerated emphasis on the morbid manifestations and on the lower aspects of human nature and the consequent generalized applications of the many findings of psychopathology to the psychology of normal human beings."[51] Further, through this approach, "many important realities and functions have been neglected or ignored: intuition, creativity, the will, and the very core of the human psyche—the Self."[52]

As intellectual hostilities soften, a healthier, more positive dialogue may emerge to encourage other regulatory values such as health care freedom, functional integration, and transformation. Such values can look to the realization of creativity and of other core aspects from the richness of the human psyche, as expressed in transpersonal psychology. In fact, the history of this process suggests an evolution in the regulatory structure that corresponds with changing social views of the motivations of complementary and alternative medical providers and with changing levels of regard for therapies outside the biomedical paradigm. Greater dialogue and tolerance create the possibility for tracing regulatory developments to the hierarchy of needs. One can draw an analogy between each set of policy needs identified in the hierarchy of regulatory values and each set of personal needs delineated in Maslow's hierarchy (see chart 5). Historical evolution along the hierarchy also may reflect increasing tolerance for diversity and pluralism in the wake of other social movements, such as the women's movement, the civil rights movement, and the environmental movement.

Beginning in the mid–eighteenth century, the earliest call for legislation to credential physicians and surgeons aimed primarily at *fraud control*. In the words of one contemporary medical historian, "Quacks

CHART 5. Comparing Regulatory Values and
Personal Needs

Regulatory Values	Historical Emphasis	Personal Need
Fraud control	Mid-eighteenth century	Physiological
Quality assurance	Mid-nineteenth century	Safety
Health care freedom	Mid-twentieth century	Belongingness and love
Functional integration	Late twentieth century	Esteem
Transformation	Twenty-first century	Self-actualization

[among us] abound like locusts in Egypt."[53] This regulatory focus on fraud control corresponds with *physiological needs* in Maslow's hierarchy. By preventing fraud, regulators could help protect patients from the physiological damage caused by the maleficent behavior of unscrupulous practitioners.

Such protection clearly remains the base of the pyramid for a regulatory system, even if additional regulatory concerns are later added on. Thus today, at a minimum, federal food and drug law provides that drugs distributed in interstate commerce must be free from adulteration, and state laws prohibit the practice of surgery without licensure as a medical doctor.

By the mid–nineteenth century, regulators increasingly focused on *quality assurance* regarding providers and therapies in the health care marketplace. This regulatory focus corresponds with the *safety needs* identified by Maslow. Licensing, for example, increasingly emphasized standardization of training and examination for physicians and allied health care providers and expanded as chiropractors and other complementary and alternative medical practitioners sought state recognition through licensure. Similarly, quality-assurance mechanisms were built in through passage of federal food and drug law, as well. Once mechanisms were created to weed out affirmative acts of fraud, it became increasingly important to ensure that health care providers were competent and could meet minimum standards imposed by the state or by professional associations, institutions, and accrediting bodies.

Again, while quality assurance began to dominate the regulatory landscape in the early to mid–nineteenth century, today it remains an important component of the regulatory pyramid. For example, federal food and drug laws continue to help protect patients from misbranded substances, from untruthful or misleading claims, and from claims leading patients to over-rely on nutritional supplements for the treatment of a disease that requires a trained and experienced medical professional. Thus, both fraud control and quality assurance have remained important regulatory values that have helped to safeguard both patients' physiological well-being and the need for safety in health care products and services.

By the late twentieth century, consumers increasingly asserted the value of *health care freedom* as a counterweight to public policy concerns for fraud control and quality assurance. As noted, the call for greater health care freedom has not always been successful. Case 1B pits patients and family against physicians and the state in a struggle for the life of a child; Case 3A similarly pits the patient against the government. From the parents' perspective, the state is emphasizing fraud control at the cost of personal choice and thus sacrificing their feelings of belongingness to a community in which personal treatment choices are respected and valued.

Thus, the regulatory value of health care freedom is analogous to Maslow's emphasis on *belongingness and love.* As reflected in the nation's founding legal documents, the notions of belongingess to a political community and freedom are inseparable. The unique constitutional liberties and other freedoms in this society create a sense of belongingness to a community in which individuals can protect and pursue that which they love—"life, liberty, and . . . happiness." These pursuits accord with Maslow's definition: when using the term *love,* Maslow is not referring to the courtly ideal of romantic love but to the "hunger for relations," the "giving and receiving affection" that removes "the pangs of loneliness, ostracism, rejection, friendlessness, and rootlessness."[54] In other words, Maslow is describing love as community. Some psychologists have described this in terms of the healing effect of social support.

Today, the value of health care freedom also is an important component of the regulatory pyramid, one built as values such as fraud control and quality assurance are satisfied. For example, the Texas state medical board rules for complementary and integrative medicine provide physicians with the choice to integrate complementary and alternative medical therapies responsibly in clinical practice. As opposed to rules and practices that label physician integration of complementary and alternative medical therapies as dangerous, deviant, inherently "deceptive," or "questionable," or that discipline physicians for *any* deviation from conventional standards, whether harmful or beneficent, the Texas rules make physicians and patients part of a community that allows choices outside of biomedicine.[55] Tolerating such choices in turn can enhance the physician-patient relationship, thus helping to alleviate feelings of antagonism and isolation and satisfying the "hunger for relations" to which Maslow alludes.

Turning to the fourth regulatory value, by the late twentieth century the birth of the term *integrative medicine* suggested a new emphasis on *functional integration* of biomedicine and complementary and alternative medicine. In its narrowest aspect, functional integration suggests the mission of evaluating which combinations of biomedical and complementary and alternative medical therapies are synergistic or adverse. For example, whereas historically few physicians asked about and few patients disclosed use of herbal medication, the analysis of potentially adverse herb-drug interactions now is becoming a routine and necessary part of clinical care.

In the broader sense, though, functional integration suggests the larger aim of a world synthesis of medicine, the potential embrace of accumulated knowledge within all global healing traditions from across time and cultures. This is the process of distilling the collective human wisdom regarding health and healing; it is multidisciplinary and revolutionary; it invokes radical combinations of perspectives on science, human purpose, and ultimate questions such as the meaning of human spiritual evolution. The regulatory value of functional integration thus is analogous to Maslow's personal need of *esteem*. Esteem flourishes when cultures, traditions, personal beliefs, rituals, ceremonies, understandings, and perspectives are acknowledged. Esteem flourishes in multiplicity and inclusive pluralism.

The value of functional integration acknowledges scientific inquiry and integrity but cautions against biomedical fundamentalism. Like other inclusive, pluralistic traditions, functional integration makes the claim that "the unity of being renders all dogmatism ineffective."[56] This regulatory value respects the essential unity of the patient as a person whose esteem is recognized by honoring not only individual autonomy and personal freedom of choice but also the larger cultural, social, and philosophical matrix comprising the person's belief systems governing health.

Turning to the fifth regulatory value, an emphasis on *transformation* is emerging. Once fraud control, quality assurance, health care freedom, and functional integration are satisfied, questions regarding such issues as the meaning of disease, and spiritual issues potentially underlying it, begin to take shape—both for the individual and for the species. The ultimate nature and purpose of illness and suffering; the human's struggle to transcend them; and the place of a finite human being in an apparently infinite cosmos—all these claim the theme of human transformation. Generally speaking, once physiological, safety, belongingness, and esteem needs are met, the inquiry crosses into spiritual realms, and the person is ripe for what Maslow calls *self-actualization.*

The regulatory value of transformation acknowledges that self-actualization takes place on macrocosmic as well as microcosmic levels, in the social order as well as in the individual patient. Thus, transformation as a regulatory value expands out, at the broadest possible level, to actualization for the society, for the nation, for the global order. It bespeaks the collective liberation to which the Buddhists allude; the coming of the cosmic Christ in allegorical terms; the goals identified as universal peace, harmony, brotherhood and sisterhood, enlightenment, *sartori,* and illumination on a world scale; and the advent of universal spiritual values within a climate of pluralism.[57] This is a worldview of Maslow's description of the "farther reaches of human nature."[58]

Far from being some tangential, idealized description, the regulatory value of transformation is an important component of integrative care and reflects the fact that the word *health* is etymologically related to the words *whole* and *holy.* As an implicit and sometimes explicit goal of complementary and alternative medical therapies, and as an integral component of the notion of "healing," human transformation receives recognition as an important component of the regulatory pyramid—at the very least, as one that may begin to be addressed once other, more primal regulatory needs are satisfied. Indeed, one could argue that politically, human transformation is the logical extension of ideals such as the pursuit of life, liberty, and happiness. This argument is advanced by Robert Thurman, who claims that a "society's top priority is to provide all the means for each individual to achieve this inner revolution," which consists of "coups of the spirit in which we are freed to be as happy, good, and compassionate as we can evolve to be."[59] In this respect, political freedom allows the capacity for untrammeled pursuit of inner freedom, leading to a realization of happiness at core levels of being.

Personal Political Philosophy and the Hierarchy of
Regulatory Values

Because the regulatory framework, to date, has barely begun to address the value of transformation, it is worth attempting to elaborate how it might do so. But first, as a basis for such elaboration, the proposed hierarchy of regulatory values can be tied in to the questions in chapters 1 and 2 regarding the ethical propriety of delivering, or referral for, complementary and alternative medical therapies that may lack sufficient evidentiary support to furnish a government agency, a professional medical organization, or an individual physician sufficient comfort in permitting or recommending such therapies.

Ethics is a slippery field, presupposing personal preferences that underlie the framework one chooses to use to answer any given question. More specifically, the way one answers the ethical question concerning complementary and alternative medical therapies may correlate with the personal need that predominates the analysis. In other words, the regulatory value that predominates in any given clinical situation may depend not only on contemporary biomedical consensus, together with historical, political, and cultural factors, but also on the dominant personal need of the regulator as it affects his or her view of government and overall approach to regulation. Some generalized observations will flesh out this point (see charts 6 and 7).

First, if the personal need one predominantly emphasizes in regulatory analysis is physiological, then, as noted, one tends to focus on the value of fraud control. In other words, assuming one's primary regulatory value is fraud control, one tends to adopt a paternalistic approach and view the government as a benevolent parent. From this perspective, it is *absolutely unethical* to tolerate, encourage, or refer for therapies lacking a satisfactory evidentiary base. This is the perspective of the FDA in case 3A. This view, as noted earlier, is supported by a chain of cases, including the U.S. Supreme Court's interpretation of the federal Food, Drug, and Cosmetic Act in *Rutherford*.

CHART 6. Dominant Personal Need and Approach to
Health Care Regulation

Predominant Personal Need	Controlling Regulatory Value	Dominant Regulatory Approach	Quintessential View of Government
Physiological	Fraud control	Paternalistic	Benevolent parent
Safety	Quality assurance	Structural	Social architect
Belongingness and love	Health care freedom	Libertarian	Guarantor of liberty
Esteem	Functional integration	Pragmatic	Cultural mediator
Self-actualization	Transformation	Transcendent	Crucible for change

If, on the other hand, the predominant personal need one emphasizes in regulatory analysis is consumer safety, then one's primary
regulatory value is quality assurance. One tends to view the government's role as structural—for example, as that of a social architect for
the emergence of complementary and alternative medicine in ways
consistent with the biomedical tradition. From this perspective, it is
probably unethical to encourage or even allow complementary and
alternative medical therapies that have not been proven to the complete satisfaction of biomedical authority. Although the risk/benefit
data is helpful in making a thorough assessment, this perspective
prefers to err on the side of a conservative approach to integrative and
energy medicine.

Next, if the predominant personal need one emphasizes in regulatory analysis is the sense of belongingness to community and love, then
one's primary regulatory value is health care freedom. The community
here refers to the individual's relationships with health care givers (for
example, physicians, allied health professionals, complementary and
alternative medical providers, proprietors of health food stores, spiritual caregivers, family members, friends, and others). One tends here to
be more of a libertarian and to view the government's role in health

CHART 7. Political Philosophy and Regulatory Posture toward Complementary and Alternative Medicine

Primary Regulatory Value	Fundamental Philosophical Approach	Position on Ethics of Tolerating, Encouraging, or Referring for Therapies Lacking a Sufficient Evidentiary Base
Fraud control	Paternalistic	Absolutely not. The patient must be protected at all costs.
Quality assurance	Structural	Probably not, but all risk/benefit data should be obtained.
Health care freedom	Libertarian	Absolutely. The patient's autonomy interest trumps medical and scientific majoritarian consensus.
Functional integration	Pragmatic	Sometimes. It depends on the balance among patient needs; government interests; medical responsibility; and environmental, cultural, societal, and religious factors.
Transformation	Transcendent	Generally, when a patient's physiological, mental, emotional, and spiritual needs align with a health care need or request, it is important to respect that request.

care regulation involving complementary and alternative medicine as that of a guarantor of the individual's liberty interest in selecting that combination of modalities that personally seems best.

From this perspective, provided appropriate risk-benefit disclosure is made, it is *absolutely ethical* to offer complementary and alternative medical therapies to the individual. A person in a healthy society has an absolute right to make a voluntary, knowing, and intelligent decision regarding personal use of such therapies, and this autonomy-interest right trumps medical and scientific majoritarian consensus to the contrary.

Such a perspective is partly reflected in cases such as *Schneider v. Revici*. In this case, the Second Circuit Court upheld the doctrine of assumption of risk in health care choices involving complementary and alternative medicine. Specifically, the court held that the physician who provided a complementary and alternative medical cancer therapy would have a complete defense if the patient had knowingly, voluntarily, and intelligently chosen and accepted the risk of choosing such a therapy in lieu of conventional cancer therapy.[60] The right to assume the risk of injury implies freedom to choose among therapies.

If the predominant personal need one emphasizes in health care regulation involving complementary and alternative medical therapies is esteem, then one's primary regulatory value is functional integration. One's approach to government regulation generally is pragmatic, viewing the government as a cultural mediator among differing health care perspectives and traditions. In this view, it is *sometimes ethical* to offer therapies that fail the standards of biomedicine; the ethical analysis depends on the balance among patient needs; government interests; medical responsibility; and environmental, cultural, societal, and religious factors.

This perspective is reflected in a proposal of the Hawaii legislature to develop a health care system that emphasizes a "collaborative approach, utilizing health care professions from a variety of disciplines, embracing native Hawaiian kahuna, eastern (e.g., acupuncture, Honetsugi, Reiki, Chinese herbal medicine, shiatsu, Ayurvedic and Tibetan medicine), alternative (e.g., massage therapy, Rolfing, art, and music therapy), western (e.g., medical/osteopathic physicians, psychotherapy, pastoral counseling), and nutritional approaches."[61] The bill reflects a pluralistic perspective on what health care may be appropriate for a given patient and condition; the state is seen as a cultural mediator among biomedical, native Hawaiian, and other complementary and alternative medical approaches to health care.

Finally, if the predominant personal need one emphasizes in regulatory analysis is self-actualization, one's primary regulatory value tends to be transformation. One's regulatory approach is transcendent, viewing the government as a crucible for change. Given the emphasis on individual wholeness at all levels, this perspective suggests that generally, when a patient's physiological, mental, emotional, and spiritual needs align with a health care need or request, it is important to respect that request. Since patient preferences cannot always be evaluated solely on the physical level or in biomedical terms, then so long as the proposed therapy is not blatantly dangerous, it is *usually ethical* to honor such preferences (even if they contravene conventional medical judgment). Again, while this position accords autonomy respect, it is based on respect for the possibility of human transformation.

Although this discussion begins to formalize a set of relationships among Maslow's personal needs, the five regulatory values, and individuals' political philosophies and preferences, these are generalized possible webs of connection. In fact, all five sets of personal needs coexist in varying degrees alongside all five regulatory values. One may be, for example, transcendent in some respects; pragmatic in others; and libertarian, structural, or paternalistic in others. A person might apply a more libertarian approach to licensing but a more paternalistic approach to food and drug law; or a more tolerant and transcendent approach to spiritual therapies so long as the patient's pragmatic interest in full disclosure of risks, benefits, and unknown factors is met. Therefore one's ethical perspective may fluctuate according to which personal need and regulatory value assume predominance in any given clinical situation.

The discussion also suggests that the ethical perspectives of providers, regulators, and patients are not static but dynamic. They depend on changing personal philosophies and preferences. In addition, the discussion suggests a way of emerging from an ethical analysis grounded in a late-nineteenth-century regulatory framework, in which all "untested" therapies were proscribed. A more enriching dialogue will account for personal views of the problem, as clinical practices continue to evolve.

Of Human Wholes and the Transcendental Objective of
Government Regulation

Long before the term *holistic* was used to described nonbiomedical modalities, Maslow placed emphasis on human holism for fashioning a psychology of motivation based on a hierarchy of personal needs. Maslow saw the human being as a unified whole organized by the satisfaction of ever-higher needs. He notes: "The single holistic principle that binds together the multiplicity of human motives is the tendency for a new and higher need to emerge as the lower need fulfills itself by being sufficiently gratified."[62] When Maslow wrote of "higher" needs, the words "higher" and "lower" were not meant to be pejorative. In this respect, the discussion of regulatory values does not debate whether one such value—for example, autonomy—is more important than another, such as fraud control. Rather, the notion of a hierarchy suggests that a "higher" need or value can become foregrounded once a "lower" one is satisfied.

On the other hand, the "higher" needs and values reflect increasingly more refined levels of participation in human existence. Maslow viewed human beings as able to gratify the entire panoply of personal needs and thus to express the most refined as well as the most coarse dimensions of human nature. Yet just as the human being evolves from struggling to satisfy the most basic physiological need potentially to expressing the most sublime, the regulatory system can similarly be said to evolve from satisfying the most primal concerns—for the patient's physiological well-being and safety—to more refined interests such as the spiritual welfare of the person in the social order. Thus, the provider using a Chinese herb is more likely to ruminate on subtle questions of stimulating meridians or the gift of the plant's consciousness only once satisfied that the herb will not produce a toxic reaction. Likewise, while St. John's wort derives its name from the fact that in medieval times, the flower was picked on the feast day of John the Baptist, this fact has little clinical relevance to the clinician focused on the possibility of adverse reactions.

Maslow describes the process of moving through the hierarchy of needs as follows: "The child who is fortunate enough to grow normally and well gets satiated and *bored* with the delights that he has savored sufficiently, and *eagerly* . . . goes on to more higher complex, delights as they become available to him without danger or threat."[63] This suggests that when "lower" regulatory values are satisfied easily, routinely, and mundanely, it becomes boring to maintain an intense regulatory focus on such values. The hierarchy of regulatory values offers the hope that our culture "eagerly" will move on to "more . . . complex, delights"—namely, that of contemplating the role of human spiritual evolution in health care regulation.

The process is not inevitable, however. The modern media culture expresses delight in pointing out, prosecuting, and publicly humiliating those who transgress professional boundaries. Hence, it is doubtful that this culture will get "satiated and bored" with fraud control in the near future. According to Maslow, this is not uncommon. He hypothesizes about the regressive tendencies that prevent a focus on higher needs from emerging and keep human beings stuck in a focus on lower, less complex needs:

> [The child] *wants* to go on, to move, to grow. Only if frustration, failure, disapproval, ridicule come at the next step does he fixate or regress, and we are then faced with the intricacies of pathological dynamics and of neurotic compromises, in which the impulses remain alive but unfulfilled, or even of loss of impulse and of capacity.[64]

Similarly, one could hypothesize that legislators, administrators, medical boards, judges, and other institutional actors want to "go on, to move, to grow" past the late-nineteenth-century regulatory framework. Chiropractors are licensed in every state, even though terms such as "quackery" still appear; practitioners of acupuncture and traditional oriental medicine are licensed in well over half the states, even though many physicians still believe acupuncture has entirely a placebo effect; massage therapists also have licensure in well over half the states, even though relatively few physicians presently refer their patients to massage therapists. Integrative and energy medicine are emerging, even though some indicia of medical acceptance (for example, conclusions of an NIH Consensus Panel) may acknowledge only specific modalities for particular conditions.

In Maslow's terms, only "frustration, failure, disapproval, ridicule" cause fixation or regression; without them, the impulse is to move on and evolve. One wonders whether a proclamation such as, "There is no alternative medicine. There is only scientifically proven, evidence-based medicine supported by solid data or unproven medicine," would qualify for Maslow's "disapproval, ridicule."[65] From this perspective, such language may be not only depreciatory rhetoric but also, in Maslow's terms, "neurotic"—an attempt to defeat, "frustrate," and create "failure" for integration of therapies outside the present conceptual borders of consensus biomedicine. In Jung's terms, the shadow may come masquerading as defense of scientific truth.

This application of Maslow's argument helps explain why fraud control has been the dominant voice in regulation of complementary and alternative medical therapies for so long. Legal authority follows biomedical authority. Legislators, judges, and agencies turn to medical leadership for guidance concerning health care policy. Such guidance is precarious when some medical leadership makes statements attributing, for example, some of consumer interest in complementary and alternative medical therapies to "New Age interest in 'channeling' and astrology, modern 'witch trials' concerning Satanic child abuse rituals, and alleged capture by space aliens."[66]

While such extreme attitudes undergird a regulatory fixation on fraud control, Maslow addresses paternalism itself more directly. Maslow generally disfavors the use of excessive paternalism as a philosophy for protecting individuals from their own errors. In fact, he not only promotes autonomy but also asserts that individuals must be *allowed* to make bad choices. His position is not libertarian: he maintains it not because he believes choice in itself is to be honored but because he finds there is learning in every choice, whether we label the choice good or bad, beneficent or destructive. Maslow observes:

> If grief and pain are sometimes necessary for growth of the person, then we must learn not to protect people from them automatically as if they were always bad. . . . Not allowing people to go through their pain, and protecting them from it, may turn out to be a kind of over-protection, which in turn implies a certain lack of respect for the integrity and the intrinsic nature and the future development of the individual.[67]

Applying Maslow's analysis, merely because the choice of an "unproven" therapy causes the patient harm does not mean that the state should protect patients from such choices at all costs. This posture is more than paternalism: it is "over-protection," which disrespects not only the value of autonomy but also the individual's core essence and capacity for further personal development. Some patient choices of "untested" therapies—even those with some evidence of lack of safety and/or inefficacy—must be tolerated, or regulation will stifle not only personal choice but also personal growth. The foregoing presumes that sufficient truthful and nonmisleading information is available to facilitate an informed decision. Notably, this argument resounds as heresy in much conventional medico-legal thinking, which argues that patients must be protected from unsafe, ineffective therapies at all costs.

Maslow observes that choice itself promotes individual health and a healthy society. He comments that if the "essential core of the person is denied or suppressed, he gets sick sometimes in obvious ways, sometimes in subtle ways, sometimes immediately, sometimes later."[68] Finally, Maslow addresses the way individuals find a healthy core and learn to evolve in the absence of regressive external forces. He notes that the "healthily spontaneous child, in his spontaneity, from within out, in response to his own inner Being, reaches out . . . [t]o the extent that he is not crippled by fear, to the extent that he feels safe enough to dare."[69] An analogy may be drawn between the child and the regulatory structure. The child represents the health care regulatory system. The unhealthy system is dominated by fear (viewing everything through the lens of fraud control) and crippled by neurotic tendencies (the tendency to characterize everything unfamiliar as deviant—in other words, as "quackery"). Fear protects entrenched interests and blocks innovation. The healthy system reaches into the highest, most refined values of its members and regulates from there. Maslow's note that the healthy child "reaches out . . . [t]o the extent that he is not crippled by fear" suggests that the evolutionary impulse behind regulatory change takes one direction when driven by public health disasters and "what-if" scenarios and another when driven by imaginative, forward-thinking conceptualization. Maslow's final comment, "to the extent that he feels safe enough to dare," opens the discussion to the value of transformation.

Elaborating on the Regulatory Value of Transformation

The regulatory goal of transformation helps safeguard, at a societal level, Maslow's value of self-actualization. Persons have the capacity for self-actualization when transformation on all levels becomes an explicit goal of the healing process. However, to define self-actualization in health care requires reaching beyond current biomedical inquiry and exploring psychological, transpersonal, and philosophical notions about health and consciousness. Transformation moves beyond physical cure. Maslow observes: "The goal of . . . self-actualization . . . [and] individuation . . . seems to be . . . the Eastern one of ego-transcendence and obliteration, of leaving behind self-consciousness . . . [and] of fusion with the world and identification with it. . . ."[70] The goal of empowering transformation is likely to challenge a regulatory system premised on biomedical notions of health and disease and the marginal role assigned to both the individual's emotional life and spiritual consciousness. Maslow ties self-actualization to aspects of Eastern philosophy. Where he uses the term *ego-transcendence,* some of these traditions use *Self-realization* or *God-realization* to denote the obliteration of the personal ego and the individual's total and permanent establishment in the awareness of his or her union with God.[71] According to one definition, Self-realization is

> the recovery of one's authentic Self, *not* the ego-personality bound by one's individual circumstances. This greater Self is an aspect of transcendental Reality. The recovery of this Self, synonymous with enlightenment, is the mystical experiential knowing and remembering in mind, body, and soul that we are one with God.[72]

Thus, the highest need in Maslow's hierarchy ultimately implies the individual's full realization and actualization of the innate potential to embody divinity. Such a state, according to Maslow, is characterized by "peak experiences," in which the individual becomes "poetic, mythical and rhapsodic, as if this were the natural kind of language to express such states of being."[73] These ideas find analogues in Western as well as Eastern religious literature. In Christianity, for example, saints such as Teresa of Avila and John of the Cross describe such "interior castles" of consciousness. In Judaism, the Baal Shem Tov and other Hassidic as well as Kabbalistic masters describe their experiences of union with God. In India, Patanjali also made the case for Self-realization as an integral component of human life.

According to such mystics, contentment, ecstatic poetry, divine virtues, and awareness beyond the small self emanate organically from the consciousness of eternal bliss that permeates an organism drenched in the permanent state of Self-realization. As Paul asserts in the New Testament, "It is not I who live, but Christ who lives within me"; as Robert Thurman states in a Buddhist framework, "Freedom from enslavement to the ego as center of the universe becomes the bliss of union with the free-flowing energy of the world."[74] When reaching this state, the ordinary ego-consciousness of the person no longer dominates the psyche; rather, mystics assert, the personality is extinguished in favor of the bliss consciousness of the Godhead that shines through the person's being.

The mystical literature of all traditions can be combed for further clues as to what is encompassed by the goal of "self-actualization" that supports a regulatory value of transformation. This chapter will not advance too far in that direction, except to note that a dialogue among clinicians, attorneys, ethicists, and mystical leaders may help further to clarify what it is the regulatory structure *ultimately* ought to promote. Such a dialogue, in fact, is called for by the very inclusion of prayer, meditation, visualization, biofeedback, hypnotherapy, yoga, and other spiritual disciplines within the Chantilly Report's categorization of complementary and alternative medical therapies. Further, such dialogue is logical: one cannot separate autonomy interests, from values relating to health care freedom, from the ideal of synthesizing all world traditions to distill what humanity has learned about health and healing, from the "higher" value of creating a system in which the highest aspirations of the individual can be realized. The patient in case 3A, who seeks a non-FDA-approved therapy that is biologically based, and the patient in case 3C, who "hallucinates," "hears voices," and seeks therapeutic guidance from the spiritual realms, manifest in different ways the realm Maslow expresses as the "farther reaches of human nature." Yet, in a health care system that denies the reality of these experiences, patients who pass through these realms can feel bereft, without empathy or support.

These cases may seem odd to health care providers engaged in the process of helping the patient survive, curing the disease, or otherwise attending to necessary, physiological functions. The demands of modern, conventional care require attention to these levels, yet the earlier discussion suggests that such a focus can broaden to include the "farther reaches" of human nature and potentially incorporate these dimensions into its therapeutic repertoire. This has particular implications for mental health care, a topic that receives further exploration in chapters 4–6.

Case Histories of Transformation, Ancient and Modern

Cases 3B and 3C provide examples of what it might mean to honor the regulatory value of patient transformation. In case 3B, one could choose to honor ideomotoric signals as evidence of a patient's wishes; the phenomenon is well known in hypnotherapy and captures choices made while an individual is in a trance, or an altered state of consciousness.[75]

The problem with such experiences is that they require interpretation of internal cues, along with a certain tolerance on the part of the provider for realms of consciousness other than those ordinarily involved in conventional care. Arguably, rapport would be better still than tolerance. The ability to transverse states of consciousness cannot be understood entirely through intellectual analysis, but requires experiential familiarity. Such ability does not necessarily preclude necessary attention to the details of conventional care. A CAT scan is not contraindicated, for example, because the patient has an out-of-body experience (OBE), but the physician discussing the results of the scan with the patient may be able to deepen the therapeutic relationship by being sufficiently conversant with OBEs to discuss the experience meaningfully with the patient and/or guide the patient to further resources for exploration.

Further incorporating experiential study of such modalities as hypnotherapy and guided imagery into the curricula of medical and allied health professional schools would help enrich providers' understanding of altered states of consciousness and their role in disease and healing. Such curricular integration would also help bridge biomedicine and such complementary and alternative medical practices as "soul retrieval" in shamanism and thus bring "outer" and "inner" technologies into greater balance.[76] While guided imagery is becoming part of palliative care (as well as dental care, pediatric care, and other aspects of conventional care), the experience of the trance state is crucial toward engendering respect for practices that may or may not be biologically mediated (or explainable) and that may demand clinical observation of one's self in the area of human consciousness.

A second preliminary foundation for conventional providers would be giving up the "frustration, failure, disapproval, ridicule" that typically accompany reports such as in case 3B and opening to the possibility of new paradigms of consciousness. Many dying patients, for example, report departed relatives coming to their bedside in spirit form; since such reports cannot be validated by scientific instruments, given objective content, or made to fit within the personal belief systems of many physicians, they usually are assigned no value. Yet such experiences are familiar even to Western religious traditions.[77] In death and dying and in health care generally, the culture tends to view pathology largely in material terms, define scientific truth in biophysical realities, and dismiss the "irrational" and the "mystical" as unworthy of medical credence or more than casual attention.

From the perspective of transformation, the appearance of Elijah, Buddha, Jesus, or Kwan Yin in the dying person's room might have greater significance on a soul level than the cessation of brain waves, which marks the advent of death in the latest clinical definition. It is difficult to speculate, but that does not mean the matter should be immune from inclusion in regulatory (or hospital) policy. Similarly, while the evidentiary value of the sister's report from meditation in case 3B might or might not have any weight toward a judicial determination of the patient's wishes, it might have bearing on the timing of the decision to disconnect life support or to move the physical body from its hospital bed. The subjective report of her brother's present consciousness might have bearing on the determination of how the expiration of life might be accomplished from all vantage points and on what is truly meant by "best interest of the patient" at this moment in time. Certainly, the sister's experience has weight; the question becomes how legal, ethical, and biomedical systems can assign significance from all perspectives along the hierarchy of regulatory values.

In short, cases 3B and 3C provocatively raise the question of the role of internal experience in assigning a value to aspects of human transformation. Health care presently grants internal experiences little validity—except, perhaps, to the extent of suggesting a need for a "psych consult" when patients insist on their reality and insist that these experiences govern their medical decisions. A patient who proceeds with a recommended psychiatric consultation and continues to insist that such internal experiences are valid risks being declared incompetent and thereby having his or her medical decisions made by another.

Curiously, the criteria applied to patients in health care policy differ from criteria applied to personal views in other realms. Legal rules have always regarded medical choices with greater paternalism than other choices. For example, the choice of belief in internal experience in the religious realm has met greater tolerance. From one perspective, leaders of major world religions each founded a canon based on "hallucinatory" experiences—whether these included a voice claimed to emanate from God or words alleged to be spoken by angels. Many saints from various traditions have also claimed to receive divine guidance from visions and voices that no other individual could hear. Yet it would be unthinkable to ridicule or demean such claims. In other words, there is a double standard for religious and medical choices; the culture follows a "reverse–Jehovah's Witness" morality—choices involving the body are suspect, but choices involving the soul are not. Thus, saintly claims to visions and voices are protected under the banner of religious freedom. The same claims made by the deceased patient's sister in case 3B or by the professor in case 3C could be treated much differently in a religious setting.

A double standard also exists in the way meaning is assigned to evidence in health care as opposed to religion. For example, as suggested, so-called anecdotal evidence involving "hallucinatory" guidance forms the basis for many world religious traditions. Some scholars have argued, for instance, that gospel assertions of "truths" underlying Christianity are based on the anecdotal reports of a handful of individuals who claimed to see a resurrected Jesus.[78] Yet faith in such reports is held by those who simultaneously only accept the validity of therapeutic practices based on rigorous scientific trials. No doubt there are good reasons for holding both beliefs—belief in anecdotal reports of a resurrected divine being and belief in a hierarchy of scientific evidence.

The contradiction need not be pursued in depth, since pursuing contradictions too far in any one religious path or another risks offending its adherents. Further, the purpose in presenting the analogy is not to comment unfavorably on such beliefs but simply to observe a contradiction between the way legal, ethical, and medical norms handle religious as opposed to scientific assumptions. This observation, in turn, may help facilitate *increased* respect for "religious" beliefs, even if such beliefs fall outside the realm of commonly accepted religious *or* medical systems. For instance, we do not know whether the "voice" heard by the patient in case 3C was that of Jesus or not, but we can hesitate prior to dismissing her "symptoms" as delusional or presuming them dysfunctional. Such patients might not be neurotic, dysfunctional, or diseased; they might be self-actualized. Belief in their experience might be no more absurd and no less sublime than belief in experiences reported by religious figures. Dismissal of one might imply dismissal of the other; tolerance for one might imply tolerance for another. Labeling one true and the other crazy might suggest biases underlying the search for neutral, "objective" principles.

The notion that the use of clinical terms such as "hallucinatory" to describe patients' internal states can sometimes be misleading (or even ethnocentric) has been raised in various disciplines, such as psychiatry, sociology, and anthropology. This contributed, in fact, to R. D. Laing's critique of "schizophrenia" as a label for a distinct psychotic state.[79] As one ethnographer observes:

> Michel Foucault . . . has traced Western society's altering perceptions of the schizophrenic from the concept of the "madman" as a moral renegade, to that of a romantic tragic hero, and finally to his confinement as a "diseased" member of a wistfully healthy society. . . . However, in many non-Western and so-called primitive societies, the symptoms of life-crisis "reactive" schizophrenia are often identified with religious conversion or mystical experience, and the individual may be elevated to the role of prophet or shaman. . . . The fact that the hallucinations or "visions" of the shaman often provide a focus for the integration of a troubled community has resulted in a continuing scholarly dialogue regarding the "creative psychosis" and the "myth of mental illness."[80]

It could be said that while psychopathological symptoms are regressive, the extraordinary experiences that accompany movement toward Self-realization are progressive. The difficulty lies in mapping the borderland between the two. The latter call for therapeutic acknowledgment rather than elimination, for a nurturing of the individual toward personal and spiritual psychosynthesis rather than suppression or reinterpretation.[81]

If transformation ultimately implies allowing human beings to expand and open different channels to multidimensional levels of spiritual experience, then the sister in case 3B and the professor in case 3C are to be encouraged in their health care choices, and not frustrated, rejected, disapproved, ridiculed—or medicated. Again, a focused dialogue between scientists and mystics might open the regulatory structure to considering the farther reaches of human health and wholeness and ways in which the law can support the human being's realization of these diverse domains of consciousness. The writings of mystics provide ground for contemplating how modern labels of pathology might miss important internal experiences that feed positive aspects of spiritual transformation.

Compare the experiences, for example, of the individuals in cases 3B and 3C to that of the twelfth-century mystic Hildegard of Bingen. Hildegard is remembered not only for her written recording of mystical experiences but also for her classification of plants according to their medicinal properties; she was an early herbalist who traced connections among physical, emotional, and spiritual factors in human disease. Hildegard began her book *Scivias* (Know the Ways) with the following description of her psychic opening:

> And behold, in the forty-third year of my life's course, when I had fixed upon a celestial vision with great fear and trembling attention, I saw a very great splendor, in which sounded a voice from Heaven, saying to me:
>
> O frail mortal, ashes of ashes and dust of dust, say and write what you see and hear. But since you are fearful of speaking, artless at explaining and untaught at writing, speak and write not according to human words nor following the understanding of human intelligence, nor according to the rules of human composition, but according to what you see and hear in the heavens above and in God's wondrous words. Offer them to be understood as a listener, perceiving the words of the teacher, transmit them according to the tenor of that speech, subject to this will, showing, and instruction. So, O mortal, shall you speak what you see and hear; and write such things not after your own fashion, nor that of any human, but according to the will of Him who knows, sees, and arranges all things in the secrets of His mysteries.[82]

In this paragraph, Hildegard acknowledges that, like the patient in case 3C, she perceives herself as a channel, or instrument, of some other intelligence. It is not her words that flow onto the pages; she is merely a receiver. Hildegard's "peak experience"—in Maslow's terms—consists of revelations accompanied by great light and intuitive grasping of texts, ideas, and situations in their totality, from a perspective of divine omniscience.

While regarded by some as a prophet and saint, today this practitioner of herbal medicine might be classified as psychotic. Her delusion would be regarded as especially dangerous, as she claimed that her insights came directly from God and that these revelations gave her special knowledge of both religion and medicine. This could lead to legal and ethical trouble. But Hildegard insisted on the possibility of personal revelation from the divine. Once, Hildegard saw that

the heavens were opened and a blinding light of exceptional brilliance flowed through my entire brain. And so it kindled my whole heart and breast like a flame, not burning but warming, as the sun warms anything on which its rays fall. And suddenly I grasped the underlying meanings of the books—of the Psalter, the Gospels and other catholic books of the Old and New Testaments—not, however, that I understood how to construe the words of the text or their division into syllables or their cases and tenses.[83]

Hildegard located her identity other than in the ego, the functioning part of identity our biomedical culture considers as "normal." She thus challenged conventional structures. Yet were Hildegard to choose an herb for her patients based on the kind of experience just quoted, her prescription would challenge current regulatory values.

Without intending to deceive, she would not be committing fraud; hence fraud control would not entirely control. Nor would quality assurance necessarily apply to an herbalist claiming to derive information directly from God and making recommendations to an individual patient on that basis. While the value of health care freedom could support the patient's right to choose a healer such as Hildegard, neither this value nor functional integration adequately would account for the claimed source and nature of Hildegard's health care expertise. But the value of transformation, informed by Maslow's notion of self-actualization, could embrace Hildegard's practice and experience. In other words, while Hildegard might be liable under a variety of statutes, a vision of transformation might grant her leniency. Hildegard here stands for many other healers who were driven intuitively and who served as progenitors for many of today's health care providers. Hildegard's writings suggest that she lived a self-actualized life, replete with "peak experiences."

One reason Maslow's work is particularly helpful in bridging complementary and alternative medicine and biomedical therapies and in considering what synthesis might emerge beyond both is that it bridges psychology and spirituality and thus regards experiences such as those of Hildegard as part of our essential, common human heritage. Maslow remarked that he did not discover self-actualization or peak experiences; he simply coined terms and used language familiar to his time and culture to explain mystical phenomena in humanistic terms. By translating religious experience into contemporary psychology, Maslow helped to remove mystical phenomena from the exclusive domain of rare saints and canonized beings and to place these experiences within the reach of ordinary persons. He thus not only helped birth transpersonal psychology but also helped reclaim intuitive and psychic openings as a natural part of human existence.

Maslow's contribution prefigures the unification of the physiological, the mental, the emotional, and the spiritual in understanding the web of factors comprising health, wholeness, and disease. It is not merely a matter of grafting spirituality onto biomedicine and then reinterpreting spiritual phenomena in biomedical terms; again, the reduction of acupuncture to the placebo effect, the interpretation of the atheist professor's vision as a result of "too much carbon dioxide," the attribution of spiritual experiences to stress—all bespeak a paradigm that cannot reach beyond itself but must confine new insights to conventionally packaged understandings.

Thinkers such as Maslow and Patanjali; explorers of consciousness such as Hildegard, the sister in case 3B, and the professor in case 3C; and potentially many patients (and their families and caregivers) today present the possibility that self-actualization—as protected and nurtured by the regulatory value of human transformation—is reachable by an individual who might otherwise be seen as deviant, subversive, or downright mad. Self-actualization may be a gift in the process of healing from disease, as the wisdom that comes from healing includes the possibility for transcendence. Maslow comments that peak experiences are available to all and that any person in the midst of a peak experience temporarily takes on many of the characteristics of the self-actualized person.[84] Not only are these instances the individual's "happiest and most thrilling moments, but they are also moments of greatest maturity, individuation, fulfillment—in a word, his healthiest moments."[85]

Maslow is not unique in offering this possibility. Ideally—religious thinkers, mystics, saints, and liberating beings from many cultures assert—such transcendence asymptotically approaches permanent establishment in a perfected, divine consciousness. An Indian writer, Gopi Krishna, asserts that "the illuminated mind has been a regular feature of human life, at least, since the Vedas"; he claims that illumination and genius are the product of mystical ecstasy, which in turn is produced by the natural, organic evolution of the human brain, as stimulated by the flow of God-consciousness known in mystical Eastern texts as kundalini.[86] Krishna agrees with Maslow's notion that this place, from which divine virtues and ecstatic inspiration spring, is not the exclusive domain of a handful of artistic geniuses but rather the heritage of the common person. Like Hildegard, Gopi Krishna states that poetry and transformative perceptions in his consciousness

> came from the depths of my own transformed consciousness, but . . . [were] monitored by some other will than my own. A higher personality has been guiding the whole operation. I erred and blundered . . . failed to co-operate or . . . learned, doubted, questioned and rebelled. But every time, by a Grace, I have no words to express, I was led by the hand back to the path and again instructed and taught until slowly I learned the hard lesson which the skeptical climate of our time made it harder for me to grasp.[87]

Krishna finds that his own blundering personality was not the source of his inspiration; rather, he became the receiver of personal revelation.

While Hildegard and Gopi Krishna span centuries and cultures, some of their experiences are parallel. If the visions and voices and awakenings of mystics from across human experience were to be compared, contrasted, and added to the storehouse of information concerning human potential and then incorporated into models of health and wellness, such analysis would help us implement the values of functional integration and transformation and possibly radically alter contemporary visions of health and health care. Further, as Patanjali and others suggest, the state we define as "normal," "healthy," "well-adjusted," or "cured" might be recognized as a distortion of the essence of human nature. The potential for a breakthrough to what Patanjali considers a "normal" state—bliss—provides yet another rationale for implementing a regulatory value of transformation within a hierarchy of regulatory needs.

Maslow's description of self-actualization offers reasons for pursuing this possibility. Maslow describes self-actualized individuals as having qualities that include the following: "[accurate] perception of reality, acceptance, spontaneity . . . solitude, autonomy, fresh appreciation, peak experiences, human kinship, humility and respect, interpersonal relationships, ethics . . . humor, creativity, resistance to enculturation. . . ."[88] He seems to share Patanjali's belief that when humans are in this state, they are abiding in their true nature and that when they are not, individuals are caught in fluctuations of the mind (such as anxiety, depression, and all the inner chaos that accompanies daily living). Ultimately, the contributions of these thinkers suggest that if the regulatory structure aims to promote patients' well-being, it ought to promote the highest stages of health and healing, and not be dominated by a possibly pathological view of health and human nature.

And yet the tantalizing question remains: how *would* the regulatory structure protect the value of human transformation? Even with the creation of a White House Commission on Complementary and Alternative Medicine Policy—whose ultimate report and effect on legislation will inform future legal scholarship—and with the creation of similar bodies in the United Kingdom and elsewhere, the field is young. Full integration of spiritual teachings into conventional care barely has begun. It is the present human condition to gasp, struggle, and toil somewhere between physiological needs and self-actualization; at least in this society, we have yet to see what happens when illuminated regulators make laws whose very *object* is to cultivate illumination.

Conclusion

A new understanding of medicine calls for a new understanding of law and regulation, in turn supported by new paradigms in ethics. Thomas

Kuhn stated that new paradigms occur by revolution, not by accretion.[89] Such a revolution, however, need not be bloody. It may be a "cool" revolution, one of spirit, not flesh.[90] Gopi Krishna describes such a change this way:

> One flash of genius or one instant beam
> Of Revelation, like a vanished dream,
> Heaps of pedantic dross can melt away
> And thought of centuries change in a day.[91]

As human consciousness expands, shadows remain. Fraud control remains a valid and important regulatory objective, and abuse of spiritual power, a human delimiter. Yet describing the unbounded possibilities through the lens of Maslow's hierarchy helps further enlarge the discussion of legal and ethical parameters of integrative and energy medicine. As succeeding chapters suggest, describing the regulatory value of human transformation in this way may help open the door to new understandings of therapeutic boundaries, placebo encounters, and the biofield and of the way these concepts potentially can enrich the regulatory container for future expansions in health and human consciousness.

PART 2

Implications for Mental and Spiritual Health Care

4

Energy Healing and the Biofield

Case 4A   The Physical Therapist Who Integrated Reiki

 An attorney telephoned for the following consultation:

"I represent a licensed physical therapist. The physical therapist has been treating a client for a sports injury; the client also is seeing a psychiatrist for emotional dysfunction. The physical therapist has taken some weekend workshops in Reiki. While using traditional physical therapy techniques to help the client regain flexibility and range of motion in the arm, the physical therapist, with the client's consent, 'ran energy' using Reiki. The client felt warm, tingling energy and found that it increased the rapidity of her healing.

"As the sessions continued, the client grew more relaxed and in fact began experiencing regression into deep trance states where she connected to previous traumas to the arm and the symbolic meaning of her injury. Some of these experiences involved childhood traumas, while others reached into what the physical therapist explained and the client understood as 'past lives.'

"Simultaneously, the client began experiencing symptoms of multiple personality disorder in her psychiatric sessions. The client has sued the physical therapist for malpractice, alleging that the physical therapist's use of Reiki—a modality not generally accepted within the profession—caused her unwarranted emotional injury.

"The physical therapist had had her client sign a consent form agreeing to the use of Reiki treatment. Now, I don't know much about Reiki and less about past lives; do you think my client has a defense?"[1]

Case 4B   The Healer Whose Intuitive Guidance
           Contradicted Medical Advice

 A healer related the following:

"I was working with a young woman who had multiple physical disorders. . . . I asked for specific guidance. . . . I heard the following words: 'Tell her to reduce her thyroid medication by one-third.' At the time, I was completely unaware that she was taking it. In a rather embarrassed manner, I asked her about it. She confirmed that she was taking it. In the next few weeks, with the consent of her physician, she reduced her intake of the medication according to the guidance channeled and proceeded to regain more health. After five months it was necessary to make another reduction. Shortly thereafter, she left treatment, satisfied with her health, having decided to go to college."

The healer then described a second client:

"Before Jennifer arrived in my office for her first appointment, I received information that she should choose the type of chemotherapy that lasted three months and used two drugs, rather than the one that lasted two months and used three drugs. I had never met Jennifer and didn't know why she was coming to receive healing from me. When Jennifer told me her presenting complaint, she stated that just a week before, she had been given the choice by her oncologist of two different chemotherapies for cancer treatment. One was to use three drugs and last two months, while the other was to use two drugs and last three months. She had come to me to help her make the decision."[2]

Case 4C   The Father Who Was "Guided by an Angel"

Recently, while purchasing a plane ticket at an airport, I produced a photo ID from the hospital where I work. The ticketing agent smiled and began to lavish praise on that institution. "Both my kids were born there," he said, "and they treated my wife like a queen. . . . In fact, she was in labor for *twenty-six* hours, and the doctors didn't give her any medication to induce labor." He smiled proudly. "And guess who held her hand the whole time?" He went on. "My son was a big guy, ten pounds, twenty-one inches, and my wife, she's petite. There wasn't enough room for him to come out, so the doc said to me, 'What do you want to do, Manny?' See, this isn't the kind of place where they just rush and cut people up, so he asked me.

"I was about to say, 'Gee, doc, I want to do whatever's safe for my kid, *you tell me* what I should do,' when I suddenly felt a presence beside me. I grew calm. 'It's going to be okay,' I heard, out of the blue. 'Give her another half hour.' Turned out she never even needed the C-section.

"Anyway, I'm telling you this because you're a representative of that institution." He gave me a warm look. "Aisle 16C," he said. "It's an emergency row, extra leg room. You should be quite comfortable there." He returned my photo ID. "Have a nice flight, *doc*."

Public Policy and Energy Healing

Earlier I defined the term *energy medicine* as that subset of therapies within the spectrum of complementary and alternative medical therapies that primarily are based on the projection of information, consciousness, and/or intentionality to patients. As noted, laying-on of hands, intuitive medical diagnosis and distance healing, and aspects of traditional oriental medicine, Tibetan medicine, and herbal medicine all come under the rubric of energy medicine. While this definition doubtless will evolve over time, the thrust is an understanding of medicine and healing that incorporates and simultaneously transcends the physical world as presently understood, including known biological, chemical, pharmacological, and other mechanisms in our human anatomy and physiology. Energy healing, as mentioned, is included as a subset of energy medicine and denotes a set of therapies based primarily on the projection of spiritual or mental energy through intentionality and consciousness.

The research literature on energy healing to date includes evidence-based reviews, case reports, and other studies, both on energy healing itself and on nonlocal effects of consciousness and other so-called psychic phenomena, as well as on the application of energy healing in clinical settings such as operating rooms, critical and intensive care units, and elsewhere.[3] This literature is complex and beyond the scope of this book. To quote a recent meta-analysis, although approximately 57 percent of the randomized, placebo-controlled trials of distant healing reviewed showed a positive treatment effect, "the evidence thus far warrants further study."[4]

The National Center for Complementary and Alternative Medicine (NCCAM) at the NIH has defined "energy therapies" as therapies in one of five major domains of complementary and alternative medical therapies and has further subdivided the domain into therapies that

focus either on energy fields originating within the body (biofields) or those from other sources (electromagnetic fields). . . . Biofield therapies are intended to affect the energy fields, whose existence is not yet experimentally proven, that surround and penetrate the human body. Some forms of energy therapy manipulate biofields by applying pressure and/or manipulating the body by placing the hands in, or through, these fields. Examples include Qi gong, Reiki and Therapeutic Touch. Qi gong is a component of traditional oriental medicine that combines movement, meditation, and regulation of breathing to enhance the flow of vital energy (qi) in the body, to improve blood circulation, and to enhance immune function. Reiki, the Japanese word representing Universal Life Energy, is based on the belief that by channeling spiritual energy through the practitioner the spirit is healed, and it in turn heals the physical body. Therapeutic Touch is derived from the ancient technique of "laying-on of hands" and is based on the premise that it is the healing force of the therapist that affects the patient's recovery and that healing is promoted when the body's energies are in balance. By passing their hands over the patient, these healers identify energy imbalances.[5]

NCCAM has identified energy therapies as falling under the rubric of "frontier medicine."[6] NCCAM defines frontier medicine as including those complementary and alternative medical practices for which there is no plausible biomedical explanation; examples include bioelectromagnetic therapy, energy healing, homeopathy, and therapeutic prayer.[7] NCCAM has established a Frontier Medicine Program to "create a stable infrastructure to nurture and therefore advance this field of biomedical research by providing the institutional support and resources necessary for rigorous scientific investigation."[8] In short, despite the fact that "in the Frontier Medicine area, where, by definition, we do not really have a generally-accepted and understood series of mechanisms of action," NCCAM has identified these areas as merit-ing research attention and funding.[9] On June 12, 2000, NCCAM issued a request for applications to provide exploratory program grants for frontier medicine research.[10] Efforts by NCCAM to address these "fron-tier" areas of medicine and science contrast with other efforts, by some within the scientific community, to disparage these therapies as not even meeting the crucible of plausibility.

While these efforts are ongoing, the existing literature to date has failed to convince much of the scientific community that energy healing is anything more than "placebo responsiveness" or something that should be "debunked."[11] From the perspective of the skeptical research director looking for sufficient large, controlled, double-blind, random-ized trials to validate assertions made by energy healing, there is noth-ing further to say, and the book could end here.

But this is not the whole picture. One of the regulatory goals offered in earlier chapters is that of functional integration, defined as including appropriate integration of all world systems of knowledge about healing. Another regulatory goal involves facilitating human transformation at the broadest and deepest levels. The scientific agenda for energy healing has not controlled the public policy debate. As sug-gested, it is often the case in complementary and alternative medicine that "legislative recognition trumps medical recognition."[12] State legis-latures have granted legal recognition to energy healers in a variety of ways. For example, a house bill in Maryland has proposed to require the state Board of Chiropractic Examiners to adopt regulations for the registration of "energy practitioners," to define the term *energy therapy*, to define an "Energy Practitioner Advisory Committee" within the board, and to prohibit the practice of energy therapy (with specific exemptions) by individuals lacking registration.[13] The bill defines energy therapy as "the laying of hands on a clothed individual to affect the human energy field" and includes modalities such as Shiatsu, Polarity, reflexology, Reiki, Jin shin jyutsu, Healing Touch, zero bal-ancing, kinesiology, Bowen technique, and "therapeutic touching."[14]

Energy healing has sufficiently penetrated legislative, consumer, clinical, and research arenas to fuel contemplation of what it might por-tend for health care generally, even as research continues to help define its parameters and permutations. From a policy perspective, the range of this penetration suggests not only the plausibility of these means of healing—at least in the minds of a good segment of legislators and the public—but also the importance of information regarding (and experience with) these therapies becoming part of the medical corpus. Although definitional terms such as *integrative* and *energy* may change, such words presently serve as place-markers—verbal bridges to a future world of medicine and healing in which the physical and non-physical are understood as components of a spectrum of therapies, to be utilized, as appropriate, along a spectrum of consciousness of healing. In this spectrum, practices including clinical experience, observation, judgment, and intuition may be important. In short, perspectives from vitalism—"the proposition that more is needed to explain life than just physical or mechanical laws"—will play a more prominent role.[15]

Both educationally and clinically, energy healing is particularly significant among complementary and alternative medical therapies because of its potential universality, accessibility, and versatility. If, as many instructional courses assert, energy healing can be learned by any individual in a short period of time, its permutations potentially may be incorporated, in some form, into nearly any health care modality or practice and thereby require the fashioning of hospital policy for its use by physicians, physician assistants, nurses, and others. Further, energy healing conflates distinctions between therapies on physical, emotional, and spiritual planes and thus, by attempting to unify these various dimensions, potentially forms a potent bridge between medicine and spirituality—between the biophysical and the biopsychical. In regulatory terms, energy healing conceivably could fall within the scope of practice of any complementary and alternative, as well as conventional, health care profession. For example, the Massachusetts Board of Registration in Nursing issued an advisory ruling that it is within the scope of an R.N. or L.P.N. practice to employ complementary therapies, including "massage, Therapeutic Touch, Reiki, reflexology, imagery, hypnosis, music therapy, shiatsu, and aromatherapy," as "part of an overall plan of nursing care for which clients have granted informed consent."[16] Thus, far from being the most "extreme" or arcane modality within complementary and alternative medicine or health care generically, energy healing may be one of the most integral. This suggestion itself justifies a multifaceted consideration of the "farther reaches of human nature" that energy healing potentially presents and the most futuristic implications for health care and policy.

Energy Healing and Medical Education

Even though to some, scientific research has neither validated nor justified inclusion of energy healing in clinical care, perspectives from energy healing increasingly are informing even the conventional medical setting. Recently, at a fund-raising event, a medical school dean framed his speech with the story of a patient who had developed thyroid problems. The patient's doctor informed her that her thyroid was "being invaded by foreign cells." In narrating the history of her diagnosis, the patient told the clinician that she had suffered from sexual abuse as a child; that the notion of *invasion* was traumatic to her; and that she felt there was some connection between the physical, emotional, and psychological invasion during childhood and her present medical condition. The patient concluded with a request for a referral for acupuncture, as one means of resolving this connection. She then asked, "Doctor, do you know what *chi* is?"

The dean explained that a few years ago, such a question would have been mystifying, but that in the present environment, the question stimulated the clinician to consider the possibility that understanding the mysteries of *chi*—universal life energy—might provide some clues to the underlying etiology of a particular disease. The question of *chi* well may become more standard, as patients increasingly explore therapies such as *qigong* and other forms of energy healing for themselves and ask their physicians and other allied health providers for information, referrals, and meaningful ways to integrate such therapies into their conventional regimen. This reflects two civilizations colliding—or perhaps converging.

Health care educational institutions then would have responsibility to provide sufficient education to physicians and other conventional providers concerning the potential role of energy healing in clinical practice, as well as the theoretical underpinnings of energy healing and a practical experience of its parameters. Recently the Select Committee on Science and Technology in the United Kingdom's House of Lords devoted a lengthy report to complementary and alternative medicine.[17] In this report, the committee recommended that "every therapist working in complementary and alternative medicine should have a clear understanding of the principles of evidence-based medicine and healthcare," with such principles being "part of the curriculum of all complementary and alternative medical therapy courses."[18] The committee also recommended, however, that "if CAM [complementary and alternative medicine] is to be practiced by any conventional healthcare practitioners, they should be trained to standards comparable to those set out for that particular therapy by the appropriate (single) CAM regulatory body."[19] In short, medical (and other professional health care) education in the future would have to include not only information about what energy healers purport to do and to what extent the literature supports (or fails to support) specific therapeutic claims but also training of medical students (and students in other health care professions) to standards "comparable" to those established for energy healers by an appropriate regulatory body. It remains to be seen to what extent state legislatures (and professional bodies) in the United States will require (and promote) standards of education and training for energy healing practices that then could help create standards for medical education.[20]

Energy Healing Theory and Practice

The Chantilly Report provides one starting point for health care providers to understand the parameters of energy healing theory and practice. The document was drafted in a quasi-governmental context—as a summary of fields of practice by leaders in complementary and alternative medicine, in conjunction with academic institutions and representatives from the NIH—and thus blends research and governmental concerns and perspectives. The report includes "biofield therapeutics" (by which it refers specifically to energy healing) in the category of manual healing methods.[21] The report also notes that peoples and cultures in every sector of the world have had names for the biofield, or human energy field. These include ancient Egypt (*ankh*), South America (*gana*), Japan (*ki*), Polynesia (*mana*), ancient Greece (*pneuma*), India (*prana*), China (*chi*), and Native American Indian cultures (*ton; wakan*). The report describes biofield therapeutics (energy healing) as

> a process during which the practitioner places his or her hands either directly on or very near the physical body of the person being treated . . . [and] engages the perceived biofield from his or

her hands with the recipient's perceived biofield either to promote general health or to treat a specific dysfunction.[22]

The report catalogues a range of therapeutic intentions, including those regarding general health (such as stress relief and improvement of overall health and vitality), biological well-being (such as reduction of inflammation or pain), vegetative functions (such as improvement of digestion and sleep patterns), emotional states (such as changes in anxiety or grief), and dysfunctions often classified as psychosomatic (such as eating disorders and post-traumatic stress disorders). The report further offers some statistics on the use of energy healing: for example, in the United States, approximately fifty thousand practitioners provide about 120 million sessions annually. In addition, student nurses receive training in courses involving hands-on healing in more than ninety colleges and universities around the world.

In the United Kingdom, over eighty-five hundred registered healers may give healings at patients' request, and over fifteen hundred government hospitals have approval to use such healers.[23] In the United States, healings occur more informally. As a starting point, the Chantilly Report catalogues major therapies within the field. These include Barbara Brennan Healing Science (1978); Healing Touch (American Holistic Nurses Association, 1981); *huna* (traditional Hawaiian); Mariel (Ethel Lombardi, 1983); natural healing (Rosalyn Bruyere, 1974); *qigong* (traditional Chinese); Reiki (Japan, 1800s); SHEN therapy (Richard Pavek, 1977); and Polarity therapy (Randolph Stone, 1950s). Another major therapy is Therapeutic Touch, systematized in the early 1970s by Delores Krieger, R.N., and widely taught as part of the nursing school curriculum and considered by many to fall within the scope of practice for nursing.

Today, energy healing largely remains at the fringe of complementary and alternative medical therapies, in the sense that it lacks mainstream approval; functions without independent licensure for healers; and usually occurs covertly, tucked into another clinical practice. At least three reasons may account for this situation. First, there is a relatively small body of scientific literature validating human energy fields and/or explaining the nature of "spiritual energies" and the mechanism by which they are transferred from healer to patient. Some might argue that the literature exists, but that cultural bias precludes its more ready acceptance. It is not generally accepted, at present, that human energy fields are conclusively "proven" to exist by contemporary scientific tools; nor is it generally accepted that accounting for such energy fields should be an important component of clinical care.

A second reason for the relative obscurity of energy healing in clinical care is the lack of interdisciplinary research in exploring the potential role of this "technology of consciousness." Many of the phenomena proposed by energy healing, while perhaps antithetical to prevailing medical orthodoxy, find congruence in descriptions of reality proposed by physicists, mathematicians, anthropologists, psychologists, and individuals in other disciplines. For example, one proposed model is found in the writings of David Bohm. His notion of an implicate enfolded order, with layers of successive realities unfolding through multiple dimensions, coincides with the holographic notions of space, time, and information that the energy healer apparently experiences in accessing different states of consciousness with a patient.[24] Such models have not found much resonance in medical circles nor created impetus for translating their social and philosophical suggestions into provider-patient interactions in mainstream clinical care.

Third, energy healing has metaphysical and mystical implications and does not confine its descriptions to biochemical phenomena. This makes any embrace of the field practically heretical to the "objective" processes of scientific method and investigation. In fact, nurses who have been overt about their use of Therapeutic Touch in hospital systems sometimes have found themselves under investigation (or fired) for using "unscientific" approaches to patient care. Some of their detractors have found something about "waving one's hands" over the surface of a person's body that signifies the occult; that heralds the practice of magic, ritual, or witchcraft. Since there is no generally accepted scientific explanation for any benefit from such a practice, the presumption is that the individual practicing the craft must be delusional, dysfunctional, or otherwise creating a danger to patient safety. In short, a metaphysics that has no basis in physics must be crazy; hence, an early appellation for students of Delores Krieger who learned Therapeutic Touch was "Krieger's Crazies."

Many healers have suggested that the human energy system is best understood experientially, through meditation and exercises, as amplified by readings in the spiritual literature, together with some articles about research and models of care. In this vein, it might be argued that an academic, intellectual, and nonexperiential approach to energy healing confines understanding to the head, not the heart and spirit—to use a scriptural metaphor, such an approach is like describing the sunset to a blind person or music to one who is deaf. The inadequacy of such an approach is akin to the difference between reading studies concerning the efficacy of massage for a specific condition and getting a massage. For descriptions and illustrations of the energy system, the explorer of consciousness apparently must turn within and regard external indicia as secondary sources for explication. Nonetheless, a summary of relevant principles and practices may help guide conventional providers and complementary and alternative medical professionals who will be utilizing such modalities or contemplating referrals to providers offering such modalities, either within the hospital or outside its walls.

The Human Energy Field (or Biofield)

Energy healers assert that our physical anatomy has a bioenergetic component, a human energy field (or biofield) composed of centers of psychospiritual energy known as the chakras. *Chakra* is a Sanskrit word for "wheel."[25] The notion that humans have wheels of spiritual energy is not unique to Hinduism or any other Indian religious tradition. For example, the "emanations" of the mystical Kabbalistic teachings (the *sephirot*, or "wheels") and even the Christian sacraments are said to have correspondences to the chakras.[26] Although chakras have correspondences in other traditions, some of the terminology and framework for understanding their relation to human evolution, consciousness, and health come from Sanskrit writings.

The chakras are said to absorb, metabolize, and distribute universal life energy through the body and the energy field.[27] Healers describe at least seven major chakras going up the body—root, sacral, lumbar, heart, throat, brow, and crown—as well as numerous minor chakras, such as the energy centers in the palms of the hands, the fingertips, and at the bottom of the feet. Each chakra involves a different aspect of human experience (see chart 8).[28]

Healers also draw correspondences between the individual chakras and glands and areas of the body these chakras nourish (see chart 9).[29] These links create correspondences between diseases affecting glands, organs, and parts of the body and the emotional and spiri-

---

CHART 8. The Chakra System

First ("root")	Relates to the physical body and to the instinct for self-preservation
Second ("sacral")	Relates to the emotional life and to sexuality
Third ("lumbar")	Relates to the intellect and to one's sense of security or boundaries in interactions with others
Fourth ("heart")	Involves relationships and the experience of love
Fifth ("throat")	Relates to communication and expression
Sixth ("brow")	Relates to the ability to envision and translate ideas into reality
Seventh ("crown")	Relates to the ability to integrate all aspects of one's being

---

tual issues associated with the specific chakra affected. For example, kidney disease is said to be associated with dysfunction in the second chakra, indicating that the individual may have fundamental unresolved emotional and spiritual conflicts relating to matters of money, sex, and personal power. Similarly, digestive problems suggest difficulty "digesting" the input one receives from others; they are "third-chakra" issues, being concerned, among other things, with personal boundaries in relationship to others.

Healers perceive blockages and distortions in chakras accompanying (or presaging) disease. Barbara Brennan states, "Everyone who has angina has clogged, darkened energy in the heart chakra."[30] From her perspective, there is a correlation between an energetic stance ("clogged, darkened" heart energy) and a physical condition. Brennan views heart "attacks" as literally the effect of congested energies in the fourth chakra, which are blocking the free flow of love in relationships with others.

The logic and theoretical appeal of the chakras is the suggestion that this system can help bridge the physical and metaphysical—can mediate among the physiological, emotional, and psychospiritual aspects of human existence. More specifically, each chakra is said to mediate a particular kind, or quality, of spiritual energy; it "holds a note" for a particular band or frequency of consciousness.[31] In total, the

CHART 9. The Chakras, Glands, and Associated Areas of the Body

Chakra	Gland	Associated Area of the Body
First	Adrenal	Spinal column, kidneys
Second	Gonads	Reproductive system
Third	Pancreas	Stomach, liver, gall bladder, nervous system
Fourth	Thymus	Heart, blood, vagus nerve, circulatory system
Fifth	Thyroid	Bronchial and vocal apparatus, lungs, alimentary canal
Sixth	Pituitary	Lower brain, left eye, ears, nose, nervous system
Seventh	Pineal	Upper brain, right eye

seven major chakras are said to give us a physical experience of our consciousness (first chakra); an emotional and sexual experience (second chakra); a mental experience (third chakra); an experience based on relationships with others in our environment (fourth chakra); an experience based on expression of our essence (fifth chakra); an experience based on our personal vision of consciousness (sixth chakra); and finally, a fully unitive and integrative experience of consciousness (seventh chakra). Further, the second, third, fourth, and fifth chakras are said to have a front and a back—reflecting, respectively, the aspects of "feeling" and "will" for each of these chakras.[32] The flow of energy among chakras is said to be dynamic, fluid, and observable to healers as exchanges of color, light, and patterns of information between individuals and others and between individuals and their environment.[33]

The chakras also are seen as gateways to higher consciousness. Each chakra embodies a mode of experience and an archetypical theme through which the individual consciousness passes as up an "evolutionary ladder," from mere struggle for survival through unitary consciousness (see chart 10).[34] An individual suffering from a particular disease can be said to be learning an individualized form of an archetypical "lesson"—from a soul's perspective—of a particular chakra; families, friends, and caregivers of the afflicted person perhaps are sharing in the wisdom of that journey. Similarly, certain cultures may be predisposed to certain types of diseases and in this way may be collectively running through archetypical lessons specific to those civilizations. Thus, certain peoples may share certain kinds of collective medical pathologies or be more prone than others to a particular form of disease or infirmity. Even though such predispositions may be traceable to environment, diet, genetics, or some other observable factor, they also are said, in the chakra system, to reflect specific lessons common to a culture or social group. The term "lesson" is not meant to reduce suffering to a ready, pseudopsychological answer but rather to reflect in larger terms on the course by which peoples evolve, mature, and assimilate normative growth.

One can see how easily the chakra system lends itself to spiritual interpretation of medical phenomena in a way that facilitates healing. Among other functions, the system helps the individual address the anguishing question, "Why did *this* happen to *me*?" Or, put in a more uplifting way: "Is there some design, purpose, or pattern behind this suffering? What is the gift behind my illness, and what, for me in this specific situation, is the meaning of healing?" Of course, a good "bedside manner" in medicine might include an attempt to help the patient wrestle with such questions; on the other hand, the chakra system focuses specifically on the interaction among the physical, emotional, and spiritual levels. The system thus orients the provider to a different set of questions than other health care disciplines may suggest.

Like Maslow's hierarchy of personal needs, the chakra system expresses a fuller range of human potentiality than care pitched at the "first-chakra" level (concerned with struggle for survival) sometimes allows. Again, the chakras give clues to the meaning of "healing" as a different order of process than "curing." Healing may involve lessons of the soul, whereas curing primarily serves at the level of the body. The two are permeable as body and soul interpenetrate, although the primary focus of each differs. In this sense, the chakras of energy healing are similar to the anatomical maps and disease correspondences in other systems of healing within energy medicine, such as the acupuncture points and meridian system of traditional oriental medicine. Simply put, like these other systems, chakras link spiritual and emotional imbalance to physical disease. Presently, even with disciplines such as psychotherapy and psychoneuroimmunology, conventional care rarely assigns such meaning, value, or interpretation to the lessons of the soul.[35]

CHART 10. The Chakras and the Archetypes

Chakra	Mode of Experience	Archetype
First	Struggle for survival	The victim
Second	Sensory pleasure	The hedonist
Third	Mastery, domination, conquest	The hero
Fourth	Compassion, generosity, loving service	The liberator/ liberated one
Fifth	Devotion, surrender, creativity, grace	The child
Sixth	Insight, witnessing	The sage
Seventh	Unitary consciousness	Beyond form

The chakra system presents yet an additional complexity, however, in that each chakra also relates to a specific layer in the human energy field. These layers of the field are known in Eastern scriptural traditions as independent energy bodies corresponding with our physical body. In other words, in addition to our physical body, we are said to have at least seven different energy bodies surrounding and interpenetrating the physical body. Each chakra, in this system, thus runs both through the physical body and through all of the energy bodies. The seven energy bodies of the biofield are said to relate, respectively, to (1) an etheric body, containing lines of force to shape and anchor the physical body; (2) an emotional body, appearing to the healer as "colored clouds of fine substance in continual fluid motion"; (3) a mental body, associated with thoughts and mental processes; (4) an astral body, associated with literal cords of relationship binding individuals to others; (5) an etheric template, creating the matrix for the physical body as a whole; (6) a celestial body, constituting the emotional body of the spiritual plane and connecting individuals to experiences of spiritual ecstasy; and (7) a causal body, which is the egg shape of the aura body, appearing to the healer as "tiny threads of gold-silver light of very strong durability," containing "a golden grid structure of the physical body and all the chakras."[36]

The biofield system, as delineated to date by a combination of scriptural traditions, descriptions by healers, reports from patients, and research in a variety of disciplines, is dynamic, complex, and not fully understood. Many ancient texts describing the features of the field and the further reaches of human awareness remain untranslated—or lost. Some researchers suggest that the biofield carries extremely high frequencies (at least double, for example, those of electric signals in the heart, muscles, and brain) and that such frequencies can be characterized and differentiated across different patients through properties such as coherence, flow, strength, and range.[37] Lacking instruments to measure each aspect of the chakra system and energy bodies, it is difficult to be "scientific." Known observations come from highly focused individuals, often in trance states, and thus at first appear inaccessible to consensus experience based on repeatable, objective verification. As another complication, different teachers of energy healing describe their craft differently. They vary in description of the number of chakras, the functions of each chakra, the relationship of one chakra to another within the biofield, and the specific meanings different chakras hold. The very diversity of perception, interpretation, and analysis of the chakra system frustrates those who only trust reproducible results, "objective" validation of experimental reports, and announcement of scientific data by publication tested in the crucible of peer review.

Experiential Views of Energy Healing

Although the description of the biofield challenges biomedicine, existing scientific instrumentation, and contemporary beliefs about the existence of subtle bodies beyond the physical, those who explore energy healing experientially do seem to have ready, subjective experiences of the biofield and of the perceived ability to direct healing energy to another individual's biofield. This occurs even with a modicum of training (in other words, a few hours). For this reason, workshops in Reiki, Therapeutic Touch, and other modalities are highly popular, both for health care professionals and lay individuals, internationally. Many attend weekend workshops and as a result call themselves "healers," "Reiki masters," and the like, independent of direct medical or governmental recognition.

There are several possible explanations for the ease with which people can experience transmission and effects of energy healing. One could be that the experience of energy healing is delusional and humans easily are prone—as the placebo effect demonstrates—to imagine, fantasize, project, idealize, and otherwise distort objective reality according to the desires of their hungry minds. This is an explanation that many individuals tend to adopt, even once they have experienced the projection of *chi* by others or within themselves: it must be a trick of the mind.

A second explanation is that experiences of energy healing are a matter of belief, as are such experiences in any religion. This objection is familiar to those who label complementary and alternative medical modalities generally, including chiropractic and acupuncture, as "cult" therapies; such language was part of the American Medical Association's diatribe against these professions for much of the twentieth century. In this respect, "faith" in energy healing is like "faith" in God. To quote the Catholic saint Bernadette Soubirous:

> For those who believe in God, no explanation is necessary.
> For those who do not believe in God, no explanation
>   is possible.

More likely, however, although a satisfactory and comprehensive explanation is not yet available, explanation is both necessary and conceivable, yet experience makes a difference. As Groucho Marx said, "Who are you going to believe—me or your own eyes?" From a more established philosophical tradition, the work of William James in exploring the phenomenology of religious experience validates the importance of subjective experience in uncovering knowledge.[38] "Subordinating intellect and preconception to feeling and faith," James rejected "any system of thought whose chosen preconceptions make the very real facts of experience, religious or otherwise, vanish before one's very eyes."[39]

Yet a third possible explanation is that the ability to project felt healing, or spiritual energy, by hand, heart, or thought is an organic and inherent component of the human organism. Such powers, however, remain undeveloped, particularly in a society oriented toward external things and dominated by technology. Further, such abilities, if manifested, are ignored or squashed, because the consensus culture does not accept the validity of such experiences. For example, perceptions of other realities in children tend to be squashed or ignored among the demands for intensive, mentally-based homework and chores and the lure of technologically based entertainment, all of which steer the mind toward external attainments (for example, a good score on a quiz) and away from internal experience. Children have their energies directed away from *being* and instead focus their sensitive perceptive apparatus toward *analytic* functions (such as learning algebra and memorizing the date that Columbus discovered America).

Although the potential role of energy healing in secondary education deserves much fuller treatment, suffice it to say that contemporary education assigns a marginal role to cultivation of sensitivities toward spiritual realities and dimensions of intelligence that enhance extraordinary perception and expression.[40] In fact, the separation of church and state assures as much: secular education is directed away from anything that could be construed as bringing God into the classroom. This clear division—although it finds some justification in First Amendment precepts—creates, as a by-product, dissociation from abilities that might lie beneath the surface of ordinary consciousness and thereby exist independent of any particular religiosity.

Again, the possibility for (and implications of) a more generalized *mysterium tremendum* within the human organism, apart from any one religious perspective, deserves fuller treatment. As far as early development of such abilities is concerned, much of present education and the social milieu force us to abandon the ideas, for example, that we have angel playmates; that we can see a rich world of colors that is produced by objects, persons, and social interactions; that we live simultaneously in multiple dimensions; or that we can communicate with nature in ways the intellect cannot fathom. This creates an immeasurable loss. Such experiences "suggest that our ordinary experience 'may be only a fragment of real human experience,' and that an intellectual logic which ignores such experiences will never be able to 'reach completely adequate conclusions.'"[41]

While there are numerous philosophical and psychological models for explaining the difference between experiential knowledge and deductive, logical knowledge (for example, the distinction between empiricism and rationalism or William James's pragmatic interest in the experience of religious states of consciousness), the argument that other ways of knowing and seeing are possible—beyond the five senses—can inform health care practice and policy.[42] Sometimes a metaphor helps—this one involves an attempt to research intuitive aspects of communication in dolphin populations:

A researcher on dolphin communication recorded hundreds of hours of dolphin sounds, and analyzed these sounds on her computer to determine whether the complex set of signals contained reproducible patterns, corresponding with specific behaviors. At length she was able to decode certain clicks, high-pitched squeals, and other noises associated with certain social interactions between dolphins.

Later, she decided to view the dolphins' sounds and movements from the perspective of *music and dance,* rather than *language.* She swam in the circle of dolphins, using a water fan that allowed her to flow with them as they frolicked together. In so doing, she changed her position from one of *observer,* to *participant.* In short, she became one of them. She noticed that their awareness of her, and interaction with her, changed as well. It became friendlier, warmer, richer with emotional exchange.

She then understood them in a more intuitive way. She lost herself in the whirling movements. When her morning of "research" was over, she felt exhilarated: she had become part of the dance. And her scientific investigation was enriched by her ability to *merge with the object of her study.*[43]

Centering, Assessing, Directing

Delores Krieger described Therapeutic Touch as a process involving several essential steps that generate the experience of transferring energy from healer to client. The first stage, *centering,* involves calming the healer's mind and body and preparing his or her own energy field to absorb universal life energy that can be channeled to the client or patient. This means "being at a quiet place within ourselves from which we can focus completely on the person before us."[44] Meditation, yoga, and prayer help individuals find and maintain a state of centering.[45] The second step, *assessment,* involves scanning the patient's energy field. Some healers scan visually, others kinesthetically. The sensations healers might detect with their hands include "tingling, pressure, shock, pulsation, heat, or coolness" in various locations in the biofield; such irregularities in the biofield indicate energetic blockages or imbalances.[46] The third step, *unruffling,* involves sweeping the biofield in smooth, rhythmical motions to help loosen congestion and begin to remove blockages.[47] The final step, *directing and modulating energy*, involves "sending" energy into the patient's biofield.[48] A study of the effects of Therapeutic Touch on bereaved recipients summarized the four-step protocol as follows: the practitioner "moves the hands over the body of the subject from head to feet, attuning to the condition of the subject by becoming aware of changes in sensory cues in the hands."[49]

Patients have reported common experiences as recipients of energy healing. For example, a research physicist described her experience as a recipient of Therapeutic Touch as follows:

> Within minutes of [the healer] placing her hand on my knees I felt a sensation of tingling heat, and experienced a spontaneous decrease of pain in my knees. Being a scientist, I was intrigued . . . by the fact that this was not explainable within current scientific or medical theory.[50]

A study of premature babies at Stanford Children's Hospital described the healer's transfer of energy as follows:

> Cupping one hand above the body's head, [the nurse] slowly sweeps the other hand down the baby's body, above the surface of the blanket.[51]

Practitioners have noted few observed contraindications to Therapeutic Touch. Among other things, practitioners are advised to stop directing energy once the biofield is balanced; to direct energy to the head for only a short time; and to make the process brief for infants, very debilitated patients, and the elderly.[52] Therapeutic Touch and related modalities may have specific effects on dying patients (see chap. 7). As research accumulates, the field of energy healing, like massage, may create a more comprehensive list of contraindications and of adverse events that could be attributed to the application of energy healing.

Disease: A Perspective from the Biofield

Both ancient texts and modern healers insist that domains of knowledge regarding the chakras provide specific technologies for the preservation and restoration of physical health and mental well-being. Significantly, the chakras and energy bodies are described as extremely sensitive barometers of information the human organism receives and integrates, both internally (generated from the body-mind) and externally (accumulated from others).

William Tiller, of Stanford University, analogizes these systems to electromagnetic energy radiated from the human body, as well as to "sonic fingerprints" associated with physical movement of cells and body systems.[53] Tiller believes present scientific understanding of human energy fields is inadequate to account for the phenomena experienced and observed:

> So many things seem to happen that are not explicable in terms of electromagnetic energy or sonic energy that, by trying to squeeze all these new aspects into that very small mold, we shall get lost (because they just will not fit). Thus, the place where I have started is to take the yogic philosophy . . . and hypothesize that this really means that there are seven different levels of substance, and that these different substances are unique and have different types of configurations. They obey entirely different kinds of laws and they have unique characteristics of radiation (absorption and emission). I further postulate that they operate in different kinds of space-time frames in the universe and so are distinct from each other.[54]

Healers suggest that both positive (healthy) energies and negative (unhealthy) energies can, respectively, balance and energize or invade and deplete different chakras and layers of the field. In common parlance, we note that we are "drained," for example, by large crowds, airports, and needy people who "steal" our "energy" (for example, those with "vacuum-cleaner eyes," also known as "psychic vampires"). Thus, from the healer's perspective, disease can originate in and manifest in the human energy field, as well as in the physical body. The notion of imbalance is crucial. From the healer's perspective, energetic imbalance leads to disease, and disease leads to further energetic imbalance.[55] While the relationship between energetic depletion, or imbalance, and disease is familiar to complementary and alternative medical disciplines such as traditional oriental medicine, the chakra system provides another set of unifying energetic principles for integration of the notion of energy medicine with conventional therapeutic disciplines.[56]

To illustrate the potential relationship between chakra or energy field imbalances and disease, consider the heart patient. According to the chakra system, a person with intense unresolved anger, frustration, and grief will carry blockage or stagnant, dark energy in the solar plexus and heart chakras. A healthy heart chakra spins clockwise (drawing in universal energy, or *chi*). A heart patient's chakra will spin counterclockwise, in a wobbly fashion, or not at all. Chakra dysfunction destabilizes the physical heart and surrounding organs and systems. Therefore, by failing to discharge or resolve the negative emotions in a healthy way, the individual literally blocks and shuts down the chakras. He or she thus fails to take in sufficient universal life energy, in that chakra, to sustain the system.[57]

Brennan summarizes the process as follows:

> Whenever a person blocks whatever experience he is having, he in turn blocks his chakras, which eventually become disfigured. The chakras become "blocked," clogged with stagnated energy, spin irregularly, or backwards (counterclockwise) and even, in the case of disease, become severely distorted or torn.[58]

Thus, the cardiac patient literally experiences an energetic attack on his or her own heart—the blockage stems from accumulation of stagnant energies; the clot begins on the energetic level. If left unaddressed, the energetic blockage manifests in the physical body. From a preventative perspective, healers would encourage such individuals to seek counseling to clear these blockages long before they manifest in disease.

Parenthetically, it should be noted that animals, too, are said to have chakras and that the chakra system and associated disease theories also would have potential application to veterinary medicine. The question of emotional and spiritual release with animals is more complicated, however, since animals do not communicate in human language and thus do not process their emotional realities in the same way as humans (see chap. 8).

Brennan further describes a subtle aspect of the chakras as the cords of biofield energy that connect the chakras of human beings in relationship to one another.[59] Damaged cords from each chakra are said to result in propensity for different kinds of diseases (see chart 11).[60]

Despite the attempt to map such correlations, the chakra system does not purport to create a dogmatic and exclusive orthodoxy. First,

CHART 11. Damaged Chakra Cords and Associated Diseases

Damaged Cords	Represent	Some Common Resulting Illnesses
First chakra	Weakness in will to live and in physical function	Cancer, AIDS, rheumatoid arthritis
Second chakra	Lack of fecundity in sensual relationships	Sexual infections and diseases
Third chakra	Trauma from parental overcontrol, or from lack of nurturing or contact	Diabetes, ulcer, liver disease
Fourth chakra	Damage during unhealthy love relationships	Heart disease
Fifth chakra	Failure of trust and communication in relationships	Thyroid problems, misalignment in neck, lung diseases
Sixth chakra	Betrayal and coercion in religious experience	Headaches, learning disabilities, schizophrenia, brain disorders
Seventh chakra	Inability to integrate physical and spiritual worlds	Depression, stunting of physical development, mental disorders

the chakra system arose prior to modern medicine and remains to be integrated with modern medical knowledge and care. Second, as noted, the relationship between the chakras and energy bodies and the physical organs and body is understood to be reciprocal, not exclusive. Dietary deficiencies, environmental disturbances, or dysfunctions in the mental or emotional life in turn contribute to chakra and energy field dysfunction.

For example, according to Roslyn Bruyere, cancer indicates, among other things, a lack of vitality in the first and second chakras. Bruyere explains this lack of vitality as corresponding, on an emotional and spiritual level, to the patient's inappropriate use of power and to grief and fear, all of which are associated with these two lower chakras.[61] Bruyere opines that in addition to treating the cancer on a physical level, the energetic level should be addressed. For example, she states that healing sessions can increase the energy in the lower chakras and balance the energy field to help the body overcome the cancer.[62] In this respect, energy healing becomes an adjunctive therapy—it is not claimed to "cure" cancer but rather to help heal imbalances underlying and corresponding with the physical manifestation of the disease.

Bruyere's analysis is not limited to cancer; she explains other diseases in terms of energy field imbalances. For example, she views arthritis as representing energetic resistance to expressing anger: the arthritic diverts his or her life-force (red energy) to the joints.[63] Her energetic understanding of arthritis is as a disease of resistance. Similarly, she views colitis as an inflammatory disease: the colitis patient has a second chakra that runs counterclockwise, representing a way of warding off emotional information.[64] According to Bruyere, this destabilizes the first chakra, which causes the intestines to be inflamed—literally, "full of red," the color of the first chakra.[65] If the patient allows honest feelings to flow—such as anger (which appears to the healer as red)—the chakra begins to spin properly, and healing begins.[66] Bruyere's descriptions accord with Brennan's notion that different diseases are associated with dysfunction in different chakras; the causal relationship, though, is not completely explained.

While Bruyere, Brennan, and others have articulated new models linking the biofield to disease, these models have not resulted in any systematic study of the field. Energy healing is relatively undeveloped professionally—it is far less professionally developed than chiropractic, acupuncture, naturopathy, or massage therapy. There is a lack of commonly agreed-upon training among schools, and professional bodies—to the extent that they function and garner internal consensus—have failed to agree on common standards for training, skill, and eventual licensure. Subjectivity is an inherent part of the field, at present. Further, many providers of energy healing practice clandestinely (for example, while the nurse supervisor is not watching); the fact that a given provider knows about Therapeutic Touch may be whispered about in the hallway, the information offered quietly to the patient. Nonetheless, some health care professions have attempted to delineate more formal parameters for delivery of energy healing within the health care institution.

In the field of nursing, for example, it has been suggested that basic professional parameters for practices involving energy healing include the following: ensuring that the practice abides with the provider's scope of practice; ensuring that the practice does not exceed the limits of the provider's competence; recognizing contraindications to treatment; demonstrating the ability to perform therapeutic techniques that can be evaluated and meet established educational criteria; ensuring that use of their therapies is safe and effective.[67] These suggestions help codify a set of practices that have flourished largely outside regulatory review. Yet overall, the lack of a mature, stable professional body to regulate energy healing, combined with the inherent subjectivity and lack of reproducibility in the techniques, create obstacles to the standardization, professional consensus, and reliability associated with governmental and institutional credentialing of providers and typically considered necessary for the regulatory goal of quality assurance.

The Spectrum of Healing

The Chantilly Report draws a distinction between curing and healing. Curing, as suggested, involves eradication of disease at the physiological level, while healing involves a movement toward wholeness, growth, or greater balance on physical, mental, emotional, and social levels, rather than just focusing on curing a given condition. Curing, for example, might involve treating breast cancer through radical lumpectomy; healing might involve addressing underlying psychospiritual issues. Thus, a patient may be cured without being healed and conversely may experience healing without being cured. From the healer's perspective, cure without healing ultimately leads to only temporary relief: the residual imbalance ultimately will manifest in another form of physical or mental disease. In short, both curing and healing are important. Further, curing occurs on the physical level, whereas healing involves the emotional, mental, and higher spiritual bodies, which may lead to curing.

The distinction between curing and healing provides a basis for reconsidering legal definitions of medicine and its unauthorized practice and the potential application of these rules to energy healing. Typically, medical licensing law defines medicine in terms of "diagnosis" and "treatment" of "disease"; anyone who practices "medicine" without a license to do so commits a criminal act. These statutes were enacted during the late nineteenth century, when groups of physicians lobbied legislatures to exclude all other practitioners. Therefore, the licensing laws attempted to define all healing as "medicine" and assign all diagnosis and treatment to the licensed class. As chiropractors, acupuncturists, and other providers entered professional health care practice, they were legislatively limited to a scope of practice narrower than the limited practice accorded to "medicine." Yet in order to define these professions, terms such as "chiropractic diagnosis" and "acupuncture diagnosis" became necessary—the underlying notion being that "diagnosis" and "treatment" would be limited to one's training and skill. These terms inherently challenged the original notion that only licensed medical doctors applied diagnostic and treatment skills to the complex phenomenon of disease. In short, as complementary and alternative medical providers gained licensure, the original language for medical licensure, and the conceptual framework surrounding such language, became anachronistic. Nonetheless, it left providers at risk of prosecution for unlicensed medical practice and continued a hegemonic perspective on the art of healing.[68]

Because medical licensing laws continue to prohibit other providers from attempting to "cure disease," the healer who purports to cure *and advises the patient to ignore medical advice* faces risk of prosecution for unlicensed medical practice. This legal rule deters overreaching by healers who would purport to *substitute* for medical diagnosis and treatment. In other words, because we live in a technological age, with scientifically validated methods of addressing disease, and not in an ancient culture governed by the tribal shaman, the practice of energy healing in this culture must be "integrative"—adjunctive to scientific interventions. From the perspective of giving the patient truthful and nonmisleading information (in other words, the regulatory goal of health care freedom), healers must inform their clients at a minimum that resolution of emotional and spiritual conflicts underlying the disease may or may not cure the disease; may or may not cut bleeding time, shorten postoperative pain and depression, or lessen the required amount of medication. Healers who make claims exceeding available evidence may be liable for unlicensed practice of medicine, as well as misrepresentation, consumer fraud, and other criminal and tortious violations.[69]

This is not to rule out the possibility that energy healing in and of itself may "cure"—that it may resolve an untreatable condition, shrink a tumor, or result in an unexplainable "spontaneous remission." Theoretically, by healing the trauma at the outer edges of the energy field and by treating imbalances or correcting alignment and releasing blockages, the healing works through successive layers of the energy field and ultimately could affect the physical body. Further, it is entirely possible that certain healers may have spiritual gifts focused specifically on healing on the physical level. Humans are complex. Disease is mysterious. Even the ancient seers who saw the chakras in meditation and thereafter described their qualities asserted, "The ways of karma are mysterious." In short, the curing/healing dichotomy, while useful, does not fully describe energy healing and the potential parameters of integration.

A richer taxonomy than the curing/healing dichotomy might view what energy healers do, or purport to do, as a step along a larger spectrum of healing (see chart 12). The chart suggests that energy healing potentially fleshes out portions of the spectrum of healing omitted in many conventional and complementary and alternative medical therapies.

Again, the caveat must be given that these categories are preliminary and that healing modalities frequently cross boundaries. For example, surgery also can be viewed as an intense form of acupuncture—in other words, as having effects on the flow of energy along meridian lines. Presumably these effects must be addressed along with physical and mental recovery after the surgery. Further, it is tempting to see again a hierarchy or progression of modalities, as the individual moves from the gross level (the physical body) to the most subtle (integration of body, emotions, thoughts, relationships, expression, connectedness to all things, and individuation).

But as noted, the therapies overlap and create healing at multiple levels, and as in Maslow's taxonomy, the categories are not mutually exclusive. For example, surgery can restore to the patient emotional as well as physical vitality—for instance, when after a successful operation, one learns one is no longer under a death sentence. Joy returns. Similarly, the relationship between physician and patient in conven-

CHART 12. The Spectrum of Healing

Chakra	Level of Being	Type of Wholeness	Facet of Healing	Examples of Healing Modalities
First	Physical	Physical	Body	Biomedical, some chiropractic
Second	Emotional/ sexual	Emotional	Feelings	Cathartic therapy and bodywork
Third	Intellectual	Mental	Cognition	Cognitive therapy
Fourth	Human love	Relational	Relationships	All therapies
Fifth	Communication	Expressive	Connectedness	Art and music therapy
Sixth	Vision	Centeredness	Spiritual	Dreamwork; Jungian and transpersonal psychotherapy, energy healing
Seventh	Integration	Individuation	Self-actualization	Meditation, prayer

tional care may include subtle relational dimensions that benefit from an account that includes the chakra system: the encounter is therapeutic in physical and subtle dimensions. A therapy such as bodywork likewise may function on multiple levels: it arguably relieves mental stress, promotes circulation on the physical level, and can release emotions and help the client access spiritual experience. In short, although there may be a spectrum of healing, complementary and alternative medicine is not necessarily an evolution over biomedicine—nor is scientific medicine an evolution over a therapy such as acupuncture. Rather, different therapies can affect different aspects of being. Future medicine consists of the perfect intervention, in the right dosage, at the right time, offered in the right way.

At the same time, though, the chart does reflect a movement toward increasingly more refined aspects of health and human wholeness. As with Maslow's hierarchy, the terms "lower" and "higher" express the notion that when an individual is preoccupied with a "lower" need (such as hunger), insufficient energy may be freed up to take interest in a "higher" need (such as self-actualization). Similarly, the patient who is preoccupied with first-chakra, physical survival issues may not have enough personal energy to consider his or her relationship with the cosmos. And sometimes, a person preoccupied with emotional, mental, or prayerful activities may forget to eat or sleep, becoming physically depleted.

This may be one explanation for biomedicine's historical focus on the physical and its frequent lack of inclusion of some of the insights presented within energy healing. *Because* biomedicine primarily became interested in curing, as opposed to healing, it has been preoccupied with first-chakra matters—for example, the integrity of the physical body, with all its complex, component parts. Practices such as Mesmerism—which dealt with potentialities of other states of consciousness—were regarded as inherently suspect and fraudulent. Vitalism was thought absurd. Likewise, since legal rules mirrored biomedical predominance, the law concerned itself primarily with fraud control and quality assurance (reflecting first- and second-chakra issues), rather than expressly addressing the upper chakras through articulated themes such as transformation of human potential and human evolutionary processes. Thus, legal and public policy concerns themselves represent the social order's emphasis within the chakras (see chart 13).

With Sigmund Freud and the advent of psychotherapy, medicine moved distinctively into the second chakra, addressing the impact of emotions, repression of unconscious motivations and drives, and human sexuality on health. Freud's theories initially met with much resistance, as contemporary physicians were reluctant to shift their perspective to a second-chakra analysis. Legal rules likewise compartmentalized body and mind, distinguishing between the practice of medicine and mental health care practices *not* involving a medical approach.

Later psychotherapeutic approaches incorporated higher chakras.

CHART 13. The Spectrum of Regulation and Healing

Chakra	Level of Being	Maslow's Value	Regulatory Value
First	Physical	Physiological	Fraud control
Second	Emotional/ sexual	Safety	Quality assurance
Third	Intellectual	Belongingness/ love	Health care freedom
Fourth	Human love	Belongingness/ love	Health care freedom
Fifth	Communication	Esteem	Functional integration
Sixth	Vision	Esteem	Functional integration
Seventh	Integration	Self-actualization	Transformation

Licensing laws began to embrace such healers as music and art therapists. The movement to incorporate emotional and spiritual realities also moved into medicine. For example, surgeons have begun exploring the healing effects of music, aromatherapy, and hypnosis (higher-chakra therapies) on patient recovery from surgery.[70]

The spectrum of healing thus presents one way to trace the expansion of human consciousness, and regulatory attention to such expansion via various social issues, through the chakras. This evolution accords with one understanding of disease in an aspect of Indian philosophy. Disease is considered to exist at both gross (physical, lower-chakra) and subtle (mental, emotional, spiritual, higher-chakra) levels. The most subtle, pervasive, and insidious form of disease is called bhavaroga—sometimes translated as "transmigration," or as "the disease of mundane existence"; only contact with the indwelling divinity in the human heart is said to provide a complete cure for this disease.[71] Thus, the notion that only resolving disease at the highest levels of the energy field provides a complete remedy is analogous to the healer's notion that healing must resonate on every level of the field in order for the disease to be completely cleared from potential manifestation. Yet although energy healing concerns itself with ultimate healing, it also acknowledges that the physical level must be addressed.

Issues such as access to health care, social justice, peace, and economic well-being—all of which express higher-order values—occupy the language of law, yet the actual pursuit of such themes typically has engendered conflict and been mired in duality, with proponents and opponents of various proposals steeped in "proving" which position is "right." Articulation of the conflict of high-order values can occur on the mental and emotional levels of the field, while the struggle can entail lower-level collisions (for example, survival of one idea at the expense of another). In other words, the chakra system offers one way for those in the legal system to view the process of social change and evolution. For example, from one perspective, the "trimester" rule in *Roe v. Wade* represented an attempt to craft a compromise position between the opposite poles of abortion being morally "right" or morally "wrong"; yet despite the social compromise this rule fashioned, it provided no escape from conflicting, dualistic positions, each claiming a monopoly on truth, and persisting through various changes to the rule of law. The attempt to collectively *live,* from a state of *being,* in higher-order values and *then* articulate policy has not yet occurred in contemporary American culture. What society enlightened beings might produce remains subject to speculation.[72]

Some Regulatory Conundrums

Energy healing presents at least four emerging regulatory conundrums: first, whether and how to license providers practicing some form of energy healing; second, how to define healers' scope of practice; third, how to establish a standard of care for purposes of determining the boundaries of acceptable practice; and fourth, how to appropriately document the application of energy healing.[73]

First, licensure is perhaps the most important gateway to greater acceptance and overt inclusion in clinical care. One objection to licensure comes from those who assert that spiritual healing is sacred and therefore ought not to be subject to any form of government regulation. Healers, the argument goes, have "lain hands" on human beings for millennia, across innumerable traditions; they access nonordinary realms of reality and serve as mediums for divine energies to help heal the sick. Therefore, the limited, fallible, and tainted structures of human bureaucracies ought not to touch these sacred waters.

On the other side of the coin, to the extent that spiritual healing implicates medical and not merely spiritual care, many would argue that some form of government intervention is justifiable. The regulatory system often has drawn a distinction between "medicine" and "religion"—for example, in the exemption religious healers receive from licensing statutes, so long as they are practicing a recognized religion and are not prescribing medication. In addition, licensure in complementary and alternative medicine generally is seen not only as a means of preventing dangerous and unskilled practitioners from offering health care services but also as a mechanism for providing legislative recognition, and hence legitimization, of the complementary and alternative medical profession. Licensure thus serves not only to protect the licensed profession against unwarranted prosecution for unlicensed medical practice but also to provide a gateway for inclusion in hospital credentialing schemes, referrals from M.D.s and other providers, and eventual third-party reimbursement. Thus, licensure may have advantages for healers: it provides recognition.

The impetus for licensure typically comes from within the profession itself and often involves a sorting-out among providers with differing levels of education in that profession. For instance, naturopaths who have more extensive training in naturopathy typically have been the ones to lobby for licensure, establishing more rigorous requirements for the license (for example, graduating from one of the few naturopathic colleges recognized by the U.S. Department of Education) than the "diploma mills" through which one can take a weekend or correspondence course and call one's self a "naturopath." From a regulator's perspective, some minimal level of consistency of training within the profession, together with some minimal level of educational bodies observing commonly agreed-upon, recognizable educational standards, offer a sense that a distinct professional field is evolving, capable of generating criteria that can guide practitioners toward responsible practice.

If the Reiki practitioners, Polarity therapists, individuals trained in Therapeutic Touch, and graduates of any number of schools for energy healing collectively create standards for certification and accreditation within the profession of energy healing, such intraprofessional efforts will heighten the field's candidacy for licensure in any given state. In other words, the state is more likely to recognize the profession via licensure or some other regulatory mechanism once the profession suf-ficiently organizes itself to do the work for the state. Unless and until the profession itself achieves sufficient organization and coherence, however, the state is unlikely to grant independent licensure to such providers, because there are no standards on which to base licensure. To the extent that healers do not come together to set independent stan-dards for the profession and create regulation, it is likely that *other* pro-fessional regulatory boards will take initiative and do this for them. The result will be that energy healers will fall within the jurisdiction of another profession's licensing board, as in the proposed rules for Mary-land's chiropractic board.

The second legal conundrum—how to define the scope of practice for energy healers—also implicates the question of which professions should have energy healing included within their legally authorized scope of practice. For example, is energy healing more properly a func-tion of nursing, dentistry, and other allied health professions involving close patient contact and touch? Another possibility is that energy heal-ing should be considered a component of chiropractic (which is defined, in some states, as involving a balancing of the patient's "nerve energy"); naturopathy (which involves the principle that "nature cures"); or even acupuncture (which involves projection and manipu-lation of *chi*).

Conceptually, one could link energy healing with nearly every health care profession. If the ability to heal through consciousness and intentionality comes naturally with a small amount of training, then providers in many health care professions may wish to study and incorporate these practices. Increased popularity of energy healing likely will lead to increased regulation: whatever profession claims energy healing will try to regulate it. For example, some of the chal-lenges given in the proposed Maryland legislation to the "Energy Prac-titioner Advisory Committee" are to develop and recommend to the chiropractic board the requirements for registration as an energy prac-titioner, to evaluate energy-therapy programs and modalities for approval by the board, and to evaluate the credentials required of applicants for registration.[74] As noted, though, while this legislation openly calls for credentialing standards, philosophically the idea of actually including energy healing in statutory language within various licensing laws may seem odd, since traditionally the power to heal has been thought of as the exclusive province of kings, saints, and avatars. Thus, in some states, energy healing may remain an unarticulated component of a given health care provider's scope of practice.

The third legal conundrum is how to conceptualize the standard of care in practices involving energy healing. Normally, in malpractice law, the applicable standard of care follows the profession in question. For example, an acupuncturist's conduct is judged according to community standards in acupuncture, not medicine. Expert testimony establishes the standard of care in the profession. Since energy healing is amorphous, crosses professions, and is undeveloped in terms of standard "protocols" for specific conditions, such testimony necessarily would be ambiguous and imprecise. At present, one could argue that since standards have not yet evolved sufficiently to permit even *candidacy* for independent licensure, there cannot be compelling expert testimony on standard of care in a malpractice case involving energy healing. Until standards develop, this lack of evolution in the profession will leave providers with considerable legal ambiguity. For example, Reiki probably is not presently used by many physical therapists, particularly to relieve "effects of past lives."

On the other hand, at some point it may be considered natural to "run energy" while providing massage, manipulation, or other hands-on techniques considered part of "physical therapy." The physical therapist in case 4A may be at the crossroads of changing standards of care in the profession; at best, the therapist would hope to be considered not culpable for the patient's reaction. So long as the therapist did not engage in the unauthorized practice of medicine, psychiatry, or psychology, the therapist's conduct arguably should not lead to liability. A separate point would be whether it could be proven that there was a causal link between the use of energy healing and the patient's injury. Assuming the energy healing was offered as an adjunct to necessary medical care, the patient would not have suffered the indirect adverse effect of being diverted from conventional care.

Again, however, given the lack of standards within the profession to guide the practitioner desiring to offer energy healing, liability could flow from the very uniqueness of the therapy. On a practical level, a practitioner's admission to receiving information on channels other than those of scientific research or the usual five senses may not play well before a jury. Such conduct certainly may offend regulatory bodies committed to disciplining providers for "unprofessional conduct." If even use of homeopathy as a remedy of last resort has offended a medical board, one can well imagine the results with energy healing.[75]

The fourth issue concerns documentation in the medical record. Many health care providers do document application of energy healing modalities in the patient's chart—for example:

> Eight minutes of Therapeutic Touch applied; patient seemed calmer and more relaxed following treatment.

Accurate and comprehensive documentation is the sine qua non of a strategy to prevent unwarranted malpractice liability. In fact, some recommend documentation of energy healing modalities as part of professional practice.[76] Further, state statutes or professional board regulations may specify the extent to which *any* therapeutic intervention must be charted, as well as it how it may be charted. Assuming such rules require documentation of energy healing modalities, the issue of documentation is resolved. Absent such direct guidance, documentation also creates potential difficulties. Since many providers and regulatory authorities have their own opinions regarding application of "Therapeutic Touch" or "Reiki energy," placing this information in the chart may create legal risk. At a minimum, application of such modalities might indicate deviation from conventional standards of care and thereby lead to malpractice liability, as well as professional discipline.

In short, the regulatory structure's emerging consideration of legal issues surrounding energy healing reflects evolving notions of how best to use regulation to allow spiritual energies to permeate this sector of health care. Among other things, healers differ, and their techniques frequently follow intuitive guidance, rather than any stock "protocol" about where to place hands, "how much" consciousness to invest in any given technique, how much energy to "run," and so on. Healers' methods challenge research and medical standards, upon which legal conclusions frequently are based. Whether regulating healers under one regulatory board or another truly serves patients remains to be seen—as does whether regulatory goals such as integration and transformation are served by such efforts. The prospect of having different regulatory boards compete for jurisdiction over energy healing highlights the theme that unless regulation in *this* century proceeds with wisdom and vision, it will merely re-create the sectarian factionalism, competition, destructiveness, and hegemonic tendencies of earlier rivalries in medicine.

Intuitive Diagnosis

The prospect of intuitive diagnosis raises particularly thorny legal dilemmas when treatment for disease is addressed. Intuitive diagnosis results from the premise of energy healing that disease manifests first in the biofield and therefore might be perceived by the healer *before* it precipitates into the physical body.[77] In other words, "changes in the content of consciousness" often precede, as well as accompany, neuro-physiological processes.[78] Like application of energy healing to treatment, intuitive diagnosis raises greater concern when it is used to substitute for conventional diagnosis as opposed to when it is limited to adjunctive use.

Minnesota now allows nonlicensed energy healers to practice; such practice presumably includes intuitive diagnosis.[79] In Minnesota, unlicensed providers must, among other things, disclose to the patient the nature and theory of their practice and the fact that the state has no educational and training requirements for practice. They also must refrain from making a medical diagnosis and treatment or contradicting the advice of a licensed physician. This latter requirement is, of course, implicit in medical licensing laws, since any provider who tells a patient to ignore a physician's medical prescription could be deemed to be "practicing medicine without a license."

In case 4B, the healer advises the patient to choose one course of medication over another. She claims the information to do so came, unprompted, from an intuitive source and turned out to be accurate. This case raises the question as to whether intuitive diagnosis could help in decisions that implicate the "art" rather than the "science" of medicine, and, if so, raise liability concerns.

In case 4C, the father experienced intuitive intervention during a crucial moment in his wife's labor. Whether the "voice" he heard came from within (wherever *that* may be), from a deceased relative (standing around in an energy body, but without a physical body), from "God," or from a wise spiritual guide, or simply showed he was in tune with the cosmos, it apparently guided him concerning his wife's health. This case suggests that intuition lies within the medical choices of many patients, as well as providers, and frequently guides consumers in the choice of one intervention over another.

A collaborative study between an intuitive healer (Carolyn Myss) and a Harvard-trained neurosurgeon (Norman Shealy) claimed accuracy in intuitive diagnosis of the patient 93 percent of the time.[80] The study does not definitively establish the accuracy and validity of intuitive diagnosis, but it does suggest a potential role for intuitive diagnosis in health care. One of the implications of such diagnostic techniques is that medicinal drugs *also* contain energies in the higher realms, "which then, of course, affect the higher bodies" and then redouble back to the physical body; if this is the case, then the prescribing of medicine ought to take into account the way the drug might affect the other, energy bodies.[81]

In this way, notions of the biofield challenge much of the corpus and approach of conventional health care jurisprudence. For example, returning to the discussion in chapter 1 of the meaning of "safe and effective," contemporary notions of safety and efficacy definitely fail to take into account any bodies other than the physical. Yet from the healer's perspective, what is effective on the physical level may have consequences on the energetic levels. Similarly, conventional care often relies on standardized dosages and prescriptions—indeed, this premise supports the process of FDA approval of new drugs—yet disciplines such as homeopathy take the patient as an individual and examine such nonobjective criteria as the individual's "constitution." The healer's notion of the biofield supports the notion in such therapies as homeopathy that, even as standardized diagnostic and therapeutic information are helpful in biomedicine, energy healing is tailored to the individual, who has a unique constellation of energy bodies accompanying the physical body.

Again, literature supporting such claims is either nonexistent or inconclusive. On the whole, the scientific literature on psychic research can be categorized as (1) expressing a skeptical attitude that assumes effects are totally illusory; (2) extensions of prevailing psychological models of memory, learning, or motivation; (3) theories that postulate established physical mechanisms, such as electromagnetic waves or geophysical processes, as conveying information or influencing human neurophysiology; and (4) models that entail major changes to existing scientific concepts.[82] Of these, the fourth variety is the most intriguing, because such literature suggests potential expansion of human awareness to embrace new information about matter and consciousness.

The distinction between mechanism and holism may help frame this potential. Mechanism in health care views the body as a series of mechanical parts that can be fixed like the parts of a broken car, through standardized treatments. Holism views the body as an integrative whole, in which all the parts interrelate to create a greater synthesis that is alive, conscious, and responsive at higher and higher levels of intelligence. The distinction between mechanism and holism furnishes a useful way to understand what unifies complementary and alternative medical therapies in their common attempt to view disease as imbalance and to treat the individual as a unified whole. Energy healing also can be regarded as holistic in its characterization of the human body as dwelling within (and interpenetrating) a larger web of subtle bodies, all of which interrelate in complex ways to create health or disease on all levels of existence.

Although the dichotomy is useful, mechanism also can describe a way of reducing the chakra system to an inflexible model of human potentiality and the disease process. Similarly, while conventional care has been characterized as reductionistic, energy healing also could be used in a reductionistic fashion—for example, by reducing disease to dysfunction in a specific chakra, without appreciating the complex interrelation of the physical, emotional, spiritual, hereditary, environmental, and energetic. The tendency of the mind to reduce, categorize, and simplify does not depend on the origin of the therapy. As David Reilly puts it, health care providers may simply substitute one "chisel" for another and never reach (or understand) the essence of human healing.[83]

The way healers interpret disease can generate new orthodoxies and substitute new dogmas for the old. For example, one could understand Bruyere to be saying that in every case, arthritis represents pent-up rage and that simply expressing this rage will cure the arthritis. Such reductionism would leave energy healing in infancy as a professional discipline, because its insights would be ossified in dogma. The relative lack of standardized education and training; the variability of practice among leading practitioners; the difficulty of penetrating mainstream clinical care; and the lack of politically strong, national professional organizations all would increase the possibility of energy healing remaining marginalized. Until the profession as a whole moves out of the realm of highly charismatic, gifted, intuitive healers and into more standardized, reproducible, and generalizeable methods of training and skill, there will continue to be an inadequate bridge between energy healing, the other health care professions, and regulatory authority.

Conclusion

Healers' explanations of disease may, at times, sound overgeneralized, simplistic, and even misleading, in their ascribing complex physiological processes to mysterious subtle factors. Over-reaching is a serious concern (see chaps. 5 and 6). A brief example can help illustrate the dangers of reductionism in the field:

> Recently a friend grew deaf in one ear. Her physician told her she had permanent damage; her intuitive helper told her she was temporarily 'learning a lesson on a soul level: you haven't been listening to God.'

Depending on the manner in which this information (or opinion) was conveyed, it may have been helpful or hurtful, inspiring or intrusive. Because energy healing literally *penetrates the usual relational boundaries,* its use must be monitored and applied with integrity. Each layer of the energy field apparently creates another boundary, both containing and delineating certain kinds of energies. The skill of a healer, like that of a trained therapist, includes "reading" the field and thus learning potentially private information, which requires restraint against the possibility for unwarranted intrusion.[84]

Further, like good medicine and a caring physician's touch, energy healing may be precisely targeted toward the particular emotional and spiritual lessons the patient may need to learn—or, like the wrong medication or wrong touch, be misdirected. Like wealth, power, language, and other treasures, energy healing is subject to abuse, as well as use for greater glory than that of the ego. By moving medical care and the experience of existence in a human body beyond the physical, the emotional, the intellectual, and even the religious, energy healing might potentiate transformation and move individuals and communities toward the larger ideals of self-realization, transformation, and the highest goals of human evolution. On the other hand, further legal, ethical, and clinical boundaries may be necessary to help refine this emerging field.

5

Touch, Privacy, and Intuitive Information

Case 5A   Auric Laceration in an Island Emergency Room

 After the conference, we went snorkeling. The ocean waters were rough, impatient, demanding. The schools of fish beneath our man-made fins seemed unruffled by the back-and-forth currents that assailed us.

"Don't go too far out!" my friend cried out as he momentarily removed the snorkel from his mouth. Our collective acumen was no match for the sea. She ruled—we retreated. Our third colleague—who had gone a little too far out—received less gracious treatment in her attempted exit from our common, ancestral home. (As my feet touched sand, I instinctively remembered something from childhood: "ontogeny recapitulates phylogeny." Perhaps *that* was what saved me.) Tossed like a tumbleweed by the crashing waves, wrapped around corals, our colleague stumbled shoreward. As she emerged, she dripped blood. Her leg was cut.

"Five-inch laceration," we telephoned in to the local emergency room, thirty minutes' drive away. "We're on our way."

In the car, Lila started to panic: the pain was settling in. I shut off the radio and tried to calm her. Intuitively, I started reaching in—back—through the wound. Immediately, I received images. Another time and place; an indigenous population; bloodshed, by this ancient being, in male form. An old incarnation, she (as a male) had slaughtered indigenous people, drawn their blood; now the ocean drew hers, to even the karmic score. Every action in the universe draws an equal and opposite reaction; now, the debt was being repaid in the form of a five-inch gash along her thigh. Due to prayers and good works, the burden had been lessened. Several dozen stitches, and she would be clean—*free and clear*, as property lawyers say, *of all* (karmic) *encumbrance* in this matter. I did not convey my intuitive sense to Lila: among other things, it would have been disrespectful to start spouting, "The *reason* you got hurt is because. . . ." Respectfully, I *listened* to her body—to what it had to tell me. There was no discussion. On a soul level, perhaps she experienced the events being played out; on a personality level, she only felt the pain of the gash.

In the emergency room, I laid my hands on Lila's shoulders. We had to wait. Triage. The television was blaring some violent show. Lila was in pain and panicking. The nurse barked out Lila's last name. Her tone was coarse, rude, abrupt, authoritarian, consistent with stock images of an emergency room: cold, mentally disrupting, anything but conducive to healing.

"Whatever you're doing feels good," Lila said. I could sense Lila's life energy leaking out—to the bombardment of the nurse's questions; to the assault of the television show; even to the joking, minimizing comments of friends, aimed (in good faith) at distracting her from the pain. I remembered years ago, when my friend William was dying and his family came to visit him in the hospital, how my own perception had been of how out of sync they were with *his* needs, his wishes, his desire for *silent* communion, for spoken communion in *his rhythm* (not theirs). Finally, out of frustration, William yelled, "*Please, just stop asking me questions.*" Most of his mind was on managing the physical pain, the rest on managing his dying, a small corner on how to manage his family.

I could not sew or clean a wound, provide emergency *physical* care, or perform social or "psych" functions. But I could pray. As a layperson, I could offer at least that; as a trained healer, much more. I could help mellow out a sadistic triage nurse, counteract the violent stream of bioenergetic impulses from the environment. I could work effortlessly, nonintrusively, in a supportive role, within the system. Later, Lila told me, "I don't know what you did, but it helped. . . . I wouldn't have made it otherwise."

Case 5B   The Healer Whose Touch Is
Innocently Inappropriate

 A male patient suffering from an injury to his lower back
visits a hands-on healer for energetic healing. The patient is
a professional basketball player and extremely tall. The
healer happens to be a licensed nurse who claims that the practice of
energy healing is within the scope of practice of her nursing license.
Because the patient (who is fully dressed) complains, on the table, of
being cold, the healer covers him with a blanket and begins by "running energy" up his spine to remove the pain from his energy field. The
energy is "light blue" and is said to be cleansing. Next, the patient lies
on his back, and the healer places hands on each "chakra."

The patient feels a warm, sweet sensation flowing from the
healer's hands. When her hands reach the patient's heart area, he
relives a painful memory from childhood, during which time he felt
unloved. He begins to cry. This is an unusual and strong experience for
the patient, as he has not allowed himself to cry in years. Moreover,
although the healer's hands are on his heart, he feels his feet being held
by an invisible being. He thinks it may be his guardian angel, with
whom he used to play as a child, before his parents grew "concerned."

Because the thick blanket makes it difficult to tell exactly which
body parts are underneath, when the healer's hands arrives at the
patient's "second chakra," her hands inadvertently rest above his genitals, rather than on the pubic bone. The patient is aware of this, but the
warm and sweet "energy" has created a slightly altered state of consciousness in which he feels comfortable and safe. Moreover, because
instinctively he feels the touch is healing and not sexual, he is not
aroused.

After the session, he reports that he has been suffering from a uri-
nary tract infection and that it seemed appropriate though unusual for
the healer's hands to drift to this area. The communication between
healer and client at this point is respectful and clear.

The client, however, suddenly notices that the healer's body—
which before had not been particularly accentuated by her formless
clothing—is lean and strong. Spontaneously, he shifts mentally and
asks her out to dinner. The healer gently declines, bringing her professional boundaries to bear. Again the tone is respectful and clear. But
when the client leaves, she calls her therapist/supervisor and expresses

concern about the inappropriate, albeit inadvertent touch; the possibility of transference, given the patient's heart opening to her (and of countertransference—he is handsome); and the possibility that denying an opening to the patient's feelings on a *personal* level will result in anger or retaliation by the patient, triggering an ethical complaint and the possibility of a lawsuit for battery.

Case 5C   The Complementary and Alternative Medical Provider Whose Dormant Sexual Energies Manifest

 A patient visits her cardiologist, presenting complaints of unusual heart rhythms. The cardiologist performs all reasonable and appropriate tests and finds nothing of concern. To help the patient manage anxiety and achieve greater relaxation, he refers the patient to Dr. Yang, a locally renowned practitioner of traditional oriental medicine, for acupuncture.

During the session, Dr. Yang notes that the patient's heart meridian is out of balance, possibly due to recent family stressors. As Dr. Yang begins needling, the patient feels a buzzing sensation, emanating from the needles, and heat permeating her body. Dr. Yang has a light sweat on his forehead. "I am very sensitive to *chi*," he explains, "and the current in your body is flowing powerfully."

As Dr. Yang turns to the side table to retrieve some more acupuncture needles, the patient remarks, "Dr. Yang, you have an erection." Calmly, Dr. Yang smiles and replies, "Yes, of course." He continues with the treatment. The needles are placed on the skin in locations that would not commonly be deemed sexual or erogenous. At no time does the patient perceive Dr. Yang's touch as invasive or inappropriate. She is puzzled, however, by Dr. Yang's physical reaction to the *"chi"* and his nonchalant acknowledgment of her observation and wonders whether this raises any ethical issues to be reported to the acupuncture board.

Touch and Privacy

Two of the areas in which energy healing proposes to stretch prevailing models of care are those of physical touch and concerns regarding privacy. These areas not only are heavily regulated among the health care professions but also represent "flash points" of controversy and gateways through which health care professionals can channel either healing or destructive energies to the patient.

With regard to physical touch, legal rules defining battery represent one of the most fundamental areas of regulation of human conduct, by which appropriate contact is demarcated from invasive contact. In tort law, battery classically is defined as consisting of two elements: such contact is (1) intentional contact, (2) that is unauthorized (in other words, done without consent). Some minimal level of social contact is presumed in the marketplace—for example, if two strangers accidentally brush up against each other in the New York subway, one cannot sue the other for battery. On the other hand, touching someone without their consent in the work environment, in an inappropriate way, can lead to charges of battery, as well as sexual harassment.

Battery also is the original theory used to bring informed-consent cases, the notion being that the physician wrongfully made contact with the patient—in other words, made contact without the patient's consent—by engaging in a procedure whose risks and benefits were not adequately described to the patient. Had the patient received the requisite disclosure, the theory goes, he or she never would have authorized the designated procedure but rather would have chosen another course of treatment. Although most jurisdictions use negligence as the basis for an action based on inadequate informed consent, battery remains an option in some states.

Notably, physical contact between two human bodies is not always necessary to sustain a claim for battery. Wounds caused by bullets or knives or bruises caused by sticks, stones, feet, or fists also constitute the requisite contact and injury; so does kissing someone against his or her will or spitting into another's face.[1] In some jurisdictions, it is sufficient that the contact be "offensive," "insulting or provoking," or done "in a rude, insolent, or angry manner."[2] In any event, the law governing battery creates a penumbra of protection for the integrity of the patient's personal space.

With regard to privacy (and confidentiality), legal rules also protect a variety of interests surrounding personal space. For example, the tort of privacy prevents, among other things, undue intrusion into the person's private life and his or her right to seclusion, and public disclosure of private facts. Legal rules concerning privacy and confidentiality also govern much of modern health care. For example, at the most basic level, written patient authorization typically is required in order for a health care provider to disclose the patient's medical records to a third party. Similarly, discussing patient confidences absent authorization variously is prohibited by statute, by common law, and/or by administrative or institutional rules. Such diverse theories as breach of contract, medical malpractice, and defamation can be brought for an unauthorized disclosure.[3] Analogously, the physician-patient privilege helps maintain patient confidence and encourage disclosure between the two parties by ensuring that such conversations are for the most part protected from discovery in subsequent litigation.

Again, legal rules governing touch, and privacy and confidentiality, aim in large part to protect the integrity of the person. In other words, the individual is understood to have psychic boundaries that extend past the body but are permeable and that require legal protection so that some integral notion of the patient's person remains intact. These boundaries, though, are poorly defined. The assumption is made that the person lives in a physical body, with some modicum of sensitivity to the environment. Thus, if one person verbally threatens to attack another, and thus creates an imminent apprehension of physical harm, that person may be liable for assault. Liability, however, is predicated on the threat of physical harm; psychic harm alone rarely suffices.

Energy healing poses the possibility of interaction on levels that are not explained in physical terms and do not strictly accord with present psychological accounts of mental processes. Rather, the chakras are said to exist in dimensions of perception parallel to the physical, mental, and emotional; hence, terminology used to describe chakra interactions is imprecise, nonmeasurable, and difficult to further define—for example, such interactions are described as exchanges of "spiritual energies." The challenge energy healing presents is of the potential redefinition of personal boundaries and of the potential ability to penetrate those boundaries in ways not previously acknowledged by modern medicine, legal rules, or even mental health care.

Healing Touch, Sexual Touch

One of the early points of legislative and communal resistance to the notion of licensing massage "therapists" was the difficulty in distinguishing healing touch from sexual touch. In the primordial phase of regulation (in other words, prior to any state licensure of massage practitioners as massage "therapists"), touch was undifferentiated and regarded almost uniformly as sexual. In other words, legal rules governing massage attempted to control unwanted sexual behavior by a variety of means. These included requiring that every massage room have a "peep hole" for monitoring, prohibiting cross-gender massage, regulating the amount and kind of clothing the masseuse had to wear, mandating which areas of the body the masseuse could touch and prohibiting others, or simply forbidding any form of massage.[4] Many of these restrictions have endured and some have even survived constitutional challenges,[5] while others have been successfully challenged or repealed. In fact, one court has noted that the effect of regulatory zeal in this area was to bar "any human contact more intimate than a handshake."[6] Of course, there have been cases in which the offer of a "massage" was used an excuse to perpetrate sexual violence (or misconduct).[7] By and large, however, the sensibility out of which the laws governing massage emerged was the dread of the massage parlor, which was thought to corrupt public morals.

Safeguarding "morals"—in addition to health, safety, and welfare—has been deemed the state's purview by the so-called police power under the Tenth Amendment, which reserves all rights not granted to the federal government to the states or, respectively, to the people. The legislators and judges facing the question of massage regulation hardly could have imagined that by the end of the twentieth century, the practice of massage would be considered a health care *profession*, subject to ethical codes and a national certifying exam, within a larger body of health care knowledge known as "complementary and alternative medicine."

Energy healing, like massage, raises the same unresolved specter of regulating touch in such a way as to distinguish sexual from healing contact. Sometimes that touch is above the surface of the body—as in so-called noncontact Therapeutic Touch. In such cases, the healer may scan the biofield with his or her hands and try to assess the relative balance and flow of energy. At other times, the healer may make contact with the body—for example, by placing hands on the skin where a chakra is located. In any event, the touch portends sufficient intimacy as to raise the specter of unwanted, erotic touch, rather than healthy, assented-to touch.

Parenthetically, this chapter does not attempt to draw a clear distinction between massage and energy healing, since many healers are trained in massage and many massage therapists use energy healing as an integral component of their massage session. Moreover, although frequently defined in such terms as "rubbing and stroking" the muscles, massage often is broadly enough defined to include any light contact with the skin and hence conceivably to include, within the legally authorized scope of practice of massage, such techniques as laying the hands over the surface of the body and "running energy" into a chakra.

Since energy healing, however, generally does not focus on the musculoskeletal system but instead emphasizes transfer of spiritual or psychic energies, one could argue that energy healing has the potential to be *more* invasive, more penetrating, at least in the sense of dominating the patient's psychospiritual space. In other words, it may be one thing to massage the area surrounding a person's chest and thereby loosen the muscles and another to place one's hand on the individual's heart and hold it there, "run energy" into the heart chakra, and monitor how the client reacts. Again, the intent of this analysis is not to draw a rigid and dogmatic boundary between the art of massage and what has been defined as energy healing. In fact, recipients of both types of "therapy" may react in a similar fashion—in other words, anywhere from feeling nothing to an intense emotional release. More typically, however, because the energy healer generally focuses less on the physical level (the level of the body) and more on the psychic and spiritual level (the subtle bodies described in chap. 4), the individual receiving the treatment presumably could feel intense emotional and spiritual stimulation from contact with the energies flowing through the healer. To summarize, touch is at least as problematic in energy healing as in massage and, in some contexts, may be even more problematic.

This suggestion is the import of cases 5B and 5C. In case 5B, sexual arousal does not occur; in case 5C, the therapist is aroused. On the physical level, case 5B presents inappropriate—albeit innocent—touching. The healer in fact makes unauthorized contact with the client's genitals, yet because the healer maintains a clear therapeutic presence, the gaff goes unnoticed. Only later does the client mentally shift gears. At this point, it is the *client* who is acting inappropriately. In this case, the healer maintains correct professional boundaries and declines the invitation to pursue romantic or erotic contact. This is a challenge any health care professional might face in a given situation involving private, therapeutic application of touch.

Case 5C presents converse facts: here the therapist is physically appropriate, but energetically and psychically aroused. When the matter is brought to the therapist's attention, however, the therapist honestly and in good faith explains away a natural physical reaction as unavoidable, yet of no erotic or romantic meaning. Dr. Yang could be no different than a similarly situated therapist. That is, it may be that psychotherapists sometimes get aroused when discussing certain scenarios with their clients. Yet the differences among having an internal reaction, disclosing that reaction to the client, and "acting out" an impulse generated from that reaction are well known to therapists and within their training. Again, Dr. Yang's arousal purportedly stems from the flow of *chi*, and not just from seductive thoughts and fantasies. Thus, energetic healing modalities (such as flow and transmission of *chi* during acupuncture) may raise interesting and sometimes unique questions about what is actually meant by the concept of "touch."

To recall, even the tort of battery does not require physical contact but can include contact through surrogate physical objects. In an analogous fashion, it should be remembered that flow of *chi* itself represents contact with the patient. For those who feel the flow of *chi*, such contact occurs at a physical level. For example, in his book *Encounters with Qi*, David Eisenberg reports his observation that acupuncturists in China routinely check with their patients to see if the patients are *feeling* the flow of *chi*. This feedback then enables the acupuncturist to know whether or not to reposition the needles.[8] According to Freud, libido (sexual energies) represents one form or flow of psychic energies, but not an exclusive transmission of psychic material from one individual to another. If sexual energies represent one frequency, so to speak, within a larger band of psychic energies transmitted during complementary and alternative medical therapies involving touch—especially during acupuncture, massage therapy, and energy healing—the common question among professions remains that of how to distinguish sexual energies from healing ones and how to contain the energies that otherwise may leak out in unhealthy ways during the therapeutic encounter.

Containing Sexual Energies in the Healing Process

Again, one way to think about touch in energy healing is to analogize the way touch is "handled" in other professions, such as mental health care. These professions take violation of personal space seriously and deem inappropriate touch a cause for professional censure and discipline, including loss of licensure. Teaching materials in the health care professions contain many examples of grossly inappropriate behavior—for example, having sexual intercourse with a patient or client, asking the patient out on a date, or touching any body part in a way that could be deemed sexually explicit and provocative. In clinical practice, however, aside from these gross behaviors, the line between healthy touch and unhealthy connection can be quite subtle. In fact, the attempt to delineate what is impermissible may be as difficult in this arena as it was for the U.S. Supreme Court justices to define pornography—hence Justice Potter Stewart's famous definition, "I know it when I see it."

In psychotherapy, it was Freud who initiated the debate about appropriate use of touch in mental health care. His writings raised "questions that still cannot be definitively answered: Where is the line that demarcates non-erotic touching from erotic contact or sexual intimacy?"[9] Freud's question remains applicable to energy healers as well as psychotherapists: where can the line be drawn? Regulatory language cannot easily answer this question. For example, in the draft Maryland legislation attempting to define and regulate "energy therapy," the prohibition mentions:

> Except for footwear, asking for the removal of a client's clothing, engaging in sexual contact with a client, engaging in contact with a client that may be construed as indecent, or engaging in any verbal behavior that is seductive or sexually demeaning to a client.[10]

Asking for removal of some clothing does not indicate anything suspicious, but asking for removal of all clothing may be a nonsubtle clue to motivation. The rest of the regulatory language, though it may appeal to common sense, leaves such ambiguity as to make innocent conduct potentially suspect. For example, the term "sexual contact" has no definition and begs the question as to what "sexual contact" *is*. Similarly, "contact . . . that may be construed as indecent" suggests that whenever the client subjectively perceives a sexual motivation, the provider is at legal risk. Similarly, there is no definition of what verbiage is "seductive" or "sexually demeaning." With verbal behavior, context doubtless is important. Though such regulatory language may survive constitutional challenges of being void for vagueness, the inherent ambiguity leaves room for prosecuting innocent behavior. Under such a definition, the providers in cases 5B and 5C would probably be disciplined.

More definite guidance is given by a series of guidelines published for physicians by the Harvard Risk Management Foundation. The guidelines observe that "boundary violations . . . imply physician behavior that seems to exploit a patient either sexually, financially, or emotionally."[11] The guidelines give the following examples of "boundary violations":

> Making arrangements to meet with a patient outside of regular office hours and/or out of the normal office setting . . . sharing an inappropriate amount of information about the physician's private life or using the patient for emotional support.[12]

The guidelines thus give physicians specific instances of what constitutes inappropriate, sexual contact with patients. By proscribing specific behaviors (for example, arranging to meet a patient for coffee), the guidelines help draw a clearer boundary between healing and invasive encounters.

In attempting to create a distinction between sexual and healing contact, psychotherapists have provided one definition of erotic contact in the clinical setting as "behavior that is primarily intended to arouse or satisfy sexual desires."[13] In this definition, the provider's primary intention is key. Using intention as a guide creates more difficulty than identifying problematic behaviors. The cases highlight this difficulty, particularly as applied to complementary and alternative medical practices involving exchange of psychospiritual energies.

Thus, applying this definition to case 5C, the behavior of Dr. Yang (as presented here) does not satisfy the definition: he did not touch or approach his patient with an intent to arouse or satisfy sexual desires but rather experienced a physiological reaction in his genitals as a natural result of increased flow of his *chi*. This remains true even though Dr. Yang in fact became sexually aroused while treating his client. Using *intention* to judge Dr. Yang, his conduct is free from blame.

The context is significant here. While Dr. Yang's nonchalant reaction could be taken as smug or deviant if made by an exploitative therapist, the actual words used, "of course"—taken in the context of his overall behavior (assuming Dr. Yang's reaction is honest and in good faith)—suggest that the phenomenon of his sexual arousal could be interpreted as a by-product, and not an intended outcome or focus of his therapy. In short, one might assume from the case that Dr. Yang, in good faith, honestly believed that it was natural to be aroused during stimulation of *chi* and that the best way to handle this arousal was to be nonchalant and continue focusing on the therapy. If Dr. Yang in fact was internally innocent, his external behavior might be excusable. This implies that professional boards might grant some leeway to a Dr. Yang, if regulators accepted that energy healing can stimulate sexual as well as other psychic energies and that such stimulation does not in and of itself create professional disciplinary or boundary issues.

The suggestion of a connection between flow of *chi* and sexuality—while not an *excuse* for inappropriate sexual behavior with clients—suggests some of the difficulties in adapting concepts from conventional care and ethics to an emerging field involving energy healing modalities. Other cultures that are more familiar and comfortable with concepts such as *chi* readily draw connections between the flow of psychospiritual and sexual energies. For example, one only has to view statues of the Indian god Shiva sitting in meditation with a huge, erect phallus to see that a connection has been drawn throughout history between release of spiritual energies and sexual arousal. Had Dr. Yang drawn attention to his engorged genitalia or acted out a sexual longing, for example, he clearly would have crossed the boundary to inappropriate behavior, but merely to have a physical reaction does not in itself create a status offense.

In spiritual literature from various traditions, stories of spiritual adepts being tempted by the beautiful form of a human body are legion. In some—for example, Euripides' play "The Bacchae"—the sexual energy drives seekers toward uncontrollable, orgiastic frenzy and thus leads to violence and destruction.[14] The play reveals the power of Dionysus, the Greek god of wine, archetype of everything wild, passionate, and loose. When denied and suppressed, he avenges himself by showing his power; as his spirit possesses the women of the city, they go mad and tear men from limb to limb. In the concluding lines of the play, the Chorus comments:

The gods have many shapes.
The gods bring many things
to their accomplishment.

And what was most expected
has not been accomplished.
But god has found his way
for what no man expected.
So ends the play.[15]

In other spiritual traditions—at the opposite end of the spectrum—
the sexual energy is neither denied nor repressed but rather is acknowledged, sublimated, and used for spiritual transformation. For example:

A being striving toward enlightenment wrote about how during
one phase of his spiritual practice, he kept seeing a beautiful,
naked woman in meditation. His penis grew so erect it dug into his
navel. He felt tremendous shame at having his longing for God
subsumed by this vision. Ultimately, he began to see this beautiful
woman as simply a manifestation of the archetype of the divine
feminine, the divine mother. With this realization, the woman
changed form; she was holy cosmic energy. The sexual urges sub-
sided, and the energy was transmuted into divine love.[16]

From this perspective, the energy itself is neither good nor bad but
simply a tool for human distraction or enlightenment, depending on
how it is directed. Learning to tolerate sexual energies, yet maintain a
healing focus, suggests the power of an inner attitude toward maintaining healthy boundaries. For example:

I was completing a healing on a classmate with whom I had had
some potential romantic exchange. I arrived at her heart chakra.
One of the teachers came by and saw me tentatively putting my
hand a few inches above her chest. "What's this about?" he said.
He lifted my hand and put it smack between her breasts. "If you're
clear, the client's clear," he said.

Clarity thus comes from intention. But as one group of ethicists
remarks, even "kissing, embracing, and hands-on contact can vary
from the tenderly wholesome to the imprudently impassioned. Interpretations lie both in the intent of the perpetrator and the reaction of the
recipient . . . [within the] situational context."[17] Whether professional
boundaries have been crossed and patient trust has been compromised

is contextual.[18] Thus, a warm embrace after learning that an anxious client passed a bar exam would be viewed differently than the same embrace without the contextual pretext.[19] Even in psychotherapy, the distinction between healthy and unhealthy, professional and unprofessional, appropriate and inappropriate, healing and sexual, is a matter of context. Again, the suggestion is made that in energy healing, the problem of drawing distinctions may be further amplified because the modality by its nature releases a powerful exchange between therapist and patient that potentially carries greater psychic force than in other therapeutic exchanges.

Touch Misconstrued

Can psychotherapy shed light on ways to confront and contain the dark possibilities within such an exchange? Existing data in the mental health professions sheds light on the kinds of personality issues within the therapist that tend to produce violations of professional boundaries via touch. Specifically, the data suggest that psychotherapists who violate sexual space with clients tend to have unmanageable levels of personal vulnerability, fear of intimacy, crises in personal relationships, feelings of failure, low self-esteem, poor impulse control, professional isolation, and depression.[20] It is these unresolved personal problems, rather than the fact of touch itself, that compromise the therapeutic relationship and make what might have been healing toxic instead. Presumably, healers would benefit from legal, ethical, and internal professional rules that attempt to address these kinds of dysfunctionalities within healers themselves.

Yet even innocent touch remains problematic in the context of healing. Even in the practice of medicine, touch can be misconstrued. For example, Rachel Naomi Remen, admits that on pediatric rounds, she was "a secret baby kisser," that this was "so flagrantly 'unprofessional' that [she] was careful not to be discovered." Remen tells the story of a chief resident who once bent over to kiss the forehead of a little girl who had leukemia. Although Remen had a close friendship with the resident, the incident was never discussed. Remen concludes, "Expressing caring directly . . . transgresses a strong professional code. . . ."[21]

Health care providers using energy healing may be advised to monitor the extent to which (or the way in which) they touch patients—at the very least, as a risk-management tool. This helps ensure that their touch will not be misunderstood and then raised as a basis for a malpractice lawsuit. The present *Ethics Manual* of the American College of Physicians simply states:

> Issues of dependency, trust, and transference and inequalities of power lead to increased vulnerability on the part of the patient and require that a physician not engage in a sexual relationship with a patient. It is unethical for a physician to become sexually involved with a current patient even if the patient initiates or consents to the contact.[22]

Ethical codes for complementary and alternative medical providers echo such provisions. For example, the American Chiropractic Association Ethics Committee has opined that engaging in "sexual intimacies with a patient is unprofessional and unethical" and that such conduct risks the possibility of impairing professional judgment and exploiting the confidence placed in the chiropractor by the patient.[23] Indeed, there may be times at which touch—even healing touch—is inappropriate, and the patient would benefit instead from conversation and appropriate nonverbal behavior.[24]

In mental health care, one manual for therapists advises that the psychotherapist's best protection against inappropriate touch, as well as corresponding ethical violations and liability concerns, is recognition of signs of attraction, both in the client and in oneself, and handling such feelings immediately, ideally with a competent therapist.[25] This information suggests that health care providers who offer energy healing must above all, explore and understand transference and countertransference, sort through their individual emotional issues, and clarify lurking personal issues that might sabotage a therapeutic relationship. Particularly because the exchange of psychospiritual energies is amplified in this context, healers are called on to clarify their own psychological needs and expectations. If healers gain licensure, supervision might be an important requirement, together with other tools used by mental health professionals to ensure that the therapeutic energies transmitted to the client are clear and professionally appropriate.

Sacred Touch

One area in which energy healing may furnish a revivification of understanding about potentiating human transformation—in both conventional and complementary and alternative medicine—is in presenting the experience of touch itself as sacred. In energy healing, human touch is sacred. In addition, the body is sacred, because the human being is sacred. Further, this sacredness transcends any legal or ethical notion of personal autonomy, in that it *defines* the borders of personhood, rather than the legal rights of an individual.

Moreover, "touch" in this sense includes not only physical contact with the body but also the contact that human beings can have in a variety of ways as their biofields intersect. For example, when two strangers sit together at a symphony or a crowded lecture, their biofields theoretically are touching one another. This means that even if they do not speak to one another, they are radiating thoughts, feelings, impulses, and a host of either healthy or toxic spiritual energies; the energies of one actually *permeate* the biofield of the other. The two persons also may be streaming specific bioenergetic cords toward one another. Thus, for example, if two individuals connect from a place of love, a healer might observe an arc of rose-colored light connecting the two heart chakras.[26] For this reason, touch (typically at the brow chakra) has been used as an instrument of spiritual initiation in some cultures.

On the other hand, healers may observe energetic daggers, spears, and prickly things emanating from individuals whose auric fields contain hostile energies directed toward one another.[27] From the healer's perspective, human interaction produces a palpably rich field in which to observe many subtle levels of exchange of psychospiritual energy. Further, that energy has a discernible impact on others, whether or not it is articulated, acknowledged, or brought to the conscious awareness of either party. Choa Kok Sui, the founder of "pranic healing," notes: "The study of hygiene should include not only germs and dirt but also diseased bioplasmic matter or diseased energy. This diseased bioplasmic matter or diseased energy can be transmitted to another person."[28] In short, mental pollution may be an unregulated counterpart to physical pollution of the surrounding environment. This perspective certainly lends new meaning to the tort of "battery," among other things.

The healer's perspective takes the notion of sacred touch even deeper than in some complementary and alternative medical modalities, to the extent that "touch" is directed not only to the musculoskeletal system or portion of the visible body but also to the subtle bodies—in other words, to the consciousness in which the body is housed. In

Western scriptural tradition, the body is seen as the "temple of God," since human beings are "made in the image of God." In other words, the human body houses something much larger than the human personality or ego. Rather, the finite and mortal physical body houses an infinite and immortal spirit body, reflected through multidimensional, nonphysical layers of the energy field. There are thus multiple layers of human consciousness expressed through the vehicle of the human body. From the healer's perspective, this is literally as well as metaphorically true: theology recapitulates ontology. In fact, from the healer's perspective, the human being is not limited to seven chakras and human energy-field bodies or even twelve. Rather, the being has an infinite number of such bodies. From the outermost perspective, as we are connected by cords of subtle energies to our loved ones (as well to as our enemies and anyone with whom we interact, in the physical body or otherwise), so we are all connected in the chakras of the divine. In other words, all our auric fields interconnect on some level.

The ramifications of energy healing for many different systems of thought remain to be explored. For example, in case 5A, the notion of karma—the effect that every human action has on an individual soul's destiny—implicates this web of interconnectedness. In this light, speaking about the meaning of the "soul" in medicine is no longer using a metaphor or poetry; the soul becomes an integral reality within clinical practice. Without being unduly reductionist, some action, somewhere, may lead to a clinically diagnosable and treatable event; subtle connections can be seen through contemplation. In short, energy healing purports to understand many religious and medical phenomena in terms of the biofield. Quite simply, energy healing threatens not only prevailing scientific models of understanding clinical practice and pathways but also religious authority.

But this requires further discussion elsewhere. The focus here is on sacred touch. Whenever a health care professional touches a patient, the quality of the touch theoretically penetrates all levels of the biofield. One cannot examine a patient as one examines an art object or a piece of celery. One cannot lift a patient's wrist to take a pulse the way one lifts a pencil or eraser. Although much has been written in medicine about the so-called bedside manner, the healer's perspective lends additional insight. Specifically, the human being's consciousness is theorized to be holographic. Thus, the arm, being lifted, has consciousness; the heart chakra feels the consciousness as the hand holding the stethoscope approaches the patient's chest. The caregiver projects this immeasurable spiritual energy, consciously or not. One can approach a patient along a spectrum of feeling, from the most mechanistic approach to one imbued with the consciousness of unconditional love (see chart 14).

Physical touch reflects a need for physiological security; regulation directed at inappropriate touch aims to control fraud and achieve non-sexual touch between provider and patient. But this is only a beginning layer of understanding. Caring touch provides the patient a deeper experience of safety; regulation aimed at quality assurance can help create standards for touch that help the provider convey an attitude of caring. Loving touch helps the patient experience a deep belongingness to the human community and a visceral experience of being loved. Regulation enabling loving touch reflects a regulatory goal of consumer choice and access to health care modalities that touch the heart and are backed by intellectual evidence. Regulating different professions that might implement loving touch reflects the achievement of pluralism regarding touch in health care. Healing touch provides the patient an experience of esteem and reflects integration of knowledge from different cultures across millennia, in terms of how touch can help individuals experience their own transcendence. Finally, sacred touch may play

CHART 14. Touch and Regulation

Essential Need	Met by	Regulatory Goal Reflected	What Regulation Would Achieve
Physiological security	Physical touch	Fraud control	Nonsexual touch
Safety	Caring touch	Quality assurance	Standards (for example, massage)
Belongingness and love	Loving touch	Health care freedom	Medical pluralism in touch
Esteem	Healing touch	Functional integration	Transcendent aspects of touch
Self-actualization	Sacred touch	Transformation	Unconditional, positive intentionality

a role in leading persons to self-actualized states, in which the regulatory goal of human transformation generates positive, unconditional intentionality in the caregiver and the receiver of such care.

Notions of caring, loving, healing, and sacred sensitive touch already exist in many complementary and alternative medical professions. Disciplines such as acupuncture and traditional oriental medicine suggest that the body is energetically linked by a series of pathways known as meridians. For example, if the caregiver presses a point anywhere on the body along the lung meridian, this touch should have an effect on the patient's overall health relative to the lungs. Hand, foot, and ear reflexology are based on similar correspondences among points along the body. Therefore, any time the caregiver touches the patient's body, this touch has ripple energetic effects on various organs, meridians, and other subtle pathways in the patient's consciousness. From the healer's perspective, entering a room creates a vibratory effect that travels along bioenergetic cords to the chakras and energy bodies of the patient. The medium *is* the message. The healer is always transmitting himself or herself. Energy healing explains this on the level of the biofield. Fundamentally, the health care provider's *presence*—his or her *level of consciousness*, or state of *being*—uniquely energizes, potentiates, and radiates the *process* of healing.

"Touch" as Deeper Contact

Touch, at its ultimate level, is metaphor: what we touch is what we most profoundly consider to be real. Touch involves mental, emotional, and spiritual, as well as physical and social connection; touch implies connection between forms of consciousness. An advertisement for telephone services puts it this way: "Reach out and touch someone, reach out and just say 'hi.'"

The possibility for deeper contact at all levels that energy healing presents implies the possibility not only of increased, sacred connection between clinician and patient but also of increased connection between the provider and realms of consciousness previously deemed outside the realm of conventional care. One might ask a number of questions regarding the potential implications of this touch: To what extent does touch occur on subtle levels, inaccessible to the ordinary senses, hidden from scientific instrumentation? To what extent is it felt rather than analyzed, perceived rather than measured, acknowledged in the heart and spirit rather than captured on videotape? Why does Therapeutic Touch refer to this with the seeming oxymoron, "noncontact touch?" What are the contours of this world, and what are its implications for health care generally (for example, as in intuitive diagnosis, discussed in chap. 4) or for the psychospiritual evolution of the human organism (in other words, the regulatory goal of transformation)? To what extent can "anecdotal evidence"—reports of internal experience—furnish helpful description of the workings of this dimension of connection, communication, and care?

In exploring such questions, it may be necessary to suspend the usual contours of discussion. Specifically, while more research may be required to make definitive scientific claims regarding the extent of (and mechanism for) so-called extrasensory perception, the question of how healers use subtle senses to access information ordinarily hidden to the health care provider is vital to understanding some of the broader social—as well as clinical—implications of energy healing. This means drawing on reported human experience to begin mapping the "wireless coconut," the state of mind in which others' thoughts converge. In the realm of intuition and perception, stories of the individual's experience may offer the best tool for understanding what cannot, at present, be mapped objectively.

Drawing on the discussion in chapter 3 of Maslow's "self-actualization" and of the experiences of such mystics as Hildegard of Bingen, the claims of energy healers to access extraordinary realms of consciousness share common ground with the extradimensional perceptions of sages and saints across traditions and centuries. If the regulatory goal of functional integration defines clinical integration of all world systems of knowledge about healing, then the experiences of transcendent wholeness recorded by these mystical travelers—and their modern counterparts—form part of the systems of knowledge to be studied, digested, and incorporated.

In short, the attempt here is at nothing less than drawing the mysteries of consciousness out of the fields of psychology and religious studies; suggesting that they are accessible to ordinary humans (for example, nurses performing Therapeutic Touch); and thrusting them into the modern, technological arena of clinical care as well as ordinary social discourse. In this framework, the kind of experience described in case 5A would be accessible to any individual accompanying the patient described in that case to the emergency room—as well as to the triage nurse, the emergency room physician, and the receptionist.

Touch as Experience of Subtle Perception

A British physician who had an intuitive opening (Shafica Karagulla) used the term *high sense perception* to describe utilizing the subtle senses to become aware of vital energies or subtle energies—in other words, opening the sensory apparatus to receive information not available through the ordinary five senses. There is nothing "high" about high sense perception except that the phrase forms a convenient descriptor for a nonordinary mode of perceiving that may have bearing on experiences of energy healing in clinical care.

Delores Krieger describes the process as turning attention toward interior experience and focusing on one's "latent senses."[29] The shift in perception also has been described as a natural state of expanded awareness, as heightened intuitive capacity, and as using nonordinary states of consciousness to access information.[30] High sense perception is much more familiar to cultures, such as those of indigenous peoples, that place less emphasis on the logical and analogical and more on direct perception, nonlinear thinking, dreaming, and intuition.[31] High sense perception also is accessible in a slight state of trance.[32]

The subtle senses in high sense perception are said to parallel the five senses: subtle seeing, hearing, tasting, smelling, and touching. Indeed, the role of high sense perception, including intuition, has been explored in such diverse fields as management and philosophy.[33] In management, for example, metaphors provide clues to the experience of subtle sense perception: a business relationship "goes sour"; the transaction "stinks"; things get "rough"; the deal aquires a "bad aroma" (to quote from *Hamlet*—a tale of high sense perception involving a spirit helper, the ghost of Hamlet's father—"something is rotten in the state of Denmark"). Energy healers, however, regard subtle senses as more than metaphorical. High sense perception provides a way to experience subtle shifts in chakras and human energy fields. Describing forms of high sense perception can help provide guidance to the way in which energy healing can use "noncontact touch" to reach patients at profound levels of being.

Some of the main forms of high sense perception involve *kinesthetic perception* (touching and feeling), *auditory perception,* and *visual perception.* *Kinesthetic perception* is twofold: it includes feeling (in a body sense) and feeling (in an emotional sense). The first form of the kinesthetic sense involves attuning to subtle sensory cues in the hands as the healer sweeps the hands slightly above the patient's body. As noted, in Therapeutic Touch one uses sensory cues in the hands to identify depleted or congested points in the energy field. In Brennan's system, the scan by hand may reveal weaknesses in particular chakras or disturbances in specific layers of the human energy field. For example, the second chakra may be healthy and bright on the first layer of the field but torn or ruptured on the second level. Individual vortices within the chakra may be misaligned or twisted on a specific level of the field. The healer might say, "Your liver feels weak," or "Your adrenals feel depleted," or simply receive some sense of change in pressure or tingling. Choa Kok Sui states that when someone is ill, "his or her health rays droop and are entangled and the health aura decreases in size."[34] Again, these are subjective impressions that register kinesthetically in the healer's measurement of the patient's field.

A second kind of kinesthetic sense involves sensing in the healer's own physical or emotional body what the patient is feeling. For example, a healer working on a client with digestive difficulties may feel tightness in the stomach, cramps, overall nausea, or pain and tension in his or her own body. Or the healer may experience internal anger, grief, joy, or fear—the emotions present in the client that are said to be underlying the blockage or dysfunction.

Some anecdotal reports may illustrate use of the kinesthetic sense. Some years ago, a workshop in Healing Touch offered by the American Association of Holistic Nurses provided an opportunity to explore the perception of participants recollecting a pleasant, and then an unpleasant, scene from childhood. In the exercise, the "healer" places his or her hands around the "client's" head or shoulders, connecting energetically and emotionally with the client's field, and enters an open, receptive, internally focused state to access feelings and images. Nurses and physicians in the workshop with no prior training were surprised by the accuracy and extent of information they received. For example, one healer reported of a client who had cancer, "It feels like the cells are going crazy." Placing hands around the client's head, another received an impression of tenderness and love from the client's recently deceased mother, whom the healer perceived as recently deceased. The client verified this information. Receiving such verification created confidence and further opened the participant's intuitive channels.

The *auditory* subtle sense involves being able to hear on subtle levels—for example, to access information that is received internally in the form of sound or linguistic impressions. The sounds could entail music, words, or other auditory information. A dog's hearing encompasses frequencies inaudible to human ears. Similarly, by stilling the mind and developing a state of inner silence and receptivity through meditation, energy healers attempt to develop perception of subtle sounds—in other words, information accessible to the "inner ear" that may involve music, songs, or words. Gopi Krishna writes, "One of the most amazing features of our time, in the eyes of our progeny, would be the blindness of the intellect that assumes that what it perceives with the senses is the totality and not just the tip of an iceberg of which the bulk is beyond our power to discern."[35] For example, one healer hears a high-pitched whine whenever a client has a particular kind of infection. Another reported reaching a client's sacral chakra and hearing, "She may have ovarian cancer"; purportedly, the client later verified that she was having lab tests to check for the possibility of such a disease.

The third subtle sense, the *visual,* means that when scanning the patient's energy field, the healer may receive information in the form of images, words, or sensations.[36] Such "visual" sensing may be experienced as external to the healer—in other words, as actual "seeing"—or as internal seeing, in the "mind's eye." For example, the healer may "see" a black spot in the energy field where a patient has a tumor. Similarly, the healer may "see" clogging in the center of the heart chakra. Just as kinesthetically oriented healers may experience the clogging in their own chest or sense it in the patient with their hands, the visually oriented healer will experience the blockage by receiving an internal image or by seeing the image with the eyes. Using the chakra system, healers assert that visual sensing is heightened when the healer opens the third eye—particularly, the seals between the layers of the field in the region of the sixth chakra. The opening deepens with meditation and seems to involve Grace—assistance from other, nonphysical dimensions of reality, if you will.

Again, an anecdote may help illustrate:

While studying hypnotherapy, I began entering trance states in which I felt words being channeled through me. I began to see a

field of purple surrounding the client's body. Purple is often identified in esoteric literature with sacred space. I experienced the
purple as a numinosity through which information from or about
the unconscious mind was being transmitted.

When I related this phenomenon to my instructor, who had
studied with Milton Erickson, her response was, "Yes, you can
receive information on a variety of levels." She seemed to interpret
my experience as one of receiving images from my own unconscious, whereas in fact, I was seeing the field of purple with my
physical eyes. It was not until later that I met another hundred or
so students—physicians, nurses, psychotherapists, real estate
agents, attorneys, educators, and other professionals—who had
the faculty of visual sensing. In this setting, my experience could
be validated, understood, and put in context of the human energy
field.

Following is another account of an experience of high sense perception. This one is taken from the operating room, rather than the hypnotherapy session.

A significant experience of visual sensing occurred as we
scrubbed and entered the operating rooms during surgery. I saw
energy fields around the surgeons, nurses, assistants, and
patients—the bright blue first layer, the multicolored second and
fourth layers, the bright yellow third layer, and other levels. I saw
the exchange of energies as surgeons interacted with anesthetized
patients and with the health care professionals around them.

The blue first layer was apparent even around the instruments
that were handed to the surgeons and around the patients' organs
as they were projected on an overhead screen. The surgeons'
"energy"—their conversations with colleagues, the blaring rock
music and commercials in some of the operating rooms, the fluo-
rescent lights, and the silent presence of other faculty—had visually discernible effects on the patient's energy field. Moreover, I
had my own impressions of communication with patients under
anesthesia or in the intensive care unit, particularly patients
declared "incompetent," "comatose," or otherwise inaccessible
through the ordinary five senses. However, I was not able to discuss these observations with my colleagues, as such experiences

are usually dismissed as imaginative or hallucinatory. I was told that a true account could jeopardize my reputation and career.

Though many surgeons, physicians, and other health care providers have opened their subtle sight, only a few have openly described their experiences.[37] Use of subtle senses has been greatly misunderstood in our history. The fear and resistance such practices engender are partly due to language. Words such as "clairvoyant," "psychic," "extrasensory," or "sensitive" imply abnormality. Further, reported experiences are often met with skepticism, hostility, or dismissal. As suggested, when children experience the presence of departed relatives and "imaginary playmates," their experiences are discounted by adults, and they learn to "grow up" and live in the "real world." By labeling decisions, perceptions, and actions as "psychic," our culture both dismisses and splits off phenomena that may be part of the human birthright, perpetuating the misconception that reality is limited to what we can experience with the five mundane senses.

One may wonder whether, for example, the experience described in case 5A would be considered "significant" enough by our culture's standards to be (1) reported to the patient or (2) recorded in the patient's medical record, if experienced by an attending nurse or physician. In part, the answer may depend on the way one defines such concepts as "medical necessity" and understands regulatory requirements relating to charting in a "medical" sense something that embraces spiritually cognizant notions of "healing."

One of the most controversial components of high sense perception is the experience of receiving wisdom from nonphysical beings, or "guides." Some may prefer to understand this phenomenon in terms of the notion of inner wisdom or intuition—in other words, "it's all in the mind." Gopi Krishna refers to an inner voice as a result of "spontaneous kundalini awakening"—the arousal of an inner evolutionary energy that raises the consciousness of the individual and provides a sense of an inner voice that guides the seeker during meditation, prayer, or the dream state.[38] According to Brennan, everyone has "guides" in spiritual form; because guides exist in the higher levels of the energy field, but lack physical embodiment and existence on the first three layers, their perception requires learning to perceive beyond the fourth layer of the field.[39]

The phenomenon of receiving guidance requires further attention in health care, as it may be an aspect of care that has been assumed away and not investigated. The fluidity of information in a world of expanded consciousness raises interesting challenges, as expanding psychic boundaries and concepts of the "person" change to incorporate new dimensions of knowing exactly what the self, in caring connection to another being, is. Following is an anecdotal account in this regard:

> The moment the healer put her hands over me, I felt a solid presence behind her, as if these giant wings enfolded the table. I asked the being, "Who *are* you?" and he said, "I am Archangel Gabriel." During the healing, I was puzzled that I felt a pair of hands continuously on my shoulders, when the healer was down on the other end of the table. When the session ended, I asked how her hands had reached up to the other side of the table, while her legs were planted. She told me she had seen the guide at my shoulders.

Similarly, a dancer spoke of the first time she ever saw the human energy field and of how it helped her dance:

> I went to a dance performance. When this one solo performer came on stage, I saw these beautiful colors emerging out of her being. Then there were these other beings around her, dancing and supporting the performance. I couldn't believe what I was seeing. The friend I was with later said I looked like I was in trance during the performance. She suggested that I go backstage and speak to the dancer about my experience. So I did. The dancer said to me, "Every time I prepare to go on stage, I have a list of great dancers and artists that I call upon and invoke to help me with the dance." Those were the people I was seeing.

This dancer later studied energy healing. She reported:

> When guides come during healings, I often feel them nestled around my field; my brow chakra opens, and I see my hands dissolve in white, blue, and gold light.

Western medical culture insists on a distinct separation between ordinary and nonordinary reality, between physical and nonphysical dimensions of being. The way our culture does handle such experiences—if at all—is through art and literature, through understanding them as symbolic rather than living realities. Our culture, in other words, splits scientific reality from the realities portrayed in religious iconography, transpersonal psychology, and literature. Yet if energy healing suggests that the experiences of prophets, saints, and seers in many traditions are accessible to ordinary human beings—not only in a state of trance—and can, indeed, be *learned*, then this culture falsely has labeled the *normal* as "paranormal." In short, we have stultified our organic human growth, in part through use of terminology.

Numerous psychologists have agreed that naming and labeling can shut off the capacity for nonordinary experience. For example, Robert S. DeRopp observes:

> Man . . . mistakes the word for the thing, the map for the land it represents. He thinks he knows the truth when in fact he is merely juggling with verbal symbols. . . . [One must be] ready to undertake the reeducation of his intellectual brain, a reeducation which will enable him to emerge from the fogs of verbalism. The essence of the new form of thinking is a direct awareness of process, a face-to-face encounter with actual events. . . . It is a state in which . . . forms are seen not as fixed, but as "time-shaped."[40]

DeRopp gives the following example of sensory reeducation and then comments on it:

> A rosy apple in a food store is seen in all its stages, bud, blossom, green, red, on the tree, off the tree, in the store, etc. . . . It involves awareness of time as a shaping dimension, time as a component of form. We know this theoretically. It is a principle of physics. But direct perception of "time shape" is a very different matter.[41]

Many indigenous cultures consider it natural to talk to trees, plants, stones, and animals, as well as to experience these aspects of the creation talking back to a person's consciousness. But by and large, in our culture, such an experience only is represented in a "safe" mode, such as a Walt Disney production. For example, the film *Pocahontas*, which is quite popular with children, features a talking tree that helps guide the protagonist through the forest. The ability to converse with spirits and receive communication from them is more important than pharmacological considerations to some Native American herbal traditions. Additionally, many such cultures emphasize nonordinary states of consciousness as a means of recognizing their reality. To these cultures, talking to far-away people on cell phones while standing in line for the subway or in an elevator might be a distorted reality, whereas communing with nature, talking to God, or simply sensing one's own shifting perceptions and moods would be regarded as authentic and natural. In some of these cultures, the "blessing" of a lama or priest or of medicine, embedded in a medicinal substance, can be felt and perceived on multiple levels of being; holy sites uplift and empower, "raise the energies," and help clear the biofield in a tangible way; so-called miracles occur at subtle energetic as well as physical levels.

Perspectives differ. Then again, so do the tools of the indigenous healer and the modern clinician. But something might be learned from paying attention to subtle states of consciousness, even alongside the modern inventory of diagnostic and therapeutic techniques. One can speculate as to whether such an attunement would even be possible, or appropriate, in modern, clinical care. Perhaps it is the nature of the modern social network, with its chaotic energy, demands for attention (such as constant advertising, both visual and auditory), incessant, random noise and intense stimulation, to turn individuals away from *inner* focus, toward the imminent outer reality. Our culture (the emergency room being no exception) stimulates almost to the point of psychic assault and bombardment. Intuitive information may simply represent a shift from modes of consciousness more familiar and accessible to the present acculturation of the Western mind to modes of consciousness more natural to indigenous cultures and the traditions of certain Eastern peoples.

In our culture, meditation—the art of turning attention within—is viewed as a tool for shifting from one mode of consciousness to another. This then becomes the gateway to high sense perception. The perception of the wound in case 5A exemplifies an experience of such a perceptual shift. Whether we characterize the experience in terms of a "past-life reading," "touching an archetype," "reaching into the collective unconscious," or simply "imagination," the experience took hold in the patient's being *without ever being discussed.* In short, by virtue of the healer's opening up to nonordinary channels of information, the patient experienced a healing. The exact mechanism of the healing is unknown. Again, "past life," "imagination," and even "nonspecific/

placebo" may be labels for experiences and events that, like "high sense perception," our culture presently neither fully understands nor has integrated into the experience of being human.[42]

Touch as Exchange of Information

A full-blown explanation of the *mechanism* of spiritual energy, its transmission, and the modes of perceiving these phenomena may be beyond the scope of the present analysis. Two preliminary explanatory models, however, may be useful in providing a backdrop for policy considerations regarding energy healing. As suggested earlier, physicist David Bohm's notion of a holographic universe provides one such model. Bohm describes the universe as a series of enfolded realities. According to Bohm, what we perceive with our senses and scientific instruments is merely a projection of a higher-order universe, within which ours is enfolded. Bohm's description of the holographic universe, in which each level projects into and influences the next, resonates with healers' descriptions of the energy field. The seven levels of the human energy field can be seen as successively enfolded anatomical realities, resonating downward in frequency from the highest level—pure consciousness—toward the physical.

In this model, disease manifests on the physical level only after it has been created on the higher levels of consciousness and precipitated down through the various bodies. Disease, then, must have a higher purpose and meaning. It is here that religious explanations of disease potentially can be meshed with scientific understandings and with the healer's explanation. While avoiding a strictly causal, reductionist explanation (for example, illness as punishment for a previous sin), an interdisciplinary conversation could explore the possibility that distorted belief systems can indeed translate into effects at all levels of the energy field. Of course, the role of genetics, environment, and other factors would have to be taken into account. According to energy healers, even ants, snakes, and pennies (and viruses, bacteria, and cells) have energy fields. The suggestion that everything, including inanimate objects, carries living intelligence and consciousness (a notion one finds in the Vedas and other ancient, sacred literature) makes any reductionist view impossible and implies a view that intentionality, consciousness, belief, and past and present connections with all things share a role in disease and healing. An ultimate reconciliation of new theories of physics, higher mathematics, and models of reality proposed by Eastern scriptures awaits further development.

Beverly Rubik proposes a second model for the mechanism of transmission. She proposes that humans are living informational systems, capable of transferring information simply by having their fields touch. This notion of "informational biology" would explain some phenomena in high sense perception—for example, emotionally connecting with a client and receiving impressions of a childhood accident or a recurrent problem with a certain organ. In this model, it is possible that the healer could have an experience of "hearing" the organ saying, for example, "I have been neglected. I need such-and-such care."

Such a model would create room for such seemingly "bizarre" anecdotes as the following:

A healer reported that she was sitting on a plane, on the runway, when the pilot announced that there was some minor problem with the engine. The healer "communicated" with the plane, asking what was the matter. The plane "responded": "It isn't what they're saying. I'm tired, I've worked all day, they're not taking care of me, and my throat hurts."

Having centered and having "scanned" the plane's energy field, the healer then directed energy. She further coached the plane: "I know they just see you as a mechanical object. But I know you are conscious. Know that you are loved and taken care of. You have communicated this message to me; now let your throat heal." Soon the pilot came on the intercom and reported that the problem was not with the engine but with the communications system (the throat chakra of the plane); the problem had spontaneously corrected itself, however.

Just as intuitive diagnosis would not relieve the physician from conducting conventional diagnostic tests, it would be foolish to rely on such communication and assume that the plane could fly safely. On the other hand, such an experience is closer to the shamanistic perspective that everything carries consciousness. At some level, such a notion may appear animistic and thus seem to clash with monotheistic beliefs. The overlap between energy healing and theology is a subtheme in this book, the suggestion being made that the theological discomfort energy healing engenders—both to a pure science perspective and to a Western, religious one—partly accounts for the marginalization of the field. In any event, from the perspective that everything has an energy field and that consciousness resides in everything, even airplanes have "throats," in the sense of centers of communication. The energy field of an airplane thus is perceptible through high sense perception. To the healer, such perception is not merely wishful, anthropomorphic thinking, any more than the phenomenon of consciousness as manifested through religious experience can be reduced (as Freud suggested it could) to a psychic projection of the father archetype.

Another possibility that energy healing suggests is that some of the placebo effect is bioenergetically mediated. In the chakra system, when the patient's belief system shifts (the seventh layer of the biofield), this shift transduces down into successively lower layers of the energy level and ultimately into the physical body. In other words, the *expectation* of the patient operates not only on the physical level—in terms of mental processes igniting healthy physiological mechanisms—but also on the subtle level.[43]

This expectation may be involved in such energy healing techniques as clearing "clouds" of dark or stagnant energy from the second level of the field (that of unresolved emotions); strengthening and clarifying the structured first and third levels of the field; and opening the higher levels of the field to more refined, universal frequencies, including those of angels, perceptions of extradimensional beings, and divine love drawn in through meditation and prayer.[44] The consciousness of the healer affects the consciousness of the client, which in turn stimulates movement of energy in the subtle bodies and translates (ideally) into beneficial physiological effects; the placebo effect thus is mediated by the energy field as well as the mind. Similarly, the expectation of the provider positively affects the patient's physical health because energy fields, at least according to Brennan, vibrate along principles of harmonic induction.[45] This means that if the provider's biofield resonates with an expectation of health, that vibration induces a similar frequency shift in the patient's biofield. Thus, what we call the placebo effect could in fact be a gateway to higher consciousness. In this framework, the provider's thought of health instantly communicates itself to the patient—even if no verbal suggestions are made and no nonverbal conduct indicates positive expectations.

The tantalizing suggestions of energy healing remain largely unproven; yet, it is said that the *rishis* (sages) of India developed yoga postures from meditation: as the awakened inner energy traveled through their bodies, they found themselves spontaneously moving into different asanas (postures).[46] In modern times, we can measure the *effect* of certain postures and yoga practices on specific conditions, but we do not understand why certain postures developed or exactly *how* they operate (their mechanisms). Indeed, the development of the postures in yoga was not primarily aimed at physical health, as we understand such techniques as aerobic exercise; rather, yoga aimed at awakening specific energy centers and developing the subtle bodies so as to facilitate the arousal of divine energies within the human organism and also center the mind.[47] Similarly, we may be able to demonstrate *that* prayer works but fail to understand *why* or *how*. Likewise, we may be able to license healers and teach medical students how to see the biofield but not understand the cosmic web by which clairvoyants perceive its structure. Mystery still lies at the core.

Touch as Revolution

If disease has an energetic as well as a physiological component, then clinical applications of energy healing may encompass nearly all areas of medical practice. Further research and physician-healer collaborative efforts can help identify areas in which energetic healing is most useful in conjunction with conventional medical care. Based on research, some areas may be less controversial—for example, having healers pass their hands over the biofields of wound or burn patients to help relieve trauma and pain. Others may generate greater controversy—for example, the presence of healers in the operating room to help reduce organ rejection and other complications during heart transplants.[48] The whole question of when or how energy healers will be brought into the diagnostic arena—for example, to provide opinions concerning the risk-benefit analysis for exploratory surgery—remains largely unexamined.

Any number of perspectives may come into play: medical and scientific, legal, ethical, and economic. From one perspective—that of patient autonomy (the value of health care freedom)—the debate must take into account patient as well as physician preferences and the scientific perspective; the patient, for example, may insist on his or her healer being present in the operating room during surgery. Although the exact shape of integration remains to be resolved, one can envision a number of areas in which physician-healer integration could be useful. Such visioning is based on existing qualitative as well as the limited quantitative research concerning the potential applications of the different energy healing modalities in clinical care (for example, the use of intuitive diagnosis for disease prevention).

On the social level, the spread of psychic opening, on a mass scale, may change the way ordinary human beings interact and perceive reality. For example, assume that the clairvoyant, clairaudient, and clairsentient abilities described earlier were available not only to healers in meditative (semitrance) states but also to ordinary individuals in waking realities. We then would have a situation in which laypersons were receiving detailed information regarding each others' physical and emotional health, states of mind, states of being, and psychic agendas during routine interactions. In plain terms, people would be able to "read" one another clearly—even from a distance (in other words, as a nonlocal effect of consciousness). The notion of having a certain core of "private" information would be eviscerated if everyone could read anyone with total accuracy. Legal rules governing privacy and confidentiality would have to change. So would ethical standards governing disclosure in clinical settings.

The ability to scan chakras certainly would change the therapeutic relationship as well. Physicians, even without psychotherapeutic training, would be able to access repressed psychic material of their patients more easily and then help assimilate mind-body-spirit connections to accelerate "nonspecific effects" and to stimulate emotional release and spiritual and physical healing. Certain legal and ethical rules would have to be revisited in the process. For example, Larry Dossey, has noted that a psychologist who dreams about a patient may be ethically prohibited from sharing the dream with the patient, as this might be regarded as impermissible countertransference; yet the dream may indicate that the two beings are interacting on a subtle level, on which healing energies and clues to the patient's etiology are exchanged.

If psychic opening to include high sense perception becomes an expanding social phenomenon (and not merely a phenomenon within health care), then opening on a mass scale might represent an evolutionary acceleration in human consciousness. There would be additional clinical, legal, ethical, and social implications. For example, the importance ascribed to scientific methods of validating and interpreting such information in clinical practice may shift. There might be other means, for instance, of collecting information regarding subjective experiences of states of consciousness. There might be new ways of measuring such states and of determining to what extent individual experiences provide accurate or useful models for clinical practice.

Touch and Informed Consent

One of the legal and ethical arenas implicated is that of informed consent. Suppose, for example, that we could measure the physical effect of Reiki on cancer patients and demonstrate efficacy according to the most rigorous type of evidence required. Then, under informed-consent rules, since information about Reiki would be material to a treatment decision, the physician would be obligated to disclose to every cancer patient that Reiki is an effective treatment. The physician also would have to describe the risks and benefits of Reiki and how it works in combination with other cancer treatments. The physician would have to decide whether to provide the Reiki treatment or to refer the patient to a practitioner elsewhere for treatment. The question then becomes how to disclose exactly what the health care provider applying Reiki thinks Reiki does.

Following are three sample scripts for physician-patient dialogue:

Script 1. Here is how I apply Reiki. I just put my hands on the disease spot and mentally say, "Reiki on." When I am done, I mentally say, "Reiki off."

Script 2. Reiki involves channeling universal life energy. This is what I do when I apply Reiki: I tune in to universal life energy and channel it to you.

Script 3. The best scientific evidence I can offer—studies regarding safety and efficacy—still do not address mechanism, still leave unexplained what is the substance of the "Reiki" itself, the "universal life energy." Ultimately, *chi* evades scientific description because it purports to operate only *partially* on the physical level, in the physical world.

Deeper inclusion of the phenomenon of Reiki in conventional care, and corresponding legal and ethical models, might lead providers into thinking that Reiki energy is under the control and domination of scientific instrumentation, regulatory bodies, and the human experiencer. At least for many practitioners of traditional oriental medicine, *chi* is regarded differently than the surgeon's scalpel; there is an almost religious reverence. *Chi* masters insist that we do not create *chi;* we can only be temporary storehouses of *chi* and thereby limited human instruments of greater cosmic powers. Similarly, in Eastern scriptures, the kundalini energy—the awakened consciousness of divine infinitude, said to be coiled at the base of the spine—also is addressed as Mother Kundalini, the Shakti, the creative power of God.[49] Phenomena that science might measure as corporeal realities are said to be linked to nonmeasurable, cosmic ones. In other words, the superluminous energy itself is perceived as prior to, within, and beyond the mind of the human, not the reverse. In terms energy healers use, the biofield creates the template for the physical body, not the reverse.

To take the thought experiment one step further, let us assume that a machine could be developed that measures the amount of universal life energy in any object or person: the further the needle goes to the right, the more universal life energy. In this scenario, every plant, animal, and person is assigned a universal life energy reading, like a social security number. Now collectively we may think we have captured some piece of the information puzzle. The Reiki master is asked to "channel energy" in order to test the machine. The healer, however, states, "When I call on my master guides and teachers, all available Reiki masters, they appear and assist with the transmission of universal life energy." We then need a machine to measure the presence of spirit Reiki masters or Archangel Gabriel or Jesus, Buddha, the Gaon of Vilna, or whomever one calls. Again, we are left with some particles of mystery—a spiritual Heisenberg uncertainty principle.

Now assume that through modern technology, our "universal life energy detector" machine (ULED) can detect the presence of nonphysical guides. In fact, the machine is so subtle, it can detect specific levels of vibration for different spirit beings, including those the Buddhists call "hungry ghosts." For example, there is a certain frequency when Uncle Mort, who died in a skiing accident a few years ago, is present; another frequency when Bishop Smith, who was a friend in a past life and is now between lifetimes, is present; still another frequency when Archangel Gabriel is present; and yet another when Jesus brings in his healing energy. We can have a readout of the band, much like an X ray or CAT scan, showing who is in the room sending healing. We can tell the patient, "Okay, your cancer is being addressed at various levels of being by Uncle Mort, Bishop Smith, Archangel Michael, and Jesus."

This imaginary scenario highlights the collision of civilizations when conventional care fully meets the implications of some energy healing modalities. One system purports to operate in the physical world—the only, commonly recognized, "real" universe—the other to correspond in "subtle" dimensions. This sensitivity to what beings are in the room during the healing is, in fact, what some healers purport to employ when scanning the auric field. The healer uses intuition, while the machine uses technology. The healer uses his or her own perceptual apparatus, whereas the machine is "objective." Hence the collision.

The foregoing makes a number of assumptions. It assumes that, in the words of Einstein, God does not play dice with the universe, and it is willing to hold certain natural laws in place so that the machine will detect presences accurately each time. It also assumes that we know who these beings really are—what it really means to sit in the recovery room in the presence of a Jesus, Buddha, Moses, Mohammed, Mary, Kwan Yin. One also has to consider that the machine, being in the energy field of these beings, will begin to absorb their vibrations and glow with certain high-frequency energies on a subtle level. The one who is operating this machine may be like the woman who touched Jesus' robe in the marketplace. Presumably, the Christ love will wash over her, and this experience will in fact become the object, destiny, and purpose of operating the ULED.

Taking the thought experiment one step further, suppose the healer wishes to explain what truly happens during the application of Reiki healing. The script, however, might not resemble anything familiar from informed consent. It might sound like a religious teaching. For instance, the healer might explain to the patient:

> The purpose of experiencing great beings is to attain the state of the great being. When one contemplates Christ, one becomes Christ; when one contemplates Adonai, one draws into oneself the loving-kindness, the compassion, the greatness of God; when one gazes at the Buddha, one realizes one's own Buddha-nature.

True medicine is becoming one with the patient. This is the meaning of compassion. The caretaker understands what the patient is experiencing and can heal from love for one's own being. That is why the Boddhistava's prayer says, "May I be the doctor *and* the medicine." It is a much subtler and more profound appreciation of healing than what we label "the placebo effect." The doctor is the medicine and cannot separate himself or herself from the healing process.

In the end, therefore, there is a value to the subjective experience of great beings and healing energy. Scientific measurement has its place, but ultimately, the experience of God is foremost. Great beings and angels existed long before modern science; it is folly to believe we can "capture" their reality solely by reliance on the science we know.

To learn more, we have to turn to other texts studying the science of being, such as the Yoga Sutras of Patanjali and the scriptures. All the experiences of modern energy healers are recorded in these books, even going back, for example, to Abraham and Ezekiel.

This conversation sheds light on the initial discussion of whether or how to license providers such as energy healers. Among other things, if healers gain intuitive information by "listening to their guides," by "tuning within," by "meditation," by "stilling the mind," or by some other subjective technique, one wonders whether all the accrediting and certification mechanisms our social order has developed for licensure would be beneficial in regulating the education and training of healers, as well as standardizing their ability to practice. Again, the question of regulating energy healers may be addressed differently depending on whether one assumes the goal of fraud control or of quality assurance or of a goal such as encouraging the collective evolution of human consciousness.

Touch as Psychotherapy

As suggested, energy healing may be a natural extension for mind-body therapies and mental health care, including psychology and psychiatry. This nexus is logical for a number of reasons. First, the skills a healer uses are similar or analogous to, or fall along a spectrum together with, many skills used by trained therapists. For example, the healer also relies heavily on looking and listening, using one's own perceptual apparatus to glean diagnostic information about the patient. Therapists look to body language, nonverbal behavioral cues to the client's emotional state; the healer listens to the body, to the energy field, to impressions bombarding the subconscious mind from a variety of channels and on a variety of levels. For example, in case 5A, the healer tunes in to information coming to the conscious or subconscious mind from the wound itself, from the trauma.

Second, energy healing, like mental health care, also relies on subjective testing; probes inner states rather than merely outer (physiological) responses; ferrets out emotions and confronts the emotional life; and more frequently crosses the line into nonmaterial, spiritual concerns. Third, both healers and therapists primarily concern themselves with issues of trauma, emotional pain, and the patient's alienation from a state of happiness and clarity. Fourth, both therapists and healers must distance themselves from the information received to be sure that their reading is accurate and does not unduly reflect their own biases and perceptual filters. In short, they must attend to issues of countertransference.

Psychotherapy and energy healing may provide different techniques that create a spectrum of emotional and spiritual healing, from the most essential and acute therapeutic work (for example, relieving severe depression) to the most refined and subtle (for example, putting an individual in touch with his or her deepest authenticity; removing all masks; facilitating individuation; furthering Maslow's notion of self-actualization).[50] The two systems also may have different ways of viewing the same phenomenon. For example, George Vithoulkas proposes that the psychological phenomenon known as "dissociation" is in fact a separation of one or more of the energy bodies from either each other or from the physical body.[51] According to Vithoulkas, which bodies dissociate from one another depends on whether the individual is experiencing sleep, somnambulism, fainting, surgical anesthesia, hypnosis, yogic and religious trances, schizophrenia, use of hallucinogenic drugs, or apparent death.[52]

Another basis for comparison consists of the ground rules for the healing relationship; healers may benefit from literature on psychotherapy.[53] For example, what kind of social amenities are appropriate before, during, and after the healing session? Is it appropriate for the healer to hug the client? Should the healer set an outer time limit for the session? How should healers set fees and receive payment? How should the healer frame the therapeutic purpose of the healing relationship?

To the extent that healers share with therapists the ability to "read" the patient's emotions, and thereby penetrate boundaries and invade psychic space, such questions will be useful in learning new ways to manage transference and mediate the exchange of psychospiritual energies between provider and patient. To the extent healers also are able intuitively to pick up on the past, present, and future, resolution of boundary issues may require even more novel thinking. Further, while the therapist may be trained to elicit strong emotional material while remaining in a detached, neutral, "objective" therapeutic mode, the healer may consciously be touching the place in the patient's biofield where the traumatic experience is stored and thus moving empathy into an actual personal experience of the trauma or chaos. In short, the conscious merging of two energy fields presents a potential new frontier for psychotherapeutic theory.

Energy Healing as Exorcism

More profoundly, the insights of energy healing regarding human existence within a multilayered biofield present profound implications for the understanding of psychic pathology that is currently, commonly held by many mental health care disciplines. Additionally, these insights present opportunities to bridge these disciplines with the teachings of various world religions. For example, the chakra system at first may appear to present a closed, grid-like universe with definite hypothesized pathways and correspondences. In actuality, though, the chakras merely purport to present one map, or interpretation, of the way spiritual energies flow through material reality. An infinite number of chakras are postulated, all interconnecting, as humans are seen as "souls reincarnating life after life, slowly progressing in our evolutionary path towards God."[54] Thus, while imbalances in certain chakras theoretically might be correlated with certain manifested diseases, the soul's journey, as seen through the chakra system, is far more complex:

"All these possible experiences or probable realities are stacked in the energy field. They are all designed to teach our soul certain lessons we have chosen to learn."[55]

One of the arenas in which energy healing may help bridge such disciplines as psychotherapy and world religious traditions is the way it views release of negative energies from the biofield. In many camps, exorcism is considered a religious ritual, but not a psychotherapeutic technique. Psychotherapy and psychiatry are considered to follow "scientific" principles and hence to be clear from any imputation of a "belief" system, yet the parallels between the therapeutic process and exorcism may be more than metaphor. A Native American shaman might burn incense to "clear the spirits" in a room—many healers perceive in this ritual or in an effective psychotherapy session an actual clearing of negative energies from the room.[56]

Analogously, a shaman might burn sage around an individual afflicted with "possession"; a psychiatrist would make a diagnosis under the DSM-IV and might prescribe appropriate medication; an energy healer might actually "see" the spirit afflicting the individual and use techniques to read the biofield of those troubling energies. Stories of psychotherapeutic exorcism abound in religious literature. Even Jesus meets a man afflicted by legions of demons and drives the "unclean spirits" out of him.[57] The question remains as to what extent the phenomenon of possession is strictly mental (in other words, "within" the person's "mind"); strictly bioenergetic, and thus sharing an almost physical (but more than intrapsychic) reality with the individual's body and energetic system; or both. It is also intriguing to ask whether consciousness alone can mediate the healing.

Energy healing again thus poses phenomena that may defy the best attempts to undertake "rigorous scientific research." Scientific methods used to study safety and efficacy, assess levels and types of evidence, rule out "placebo effects," randomize patients, and so on are important but may not control or completely capture subjective phenomena experienced by either healer or client on the healing table. According to energy healers, these may include:

working with spirit guides and angels;

seeing departed relatives around clients,

seeing aborted fetuses in their fields;

removing curses and entities;

removing astral gunk;

healing archetypical or "past life" traumas.[58]

To attempt to "validate" these phenomena may be similar to trying to validate religious claims or, for example, to validate transubstantiation. No chemical analysis of the holy wafer before and after communion will "definitively" resolve the theological dispute between those who believe in transubstantiation and those who believe in consubstantiation. And yet energy healing purports to be other than religion; to be based on laws of the universe and not on faith; to be grounded in realities that we eventually may be able to perceive and measure but that, like the phenomenon of love, can only be fully captured by sitting in the experience of the phenomenon. Energy healing will raise controversy in claiming as valid things dismissed elsewhere as preposterous—for example, the belief that there is anything different about "holy water," reportedly gleaned from sacred sites; or even, in homeopathy, the belief that something in the water "remembers" an energetic pattern, even though the dilution leaves the active substance below Avogadro's number; or the belief that on a bioenergetic level, such ritual tools as amulets and magical incantations actually have power. Ultimately, energy healing may pose to psychotherapy and mental health disciplines (and religious doctrinal systems) the question of whether new understandings of "mind," "body," and "spirit" can evoke bridges between different forms of knowledge.

Touch as Biofield Repair

Ashley Montagu proposed that one essential function of touch was *caring*. Without sufficient touch, Montagu pointed out, infants wither emotionally and physically. In explaining the significance of contact, Montagu notes, "The skin, like a cloak, covers us all over, the oldest and the most sensitive of our organs, our first medium of communication, and our most efficient of our protectors."[59] Moving beyond the physical body to the energy bodies, one might say that the human energy field is our first medium of communication, the place in which we first make contact with one another. Without sufficient and appropriate caressing, nurturing, healing, and touching of our energy fields, we wither and die energetically; we grow holes in the aura, which, like plaque in the gums, create a foundation for later disease.

Montagu criticized the inability of his contemporaries to recognize the importance of caring, human touch:

> The impersonal child-rearing practices that have long been the mode in the United States, with the early severance of the mother-child tie, and the separation of mothers and children by the inter-position of bottles, blankets, clothes, carriages, cribs, and other physical objects, will produce individuals who are able to lead lonely, isolated lives in the crowded urban world with its material-istic values and its addiction to things. . . . The contemporary Amer-ican family constitutes only too often an institution for the system-atic production of mental illness in each of its members. . . . The importance of tactile experience, especially in the preverbal stages of human development, cannot, in fact, be overemphasized. . . .[60]

Other anthropologists and psychotherapists have added to Montagu's analysis the importance of healthy personal boundaries, within which the person's essence can take root and be nourished in a healthy way, without undue interference or invasion.

Case 5A presents the issue of whether the significance of touching the human skin, together with ideas concerning the integrity of the per-son, can be interpreted clinically through the lens of energy healing. The case broadens the notion of healthy personal boundaries by plac-ing them within the context of a luminous biofield, composed of many layers. In this case, the *physical* care being given to the patient created *energetic* holes in the aura. Psychically, the patient was abandoned and even assaulted in the emergency room. Although the ultimate stitching performed by the emergency room physician—acute care—was profes-sional and necessary, the environment was draining the patient's life-force, also necessary for recuperation at physical and other levels of existence.

The case makes the suggestion that energetically, healers poten-tially can help perform at least four distinct functions that typically are not taken up by other health care providers in either allied or comple-mentary and alternative medicine: (1) holding the integrity of the biofield; (2) invoking and amplifying cosmic energies for healing at all levels (including physical, mental, emotional, and spiritual); (3) harmonizing the energy fields of caregivers, technological machinery, and the patient; and (4) repairing holes in the aura. Again, *all* of these proposed functions require subjective understanding, or so-called anecdotal evidence—in other words, entering into the experience. Like the parables in spiritual literature, these functions are intended to operate on multiple levels. Thus, taking the last function as an example, repairing holes can be understood literally and also can be viewed in terms of all the information that may flow through the healer as the holes are literally plugged. Case 5A gives the example of information concerning a male warrior who violates the sanctity of indigenous peoples in relationship to their land.

Most health care institutions are not set up to amplify and encourage healing of the biofield and indeed may be counterproductive to therapeutic goals that might be established if energy healing were more broadly understood. For example, the hospital space designated as a "chapel" often has been stripped of any religious symbolism and reduced to the most bare, generic framework. The sense of grandeur, majesty, and sanctity that one finds in a church, temple, or mosque is absent in the attempt to create a religious space that is not religious—in other words, that serves as a neutral setting for humanistic values that is somehow tied to theism. The presence of a Bible or book of hymns, together with a poster or two regarding a Mass or some other ceremony, may indicate the vestige of religious ritual, but the sense of private centeredness and the ability to connect quietly with God are usually different from what one experiences in a place of worship outside the hospital. Paradoxically, the hospital may be the one institution in which citizens most need sacred space—temporary housing in which to quietly seek communion and contact with energies associated with the upper chakras, higher levels of the field, and their own relationship with the divine.

As another example, most hospital rooms have television sets, the idea being that these technological boxes carrying images and sounds help comfort and care for the patient. The ubiquitous presence of the television set in the hospital is taken for granted as an aid to healing through pleasant distraction. Yet television entrains the brain. Few if any contemporary shows are uplifting. Messages typically are filled with violence. The sounds and images have particular force on the subconscious of a person who is in a weakened condition, physically, emo-

210 • Future Medicine

tionally, and psychically. From the healer's perspective, the person lying on the bed is entranced by the chatter on the "tube," and thus distracted and disrupted even as his or her consciousness may be drifting to different layers of the energy field, seeking information to assist in the healing process.

Even if the person's own television set is turned off, most rooms have more than one occupant (with a screen separating them), and sounds from the other set tend to be audible. This is just part of the culture. But just as individuals need physical rest for healing, there is similarly a need for a cessation of stimulation and for emotional and psychospiritual refreshment through silence. At least this is the teaching of generations of monastic life across the traditions: silence heals. Silence allows the body's energies to settle. But instead we muffle the spirit; anesthetize the life-force; block the flow of vital energy; and barrage the body's systems with requests for information, chatter, and distraction. Energetically, the avalanche of information coming from the television invades and overloads a system of subtle bodies that need to focus on sealing holes in the aura, repairing chakras, and doing the internal work of recovery on all levels. Consciously, the patient may not notice the confusion, the incessant flow of information, the detrimental effects; the patient may even welcome the distraction. Unconsciously and energetically, the patient suffers.

This is not to say that humor, distraction, and engagement are not positive tools that television might offer; rather, the mindless inclusion of television within the healing environment does not, from the healer's perspective, represent a choice designed to augment healing energies in the biofield. Further, from a spiritual perspective, watching television cuts off individuals from other forms of conversation—from self-examination, from communion with their families during crucial moments in the lifetime, from communion within, from conversation with God. From the perspective of transformation, the hospital environment may be functional in many physical respects, but it does not reflect healing at all levels of the field.

Conclusion

This chapter attempts to broaden the foundational discussion in chapter 4 about the potential social as well as clinical revolutions suggested by integrating energy healing into modern care. Energy healing challenges the boundaries of science, medicine, education, philosophy, law, and even daily conduct. It may create common ground among religions—or greater disputes. It may forge miracles from the crucible of the ordinary—or make the extraordinary mundane. It may bring human transformation into common parlance or remove its further reaches from our instrumentation and ken.

Whatever its power and potential, the field requires much further study and development. And yet even as health care providers collectively strive to serve as vessels for higher and more refined spiritual energies, unresolved shadows remain.

6

Fraud, Ego, and Abuse of Spiritual Power

Case 6A   Fraud: The Unlicensed Healer from Nazareth

 In health care ethics based on Christianity, the figure of Jesus is regarded as a model, as he "healed before he preached, and he went out to the lepers, the most neglected members of the community."[1] But the purpose of this memorandum is to suggest how, from a limited perspective of fraud control, a religious healer could be perceived as a dangerous and subversive agent of darkness.

To: Chief Prosecutor
From: Assistant Counsel
Date: Somewhere in Time
    You have asked me to investigate allegations of unlicensed medical practice regarding a particularly controversial individual. He came from Nazareth and moved around small towns. He called himself Yeshu—"the one who saves"; Maschiach—"The Anointed One." This previously unknown individual—whose only professional training was as a *carpenter*—performed "miracle cures" and engaged in the unlicensed practice of several professions: medicine, psychology, massage. He claimed to heal the lame, the blind, and the sick; he claimed that "greater things than these" would be performed by his devotees. Once he walked through the marketplace, felt a woman touch his robe, and said the "energy" was drained out of him; at other times he was said to walk on water, resurrect the dead, and claim a direct channel to God. In this way he defrauded millions.
    Among other state laws Yeshu allegedly violated was a

prohibition against necromancy, originally instituted by the prophet Samuel and later codified under state law as a prohibition against "fortune-telling."[2] In one incident, Yeshu took Peter and James, in collusion with John his brother, to a local mountain and fraudulently created a light show (according to the testimony at trial, he was "transfigured before them: and his face did shine as the sun, and his raiment was as white as the light").[3] There he purported to converse with Moses and Elijah, thus *channeling* in violation of the statutory proscription. To cover up his fraudulent acts, he swore his disciples to secrecy until after a promised resurrection.

Yeshu not only claimed to cure disease—a felony in most states—but also reportedly empowered his disciples to do the same. Drawing on Jewish messianic fervor and revolutionary Marxist undercurrents within his social group; openly defying convention, orthodoxy, and social, legal, and medical authority; and freely mixing contemporary rabbinic Judaism, spiritualism, Kantian philosophy, existentialism, the prophetic tradition, Sufi mysticism, and the teachings of Helen Blavatsky, he also purported to transmit to loyalists the "power *against* unclean spirits, to cast them out," and—blatantly violating medical licensing laws—to "heal all manner of sickness and all manner of disease" (not excluding such serious conditions as diabetes, cancer, leprosy, and AIDS).[4] Included in the carpenter's retinue of "healers" were a former fisherman and a tax collector.

Undercover investigators, employed by a consortium of state professional boards (known as the "Sanhedrin"), repeatedly confronted him regarding the origins of his therapeutic techniques and his identity. "Are you a healer?" they asked. "Do you claim to represent God?" "What do you mean by the statement, 'I and the Father are One'? "Have you studied witchcraft, sorcery, or necromancy?" And finally, "Do you believe in homeopathy?" To all questions he remained silent, except to reply, "So say you." On the stand he took the Fifth, refusing to answer any questions. He died in prison—his body disappeared. Some say he reappeared three days later; others say he was a Tibetan master, adept at the art of dissolving into the "rainbow body" at death. Some say he was a charlatan; others, a Self-realized being. Some say he was an avatar; others, one aspect of a triune God.[5]

According to the allegations in another lawsuit, Yeshu claimed to heal a young man in the marketplace suffering from multiple personality disorder. Yeshu, who had no licensure in psychology and no training from any accredited institution in counseling or any other form of mental health care, and who lacked certification as a rabbi or priest from any recognized religious educational institution (and therefore was not entitled to any religious exemption under a state medical practice act), put his palm on the forehead of this young man (whose name was Legion) and told him to "sin no more." Following the "healing" by Yeshu, Legion went out and stabbed a young woman. According to the complaint, Yeshu, who had *reason to know* not only that the young man was dangerous but also that he might act out his specific threats, negligently failed to inform the family of the danger.[6]

Case 6B   Ego: Nonprofessional Contact at the Firm

A businessman related the following incident to his therapist:

"The moment I met Jacqueline, we experienced soul-level recognition. Warm, rosy arcs of light passed between us as our eyes met down the corridor. We had lunch—once—three months before her wedding. Leaning back casually across the grass—my tie loosened, the slit in her skirt slightly opened—we noticed the sexual chemistry, but acknowledged implicitly that there were boundaries we could not or would not cross.

"One time Jacqueline came to my office to help fix the printer. Sexual energy passed between us, a tempting flirtation. My hand reached out and touched Jacqueline on the shoulder. Immediately, the energy was 'grounded,' through her body, into the earth, and thus dissipated. There was no longer any question in my mind: that touch released any sexual charge between us.

"And yet I wondered whether she interpreted what had happened in the same way. For example, had I been a licensed therapist, that same touch easily could have been misinterpreted (as an advance). What, then, is the difference between *healing* touch and *sexual* touch? Was I indeed appropriate or abusive? Was the touch experienced as sacred or as invasive? Does my intention or her perception control? What does it mean to touch someone *inappropriately*? Can legislative language embody the subtle distinctions among states of consciousness? How much must we rely on individual providers' motives, intent, state of inner purity? What if their explanations (for example, 'I was trying to *ground* the sexual energy') defy our belief or belief systems? At what point do we put the provider on trial and consider professional discipline?"

The therapist, consistent with his Freudian training, discreetly glanced at the clock, but said nothing. When the therapist failed to answer these questions, the client continued:

"Shortly after this incident, we got together again and stared deeply at each other's faces, until we each entered a slightly altered state of consciousness and could connect to the perceptions of other lifetimes, or dimensions of being together. 'What do you perceive?' she asked. 'You were my son,' I said. Each of us felt that linkage and sat in the heart exchange. I saw Jacqueline—in this body as a single mom, a secretary—in various realms of existence as a shaman, a scholar, a priest, a tribal leader. Many impressions flicked in and out of my awareness."

The businessman looked down at his fourteen-carat-gold Cross pen. "And then we resumed our normal work activities."

Case 6C   Abuse of Spiritual Power: The Grand Inquisitor

 Sitting at the council table, the chairman hands out a sheet and says: "And these are all the therapies that defy the known laws of physics, biology, and chemistry and for which there is not a shred of credible evidence. Yet some members of this committee would have us license practitioners of these therapies."

This man embodies the shadow, and he is out to *crush* everything he does not understand. His tirades sap the room of energy. We notice him well: the aged cheeks; the idiosyncratic, elevated speech; the hostility to matters and methods outside his familiar framework.

When the meeting ends, we—the condemned, the "alternative" healers—huddle in a corner and affirm that this dangerous, destructive individual may sabotage our cause; in muffled voices, we call him the "Grand Inquisitor." For a moment, having vented, we are quiet. We wonder whether, in labeling this representative of the current order, we, too, have erred and sinned. I look at his physical form again and send love, as a true wave of compassion floods my heart. Then one of us turns to the other and says softly, "And yet . . . consciousness expands."

The Shadow Side of Energy Healing

Energy healing—like medicine, like all health professions—has a shadow side. That shadow potential is particularly intense given the intimate and powerful psychic energies projected and exchanged through energy healing modalities.

A popular radio show in the 1950s called "The Shadow" began, "Who knows what evil lurks in the hearts of men?" After a slight but menacing pause, the voice continued: "The Shadow knows." Evil laughter followed. In Jung's system of collective archetypes, the shadow represents all that a human being has suppressed in terms of unwillingness to look at one's own darkness, or evil inclinations. Jung theorized that typically individuals—and masses—project their shadow onto others. This mechanism has stimulated the mass appeal of philosophies such as fascism, empowering totalitarian leaders, fueling racism, and encouraging genocide. According to Jung, rather than confront one's own shadow (a process that uncomfortably brings one's own destructive tendencies to consciousness), a person scapegoats and volunteers to injure (for example, lynch, mutilate, or even exterminate) others. In plain terms, whatever we hate in others, we despise in ourselves; by hating them, we protect ourselves from seeing the shadow side of our own nature.

This point was dramatically represented in the second film in the *Star Wars* trilogy, *The Empire Strikes Back*. The director (George Lucas) drew on Joseph Campbell's idea of the "monomyth": "the one, shapeshifting yet marvelously constant story that we find, together with a challenging persistent suggestion of more remaining to be experienced than will ever be known or told."[7] The *Star Wars* trilogy presents analogues for energy healing because the Jedi knight is a kind of healer, one who carries gifts of high sense perception and the ability to use spiritual energies (epitomized by access to the Force and symbolized by the mysterious "light saber") to re-create the social order.

Luke Skywalker represents the hero, the individual battling duality and coming to know his or her own nature. He is guided by Yoda, the archetypical wise being, as he learns about his healership (in other words, his powers as a Jedi knight). Luke enters a cave: the primordial womb of creation in which he encounters all that has been repressed— all that he has failed to confront. Before entering, Luke asserts, "I'm not afraid." Yoda hauntingly replies: "You will be. . . . You *will* be." As Luke penetrates deeper into the darkness, he meets an image of Darth Vader (the name is a variation on "dark father," and as it turns out, Vader is Luke's father and has turned his spiritual powers to darkness). Luke succumbs to the "dark side of the Force," to his own shadow, and lashes out at Vader. He becomes aggressive and lets his emotions run the fight. Angrily, he slices off Vader's head—only to find, when the head rolls onto the ground, that the face he sees in the mask is his own.

The "cave" sequence provides a metaphor for the individual's journey through the shadow, and it also suggests the healer's path through this part of the self. First there is only light: one uses the tools of light—the "light saber" in Luke's world; or the tools of modern medicine; or the healing power of hands, mind, or prayer. Then there is the black, velvety void: the place where one confronts one's own shadow. Western religious writings speak of "sin"—literally, "missing the mark"; Eastern scriptures describe the "enemies of the Self"—such as avarice, desire, and so on. These are the inner enemies that the outer enemies of mythology represent. The healer's journey is the hero's journey: tools of spiritual power can be abused and must be reclaimed for the task of restoring the order of the wholeness.

The energy healer is a fiduciary: one entrusted with special responsibility because of the intimate, trusting relationship engendered with the patient. In this respect, energy healers are no different than physicians and other health care providers; indeed, in *The Healer's Power*, Howard Brody expressly refers to the physician's potential to abuse personal power in relationship with the patient as the "dark side of the force."[8] Brody observes:

> The point is that the dark side of the force always exists as an impulse, usually kept well under control but always remaining not far below the beneficent surface . . . and the power of the physician gives rise to more or less fear, distrust, and resentment depending on how far below the surface the impulse is felt to be and how strong reaches the control that holds it in check.[9]

Brody identifies at least three aspects of the shadow side in medicine:

> [The] use of power against the patient, motivated by the pleasure in release of being able to use one's power and control without social repercussions—the dark side—is only one form of abuse of power. Another is to use medical power to push for a personal agenda rather than submitting one's views for open discussion in appropriate form. . . . The third and most obvious form of abuse of medical power is using such power for the physician's selfish benefit.[10]

Brody calls for a system of medical ethics that "deals forthrightly with these feelings, not one that denies their very existence."[11] Similarly, because he identified the tendency to project the shadow onto others as the root of much mass evil, Jung felt that confronting one's own shadow was "an *ethical* problem of the first magnitude," from which "neither the so-called religious man nor the man of scientific pretensions" was spared.[12] Jung's admonition pertains to energy healers as well. To handle one's shadow, Jung felt that it was "not sufficient just to know about these concepts and to reflect on them," nor to deal with them "by feeling our way into them or by appropriating other people's feelings"; rather, archetypes "are complexes of experiences that come upon us like fate, and their effects are felt most in our most personal life."[13] According to Jung, unless one *confronts* one's shadow, the shadow may suddenly appeal and *devour* the person: "This is how demonic power reveals itself to us. . . ."[14] Like Luke meeting his own dark side in the cave, the "meeting with oneself is, at first, the meeting with one's own shadow. The shadow is a tight passage, a narrow door, whose painful constriction no one is spared who goes down to the deep well. But one must learn to know oneself in order to know who one is."[15] Robert Bly pithily writes, "The brighter the light, the darker the shadow."[16]

The more energy healers exude "special powers" (for example, clairvoyance, clairaudience, clairsentience, or intuitive diagnosis), the greater the potential for abuse of spiritual power. Again, in Brody's terms, there is "pleasure in release of being able to use one's power and control without social repercussions." Such repercussions may appear absent in a largely unregulated field that occurs outside the mainstream of medical interactions and in which the healer's abilities appear highly unusual and extraordinary. The healer engages in mind reading, miracle making, exuberantly exuding the presence of God—defying known physical laws by postulating the existence of a luminous system of interpenetrating energy fields. The healer is poised to expostulate the mysteries of existence to innocent clients. Arguably, the more powerful the spiritual technology, the more its practitioners are called to examine their own shadow side.

From another perspective, the shadow also can be said to characterize attempts to denigrate healers and spiritual technologies. Bly wrote of the United States: "We're dealing with a network of shadows, a pattern of shadows projected by both sides, all meeting somewhere in the air."[17] This statement exemplifies the prominence of the shadow not only in human psychology nationally but also in the history of medicine and its regulation. The history of antagonism between the various camps of providers that runs from the beginning of colonial times through the present—the war of epithets—reflects projection by one camp of its own shadow onto others. For example, Oliver Wendell Holmes referred to homeopathy as a "delusion" of "tinsel erudition," and epithets in turn raged back from the homeopathic camp.[18] Since all human beings share the collective archetypes, and *all* healers—conventional or integrative—share the tendency to act ignobly, this kind of black-and-white, either/or thinking could reflect projection of one's own tendencies for delusion and fraud onto other practitioners. Indeed, some might argue that the regulatory goal of fraud control is itself a projection of the shadow of those calling for regulation (in other words, seeing fraud only in complementary and alternative medical therapies and providers). In any event, confronting the shadow—both individually and collectively—is a prerequisite to responsible clinical practices involving integrative and energy medicine.

Shadow tendencies include fraud, ego, and abuse of power. In spiritual writings, the term *ego* is used differently than in psychology. *Ego* does not refer to the "healthy ego," the part of the psyche that mediates between the id and superego, draws healthy boundaries, or practices appropriate psychic self-defense. Rather, *ego* is used to refer to the "garrulous, demanding, hysterical, calculating" portion of the psyche that ultimately deceives the authentic being as to the path to self-realization.[19] Thus, it is the ego that defrauds the individual of his or her authentic nature, that perpetuates abuse of spiritual powers, that deludes and thus veils the ultimate good within the person, that mires the individual in shadow behaviors. Ego, in this sense, challenges the person to confront the secret "snake" within, to find all the subtle, hissing ways one veers from truth and, in so doing, to find the inner light. It is in this sense that fraud, ego, and abuse of spiritual power are combined as terminology for the dragons on the journey, whose slaying the regulatory goal of transformation also comprehends.

Eating the Shadow

Jung and Bly also claim that by confronting the shadow, a person regains and reintegrates into consciousness the energy ceded to the archetype. As Bly puts it, "When the shadow becomes absorbed the human being loses much of his darkness and becomes light and playful in a new way."[20] In this connection, Brody argues that the physician may exercise his or her healing power in relationship with the patient so long as the physician and patient share both information and responsibility for deciding on appropriate treatment, while protecting the patient from the potential misuses and abuses of power. According to Brody, responsible use of power includes acknowledgment of that power, being accountable for the way one uses such power, and purposefully directing that power toward a beneficial and specific end. In addition, the physician should be sensitive to the sense of powerlessness often accompanying illness and should be prepared to respond by, among other things, sharing knowledge, identifying psychological states characteristic of the illness (and including their management in the treatment plan), explicitly reminding the patient of the power the patient possesses, and reassuring the patient that power is being employed to secure a favorable therapeutic result.[21]

In the therapeutic relationship, both the physician's power and the energy healer's power derive from having special information not readily accessible to the patient—in one case, scientific and medical knowledge; in the other, knowledge gained from intuitive realms of existence. The physician's knowledge may result from highly specialized training; require subjective interpretation; and involve a nonordinary, priestly language (for example, the highly complex and specialized medical terminology relevant to the particular diagnosis and chosen therapy). The physician must translate this knowledge into terms accessible to the patient—indeed, this obligation is codified in legal and ethical rules governing informed consent. The energy healer's knowledge also may involve specialized, priestly language from nonordinary realms of reality—for example, symbols; metaphors; information from "spirit guides"; sensations; unusual perceptions; or a dredging up of relevant, forgotten psychic material from the patient's past. The energy healer also is called to translate this knowledge in a way relevant to the patient—without unduly frightening the patient, without "lording over" the patient the healer's privileged access to this information.

If the healer fails to recognize the temptation to misuse power—for example, the "pleasure" of behaving in a hierarchical manner—the unrecognized shadow may devour the therapeutic relationship. The dangers may be magnified in the energy healer's case, because the imbalance of personal power in the provider-patient relationship is amplified when the provider carries spiritual power additional to technologically based information. When personal power is combined with intuitive abilities, a charismatic psychic, who provides just enough accuracy in an intuitive reading to keep followers hooked, may be difficult to resist. Quite literally, from the healer's perspective, the devotees of the false guru are attached to energetic "hooks" streaming from his or her energy field.[22] There also may be "tentacles," "oozing, slippery, silent and heavy" bioenergetic material that "reach[es] for your solar plexus in an effort to capture your essence and pull it out."[23] Both hooks and tentacles may be accompanied by such other defenses as "verbal arrows"; "power/will display"; or "boundary containment," an energetic defense used to strengthen and thicken the auric boundary to convey unaffected superiority.[24]

Throughout history, there have been individuals who have used access to spiritual forces in distorted ways. A classic example is Rasputin, whose hypnotic spell over the Romanov family purportedly weakened and confused the Tsarina, creating a legacy of social and political chaos and wreckage. Even Hitler was supposed to have stolen the spear of Longinus, which was said to be spiritually charged with the energy of Christ's blood and thus to radiate a divine power that was used by an unholy cause.[25] Such attempted use of spiritual power as a weapon is not without precedent. In the ancient Indian epic the Mahabharata, the various heroes are constantly utilizing *astras*—divine weapons—to nullify their opponents; these weapons are gifts of the gods and can be used either for dharma—righteousness—or for *adharma*—a nonrighteous cause.[26]

Perhaps the ultimate archetype of the shadowy healer who masquerades as light is the original "light-bearer" himself, Lucifer, the "fallen angel." In the Hebrew scriptures, he is referred to as *satan*, usually translated as "adversary." Indeed, Jungian thought expressly identifies the Christian idea of the Devil with the collective archetype of the shadow. The power of this "false light" to seduce, deceive, and beguile humankind is an enduring theme in Christian theology. Lucifer is the original anti–energy healer, against whom all internal rules of fraud control must be aimed. Indeed, throughout Christian history, the powerful figure of Satan is used to demonize perceived enemies of the faithful, to vindicate Jesus' followers, and to draw a "thematic opposition" between good and evil.[27]

In the Book of Revelations, this power becomes incarnate in what has become known as the anti-Christ. On the psychological level, this is the embodied shadow, capable of producing false displays of healing and false miracles and thus of falsely winning the people's confidence. The impostor's display of healership is profuse: "This . . . beast . . . extended its authority everywhere, [a]nd it worked great miracles, even to calling down fire from heaven on to the earth while people watched . . . it was able to win over the people."[28] Again, the false magician is an archetype: in the Jewish scriptures, even Aaron, brother of Moses, has to compete with the false prophets of the Egyptian kingdom, magicians who, like God's chosen priest Aaron, are able to turn their staffs into serpents, though they use "witchcraft" rather than God's holy power.[29] (Postscript: Aaron's staff swallows up the staffs of the Egyptian magicians.)

Thus, the battles (and triumphs) of Yahweh (God) in the Torah, Christ in Revelations, and Krishna in the Mahabharata all suggest that the shadow is a potent force in human existence for *negative transformation* and that humans must be sufficiently mindful of the shadow's power and allure in order to transcend its evil influence. Shadows smother light, or as Bly puts it, "the unabsorbed shadow can darken the air all around a human being."[30] The psychological lesson in these archetypical tales, however, is that once the individual confronts, inte-

224 • Future Medicine

grates, surmounts, and thereby "eats" the shadow, he or she is no longer threatened by that destructive power. This is because the most devious device the shadow has is that it remains undetected, cloaked by the individual's projection of shadow material onto others. In Jungian terms, the Devil is not so much an external force as an internal energy that the individual must learn to master in order to achieve individuation. In other terms, confronting one's own propensity for evil is a perquisite to self-actualization. In bioenergetic terms, confronting the shadow and overcoming one's own propensity for "evil" involves facing all the "terrible, dirty, bad" feelings, thus ridding one's self of the "antilife" created by chronic character armoring and reorganizing the being to allow a freer flow of consciousness and spiritual energy.[31]

The profession of energy healing—or practices by existing health care providers involving energy healing modalities—can draw on this guidance. Just as psychologists, to be clear counselors, train to understand the mechanisms of projection, transference, and countertransference, similarly, a major task of a healer—whether a physician or allied health provider, licensed complementary and alternative medical professional, or nonlicensed energy healer—is to uncover, understand, confront, and integrate his or her human shadow. Just as psychotherapists use supervision to gain clarity, the same mechanism will be useful for energy healers.

In biblical terms, energy healers confront the same choice as any individual imbued with "supernatural" abilities in the time of Aaron or the Apocalypse: to follow the witchcraft, sorcery, and magic of the false priests and the Beast or to honor the sacred energies coming from the highest source of being. The choice is the same: the Devil or God, the shadow or the self, blasphemy or salvation. One confronts oneself in the Cave of Being and aligns with Darth Vader—the "dark father" of shadowy forces—or fully becomes Luke Skywalker, the prophet-priest who has integrated the "dark side of the Force." In psychological terms, the choice is whether to continue to deny and repress one's own evil tendencies or to acknowledge them and move toward individuation in the task of transformation. In Christian terms, the choice is one of the temptations Jesus faced: to throw himself down the mountain and tempt God's power or to surrender to this larger power and understand its guidance in his earthly life. In terms healers use, the question is whether one can be a *clear channel* for healing."

The Shadow Knows: The Perils of Powers

Both psychoanalysis and religious studies can bring perspectives to bear on how (or how effectively) health care professionals handle the shadow. For example, the earlier discussion begs the question of *who judges* whether a particular healer is "clear" or is "channeling dark forces." This has always been a pivotal question in assessing religious motivation: determining whether a particular religious mind brings passionate illumination to the human condition or offers the control of a tyrannical orthodoxy. This potential for tyranny—and the concomitant desire for freedom from such tyranny—is, indeed, a major motivation behind the separation of church and state, which is codified in the establishment clause of the First Amendment.

Corollary questions include those concerning what produces the "fall" of a healer. Is "sin" something intrinsic to the human being—the inner "adversary"—or an external force? What is it that sets out to entrap, ensnare, and besiege unwary humans? The question of the shadow's origin is relevant to regulation that attempts to capture complementary and alternative medical modalities. How can regulatory authorities (the modern-day Sanhedrin) in case 6A judge whether the unlicensed healer from Nazareth has exercised fundamental rights or violated fundamental laws?

As suggested in chapter 5, energy healing does force this uncomfortable collision of religious study, psychology, mythology, ethics, regulation, and interpretation of human conduct and the human condition. In a profound sense, rather than labeling practices such as Therapeutic Touch "witchcraft" (another term is "unscientific"), regulators might do well to confront their own shadow sides and explore their own intuitive abilities, using the laboratory of their own consciousness as a battleground for the exploration of the limits and outer boundaries of spiritual experience and power. This takes theology to a personal level and transduces rhetoric down to individual experience. Such an approach is profoundly antiorthodox and prefers personal discovery to collective dogma.

Yet this approach also raises the most basic and unanswerable theological questions. No present scientific theory can account for the fact that some individuals have highly developed intuitive abilities, whereas others do not; or for the fact that refined abilities differ, like the gift for musical instruments, as some are more focused on "seeing," others on "hearing," and others on "sensing," while still others have experiences in the form of visions, meditative revelations, or dreams. Hence, while as a health care modality energy healing is located uncomfortably in the realm of medicine and the health care professions—albeit "complementary and alternative"—its true thrust and deeper implications may be transcendental and spiritual. For the present, while attempting to unlock the scientific secrets of energy healing on some objective (scientific) basis, it also is vital to draw on different disciplines to understand the potential "dark side" of the force known variously as *chi*, spiritual energy, *mana*, *prana*, and so on. In short, it is necessary to use a variety of perspectives to address the issue of abuse of spiritual power.

One Shadow, Many Perspectives

This question of abuse of spiritual power is, ultimately, cross-disciplinary. No amount of scientific investigation into the *validity* of energy healing will answer the larger question of whether, assuming human beings have within them expanded powers of perception and consciousness, the human race is ready and sufficiently mature to handle these powers. Spiritual maturity—individual and collective—is a component of transformation as defined in chapter 3; "eating the shadow" helps facilitate the regulatory goal of human transformation. Brody, in fact, has called for physicians to internalize "the responsible use of power as a self-imposed standard of scientific as well as behavioral excellence."[32] The question of transformation, therefore, may require perspectives other than scientific and legal ones.

Religious writings provide one clue toward transforming the shadow side of healership—the so-called psychic powers—into the part of human motivation dedicated to *service*, not egotism. One major impetus for such transformation lies in the healer's power to glean potentially private and confidential information from patients, loved ones, or even strangers. Even if the healer is merely in a listening posture, the healer's ability to resonate with different levels of the human energy field can, theoretically, put the patient or client deeply in touch with core, unresolved psychospiritual issues. This healer's gift—helping others feel the traumas, hurts, and soft spots that are pathways to realizing their deepest longings (such as for intimate contact with their innermost self)—itself creates potential for abuse. Having located the patient's deepest wounds, the healer is automatically in a position of power and the patient in a position of vulnerability and, usually, dependence. The healer then has the choice to help heal or to exploit the wound for a perceived psychological gain.

In other words, spiritual power, like material power, itself is neither good nor bad, but the use to which it is put can be evolutionary, revolutionary, or counterevolutionary. Guidelines exist for such matters as informed consent, both in the clinical and the research arenas. But guidelines for right use of spiritual power (apart from guidelines governing such ethical issues as informed consent) have not been developed. Another way to frame this is that each year many lawsuits are brought for malpractice violation of informed consent and for violations of medical privacy and confidentiality, but judicial opinions and codified guidelines do not explicitly address the use and abuse of spiritual power and intuitive gifts.

In the New Testament, Paul expressly addresses the subject of intuitive powers and the way they can be used for good or adversity. He begins by discussing the fact that individuals often receive different intuitive gifts. Paul claims, however, that all such gifts derive from the same divine source: "One may have the gift of preaching with wisdom . . . another again the gift of healing. . . . one, the power of miracles; another, prophecy; another the gift of recognizing spirits; another the gift of tongues and another ability to interpret them."[33] Paul's method is antiscientific, in that he acknowledges the limitations of human knowledge concerning such gifts; he also emphasizes the folly in assuming that access to transpersonal and cosmic realities gives a human any true understanding of the vast scope and purpose of these realms: "The wisdom of this world is foolishness to God . . . there is nothing to boast about in being human. . . . A man may imagine he understands something, but still not understand anything in the way he ought to."[34]

Paul's writings suggest that he had grown accustomed to the presence of miracles, to being a channel for a higher power, and yet that he also was deeply in touch with his humanness and thus aware of the potential for abusing his spiritual power. Thus, having experienced the Holy of Holies within his own heart, he ultimately urges others to be "ambitious for the higher gifts" and concludes that "the greatest of these is love."[35] In short, Paul urges that spiritual powers be put to use in service of spiritual attainments, the greatest of which is love, and not be used as ends in themselves.

In drawing these conclusions, Paul shares his own vulnerability as a healer, thus embodying the archetype of the "wounded healer." Specifically, he provides his audience with the tantalizing suggestion that he has been given a built-in corrective to potential abuses of spiritual power: "In view of the extraordinary nature of these revelations, I was given a thorn in the flesh, an angel of Satan to beat me and stop me from getting too proud."[36] This verse has led to speculation as to what exactly was the nature of the "thorn" Paul describes. For the healer, the wound typically is both the source of the gift and also that which prevents the healer from imagining that the personality and its egoic distortions are the ultimate sources of that volcanic spiritual energy. To the extent that the "thorn" Paul experienced was part of his own shadow—his own inner adversary—Paul's ability to recognize that deficiency and to see it as part of an unwanted, destructive part of himself made him a clearer healer—one who was able to conclude that of all the spiritual gifts, the greatest was the ability to love.

The clues religious writings such as those of Paul provide are highly relevant to regulating an emerging field such as energy healing, which crosses boundaries among medicine, spirituality, mental health care, and other disciplines. First, given the heightened vulnerability of those who come to healers *and* the heightened psychic powers of the healer and of forces involved in the healing encounter, the consequences of failing to confront one's shadow can be disastrous, both for patient and healer and for the environment. Again (as Bly puts it): the brighter the light, the darker the shadow. Conversely, the more the shadow can brought to light, the deeper the integration and the brighter and more pervasive the resulting synthesis. The healing relationship is a fiduciary one, with all the attendant responsibilities that attach.

Second, present health care regulation aims at managing the shadow primarily through laws aimed at fraud control, rather than through fostering greater consciousness (awareness) of the shadow at work (the latter could occur, for example, by mandating education that includes experiential exercises in consciousness). Ethical codes within the health care professions are attempts to codify the ethical impulses one hopes would lie *within* the professional rather than without, in a written guideline. Similarly, malpractice rules aim to induce a deterrent effect that ideally, one hopes, would lie within the healer. Both attempt to control outbreaks of shadow consciousness, rather than to bring the health care professional to a realization of the shadow impulses inherent within his or her nature. As Brody suggests, however, some ethical checks need be internally self-regulated, rather than managed through legal or professional rules.

Indeed, in attempting to legislate the shadow out of existence, some legal rules are so intricate, so obtuse, and—even for many health care lawyers—so layered with exceptions as to be nearly impenetrable. One example is the federal legislation and accompanying regulations known as the "Stark" rules, which aim at preventing conflict of interest among physicians who have a financial interest in products or services they recommend. It is true that physicians can find themselves operating out of the desire for financial profit, rather than patient welfare, when they have a financial interest in health care products or services they recommend to patients. But it is not entirely clear that the layers of regulations in this area either help the physician practice with a clear conscience or produce a clean road map out of the ethical morass. Among the many criticisms of these rules, it is argued that other kinds of professionals—including attorneys—are allowed take a referral fee without legal consequence, whereas the medical profession remains subject to prohibitions. The many exceptions and pages of interpretation make the prohibitions appear arbitrary and difficult to draw, leaving providers vulnerable to fines and even imprisonment for lines innocently crossed.[37] To the extent that excessive regulation burdens healers and healing, constrains innovation, unduly diminishes the therapeutic encounter, and wastes human resources on lawsuits, prosecutions, and expensive consultations with lawyers, novel regulation enabling one's own ability to understand and confront the shadow becomes highly cost-effective in human terms.

Case 6A illustrates the clash between legal rules and internal ethical challenges to the healer's sense of ego. Metaphorically, the temptations Jesus experiences in the desert are a means of testing the development of a higher ethical sense over the challenges of ego. Jesus masters the challenges and also walks a fine line in terms of refusing to make overbroad claims for his powers (thus, in today's society, avoiding potential liability of the healer for misrepresentation). Statements such as "my kingdom is not of the earth" remove him from claims that he might be trying to lead a *physical* revolt against the Romans, but they also frame him as a spiritual leader rather than as a health care provider in the physical realm. The case suggests, however, that despite the attempt to remain in the spiritual domain, Jesus' ministry does touch (in our society) on the unauthorized practice of several health care professions, including psychotherapy as well as medicine. The case thus provocatively explores the extent to which our legal rules, when applied to a religious figure, miss the mark in addressing the darker reaches of human nature in the art of healing.

One could in fact argue that, rather than addressing actual ethical violations committed by healers, many legal rules express collective cultural *fears* of healers. Healing touches the boundary between medicine and religion, science and faith, intellect and uncertainty. Legal rules also codify political attempts to preserve professional monopolies (for example, earlier use of medical practice acts to prosecute chiropractors, naturopaths, massage therapists, spiritual healers, and others) and therefore crystallize limited cultural belief systems about what professional healers can or should be able to do. If Jesus were to appear in the United States today, he would not be crucified; he would, most likely, be prosecuted under a variety of health care licensing laws—and sued. In short, the Second Coming would be accompanied by a spate of court filings.

The Shadow and Personal Needs

Once again, since energy healing has not sufficiently coalesced as a mature profession, a related profession—psychotherapy—provides an analogue for exploring how abuse of spiritual healing might be handled in the professional, regulatory domain. In the field of psychology, complaints of professional misconduct that are brought before ethics committees tend to fall into five interrelated categories: exploitation, insensitivity, incompetence, irresponsibility, and abandonment.[38] All five "sins"—categories of misconduct—involve a deviation from the standard of care and thus provide grounds for malpractice liability. Further, each category correlates with personal needs and regulatory concerns, as well as with energetic violations (see chart 15). The typology suggests correlations among the field of psychology, professional regulation, and energy healing.

CHART 15. Dominant Personal Need and Professional Misconduct

Predominant Personal Need	Controlling Regulatory Value	Category of Misconduct	Chakra Wrongfully Invaded
Physiological	Fraud control	Exploitation	First
Safety	Quality assurance	Insensitivity	Second, third
Belongingness and love	Health care freedom	Incompetence	Fourth, fifth
Esteem	Functional integration	Irresponsibility	Sixth
Self-actualization	Transformation	Abandonment	Seventh

Parenthetically, the charts are not meant to draw immutable correspondences in an orthodox fashion. As Maslow suggests, "higher" and "lower" needs freely intermingle. The point, however, is to begin drawing a conceptual dialogue among the fields of psychology, religion, anthropology, and the other humanities and medical and other health care traditions, including that of energy healing, following the goals of functional integration and of human transformation.

When therapists exploit their patients, they use their patients as a means to an end. They thus defraud patients by deceiving as to the goal and nature of the therapeutic session. Therapists who exploit their patients wrongfully invade all the chakras and energy bodies, but particularly the first: the level of physiological wholeness and integrity of the body. For example, a therapist who inappropriately touches the patient, channeling sexual energy rather than holding a clean space for healing, exploits the patient by putting personal needs first and thus weakens the patient's sense of physical integrity. The patient learns from the encounter that he or she does not own the body but can be assaulted (contacted without consent). Energetically, this is dangerous, as the first chakra connects the person to physical survival on earth; damage to the first chakra and the first layer of the field is linked to issues of (and decisions involving) physical vitality.

Therapists who manifest insensitivity to patients weaken patients' second chakras and the emotional body, which needs a coherent field to maintain, hold, sort, and clarify the many conflicting aspects of a person's emotional makeup. Insensitivity threatens the sense of personal safety. It also weakens the third chakra, which spins with a person's sense of connectedness to others. Personality types with orality tend to send out third-chakra cords, seeking energetic feeding from others; when personal power is challenged, the third chakra spins wildly.[39] The third chakra also represents control over one's environment.

Incompetence threatens belongingness and love, along with the sense of immersion in community, in which one's (fourth-chakra) heart energies and (fifth-chakra) throat-center are fed. "Community" refers both to social groups and to a sense of belongingness in the cosmos, a movement toward spiritual unity.

Irresponsibility in the healing professional threatens the sixth chakra and the sixth level of the biofield, the region in which healers—and thereby their patients—connect to the angelic realms, to the inter-dimensional unity of all beings and all creation. In the Hawaiian and other indigenous healing traditions, healing comes from the gods and is channeled through humans to human bodies. This, in fact, is one nature and purpose of a blessing: to transmute divine symphonies of order, love, and coherence into human resonance so the physical body and the soul can heal. Irresponsibility means abandoning one's connection to the angelic and transcendent and thereby abandoning one's soul's connection to the source of healing (in Hebrew, *mekor ha-brachah*, the Source of all blessing).

Abandonment implicates damaging the client's seventh chakra, the place of connectedness to one's highest self. The client is left dangling in the place of confusion, where boundaries are unclear, where the healer's personal and professional motives are an impure mixture of caring and personal gain.

Case 6B briefly explores some of these permutations and, again, attempts to elicit questions about whether present cultural and professional norms regarding therapeutic boundaries might be stretched by a paradigm of health care that includes bioenergetic fields. In this case, two individuals experience "soul recognition" within a professional setting and thereby merge at some higher level of consciousness. The love is cosmic and divine (in other words, agape) although it has a personal dimension; the gaze exchanged is powerful and profound, but not seductive, in the sense of leading to sexual intercourse. There is, paradoxically, a "respectful flirtation."

The touch on the shoulder signals a potential boundary violation—in our culture, unauthorized touch in a professional setting can
signal unwarranted invasion, can even trigger a lawsuit for sexual
harassment. In the scenario presented, however, the touch "grounds
the energy," meaning that the sexual overtones are dissipated and the
relationship is understood as friendship. The touch is followed by an
exchange of information on deeper levels of contact and consciousness
regarding the connection between the two souls incarnated as the narrator of the vignette and Jacqueline. The touch thus stimulates seventh-
chakra cords rather than second-chakra ones; in the case, as written,
there is no abuse, fraud, betrayal, ego, or incongruence between motive
and manner of contact. Provocatively, the case is framed as an
encounter between professionals rather than in the therapeutic relationship; it thus frames the problem of energetic touch—contact—
between humans at a more generic level. The problem is magnified in
the healer-client exchange, in which sensitivities, vulnerabilities, and
potential fragmentation of the client's consciousness (as a result of the
disease process) are intensified.

Case 6C reinforces the theme of the potential for divine, seventh-
chakra love to permeate an interaction that otherwise might produce
shadow effects. In other words, when individuals manifest rage,
hatred, or intolerance—all of which may show energetically, as well as
emotionally (for example, as black in the aura)—and project their
shadow onto others, it may be tempting for those accused (or those wit-
nessing the psychic attack) to project their own darkness back onto the
accuser. Thus, the "Grand Inquisitor," as he is fondly called in the case,
becomes in the minds of the providers in the case a manifestation of the
Devil, the embodiment of dark energies.

Although it may be true that the "Grand Inquisitor" aims, out of
fear, to suppress different systems of world knowledge, the case also
presents potential reactions to such an individual. The case under-
scores the tendency to engage in black-and-white, either/or thinking
and the danger of projecting one's shadow, even if potentially war-
ranted. Further, the case suggests the possibility for transcending the
tendency to act through projection and thus for achieving a higher form
of knowledge regarding the antagonist's being—thus, in religious
terms, even redeeming the Devil through God's love. Finally, even
though beings of light are tested, as was Jesus in the New Testament
story and Luke Skywalker in the cave, the whole process has a larger

form, scope, and shape: no matter what form the Grand Inquisitor assumes, or seems to assume, case 6C suggests that the finite continues to stretch to the infinite and that consciousness continues to expand.

The Shadow and Boundaries

Although there are many professional disciplinary actions against psychotherapists for sexual abuse and abundant literature exists on the problem, the question of *energetic* violation of personal boundaries is relatively new and unaddressed. Ethical dilemmas inherent in energy healing remain latent in this culture, with discussion regarding "ethics" largely limited to rhetoric regarding the use of "unproven" modalities and similar discussions either favoring or disfavoring particular complementary and alternative medical therapies. The latency of the dilemma results in part from the way in which intuitive abilities have been pushed down in this culture, particularly in health care, while the technocratic aspects of care have gained ascendancy. And although ethicists, medical historians, and others have addressed the need for greater human contact—including an "ethics of care"—in the clinical encounter, the notion that contact on the level of bioenergy fields may have something to do with the therapeutic relationship remains largely occluded.

In the present medical culture, high sense perception remains a relatively rare, occult, and prized ability. We are quite skittish in social contexts about discussing the latest revelations of our "third eye"—to the extent that these gifts are even accessible to most of us. In many ancient (and contemporary) cultures, dreams, visions, and voices from the beyond were (and are) considered important religious experiences, lending guidance, direction, and meaning to the mundane. In some cultures, such as that of the Senoi, sharing dreams in the communal setting has been an important part of the regulatory order. In our culture the clinical label of "psychosis" (or "hallucination") is much more likely for those who proclaim that they derive direction from internal sources, experienced in the form of visual, auditory, or kinesthetic experiences that cannot be objectively validated by present scientific instrumentation.

This splitting off of psychic experience is not isolated to medical education but occurs more generally as early as childhood. The ability to "perceive energy" is not cultivated in secondary education, and children who have "imaginary playmates," conversations with angels and extradimensional beings, or communications from God or divine messengers learn to "outgrow" such experiences as part of their "maturation" (or rather, enculturation) in Western society. The line between sainthood and schizophrenia still is not readily understood, and it has only been recently that the behavior, mental state, and emotional conditions culturally considered "normal"—a baseline—have been acknowledged to carry a host of pathologies and disturbances.[40]

The entire notion of the bioenergy field, in ordinary clinical practice, still is considered radical and subversive: as mind is separated from body, science is dissociated from religion. Doubtless, there are attempts to shut down the whole "extrasensory" apparatus of the human organism, rather than to acknowledge these gifts—and the accompanying communication between worlds that is an inherent part of shamanism—as an integral part of the human heritage.

In reviewing the entire history of the species and examining the full sweep of human *spiritual* evolution, there is the suggestion that humans have experienced enormous, untapped, intuitive abilities. Human beings have not, however, as a species, arguably matured sufficiently to develop these powers for beneficial purposes. Collectively, one might argue, we have not yet developed the grounding, centeredness, or anchoring of sacredness to bring these more refined and subtle states of awareness to earth and utilize these abilities for higher purposes. In most of us, therefore, the spiritual power remains dormant. This is, at least, one hypothesis that might explain the relative paucity of express use of high sense perception in medical culture, in secondary school education, and in ordinary (consensus) reality.[41]

Were models of ethics, science, medicine, and even law explicitly to incorporate high sense perception, the way the culture views such archetypical tasks as confronting the shadow in professional relationships might change. This would create new challenges to existing models of professional regulation: it is difficult enough sorting out what values such as nonmaleficence, beneficence, autonomy, and justice mean in the ordinary realm of human consciousness together with technology—let alone in the realm of superconsciousness.

In esoteric Indian teachings, such cosmic consciousness is, in fact, the ultimate goal of human existence and, moreover, a natural component of spiritual human evolution. The power that facilitates such human transformation, described earlier as the kundalini, is said to be the power of the divine, lying coiled at the base of the spine like a sleeping serpent.[42] This power apparently remains dormant until awakened by grace, often in the form of an already awakened being. In writings about kundalini, awakening brings about the opportunity to clarify intention, to separate one's ego from one's godliness, to differentiate between the unreal and the real. This awakening presents the opportunity to transform kingship into kinship and manipulation (born of fear) into service, born of love. The accompanying powers, however, may be unwieldy: the rise of the awakened energy can bring about insanity, resulting from the "inability of an individual to hold awareness on several levels of reality simultaneously."[43] This model helps explain both phenomena such as high sense perception and the individual's evolution through various chakras into the full spiritual maturity that accompanies self-realization.

The difficulty of moving through such awareness has motivated calls for clear perception of reality. In Brihadaranyaka, one of the Upanishads, the seeker prays:

> Lead me from the unreal to the real.
> Lead me from darkness to light.
> Lead me from death to immortality.[44]

But whether one calls the phenomenon extrasensory perception, latent abilities, or the slumbering kundalini, the suggestion that the power behind the creation of the universe is the same power that remains dormant within human awareness also helps explain why high sense perception remains occult. The sheer power of developing these abilities may be staggering: the psychic potencies of intuitive healing and spiritual development might topple the most stable health care provider, despite legal rules and the accompanying threat of sanctions and/or rigorous training in ethics.

Robert Assagioli suggests four dangers in exploring the unconscious. These dangers help pinpoint some of the ways in which accelerated spiritual powers might threaten the health care provider who dabbles in the psychic powers accompanying energy healing. The first is "the release of drives and emotions which were locked in the unconscious and which can flood the conscious ego before it is ready and prepared and competent to contain, control and utilize them"; this situation is that of the "apprentice sorcerer."[45] This might be analogized to what Brody formulates as the disparity in power between provider and patient and the release of pleasure accompanying such intensified power. Assagioli goes further, however, and suggests that spiritual evolution unleashes internal forces that overrun the barricades formerly placed in the psyche that previously held back material the individual was unready to confront. The result is a torrent of urges that cannot be controlled and contained.

The other risks Assagioli describes are the danger of "losing the self in the great sea of the unconscious"; excessive preoccupation with the unconscious; and excessive grandeur, or "psychic inflation."[46] Some of these themes have been described in literature written by mystics—on one side, the terrifying absorption in a greater consciousness that engulfs the individual's isolated awareness; on the other side, the loss of the soul to the "dark side of the force." Assagioli's writings insist that one must have a well-integrated, harmonious personality as a foundation for spiritual awakening; otherwise, such openings can be destabilizing. That one must "have an ego before losing the ego" has become a cliché, yet the statement represents a truth about building a foundation for spiritual advancement. Until the foundation is complete, the dangers may overwhelm the psyche and lead the provider into misuse or abuse of spiritual powers and/or into personal destruction. Again, one could conclude that powers remain dormant in humanity at large because human beings as a whole have not been sufficiently emotionally and spiritually mature to handle such experiences.

As spiritual power enters the medical and legal systems with greater force, however, it becomes increasingly important to acknowledge and discuss strategies for handling the dark side of spiritual power, particularly in the provider-patient relationship. For example, consider the following encounters with healers:

Case 1. J has been experiencing nightmares, depression, and anxiety following debilitating fatigue and a diagnosis of Epstein-Barr virus. J visits a healer, who reports that she sees "crud" around J's field and that she spends her nights battling J's demons. Further, the healer identifies the names of specific demons and says they are visible to her. The healer reports that this is an all-out battle for J's soul, but that J will emerge victorious after three months of sessions.

Case 2. D has applied for a temporary restraining order against her former husband, alleging domestic violence. D's friend refers her to a healer for social support and to help keep the husband energetically at bay. D has one session and decides not to continue seeing the healer. The healer then calls D and says more sessions are necessary: she has reached into D's energy field and uncovered more distortions. Further, the healer reports, D must "clear more karma," because otherwise the anger that D has "put into the universe" will return to her. Learning this, D's friend reassures D that the healer is unbalanced. Still, D is terrified that her husband will contravene any restraining order and lash out against her; although she does not trust the healer, she is confused and unsure about whether to return for another session.

Case 3. C, a missionary, picks up a parasitic infection while stationed in Thailand. "I am in constant pain," he tells four colleagues in an email, detailing messy personal symptoms and admissions of religious doubt and despair. One colleague forwards his email to several Internet sites that solicit prayer for those in need; he is flooded with messages from well-wishers, including a healer who says C will "die within two months" without some form of divine intervention the healer can (for a fee) offer.[47] C sues, alleging violations of privacy and alleging that the healer has committed fraud by engaging in illegal "selling of indulgences."

Whether providers witness miraculous healings, enjoy the power to project energy at a distance, or become enthralled with the ability to influence future events via cognitive and energetic processes, they are invoking forces greater than those we accommodate in mundane, material reality (or arguably, even psychotherapy). This shift augurs recognition of the fuller implications of traveling as humans through multidimensional reality.

Healing the Shadow: Designing Ethical Guidelines for Energy Healing

It may seem presumptuous to discuss the nature of ethical guidelines for energy healing when many take the stance that it is unethical, per se, even to perform an "unproven" therapy (such as Therapeutic Touch) on a patient. This contention, of course, has been addressed in prior chapters—for example, through the arguments that terms such as "unproven" often serve as conclusory rhetorical labels marking hostility to particular therapies or worldviews, that issues of patient autonomy may enter the foreground and begin to eclipse older, more paternalistic models of health care, that the countervailing value of health care freedom may be seen as balancing the values of fraud control and quality assurance, and that the existence of regulatory mechanisms such as informed consent serve to enhance flow of information; and through a discussion of the uses and abuses of spiritual power and some of the shadow aspects of the healer's power. In any event, energy healing as a profession arguably has to mature—and the profession must be integrated into conventional clinical practice—before ethical rules can be formulated and tested in clinical situations. Such ethical rules likely will be codified differently depending on the state and on the way the profession (or subpractice within an existing profession) is defined. In the meantime, a preliminary exploration will help highlight some of the interwoven philosophical, psychological, religious, and social issues that energy healing presents. Again, mental health care provides a starting point for several reasons.

First, in mental health counseling, attention is paid to the therapist's own clarity (for example, awareness of transference and countertransference) and the need to respect the client's emotional boundaries as part of the therapeutic process. The notion of respecting boundaries becomes increasingly important as the consciousness that healers manifest becomes permeable—in other words, is able to merge with the consciousness of clients, such that healers are able to "read" not only the client's mood, feelings, sensations, and perhaps physiological abnormalities but even past traumas and events.

Second, the ethics of mental health counseling emphasize personal wholeness as a paramount treatment goal: the patient ultimately should receive from the therapeutic process not only "freedom from fear, anxiety, and the entanglements of greed, envy, and jealousy" but also "the development of his capacity for self-realization, his ability to form durable relationships of intimacy with others, and to give and accept mature love."[48] In Maslow's terms, this involves moving up the hierarchy of needs into the need for belongingness and love and ultimately self-actualization. In bioenergetic terms, the healer ultimately cultivates all seven chakras and layers of the energy field.

Third, psychotherapy emphasizes the patient's vulnerability and emotional dependence on the therapist. Such vulnerability and dependence already are present in the conventional clinical world. For example, a physical exam requires that the patient be partly undressed; hospitalization usually requires exchanging that in which one's ordinary identity is clothed for standardized gowns, parted thoughtfully along the buttocks to allow medical access. Or the physician may be the authoritative dispenser of a life-changing piece of information—"You have disease X"—and the technology at his or her disposal may provide the avenue of relief or hope for continued life. On the other hand, the mental health professional may be the first to probe into the client's history of emotional or sexual abuse; or may draw up repressed memories of childhood violence, trauma, and dysfunction; or may receive privileged information concerning the marital or other family relationship. Energy healing addresses both the physical and the psychospiritual and, as noted earlier, has the propensity for invasion at still deeper levels of consciousness.

Fourth, both biomedicine and psychotherapy often trigger an unconscious regression by the patient and submission to the caregiver's authority, with accompanying phenomena such as identification, projection, and transference. Although legal and ethical rules recognize such vulnerability, and correspondingly aim to protect patients in both biomedical and psychotherapeutic situations from their relative lack of power, psychotherapy pays particular attention to the possibility that the caregiver might cause harm not only negligently but even unconsciously.

For instance, the therapist must take care not to "use dependent attitudes of patients as a means of imbuing them with his own personal set of values."[49] In other words, the exchange between psychotherapist and patient—to use the energy healer's perspective—occurs on a subtle and not gross level; the relevant scalpel consists of words, moods, facial movements, gestures, tone of voice, and other subtle tools in the therapist's emotional landscape to restore the patient to a state of psychological health. Therapists acknowledge that the goal of being the clear and neutral "observer of the emotional experiences" of the patient is an "ideal . . . which . . . none of us will consistently be able to live up to . . . [since] no amount of inner security and self-respect protects the psychiatrist from being as much a subject of and vulnerable to the inevitable vicissitudes of life as is everyone else."[50] The same goal applies to healers: the healer must continue his or her own "repeated psychoanalytic inventories" throughout professional practice.[51]

Finally, maintaining clear professional boundaries through one's own personal development and the clarity that integrity brings is essential. The healer's mental and emotional health, clarity, and wholeness are vital: healers can offer patients as much as they themselves have attained. A healer with healthy emotional boundaries can help clients achieve the same. On the other hand, a healer who has unresolved wounds will tend to attract clients who complement, trigger, and reinforce these wounds, leading to further emotional and energetic injury in the client; for example, a needy healer will overly depend on the client for emotional support, thus reinjuring the client whose core wound is ignoring his or her own needs, devaluing the true self, and adopting a false caretaking self that derives sustenance by meeting others' needs. This can be explained in a variety of ways—for example, harmonic resonance, synchronicity, "lessons from the universe," a Mesmeric kind of psychic magnetism, the "self-fulfilling prophecy" resulting from preexisting psychological propensities, or simply self-selection.

A preliminary code of professional ethics for energy healing might look like the one presented in chart 16. The code has been drawn from medical, chiropractic, and other professional codes. At its heart is the healer's commitment to assist the client in reclaiming wholeness at all levels of being.

Other ethical and legal rules may supplement the ones in chart 16. For example, the healer should have a duty to refer the patient to a proper health care professional for conditions and issues outside the healer's expertise. This is implied by the section on consultation. Similarly, the energy healer may not practice medicine or assume responsibility for the patient's medical care. The healer may provide intuitive insights, but must steer clear from unauthorized practice of psychology in states prohibiting such practice without appropriate training or licensure. The healer's role regarding recommendations involving herbs and other dietary supplements must be clarified. In short, all the legal rules applicable to other licensed professionals (for example, scope of practice) will require consideration for transfer and application to the healer's arena of practice.

CHART 16. An Ethical Code for Energy Healers

Preamble
These principles are intended to aid healers individually and collectively in maintaining a high level of ethical conduct. They are not law, but professional standards by which a healer may determine the propriety of his or her conduct in relationships with clients, colleagues, other healing professionals, and the public.

I. The Healer's Commitment
The healing profession has for its objective the greatest service it can render humanity. The principal commitment of the healer is to assist the client in reclaiming wholeness at all levels of being. A healer should strive to render service to humanity with full respect for the dignity, autonomy, and sensitivity of fellow beings. The healer, in providing care, respects the beliefs, values, and customs of the individual.

II. Education
Healers should strive continually to improve their knowledge and skill; to maintain and enlarge professional competence through supervision and continued education; and to cooperate with other healing professionals, including physicians, nurses, psychologists, scientists, and religious personnel, in the exploration of healing modalities.

III. Services
A healer may only provide services commensurate with his or her training. The healing profession should safeguard the public and itself against healers deficient in character or competence. Healers should observe all laws and uphold the dignity and honor of the profession. Healers should not make extravagant claims or promises to clients; they should present information with humility, gentleness, and sensitivity. Healers associated with the development or promotion of products should ensure that such products are presented in a factual and professional way.

IV. Clients
Having undertaken care of a client, a healer may not neglect the client, and may discontinue services only after adequate notice. A healer

should not render services under terms or conditions that tend to interfere with or impair the free and complete exercise of his or her judgment and skill. A healer's fee should be commensurate with the services rendered and the client's ability to pay.

V. Consultation
As necessary and appropriate, a healer should seek consultation with the patient's physician and other medical professionals.

VI. Confidences
A healer may not reveal the confidences entrusted in the course of the professional relationship or the peculiarities he or she may observe in the character of clients, unless required to do so by law.

VII. Responsibility
The healer is responsible to himself or herself for nurturing his or her own wholeness and well-being, to the client for competent and compassionate care, to the profession for developing a core of professional knowledge and implementing standards of practice and education, to the public for protection against misinformation and misrepresentation, and to the global community for maintaining the integrity of healing.

VIII. The Dying Client
The healer should manifest respect for the religious and personal views of clients and their families regarding death and dying. A healer honors all peoples, all paths, as sacred.

The Shadow and Cosmic Energies

Well-meaning psychologists tend to violate ethical rules when they are uninformed/unaware, troubled, overzealous, vengeful, insufficiently trained and experienced, or simply careless.[52] In other words, psychologists commit ethical violations when they themselves are unbalanced, faltering, and insufficiently mindful of their own shadow aspects and boundaries. Healers are no less fallible.

Perhaps for this reason, drawing again on biblical scriptures,

Deuteronomy and Leviticus condemn practices such as casting spells and consulting ghosts or inquiring of the dead; Isaiah condemns mediums and wizards ("why consult the dead on behalf of the living?"); and the prophet Samuel chastises Saul after Saul has consulted a necromancer.[53] Fundamentalists read these warnings literally; others see in these warnings a recognition, as Assagioli has noted, of the power of spiritual openings and the ability of spiritual phenomena to overwhelm the psyche and distract the being from its true course. Thus, when spiritual thinkers urge students not to get caught up in these powers but to see them as passing phenomena on the way to liberation, these thinkers echo the warning that opening intuitive channels can tempt seekers away from integrity and into distortion (in other words, in regulatory terms, into professional misconduct that is actionable through professional disciplinary proceedings).

The chakra system itself helps explain how healers can be simultaneously open to cosmic energies yet unconsciously harmful to patients. For example, a healer who is open on the higher levels of the field and has an expanded sixth and seventh chakra may be highly intuitive, but that individual may have unresolved emotional issues from childhood, leaving dangling or twisted second- and third-chakra cords, manifesting in attempts to sexually or otherwise exploit patients, in insensitivity to their needs, or in other violations. In other words, a healer could be competent in intuitive diagnosis but irresponsible and exploitative, or, on the flip side, could be responsible but incompetent. Similarly, a healer could take advantage of intuitive abilities to frighten a patient or otherwise to wield personal power inappropriately. The paradoxical combination of openness to higher frequencies and lack of clarity on lower levels of the field helps explain why "psychic powers" have been so distrusted (and abused) throughout human history.

One of the techniques healers use is to "ground" and "center" themselves, or otherwise to open their lower chakras, so as not to get lost in the higher frequencies. In addition to remaining sensitive to issues of transference and countertransference, monitoring potential abuse of power, and being aware of the potential for distorted and destructive interactions, healers use such "grounding" techniques to better bridge "lower" and "upper" worlds. But such techniques are aids—not panacean. At the core of such practices is remembering the healer's own humanness.

Brody has useful suggestions in this regard. He argues that physicians can move beyond the "ritual advice against overinvolvement" embedded in conventional medical ethics and adopt the virtues of compassion and sympathy by "accepting the full irony of power in humility and compassion and overcoming the fear of powerlessness in vulnerability."[54] He also urges that the physician cultivate "esthetic distance" rather than "emotional distance"— that is, that the physician be "close enough to the subject" to "feel emotional identification and to experience . . . what is happening, and at the same time . . . be just far enough away so as to be able to reflect on that experience with some degree of critical detachment."[55] Brody thus suggests sufficient humanness that the power one can experience in serving as a channel for healing does not overwhelm the psyche and inflame the ego.

To the extent that energy healers violate such guidelines, they arguably should be subject to sanction by an appropriate regulatory board. Just as professional regulatory boards can impose a variety of sanctions on licensed providers, the sanctions that an ethics committee can impose on mental health care providers range from educative/advisory to educative/warning, reprimand, censure, stipulated resignation, and expulsion from the profession.[56] Presumably, similar sanctions would be imposed on healers who delved into their shadow side and were guilty of fraud, ego, and abuse of spiritual power. Indeed, sanctions probably would flow to the extent that healers already are subject to regulation in any given state by an existing regulatory board (for example, nursing, chiropractic, medicine, acupuncture, psychology).

On the whole, energy healing, like any other health care modality, in itself must be regarded as neutral—in other words, as free from elevation as "good" and equally as free from taint as "bad." As in complementary/integrative medicine generally, the dangers are not in the therapies themselves but in their application by human beings who have light and dark within them. Like poetry, art, and psychotherapeutic modalities, the tools of energy medicine—including expanded states of higher consciousness in which different kinds of information can be accessed—simply are portals for the flow of cosmic energies.

Conclusion

Hostile skeptics sometimes perceive healers as power-hungry charlatans who thrive on denigrating rationality, preying on human gullibility, and preaching an antiscientific mysticism that characterizes the anti-intellectual temperament of pre- and postmillennial fanaticism. On the other hand, grateful clients and advocates sometimes perceive healers as powerful, charismatic emissaries of God, whose will, glance, touch, and care bring transformation. The miracles ascribed to healers include spontaneous remissions and other physical manifestations, as well as emotional relief and contact with a transcendental world of departed ancestors, spirit guides, extraterrestrial cousins, and angelic messengers.

By and large, healers are neither charlatans nor special emissaries of the Creator. Rather, like masterful surgeons and therapists, they have personalities, foibles, egos, struggles, and the same foundational biological equipment. These gods have clay feet; only their intuitive structures may be more highly refined and evolved, giving them access to other frequencies within the universal informational matrix. Heightened intuitive abilities and spiritual powers, however, bring heightened responsibilities. Just as the law recognizes that fiduciaries have special responsibilities to their clients, similarly, individuals entrusted by the cosmos with access to divine realms have an ethical obligation to be additionally circumspect regarding their use of spiritual powers.

The application of legal and ethical rules to areas of conduct previously relegated to religious proscription, however, is controversial. Some argue that because intuitive and healing abilities are gifts of the spirit, these gifts should remain beyond the reach of regulation. Others acknowledge the immense power of the unconscious. These polar arguments may reflect the fact that until recently, the archetypes of the unconscious, the substratum of human imagination and the race's collective intelligence, the soul memory of the species, and the subterranean channels of psychic activity, all have been too powerful and destabilizing to become mainstream components of the human organism in mundane life, let alone the health care system. Yet, in literature, in art, and in other guises, these forms can find controlled (and sometimes acceptable) expression. With or without eruption into conventional clinical care and concomitant attempts at regulation, the psychospiritual journey toward wholeness, integration, God-realization, and enlightenment proceeds of its own accord, both collectively and individually.

This age is bridging the biological and pharmacological, the psychospiritual and the bioenergetic; it may also find measurable correlations between the subtle energies, or energy bodies, described in Eastern spirituality and esoteric texts and the anatomical and biochemical maps provided by Western science. As energy healing moves out of the arena of charismatic, mystically charged teachers and takes its place as a set of teachable skills among the various professional providers of the healing arts, it makes good sense to fashion ethical frameworks that mediate heaven and earth and bring the potent therapies to the world in which most humans customarily dwell.

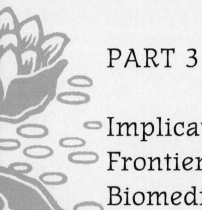

PART 3

Implications for Frontier Issues in Biomedical Ethics

7

Beyond Living and Dying

Case 7A   "Healing" Accelerates the Dying

 Phil is dying of bladder cancer. He is eighty-five years old, and his vital signs are declining. Phil's wife understands from all the physicians that Phil is dying; his son, however, continues to insist that Phil will improve and that they soon will be playing golf again together.

Although Phil is dehydrated, he is too weak to drink. A metal walker—hard fought for, from Medicare—lies abandoned in the corner. His wife holds ice cubes to his lips. She recalls his life: Phil had stormed the beaches of Normandy. She watches as the wind whips against the icy windowpanes. She invites a healer to visit. The healer places hands over the painful area and "runs energy." Phil seems to be moving between worlds—his eyes are fluttering, his sounds are incomprehensible, and he seems to be communicating with people who are not physically present. The healer wonders whether to continue. Phil's wife says, "Keep your hand there; it seems to be helping." Subjectively, the healer experiences many pairs of hands resting on top of his, each pouring energy into the field to help Phil in the process of leaving his body. Within thirty minutes, Phil dies.

Phil's son hears about the healer's intervention and reports it to the state medical board and local prosecutor. The prosecutor investigates and learns two contradictory things: on one hand, the healing has no scientific validation and therefore cannot possibly have had any effect, beneficial or adverse; on the other hand, the son feels that the healer is responsible for the timing of Phil's death and insists that the healer be charged with homicide. The wife admonishes the son and argues that the healer's presence allowed Phil to experience a peaceful and compassionate death.

251

"But Mom," the son pleads, "the *healing* accelerated his dying."
"But son," she responds, "the healing *is* the dying."

Case 7B Love between Strangers, One of Whom Is Dead

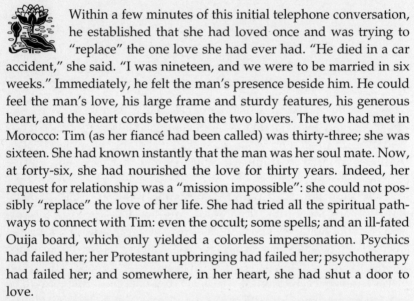Within a few minutes of this initial telephone conversation, he established that she had loved once and was trying to "replace" the one love she had ever had. "He died in a car accident," she said. "I was nineteen, and we were to be married in six weeks." Immediately, he felt the man's presence beside him. He could feel the man's love, his large frame and sturdy features, his generous heart, and the heart cords between the two lovers. The two had met in Morocco: Tim (as her fiancé had been called) was thirty-three; she was sixteen. She had known instantly that the man was her soul mate. Now, at forty-six, she had nourished the love for thirty years. Indeed, her request for relationship was a "mission impossible": she could not possibly "replace" the love of her life. She had tried all the spiritual pathways to connect with Tim: even the occult; some spells; and an ill-fated Ouija board, which only yielded a colorless impersonation. Psychics had failed her; her Protestant upbringing had failed her; psychotherapy had failed her; and somewhere, in her heart, she had shut a door to love.

The words came easily, as if from another source. "The door you shut at nineteen," he told her, "can only open in your heart." She asked what he meant by that. He replied, through the telephone cord, "You can remain in grief, shut down, closed off, afraid, unable to open yourself to life, or you can choose to connect with Tim again and thus open yourself to the fullness that is in you, to the feeling you had when in love. Reconnect with Tim—in a dream, a vision, a meditation—and you reconnect with yourself." He paused. "You have to complete this within yourself . . . and know that that relationship will endure."

"I don't have relationships with dead people."

"It's entirely healthy," he found himself saying. "People have cords to departed animal friends or to Jesus or to others who watch over them. Your heart cords are still connected, and you are still communicating to one another all the time."

"But he doesn't have a body."

"He has a *different* body, not a physical one."

She confessed then that she had felt his presence in all sorts of subtle ways. For one thing, she had miraculously escaped unscathed from a recent, near-fatal car accident. But she had not seen him directly, clearly, in the dream state. That disappointed her, troubled her spirit. Somehow, she had closed herself off—because opening up to these dimensions of being was frightening, capable of bringing up grief and other strong emotions that had been suppressed for three decades. And that was her healing.

"The cords need to be cleared before other relationships with men are possible," he said. "There is no greater gift I can give than to respect and honor your relationship with this man and your choice to do everything you can to keep the channel clear and open and have conversation."

"But why did he die? Why did he go and leave me here?"

"I cannot answer ultimate questions. But maybe there was a gift in this for you; maybe he came for a short time to ignite the flame of love in your heart—to inaugurate your spirit through this love, and its loss, into your mystical path. What is love in a body as compared with the love that spans eternity in nonphysical bodies?" He said all this feeling the man's loving presence in the room, feeling the man's love for her, feeling himself as a channel for divine love, and also feeling himself as a separate being with his own affinity for this woman and wanting to keep these things clear.

And then he said something completely uncharacteristic: "You're lucky you met me."

"That's what Tim said the first time I met him," she responded, in a quiet voice.

Somehow Tim had come so thoroughly into his field that the sense of separation was momentarily lost. "That was Tim; this is me," he replied.

Case 7C Traveling between Worlds

 Sam was dying. The stomach cancer caused him great pain. After years of separation, his parents and siblings managed a hospital visit in a belated attempt at communication.

After several rounds of question and answer, Sam finally asked his family to stop asking questions.

"I enjoy your company," he said, through gasping breaths, "but it's too much work to go inside my head and search for answers."

The family members turned to the hospital chaplain, a Zen priest, for advice. How could they reach Sam?

"Love does not require conversation," the chaplain said. "Contact does not necessitate words."

The Old Bioethics May Be Dying

Contemporary bioethics contains so many different approaches to moral questions in the practice of medicine that it hardly seems feasible or worthwhile to create yet one more approach. For example, the approach based on principles (or *principlism*) analyzes ethical issues in health care by evaluating the effect on (1) respect for autonomy, (2) nonmaleficence, (3) beneficence, and (4) justice. *Consequentialism* (or *utilitarianism*), in contrast, evaluates the balance of good and bad consequences. *Kantianism* requires that moral judgments be evaluated by generalizing the ethical choice for others who are similarly situated. *Liberal individualism* analyzes ethical decisions through the language of competing individual and group rights. *Communitarianism* looks to communal values, goals, virtues, relationships, and results. The *ethics of care* emphasizes emotional connections with and commitments to the persons in relationship. *Casuistry* reviews each case based on its own facts, with pragmatic modification of any underlying principles.[1] And dozens of other approaches exist.

Each approach provides a useful path toward resolving fundamental ethical issues—from abortion to physician-assisted suicide. An ethical theory ideally should satisfy the following criteria: (1) clarity, (2) coherence, (3) completeness and comprehensiveness, (4) simplicity, (5) explanatory power, (6) justificatory power, (7) output power (the ability to result in new judgments about issues in question), and (8) practicability.[2] While no theory is perfect, some of the theories listed earlier fulfill many of these criteria.[3] Yet each is vulnerable to criticism.

To the extent that complementary and integrative medical therapies yield one or more new ethical theories, such theories might be evaluated according to the preceding criteria, criticized, and compared to and contrasted with the many strands of existing theory. The task of articulating a complete new bioethical theory, based on one or more complementary and alternative medical modalities or systems, awaits future development. It may be that such an attempt draws on existing ethical traditions within a specific system of medicine—for example, on the discussions in ancient Chinese texts on abortion to articulate ways of analyzing modern issues in novel reproductive technologies, such as surrogacy. The teasing out of a coherent philosophical system of thought from such texts could be analogous, for instance, to the making of Jewish law by applying Talmudic texts and principles to bioethical dilemmas.

While the development of new ethical theories may be premature, energy healing suggests a number of new conceptual premises that may alter some of the fundamental assumptions underlying prevailing theories and thus shift the way physicians, ethicists, hospital administrators, attorneys and judges, and families and patients view a variety of ethical issues, from those arising during dying to those in reproductive technologies. As a starting point, consider the following questions, taken from *Healing Traditions*, by Bonnie O'Connor:

1. May we grant as serious considerations assertions that persons have (one or more) souls? That souls have obligations and destinies? That the health of souls may be as important or more important than the health of bodies? That souls and spirits, if improperly treated, may afflict or endanger the living? That spiritual salvation may take precedence over physical survival (even in apparent remediable situations)?
2. That God or other supernatural agents may intervene to heal (even in apparently hopeless or futile situations)? That there are instrumental relationships between the living and the dead? That such relationships should be taken into account in deliberations at the beginning and at the end of life?
3. That knowledge may be gained by direct apprehension, through dreams, or by supernatural agency? That such knowledge is a sound and reasonable basis for decision and action?[4]

O'Connor follows such ruminations with the provocative question: "Does exclusive application of a hegemonic ontology and epistemology in defining the field of acceptable considerations constitute in some cases a use of ideological force, and therefore a coercive action inimical to the very heart of ethical behavior?"[5]

Quintessentially, the discussion of "souls" in bioethics largely has been limited to cases involving blood transfusions for Jehovah's Witnesses. These cases inspire discussion because they directly pit the patient's *religious* choice against the obvious *medical* choice. They neatly set up an either/or decision: either the patient accepts the blood and lives—at the peril of his or her soul—or declines the transfusion and dies, saving the soul but losing the body. This paradigmatic conflict creates a neat opposition of religion and medicine and has come to symbolize the clash between "irrational" beliefs and the cool, logical imperative of life-saving technology.

But if the soul and the body are not so much in opposition as coextensive, and if choices present a more subtle range of effects on each, the case of the Jehovah's Witness who refuses a blood transfusion becomes an inappropriate model for the consideration of *soul-level* possibilities in legal and ethical decision making in medicine. The question of whether or not clones have souls, for example, raises the question as to whether genetic manipulation—with all its attendant scientific, ethical, and legal questions—fully accounts for transcendent realities beyond those any system of knowledge can grasp.[6] Even if reason is seen to triumph over emotion, more than "rational" responses are called into discussion. With an insistent hint of an offer to articulate the unspoken—a sense of what might not or could not be said—the value of transformation persists.

In case 7A, the healer provides comfort and care to a dying patient. This case can be approached as one of palliative care, the unintended consequence of which is that the patient's body ceases to function. On the other hand, the case presents other issues if the notion is taken seriously that the application of energy healing accelerated the cessation of physical life. Anecdotally, it is reported that patients who have been "hanging on" to life seem to expire when a trusted relative or caregiver, in simple language, provides *permission* to die—for example, by saying, "It's *okay* to go," or "It's fine to leave now." To quote O'Connor, what are the "obligations and destinies of souls," and how does a caregiver mind those obligations and destinies? Even more significantly, how does one do so without unnecessarily treading on "religious" ground; without invoking religious principles; without shifting uncomfortably from the logical, philosophical, and tidy world of ethical theory to the nonlogical, personal (in other words, nonuniversal), subjective, and unsteady realm of spiritual proclivity? How does a healer—one charged by profession with responsible, appropriate, and ethical delivery of health care—facilitate "spiritual salvation" as well as physical survival, without treading on individual belief systems or, in a given context, offending notions of separation of church and state; and how does such a person avoid "improper treatment" of "souls and spirits"? How might bioethics recognize such an attempt?

Duality Is Dying

No response to these questions satisfactorily can resolve the criticism that while biomedical principles provide a steady, "objective," and mutually agreeable ground—at least in pertinent part—religion leaves us stranded in the world of idiosyncratic belief. We have been stuck with this duality since far before Descartes purportedly separated mind from body. We are a post-Babel civilization: since that great biblical tower smashed earthward, we have spoken different languages.[7]

The humorous anecdote is told that once the Dalai Lama complained to his personal physician of a headache. "But from what affliction is Your Holiness suffering?" the physician inquired. The Dalai Lama opened his eyes, awakened fully from meditation, and said, "*Duality.*"

Although a scientific maxim states, "The plural of anecdote is *not* evidence," it is equally valid to state, "The singular of anecdote is a human life." The Dalai Lama's medical problem in the anecdote is a shared dilemma. This culture tends to split body and soul, medicine and spirituality. Just as Einstein failed to discover the physics of a universal energy, which he postulated unified the different forms of energy we know, similarly it may at present be impossible to discover a unifying ethical theory that satisfies all the criteria enumerated earlier. Nonetheless, one means to avoid "improper treatment" of "souls and spirits" may be to recognize their influence in bioethical processes. One can choose to avoid these aspects of the conflict or selectively to *collaborate* with the aims of spirits and souls that one might deem to be in the best interest of the patient. As the cases suggest, such recognition has the potential to expand perspectives that fail to account for noncorporeal realities, including patient perceptions that cannot be validated by objective measurement.

In short, most of bioethics to date has emerged from an understanding of the human being as limited to the body, albeit a body with some emotional and spiritual color. Incorporation of the energy bodies, of spirits and souls, and of the role of subtle energy transfers of human consciousness could represent a new understanding of how medical matters affect humans and thus should fundamentally alter bioethical norms.

The Good Death Means Dying Well

As one example, in case 7A, the energy healer assists the dying patient's death. When a medical doctor provides such assistance biologically, the term applied is *physician-assisted suicide,* with all its attendant ethical debates. The very use of the word "suicide" implies a normative judgment about what is being "assisted." Whether declared legal or illegal, ethical or unethical, moral or immoral, the concept leaves a nasty emotional residue. One could regard case 7A as a kind of *bio-energetic "assisted suicide"*: it is the healer's spiritual energy (rather than an injected drug) that purportedly pushes the patient off the edge of awareness and into the next realm. And yet the case ends with the mother's admonition that this spiritual energy enabled the patient to experience a peaceful and compassionate death and thus may have benefited the patient: healer and patient move from duality into oneness. Further, the mother responds to her unhappy son with the quizzical assertion that the dying *is* the healing.

If bioethical thought is stuck with a black-and-white, either/or paradigm of life, death, and nothing in between, then legal and ethical rules must choose between opposites: right/wrong, good/evil, moral/immoral, allowed/prohibited. Physician-assisted suicide either is or is not made legal. In terms of the Dalai Lama's proverbial headache: duality. But the "pairs of opposites" find reconciliation in the yin/yang symbol, with one flowing into the other. In bioethics, delicate distinctions are drawn between physician-assisted suicide and euthanasia; philosophical niceties explain whether one is more or less appropriate than the other or the two are the same.[8] In case 7A, the dying is the healing; the healing is the dying.

This implies that from the healer's perspective, sometimes it is not so much the *fact* of death that matters as the *manner* of death. On the physical plane, the energy healer's application of spiritual energy seems to accelerate the cessation of life. On the emotional and spiritual planes, the application of this energy facilitates the patient's transition to another form of consciousness.

Other than a recent emphasis on the importance of palliative care *while the patient still remains alive*, Western medicine typically does not recognize the significance of the patient's state of consciousness at death for the future evolution of the person's spirit. What matters is whether and not how one dies, since everything thereafter is regarded as speculative. In religious traditions such as Buddhism, however, the state of consciousness at the moment of death is vital—it is the crucial, defining moment of a person's existence; it determines the relative favorableness of the person's rebirth. The regulatory goals of integration and of transformation presented in chapter 3 argue for recognition of such diverse perspectives as part of the total picture of how health care practices and their regulation affect the human being. Such perspectives suggest that even at the moment of death, there may be more to be gained than even compassion. The clarity of mind with which the soul leaves the body is, in various global traditions, just as important as the timing of death and the manner in which relationships are handled (and healed) during the final period of one's life.

Following this line of thinking can lead to other conclusions. For example, to what extent does medication block the necessary tranquility of mind that a calm, clear death requires? To what extent are heroic efforts to salvage the body counterproductive—not because they are "futile" in a medical sense and therefore problematic in an economic sense but because they cloud and obscure the ultimate path of the patient's consciousness? Might some medication be nonmaleficent on the physical level but detrimental on spiritual levels? Might some medical orders be contraindicated on a spiritual level, and how can this information be integrated into a medical system that does not—yet—incorporate spiritual perspectives so as to explicitly acknowledge these dimensions of being? What is the deep ecology of a true commitment to do no harm?

Sogyal Rinpoche, a teacher of Tibetan medicine, asserts that narcotic pain medication dulls the mind and the senses, immerses the dying person in a narcotic fog, and thereby invades the patient's need for privacy and calm. He writes that modern hospitals make spiritual practice at the moment of death—the most important moment in a person's spiritual life—virtually impossible:

> As the person is dying, there is no privacy. They are hooked up to monitors, and attempts to resuscitate them will be made when they stop breathing or their heart fails. There will be no chance of leaving the body undisturbed for a period of time after death, as the masters advise.[9]

In similar fashion (but perhaps with different objectives), the American Academy of Pediatrics notes that if the child suffering from a terminal condition is given too much medication and sedation, the parents may blame the death on the medication rather than on the disease process; this is known as "terminal sedation." Deep sedation therefore is recommended only rarely; "dying with dignity and without pain or distress is the primary goal."[10]

With regard to the dying process, where death is imminent, Rinpoche suggests:

> While the person is actually in the final stages of dying, all injections and all invasive procedures of any kind are discontinued. These can cause anger, irritation, and pain, and for the mind of the dying person to be as calm as possible in the moments before death is . . . absolutely crucial.[11]

As noted, the moment of death, for Buddhists and members of many other religions, is crucial. From a medical perspective, these attitudes might be disregarded as religious and hence speculative and unworthy of attention. Yet present conventional medicine lacks the means to either prove or disprove these ideas. Is it possible that these religious traditions express a collective wisdom of humankind that is not simply a matter of belief or faith but a living, vibrant truth of existence, one that Western medicine, almost by definition, lacks the capacity to validate or embrace? The regulatory goal of integration expresses more than respect for cross-cultural perspectives; it entails bringing together all the diverse frames of references the human race has organized regarding a particular medical issue—for example, dying—and drawing conclusions from disciplines other than the medical one (for example, sociological, anthropological, psychological, and philosophical). The regulatory goal of transformation goes still further.

Rinpoche is critical of the lack of attention in conventional care to spiritual aspects of the dying process. He describes his deep disturbance at the "almost complete lack of spiritual help for the dying that exists in modern culture."[12] He further asserts that spiritual care is not "a luxury for a few" but is rather "*the* essential right of every human being, as essential as political liberty, medical assistance, and equality of opportunity. A real democratic ideal would include knowledgeable spiritual care for everyone as one of its most essential truths."[13] But again, a health care provider can only offer "knowledgeable" spiritual care if he or she personally has experienced transformation: has reached a state of consciousness that comprehends dying. It is not enough to read a few books about Buddhism or to respect the shaman's bedside ritual from behind the white coat.

According to the chakra system, psychospiritual energies—whether supportive or skeptical, contributory or antithetical to progress, pro-life or anti-life—are transmitted through the biofield, whether supportive or skeptical. The energies of the attending physician, nurse, relatives, and even the machines and inanimate objects, too, can store the accumulated crusts of impressions from actions present and past and permeate the dying patient's consciousness through the biofield. Energetically, they all affect what happens during death—and presumably, beyond. Further, little training is required to comfort (or otherwise potentially help) dying persons by the laying-on of hands, as described in case 7A.[14]

Prevailing ethical writings recognize the importance of spiritual values *generally* in end-of-life care. For example, the American College of Physicians offers the following suggestion: "To care properly for patients near the end of life, the physician must understand that palliative care entails addressing physical, psychosocial, and spiritual needs and that patients may at times require palliative treatment in an acute care context."[15] This represents the kernel of an approach to end-of-life care that can incorporate the kind of therapeutic attention described in case 7A. But again, the notion of "palliative care" provides a beginning foundation, not an experiential exploration of realities derived from contemplative, meditative, or energy healing practices. The application of prevailing ethical rules to dying persons, based on existing philosophical distinctions, represents use of ethical perspectives based on the person in absence of a theory of the biofield. If humans have biofields, they transcend the body; they may have spirits and souls that exist independent of the body and that predate and postdate physical existence.

In other words, quoting O'Connor, applying body-based ethical rules to the death of the body may be nothing more than "application of a hegemonic ontology and epistemology" through the "use of ideological force, and therefore a coercive action inimical to the very heart of ethical behavior." For example, in case 7A, continuing medical care up and through the moment of death may be hegemonic and inimical to the heart of the being; such care may be denying Phil the peaceful and coherent transition that, to Phil's being on the higher layers of the field, would be the most ethical and compassionate response. On the other hand, truly to integrate what the healer is doing, what the family wants, what Phil may appear to wish for, and the patient-centered objectives of attending medical personnel would require respect for many different and perhaps conflicting ideologies, a medical understanding of energetic healing, and a shared perspective on the articulated values of integration and transformation.

Dying into the Light

Dying, for most human beings, is a terrifying experience. No matter what religious beliefs one holds consciously, usually there is terror alongside. Mystery, too. But usually terror multiplied by cultural assumptions about what lies beyond mires the experience of dying in fear. Terror pushes out mystery, obscuring the potential transformation that occupies mystery's core. Modern medicine also ensures that no matter what exit point one takes, it likely will be far from gracious; rather, technology ensures that one faces "the full downhill course of the disease."[16] Again, *whether* and not *how* we die is the focus of most bioethical debates; yet from the regulatory values of integration and transformation, there is much to learn from ancient cultures and contemporary healing techinques.

Daniel Callahan has observed that a "peaceful death," one involving "dying with dignity," is preferable to a wild, violent death characterized by technological invasion. Callahan articulates the virtues of the peaceful death as able to "bring life to a fitting close, marked by connection to the self through reason and self-consciousness, and by connecting to others through dying within the circle of human companionship and caring."[17]

Energy healing sheds light on this notion of the peaceful death. Healers interpret the long tunnel with the brilliant light at the end, reported by persons who have had near-death experiences, as the soul's exit from the body through the crown chakra.[18] They see death as "a transition from one state of consciousness to another [state]," in which the person has greater awareness; death brings a "washing of the field . . . a clearing, an opening of all the chakras," which begins as a dissolution of the three lower chakras and three lower bodies.[19] The opalescent quality of the hands, face, and skin of the dying person suggests the disintegration of these lower bodies, until at last the body is "flushed through like a fountain right up the main vertical power current" by a stream of gold light: this is the experience of having one's life "flash before one's eyes," as all the blocks of consciousness are cleared.[20]

Whether taken as metaphor or fancy, this represents several healers' observations of dying, using high sense perception.[21] While perhaps suggesting an outcome similar to that described by Callahan—that the peaceful death is beneficial and important—these are transformative descriptions of human potentiality based on observation of human consciousness, rather than on a rational argument for defining compassion during the dying process. These visual images also resonate with descriptions in religious literature and art. This perspective thus lends credence to the *possibility* that some of the descriptions of what happens after dying—for example, in the Tibetan Book of the Dead—are actual technologies (or manuals) for soul traveling, rather than dogmas and doctrines created to bind adherents to a blind faith or state religion. In other words, these may be spiritual technologies, sometimes delivered in an ideologically coercive manner.

In fact, when one examines the esoteric literature of different religious traditions, one can find points of commonality around dying, even though the particular deities and aspects of ritual may be cloaked in the garb of the different cultures. For example, in *Jewish Views of the*

Afterlife, Simcha Paull Raphael compares ideas found in the Torah, the Apocrypha, rabbinic literature, medieval philosophy, medieval Midrash, Kabbalah, and Hassidism to those found in the Tibetan Book of the Dead and other traditions regarding what Judaism calls *olam ha-ba* (the afterlife).[22]

According to Raphael, beginning as early as biblical Israel, a living person was considered a *nefesh hayyah* (living soul) and a dead person a *nefesh met*—a "depotentiated psychophysical entity" who eventually dwelt in Sheol, the abode of the ancestors.[23] By the time of rabbinic Judaism, a whole body of writings described such matters as the soul's escort during death by *malakh ha-mavet* (the Angel of Death), the post-mortem life review, the dead person's ability to contact the living, and the experience of the soul after dying; thus, "the Rabbis operated from the assumption that there continued to be conscious awareness long after the demise of the body."[24]

In the Kabbalah, the Jewish mystical tradition, the dying person is understood to experience such phenomena as visions of deceased relatives and friends, a life review, and a dissolution of physical, bodily elements as the person moves into *guf ha-dak*, the "transparent [spiritual] body."[25] The process has parallels with the healer's description of dying noted earlier, as well as with Tibetan Buddhist descriptions of the dissolution of human body consciousness, internal subjective phenomena during the process, and the journey of the soul into new realms of awareness.[26] In the Kabbalah, death itself is viewed as a transition to another state of consciousness. Separation from body consciousness is seen as a "gentle, painless, experience . . . 'like taking a hair out of milk.'"[27] The afterlife journey of the soul, according to these sources, can be described as having seven stages:

1. The dying process;
2. *Hibbut ha-kever* (separation from the physical body);
3. *Gehenna* (emotional purification);
4. Lower *gan eden* (final completion of the personality);
5. Upper *gan eden* (heavenly repose for the soul);
6. *Tzor ha-hayyim* (return to the source); and
7. Preparation for rebirth.[28]

Raphael makes clear that these seven stages describe a path of healing for the soul from all accumulated and unfinished emotional business during the physical incarnation. According to Raphael's research, the first stage (the dying process) has four subjective experiences: (1) a vision of the "river of light" that is the *Shekinah*, or the presence of the divine; (2) an encounter with angelic spirits and deceased relatives; (3) a life review; and (4) dissolution of the elements of the body, together with passing through the "tunnel," the silver cord of consciousness that connects the soul to incarnation.[29]

Synthesizing Jewish teachings about these events with insights from both Tibetan Buddhism and the literature on near-death experiences, Raphael concludes:

> As we study ancient esoteric models of the afterlife, it becomes increasingly clear that dying is not simply a momentary event that takes place only on a physical level, but rather a complex process of consciousness transformation. Although scientific instrumentation cannot record physiological activity after the advent of biological death, it seems that, nonetheless, the more subtle and gradual internal aspects of dying continue for some time after pulse, heartbeat, and brain wave measurements go flat. In fact, some traditions teach that it takes anywhere from twenty minutes to several hours for consciousness to leave the body. . . .
>
> We need to learn more about the naturally occurring visionary phenomena associated [with] dying and continue to develop more elaborate cartographies of inner experience for this phase of the postmortem journey.[30]

This is an area in which modern medicine presently lacks competence. What happens to the subtle bodies during the dying process, and what happens to the soul *after* the dying, are beyond the limits of a rational, technological worldview to explain. Nonetheless, in O'Connor's terms, it may be "hegemonic" to dismiss all the information—gleaned through millennia of planetary experience, accumulated in multitudes of cultures and traditions—by assigning such information to the "religious" sphere. Such a stance—embedded in hospital regulatory policy—risks deleting important insights into the human condition from contemporary conversation, merely because the intellectual framework underlying such insights comes from different disciplines or cannot be accommodated by "objective" criteria. Perhaps in our reaction to the coercive effect of religious doctrine, the beneficial insights from religious traditions have lost their capacity to influence health care systems, and thereby have been relegated to the ash-heap of bioethical inquiry, where they rest amidst the dung of human credibility.

From the regulatory goal of integration, articulated in chapter 3, all world knowledge regarding systems of healing has some relevance. From the regulatory goal of transformation, the human being's potentiality does not necessarily have to end at death simply because Western medicine's capacity to measure such transformation comes to an end. Again, using O'Connor's opening challenge to frame the discussion, may we grant as serious considerations assertions that persons have (one or more) souls? That souls have obligations and destinies? That the health of souls may be as important as, or more important than, the health of bodies? From the healer's perspective, the soul's journey at death is a component of the definition of health: health of soul is important as is health of body. Returning to the notion of nonmaleficence as having at least five dimensions, attending to some aspects of health during the dying process expresses the spiritual aspect of "doing no harm."

Raphael, as noted, derives from his synthesis the notion that healing continues on the postmortem journey. Thus, beyond the beginning stage of death, the middle stages have to do with emotional purification, with healing the "unresolved emotional dimensions of one's being": these transit stages provide "a concentrated opportunity to encounter the dark and dishonorable, unresolved negative emotions."[31] Raphael explains:

> It is easier to deal with intense and conflicting emotions when you no longer have to attend to such irritations of embodied life as flossing teeth, answering the telephone, taking a car in for repairs, or paying Visa bills. Even though it may feel like hell, the experience of consciousness without a body allows for a much more intense connection with one's previously hidden inner reality. . . . The deceased being can no longer hide from years of accumulated and unexpressed anger, rage, fear, sadness, pain, desire, grief, guilt, and shame.[32]

Raphael describes this phase as a "prolonged psychotherapy intensive" for the dead person, concluding that *Gehenna*, often translated as "hell," is "not a locale, so much as a state of consciousness, an experiential realm reflecting one's own emotional state"; the torments of this state, "like the *bardo* visions of the *Tibetan Book of the Dead* and Titian images of hell . . . describe in allegory and metaphoric language different aspects of the process of purgation and emotional purification."[33] The later stages of transit are said to involve a second life review (using the perspective of multiple lifetimes); being with God (abiding in *tzror ha-hayyim*, or the storehouse of souls); and preparation for rebirth (*gilgul*, or reincarnation), including a prelife review.[34]

The journey ends with the experience of the soul in utero, as described in a medieval text entitled *Seder Yetzirat Ha-Vlad* (The Creation of the Embryo):

> Between morning and evening the angel carries the soul around and shows her where she will live and where she will die, and the place where she will be buried, and he takes her through the whole world, and points out the just and the sinners and all things. In the evening, he replaces her in the womb of the mother, and there she remains for nine months. . . .
>
> Finally, the time comes for the soul to enter the world. It is reluctant to leave; but the angel touches the baby on the nose, extinguishing the light above the head and sends it forth into the world. Instantly, the soul forgets all that it has seen and learned and enters the world, crying have just lost a place of shelter, rest and security.[35]

The tale may be familiar to some readers from childhood, in one version or another. Whether regarded as fanciful, as a "fairy tale," or as speculative and "unproven," such descriptions do record the observations and conceptions of different systems of health care and belief regarding the soul's journey before birth and after death. From the vantage of integration and transformation, such information must be assimilated, digested, and reconciled with other forms of knowledge (for example, scientifically validated information) about human health and possibility. The suggestion that consciousness both continues after death and begins at a soul level before birth also has implications for bioethical issues such as organ transplantation, reproductive technologies, and stem cell research.[36]

Healers Help the Dying

Case 7A presents a scenario in which an energy healer helps the dying patient by creating a clear and calm environment in which to make the transition from one state of consciousness to another. The case further suggests at least four potential roles during the dying process. The first involves using energy healing to provide comfort and care: the experience of caring touch brings calming, a reduction in anxiety, and a feeling of being comforted and cared for. The second potential application is reducing pain or potentially medication. Healers have suggested that energy healing might help reduce medication requirements by, among other things, stabilizing the patient psychologically as well as strengthening the energy field and/or reducing harsh side effects of such treatments as radiation and chemotherapy.37

The third way healers potentially may help the dying is by holding a state of consciousness of calm, peace, and wisdom and thus affecting the energy field of the dying patient in a positive, beneficial way to help facilitate a peaceful death. The healer's presence also may help move the patient through the fear associated with dying, particularly since the healer presumably has knowledge of other realms of existence, including those not associated with a human, physical body.

The fourth potential source of assistance is closely related and involves connecting with the patient on higher levels of the field. As described more fully later, this has application if the dying patient is transitioning to an existence that takes off from these higher layers of the field and is less connected to the first, second, and third chakras and levels of the field—in other words, to the mundane physical world. In case 7A, the dying patient can almost be seen traveling between worlds, as the eyelids flutter and less attention is paid to things, physical desires, and conversation of relatives involving events in this world and more attention is paid to inner processes, emotions, and residual cords of emotional contact with those in the room.

In case 7C, the Zen chaplain's response is simple: "Love does not require conversation. Contact does not necessitate words." From a healer's perspective, the experience of love may be palpable to the dying patient; but being forced to articulate mentally, when the third layer is beginning to *dissolve,* is not only painful but also potentially impossible. The necessity of focusing on external stimuli may pull the dying patient out of the internal focus on changing realms of consciousness. The healer's contribution here may be to let the dying patient know—verbally or otherwise—that there is permission to follow the wave of being, right into dying. The healer could affirm that mental articulation of concepts is unnecessary; that love *is*, in fact, present; that there is support for the dying process; and that whatever religious metaphor or tradition is useful and used, dying can be filled with grace.

A nurse who applied energy healing to her first hospice patient reported the following experience:

> I could tell the patient was ready to go. He was skeletal, emaciated; his face carried suffering; his breathing was agonized. I put my hands over his chest, scanned the field, and began to run energy. At that point, he opened his eyes, looked up, let out a huge sigh, and died. . . . I swear I could feel his soul rise up at that moment. It was if he had been waiting for that moment to die—needed one last experience of human connection—needed permission to die. . . . I had such a good feeling, knowing that he went in peace, relieved of some ineffable suffering. At the same time, I had that societal voice in my head, as though I bore some guilt for his death.[38]

Another healer reports a woman whose father was lingering with a terminal illness; the woman mentally asked her father what color he needed to be well. The father asked for pink, which the woman sent mentally, "feeling that at last there was something she could do for him."[39] Chris Griscom explains:

> What usually happens when someone becomes ill is that everyone around them is clutched by an uneasy sense of guilt . . . that we are somehow complicit in their illness through all our negativity. Deep within us we know that our thoughts and intentions toward them are sometimes filled with the shadow side of our being. . . .
>
> We may begin a crisis situation with love and the earnest intention to support, but all too quickly . . . become restless . . . feeling that we only have a certain amount to give or that we only owe so much. . . .
>
> If you send healing energy to someone, you are releasing and dissolving your indebtedness to them. . . . As you learn to send

healing energy, you might be brave enough to suggest that all the members of the family replace their worrying with this active form of healing.[40]

The notion that individuals can use specific intuitive and healing gifts and processes to help the dying "cross over" the threshold of life and death has resonance in various spiritual traditions. For example, the Tibetan Book of the Dead contains explicit instructions for assisting the dying (and dead) person through various *bardos*—states of consciousness between realms of existence. The *bardos* are said to represent flash points during which the individual—if properly guided (either from within or without)—has potential for accelerated spiritual growth and evolution. Frequently, in other traditions as well, a specific time period following the physical death is viewed as especially significant in terms of the individual's resolution of latent emotional issues from life. For example, following death, the dead person is said to communicate to loved ones and energetically transmit life knowledge and lessons. According to Raphael, the first year is particularly significant, in that it marks attempts by the departed individual's spirit to resolve emotional difficulties with other beings that were left hanging during his or her life.[41]

Jewish sources describe this stage of the postmortem journey, *Gehenna* (usually translated as "hell"): in this phase, the "individual soul has to deal with unresolved emotional dimensions of one's being . . . emotional and psychological wounds, disappointments, rejections, missed opportunities in relationship, deaths of loved ones. . . ."[42] This marks "a concentrated opportunity to encounter the dark and dishonorable, unresolved negative . . . intense and conflicting emotions . . . a prolonged psychotherapy intensive . . . [that] moves the soul toward healing, transformation, and completion with the past."[43]

In case 7B, the healing friend can access information regarding someone's relationship to her deceased fiancé of decades back. This case suggests that healing relating to deceased loved ones might have more dimensions than therapeutic value for the living person (in a psychoanalytic sense): since the dead person *also* is in psychotherapeutic process, energy healing might play a role in *mediating relationships* between the living and the dead. This might, in fact, be one purpose behind such larger public functions as a presidential talk regarding war victims—for example, one might view Lincoln's Gettysburg Address as healing both the living and the dead—releasing trauma both from souls living in physical bodies and from those living in spiritual bodies.

These ideas find some grounding in energy healing and the chakra system, in that these healing modalities define the human being in terms additional to the biological, chemical, and physical (as defined in medicine). For instance, the person is viewed as having multiple energy centers; according to Barbara Brennan, as noted, at death, the first three layers of the human energy field dissolve—the person still exists, but only at the fourth level and higher.[44] Brennan reports that at the death of two individuals from cancer, she observed that the

> lower three bodies were breaking up and coming off the body as opalescent cloudy blobs. . . . The lower three chakras were also breaking up, with long threads of energy coming out of the solar plexus. The upper four chakras appeared to be very wide open, almost like gaping holes. There was no longer a shield over them.[45]

She describes the breaking apart of the lower portion of the human energy field as accompanied by a flushing of the entire system with golden light, cleansing the dying person and releasing old blocks; this, according to Brennan, creates the near-death experience many individuals have reported of seeing all the "unblocked" and "forgotten experiences of that lifetime" as they go through a tunnel of light.[46]

Similarly, Raphael describes how Tibetan teachings understand the dying process in terms of the dissolution of earth, water, fire, and air and how the Zohar, a Jewish mystical text, states that "when a man's time comes to depart from the world, four quarters of the world indict him . . . and four elements fall to quarreling and seek to depart each from its own side."[47] Raphael notes that Ken Wilber provides a similar description: "the more subtle dimensions of consciousness—bodily awareness, sensation, perception, impulse, and eventually, the capacity for gross conceptualization . . . [and] the elemental foundations of the human psyche unravel."[48]

Again, Raphael concludes from these comparisons that

> the inner experience of dying is far more complex, than evident to objective observation. . . . Obviously, our current state of knowledge about dying is still incomplete. . . . However, a synthesis of Tibetan Buddhist and Jewish afterlife sources can help us to com-

prehend more fully the inner dimensions of the dying process. . . . Ultimately, through thorough knowledge and a deeper understanding of these inner experiences, we can help alleviate the fear individuals often experience on the deathbed.[49]

Raphael, like modern healers, describes the role of nonphysical beings during the dying process. Brennan reports observing the dying person transitioning between worlds and communicating with nonphysical beings: "The people who were crossing over spent most of their time out of the body and away. Apparently they were off with their spirit guides somewhere."[50] Further, according to Brennan, some of these nonphysical beings are discernible only once an individual turns his or her perception beyond the first three chakras and layers of the field. Brennan even goes further, to suggest that various beings (in other words, "guides") "live" in various levels of the energy field and have characteristics or qualities according to the respective layer of the field in which they reside. (For example, "fifth-level" guides attend to issues relating to the template for specific endeavors—such as musical composition—whereas "sixth-level" guides are luminously celestial in nature.)[51] Raphael does not systematically distinguish types of nonphysical guides, but compares Jewish sources to studies of near-death experiences, deathbed observations, and other religious literature, and concludes:

A disembodied being, or guide—either an archetypical, angelic wise being or a beloved parent, grandparent, or special friend— makes its presence known to the dying individual and actively assists in the transition from the world of the living to the world beyond. These guides have a very specific function: to initiate the neophyte into the realm of post-mortem consciousness.[52]

Again, these various perspectives can be incorporated from a regulatory perspective into the field of bioethics, depending on which regulatory value in the hierarchy one takes as a launching point for consideration. For example, from the perspective of fraud control, cases 7A and 7B are hokum, simply not worth considering. On the other hand, from the perspective of integration, what Tibetan medicine; Talmudic, Midrashic, and rabbinic sources; and contemporary healers have to say about the postdeath experience of a patient is highly relevant to such ethical questions as, for example, the determination of when death occurs. Similarly, from the perspective of human transformation, definitions of death that rely on biological or technological assessments alone, even if the most current and sophisticated—for example, "whole-brain" death versus heartbeat cessation—may not adequately capture the experience of being human or the timing of the dying process. It is difficult, at present, even to speculate as to what a bioethics might look like that emerges from integrating present ethical systems with the teachings of medical systems such as those from Tibet and with perspectives of scholars such as Raphael and healers such as Brennan. Integration is a process of assimilating knowledge, not an end result.

If what happens to a human being after physical life as we understand it ceases is relegated to the realm of belief and religion and hence considered—from the perspective of regulatory and ethical analysis—to be "untouchable," or beyond meaningful discussion, then discussion must cease. On the other hand, if regulatory values of integration and transformation are broad enough to embrace perspectives that cross cultures, civilizations, and epistemologies, without dismissing some of these perspectives as sheer hyperbole, speculation, or unreachable mystery, then other conclusions are possible. If a human being is postulated to exist beyond the cessation of physical life, then regulation and ethics might conceivably attempt to incorporate the phenomenon of such existence and to help living souls (in other words, those presently incarnated in physical bodies) to mediate psychosocial issues across the veil and between the worlds. Some of the present boundaries between medicine and religion—which did not exist in the world of some ancient forms of medicine—may collapse or fuse.

William James proposes one criterion for evaluating whether such philosophical bridging between material and nonphysical reality might be useful: "By their fruits ye shall know them, not by their roots."[53] From his analysis of a variety of subjective, religious experiences, James concludes that the seen world depends on an unseen order beyond the usual sense experience.[54] His approach to study of religious experience provides a pragmatic way to evaluate the experience of healers in working with the dying; including such experiences in bioethical norms is justifiable if this leads to a more compassionate view of the dying process. More information should be gathered to assess the extent to which energy healing—and the compassionate presence that may transmit information through the biofield—can facilitate transformation of the dying person, the family, the caregiver, the healer, and the experience of dying.

The Culture's Handling of Dying

Palliative care unquestionably has relieved much human suffering and arguably represents a leap in the culture's recognition of various ways to care for the dying. In recent times, open discussions of legal and ethical issues raised by requests for "physician-assisted suicide" also have created opportunities for clearer patient decision making and greater awareness of patients' emotional and spiritual needs surrounding the dying process. On the other hand, dying—at least in the hospital setting—still remains, to a large extent, medicalized, technological, and alienated from psychospiritual realities.[55] Further, religion by and large remains split off from scientific and medical approaches to patient care at death: although religious preferences are in some ways respected, debates continue, for example, about whether it is appropriate for the physician to do such things as pray for the dying patient, decline to pray for such a patient, or be neutral regarding a request for prayer. One could argue that such debates reflect both a fear of death and a fear of religion—or at least of religious coercion.

Contemporary perspectives on death could be expanded, however, if regulatory and ethical approaches more fully honored the goals of integration and transformation by incorporating a cosmic, transpersonal, and/or soul-level approach to dying, death, and the beyond. For example, in one scriptural source, the Bhagavad-Gita, the hero (Arjuna) is asked to lead his people into battle against their enemies, who include Arjuna's grandfather and cousins. Dejected, Arjuna throws down his bow and arrow and refuses to fight. Krishna, who is represented as an incarnation of God, grants Arjuna a vision of Krishna's true form and the nature of the battle. Krishna graphically shows Arjuna that all the warriors slated to die have already met their fate. Arjuna is terrified by the vision. He exclaims:

> [C]hief warriors . . . quickly enter Your fearful mouths, which gape with many tusks; some are seen with crushed heads, clinging between Your teeth. As the many torrents of the river flow toward

the ocean, so those heroes of the world of men enter Your flaming mouths. You lick them up, swallowing on all sides all the worlds, with Your flaming mouths.[56]

The vision is sufficient to shake Arjuna out of his depressive episode—a kind of cognitive therapy directly from God. On a psychological level, the Lord's therapeutic intervention is efficacious (and safe—Arjuna is overwhelmed and terrified but holds on to consensus consciousness). On a spiritual level, the dialogue becomes a teaching about the nature of life and death and the reality that transcends each. Arjuna realizes that what has been ordained must come to pass and that he, Arjuna, is merely the instrument through which Krishna will accomplish what has been planned. Krishna goes on to teach Arjuna that what has never been born can never die; that although the physical passes, the soul continues. Krishna tells Arjuna: "You have mourned those that should not be mourned. . . . Truly there was never a time when I was not, nor you, nor these lords of men; and neither will there be a time when we shall cease to be from this time onward."[57] The purpose of human life, according to Krishna, is God-realization: "He who does all work for Me, considers Me as the Supreme, is devoted to Me, abandoning all attachment, and is free from enmity toward any being, comes to Me, Arjuna."[58]

Both the Bhagavad-Gita and Hinduism—the religion within which the sacred text is framed—challenge Western medical concepts by offering a representation of a different perspective on death than that presented in the modern hospital, even under palliative care. A spiritual understanding of death does not permeate the psychology of caregiving in the hospital; rather, more frequently the culture attempts to distance the provider from the experience of dying. This is in part due to ignorance regarding the nature of death and what comes after. This is, again, a function of both lack of competence and the enforced professional neglect of the soul that comes from inability even to speculate.

Biomedicine refrains from speculation almost by necessity, because these domains of knowledge exceed medical education, training, and epistemology. It is therefore questionable whether these professions are entitled to demand "validation" of domains of knowledge beyond their ken or whether they might benefit from a more synthetic, integrative approach that, at the very least, contemplates other systems of world knowledge concerning the soul's journey prior to, during, and just after death. That reincarnation makes an appearance not only in Judaism (*gilgul*), Christianity (before the Nicean council), and even the foundations of Western philosophy (for example, Plato's notion of "transmigration of souls") suggests that medical education and training might fruitfully incorporate study of some of these systems. The key here is sufficient flexibility—coming from the regulatory values of integration and transformation—to consider these topics not as religious dogma but rather as a harvest of the collective experience of humanity, the common substratum of ancestral wisdom. Being curious about how these might enrich and inform modern scientific approaches to health care will broaden and enrich caregivers' approach to the dying. Notably, energy healing techniques may be, as mentioned, available to all health care providers, with limited training, and thereby provide a window into the neglected dimensions of the patient's soul.

Conclusion

Future medicine includes investigating potential contributions of energy healing to the dying process, since such investigation has the potential to transform the view of how the culture should handle death and dying. Of course, there remains a role for fraud control, quality assurance, and health care freedom. For example, if, in the guise of palliative care, a healer offers a dying patient a vial of "holy water" that is shown to contain toxic substances, the value of fraud control—and all the attendant legal consequences of such wrongful behavior—would come into play. The recognition of fraud, ego, and abuse of spiritual power remains an important correlate to the notion of expanding paradigms, consciousness, and models of treating the living and the dead.

Reproductive Technologies and Spiritual Technologies

Case 8A   Multiple Fetal Pregnancy "Reduction"

 In his declining years, Abraham prays for a miracle to help ease his wife's old age. God tells Abraham that his seventy-year-old wife, Sarah, will have at least six children: "Although you will be back with Me at that point, your wife will face ethical choices, and her soul will continue to grow during her remaining days on earth." Six months later, Abraham has passed. Thanks to a new "miracle" fertility drug, Sarah finds herself pregnant with sextuplets. Joyously, Sarah names the embryos: Isaac, Jacob, Noah, Moses, Elijah, and the youngest one after her beloved husband, Abraham. The doctor informs her, however, that because of her age, she can only bear *two* safely. Four must be sacrificed. "Sacrificed!" Sarah exclaims. "We prefer to say 'selectively terminated,'" the physician says, in a quiet voice. "After all, we are talking about pre-embryos."

(Abraham, standing around Sarah as a spirit guide, gently places his hand on her shoulder. He smiles, remembering God's words about giving Sarah a crash course in bioethics. The sixth level of Sarah's energy field glows with pink radiance. Her mind, though, is troubled.)

"But what do you mean?" Sarah asks. "Don't my future children have the right to live?"

The physician lowers her voice even further. "In our state, abortion is legal. In fact, the government will pay for your abortion prior to the conclusion of the third trimester. Fetuses are not considered 'persons' under the Fourteenth Amendment and therefore are not entitled to due process. Courts regard *potential beings* as having a status somewhere between *property* and *life*, deserving greater respect than accorded to human tissue but not the respect accorded to human persons."[1]

"*Potential* beings?" Sarah exclaims. "Do you mean Isaac, Jacob, Noah, Moses, Elijah, and Abraham?"

The doctor lowers her eyes. "I'm sorry," she says. "We must selectively terminate four of them."

"But which ones?" Sarah asks, thinking: *Must I sacrifice my own sons to appease God? How have I offended him? What sin must I deconstruct? Is there no act of mercy to heal the split—the blessing of pregnancy, the burden of sacrifice?*

The physician responds, "It is still problematic as to which particular fetuses should have their existences terminated."[2] She pauses, letting the words sink in. "The choice is up to you." She smiles gently, removing a set of instructions from her clipboard. "Our hospital therapeutics committee has enumerated criteria by which we are guided to decide. You can take this sheet home with you. As you'll see, the guiding star is safety. We eliminate—I mean *terminate*—the pre-embryos that are weakest and let the healthiest two children survive." She adds, "We do not discriminate based on gender, but this is not an issue in the case of your pre-embryos, as they are all boys."

"Safety?" Sarah asks, blinking rapidly. She thinks: *I remember the biblical story. Jacob and Esau struggled in utero. One got hold of the other's ankle and came out first. Extremely important in the days of primogeniture. What's going to happen in my womb? Are they already competing for oxygen, blood flow, nutrients . . . knowing that four will be sacrificed—terminated—so the others might live?*

"There's nothing more I can do," the physician concludes, wrapping up—she is behind on her HMO schedule and does not wish to be reprimanded yet again. "But I can refer you to our complementary medicine clinic; there is an acupuncturist you might consult. He has helped many women with fertility problems—a few needles, and they get pregnant. Maybe he'll have some advice for you." She makes a few notes on the computerized chart. "While you're there, we'll make sure you see the mind-body specialist; she is a rabbi, with training in pastoral counseling, hypnotherapy, shamanism, and energy healing. She might be able to help you make your decision."

Case 8B   Delivery

 "We know how much you love this child," the Beings said to the brother-in-law, "and how you have welcomed her into her physical embodiment on this plane." They stood around the hospital bed—his grandfathers, his deceased uncles, other ancestors, and still other unidentified beings—as she endured her next set of contractions. He could see them, although he was five hundred miles away. *Labor pains,* he thought, *are as old as the expulsion from Eden. Probably older.* He looked to the stars. *I wonder whether inducing labor will change the child's astrological forecast.* No worries—he had surrounded the child with mantras of protection. The moment his mother had called to say his sister-in-law's delivery was late, he had begun to chant. Medically, they were discussing a C-section. Telepathically, he was in unbroken contact with the whole situation.

"I want you to know," he said to the child, whom he could sense hovering around, "that you will be welcomed and loved in this incarnation. I will be here for you. You will be loved. May you be blessed with physical health and abundant spiritual gifts so that you will always know your secret closeness to God's heart."

He had invoked holy ones from every tradition: from Judaism, Adonai; from Christianity, Jesus; from Hinduism, Krishna, Rama, Shiva, and the Divine Mother; from Buddhism, Buddha; and also Kwan Yin, Confucius, and others, along with all the Archangels. Tears came: his arms were upraised, like those of Moses during a crucial biblical battle. Slowly they encircled the tender auras of his family and of the caregivers, and when his hands came together in *namaste*—the prayer position—the healing was complete. Then, arising, he found himself folded over his arms, which were outstretched as if holding a globe: he was holding the earth in a *mudra* (gesture) of compassion. His love for the child, for the earth, for his brother, for his family, merged into divine love for all children, all beings, the intergalactic family: he loved them as a mother could love, a divine mother, a mother of all beings. A divine mother archetype engulfed him with her compassion, with universal caring. He wept.

"She's going to deliver *today,*" his brother said.

"Your intent is strong," he replied.

"So," said his brother, "is the doctor's."
The radiant child emerged.

Case 8C   Pediatric Care

 Mary, a three-week-old baby, was born with a herniated diaphragm. The baby lay for months in intensive care, with seven tubes radiating from her body like spokes of a wheel and constant mechanical monitoring of her vital organs. Mary's mother stroked the baby's head tenderly, while the physician, in tandem with conventional monitoring and treatment, applied Reiki. The mother and healer formed a beautiful unit. Mary seemed to relax. The physician alternatively scanned the child's field and then made long brushing strokes on the child's energy field. She placed one hand over the area of the infant's lungs.

At one point, as the physician "ran energy," the child's level of oxygen intake began severely dropping. Mary's nostrils flared as she worked to consume more oxygen. The nurse, concerned, came by and muttered that the child was having "too much stimulation." The physician immediately backed away. She then let the mother know that she could "send good thoughts" from a distance. This seemed to resolve any apparent conflict between the biomechanical world of the nurse and the monitors and the world of subtle energies in which the physician was working. After the healing, the mother spoke with the physician. She said that initially she had held back emotionally from wishing Mary healing—not knowing whether her child would make it, not wanting her heart torn—but now felt optimistic that Mary was going to make it. Her husband now had also healed his heart and was preparing the child's room for her return from the hospital.

The physician saw a golden arc of light surrounding the fields of the instrumentation, the mother, and Mary. She had a vision of Mary in her twenties or thirties. She told the mother that she saw the child's "spirit" as strong and healthy and perceived with high sense perception (not medical training) that the lung would develop normally. Meanwhile, the oxygen intake remained stable. A few weeks later, Mary was strong enough to return home.

New Ideas and Values in Bioethics

As is discussed in the preceding chapter, the application of "ideas and values which have not heretofore formed a part of the essential framework upon which bioethics is founded" could change debates over fundamental bioethical questions.[3] Some of the major principles suggested as a starting point include the following:

1. that God or other supernatural agents may intervene to heal (even in apparently hopeless or futile situations); that there are instrumental relationships between the living and the dead; and that such relationships should be taken into account in deliberations at the beginning and at the end of life;
2. that knowledge may be gained by direct apprehension, through dreams, or by supernatural agency; and that such knowledge is a sound and reasonable basis for decision and action.

These principles represent a shift from the biological, physiological, and technological approach of biomedicine to a suggested synthesis of the material and spiritual. Such things as relationships between the living and the dead are posited to influence bioethical decisions, even though biomedicine might regard even the existence of life after death to be improvable speculation and hence inappropriate for bioethical consideration. The deep consideration of spiritual relationships and the dissolving of the veil between the so-called spiritual and material worlds will infuse bioethics with new vitality and allow additional realms of heart, mind, and spirit to enter discussion. This, in turn, may change the way bioethicists frame debate, or even the inner processes associated with such debate.

For example, conventional bioethical thinking on reproductive and other emerging technologies tends to emphasize, among other things, the relative legal interests of various parties. A particular issue that may arise is the conflict between legal rights of the mother and of the fetus when their medical needs collide. Similarly, legal debates over abortion have employed a "rights" analysis to determine the relative legal interests of the mother, the potential child, and the state. After all, it was in *Roe v. Wade* that the U.S. Supreme Court held that a fetus was not considered a "person" for purposes of entitlement to due process rights under the Fourteenth Amendment.[4] Although *Roe* did not grant the fetus Fourteenth Amendment rights per se, the opinion did hold that the state had a compelling interest in the potential life from the point of viability. Further, while subsequent cases—such as *Planned Parenthood of Southeastern Pennsylvania v. Casey*—placed less emphasis on "fundamental rights" and the "right to privacy," such cases retained the notion of balancing interests, including the woman's personal liberty interest in making a choice regarding carrying the fetus.[5]

Courts frequently rely on a balancing of interests in reproductive issues to fashion legal rules capable of deciding which party is entitled to have its way. For example, in *Davis v. Davis,* a case involving a dispute between a divorced husband and wife over seven stored, frozen embryos, the courts variously analyzed attempts to use property law, constitutional law, tort law, and contractual analysis in an attempt to determine which party should have control over disposition of the embryos.[6] Ultimately, the Tennessee Supreme Court decided to balance the parties' interests in the embryos and concluded that Mr. Davis's interest in avoiding parenthood had more weight than Mrs. Davis's interest in donating the embryos to a woman who would bear them. The court also noted that had the parties previously contractually decided on disposition of the embryos, such contractual agreement would control the dispute. The court further regarded the frozen embryos as having a status between "property" and "life."[7]

Such an analysis may be criticized on a variety of grounds, including the assumption that the right *not* to be a parent outweighs the interest in having the children be born. One may critique the way the court (1) chose the area of law that would control the case, (2) defined the interests to be balanced, and (3) weighed the interests it chose. Or one can shift the framework for the debate. While honoring the various needs of the parties, the court's balancing-of-interests analysis—like the "rights" approach—fails to address the essential question: *What is a human being along the full spectrum of consciousness, and how might legal rules account for a more expanded view of the consciousness embedded in being human?*

Such a question changes bioethical perspectives. It incorporates such premises as, for instance, the notion that relationships between living and dead (or not-yet-living) persons are important. It suggests that apprehension of such relationships might be gleaned through such therapies as hypnosis and guided imagery, homeopathy, and energy healing. It suggests that an entirely different framework could be added to conventional bioethical inquiry. This is quite different than relegating such inquiry to the realm of speculation or even incorporating these ideas conceptually, but only from the perspective of neutrally respecting others' belief systems.

Framing the question according to the notion of a human-energy-consciousness system becomes especially intriguing when one considers such emerging technologies as multifetal pregnancy reduction (raised in case 8A), in which the essential conflict is not between mother and fetus, mother and state, or wife and husband. Rather, here the conflict is one *between embryos*—in other words, between entities who are only considered to be *potential* lives: in the language of *Davis v. Davis*, only just more important than "property." Can such beings—or rather, *potential beings*—be said to have rights and interests and spirit wishes, or does legal analysis fail in the indeterminate zone between existence and potential existence?

As suggested, integrative health care and energy medicine may provide some novel ways of exploring ways of expanding jurisprudence, so as to reach a more expanded view of human consciousness and existence. One way to approach the question of what a human being is along the full spectrum of consciousness, and how legal rules might account for a more expanded view of the consciousness embedded in being human, involves comparing the court's analysis in *Davis v. Davis* with Maslow's hierarchy of personal needs and the hierarchy of regulatory needs outlined in chapter 3. Chart 17 presents one scenario for aligning predominant personal need, controlling regulatory value, dominant bioethical approach, and one's perspective on bioethical conflicts.

Again, chart 17 presents only an exploratory (and not definitive) framework to help move the conversation beyond such values as fraud control or even autonomy and health care freedom. Further, the chart (and the discussion following) do not purport to provide conclusive answers to such questions as whether such matters as abortion or stem cell research are "ethical" or "unethical." A more definitive framework might require parallel developments in disciplines such as biology and physics, as well as philosophy, sociology, and psychology, that would help broaden the way humanity understands different regions of consciousness and the advantages or disadvantages of relating to such realms in a particular way in a given circumstance. Ideally, though, such a preliminary framework can help tease out some of the implications of approaching emerging reproductive and other technologies from the perspective of self-actualization and human transformation.

In this framework, the physiological need drives a controlling regulatory value of fraud control, which in turn leads to a bioethical approach that is predominantly paternalistic and a view of conflict from the perspective of rights and interests. By and large, this is where regulatory and ethical analysis of issues such as multifetal pregnancy reduction (case 8A) began. It could be characterized as a "first-chakra" approach, the emphasis being on the physical body and the instinct for self-preservation. The debate pits mother against child, embryo against embryo, and tries to reconcile their relative desires. But it cannot account for subtle realities such as the potential psychospiritual dynamics between "potential beings." This point is illustrated in rather a tongue-in-cheek fashion by the mother's stream-of-consciousness inner monologue and by the physician's basis for decision making (in other words, her decision to "eliminate— . . . *terminate*—the pre-embryos that are weakest and let the healthiest two children survive").

Closely related is the second predominant personal need, that of safety. This need is often related not only to the first chakra—that of survival—but also to the second, that of emotional safety and sexual

CHART 17. Values and Bioethical Perspectives

Predominant Personal Need	Controlling Regulatory Value	Dominant Bioethical Approach	Regards Conflict as Involving
Physiological	Fraud control	Paternalistic	Rights and interests
Safety	Quality assurance	Structural	Social choices
Belongingness and love	Health care freedom	Libertarian	Personal choice
Esteem	Functional integration	Pragmatic	Human relationship
Self-actualization	Transformation	Transcendent	Relationship to God

gratification. This need drives the regulatory value of quality assurance, in which the dominant bioethical approach is structuring relationships so as to maximize appropriate social choices. In case 8A, this approach is satisfied by recommending access to a variety of appropriately credentialed health care providers (the acupuncturist and the mind-body specialist with training in pastoral counseling, hypnotherapy, shamanism, and energy healing).

The regulatory value of health care freedom, driven by the third predominant personal need—the need for belongingness and love—suggests a more libertarian approach to bioethics, in which autonomy and the individual's personal choice are most important. For example, this approach would place greater emphasis on Sarah's ability to choose the wisest course of action in case 8A; this accords with the contractual approach suggested in *Davis v. Davis*—namely, that in the future, these disputes will be resolved by prior agreement between the relevant parties. The third chakra relates to the intellect and also to one's place in the universe and personal boundaries with others. Intellect (rationality) dominates much contemporary bioethical analysis, and contract law concerns itself with using intellect to arrange personal boundaries between potential disputants. The numerous debates concerning the form and scope of informed-consent protection for human subjects involved in such related issues as human-embryo research also fall within this sphere: such guidelines reflect concern for patient choice and autonomy, issues that resonate with the relationship boundaries between persons and the relationship boundaries between individuals and institutions.[8]

Although love is a component of Maslow's third personal need, the notion of esteem suggests a fuller gateway to the heart, the region of the fourth chakra in the energy healing system outlined in chapter 4. The dominant bioethical approach is pragmatic, but concerns itself with ordering human relationships according to the felt perception of connectedness between individuals. Such an approach enables the experience of love to flow from contemplation of which embryos, for example, should be terminated, and of the larger implications of use of this technology for the embryos' being as well as the mother's. For instance, in recent congressional testimony concerning stem cell research, the father of twins conceived through in vitro fertilization and adopted when they were embryos held the toddlers in his arms and asked lawmakers, "Which one of my children would you kill?"[9]

Although the reference to killing does not resonate with love, the statement reflects a felt perception of connectedness even with life forms at a level of evolution many would consider only appropriate for scientific research.

Finally, the values of self-actualization and transformation express a transcendent approach to ethical analysis, ultimately implicating the individual's relationship to the divine. In other words, while categories of "ethical" and "unethical" reflect an either/or analysis (black-and-white decision making), the transcendental approach may reflect an underlying unification that allows both perspectives to be held in harmony. Such an approach also potentially may evoke the development of resolution that incorporates all the chakras and levels of the human energy field—in other words, the full range of human wisdom within the circle of cosmic unity. As one example, the biblical allusions in Sarah's inner monologue suggest that ultimately, the bioethical decision is a function of her relationship with God, the way she experiences that relationship, and the presence of Spirit in the interaction between Sarah and her potential children. That relationship is the heart of all decision making; it cannot be eroded or eradicated by reliance on rights, interests, or intellectual criteria. By considering that relationship at the heart of decision making, Sarah invokes the ultimate ground of being, as well as her reason and emotion.

This is not to say that fundamentalist religious perspectives should control resolution of bioethical issues but rather that taking spiritual understandings seriously can infuse bioethical issues with new light. Presently, in bioethics, religious preferences are respected *apart* from content; once preferences are labeled "religious," they are given deference only insofar as respecting them manifests respect for personal choices (in other words, the value of autonomy). Further, if they conflict with medical priorities, such preferences frequently are not given recognition. In case 8A, although spiritual values in this context do not necessarily implicate religious preferences, they do suggest that spiritual realities underlie medical ones. Even if safety and efficacy are assured, emerging technologies leave unresolved spiritual issues, requiring a more expanded framework that takes into account the role of consciousness in healing.

This theme is picked up in case 8B, in which the possibility of a C-section ushers in the drawing-down of spiritual realities to facilitate physical processes. Indeed, if the human energy field is a reality, then a physical procedure (such as the C-section) will have ripple effects on other levels of the field, and the tearing of the flesh will be mirrored in a tearing of the second chakra and the first layer of the human energy field, which is associated with surgery and physical trauma. Healing at these levels of consciousness therefore would have to accompany physical healing. Other levels of the human energy field also may be implicated, such as the fifth (in which the energetic template for physical reality is said to reside), the sixth (in which angelic entities are said to reside or be contained), and the seventh (in which human connection to the cosmos is said to be made manifest).[10]

Turning to the higher levels of the field suggests that the role of energy therapies in bioethics is partly redemptive, in the sense of reconciling earth and heaven and thus uniting physical and spiritual realities, ideally in beneficent ways. In Jewish mysticism, this process is known as *tikkun olam*—literally, the "correction" of the world. Such correction involves reaching to other worlds, other dimensions, for spiritual assistance with material realities. Thus, though rife with potential for shadow manifestations, energetic modalities also express the hope of healing the darker reaches of human nature and of letting in the light.

Emerging Technologies

Emerging technologies present an opportunity for deeper contemplation of the meaning of what it is to be a human being and of the role of the awareness of health and healing in human transformation. For example, bioethical issues associated with the human genome project have brought to the fore not only new issues regarding privacy and confidentiality but also the role of the state in regulating the frontiers of human knowledge. Similarly, cloning raises questions tied to the essential identity of a human being.[11] Likewise, the advent of prenatal screening and diagnosis has raised questions regarding the limits of so-called selective abortion and has triggered debate about the scope of allowable human choice in deciding whether (or which) prospective children should live.[12] Ethical debates to date have focused around competing dualistic perspectives (for example, the "right to life" versus "pro-choice" approaches), but have failed to resolve more fundamental issues such as the assumption, for example, that fetuses diagnosed with severe disabilities should be terminated because "life with a disability is not worthwhile and is primarily a source of suffering."[13]

The question of consciousness threads, almost invisibly, throughout these debates. For example, why does a body house consciousness, and what bioethical choices reflect the evolution of all consciousness associated with that body? Does the suffering behind disability have a spiritual purpose, and does it invoke relationships between material and spiritual agencies? Does the soul of the child hover around the parents prior to incarnation, and is the not-yet-incarnated being somehow a part of the process of decision making?[14]

Other new technologies also suggest that questions concerning the nature of being and the boundaries between embodied, human existence and disincarnate, spiritual existence permeate a new bioethical inquiry. For example, the possibility of implanted brain chips will change the way the self is viewed. Such implanted chips will allow persons not only to fuse mind with technology but also to connect minds directly via implants. In this way, the future experience of personhood itself could be different. As one author suggests:

> If people are actually connected via their brains, the boundaries between self and community will be considerably diminished . . . [and] the pressures to act as part of the whole, as a "collective consciousness," rather than as an isolated individual would be increased. The sense of self as a unique and isolated individual might be changed . . . [and this] could change our psychic state and understanding of what it means to be human.[15]

Mystical traditions in many religions have spoken of a unifying ground of being underlying all experience and of the human ego as creating an artificial boundary between the individual personality and the rest of creation. The unifying ground of being has been articulated as based in a state of cosmic, unconditional love for all things. When minds fuse, the experience of the self may differ from that classically experienced as the individual. In other words, individuation and transcendence potentially constitute states of being from which future perspectives on ethical/unethical may emerge. By changing perceptions of the self, such future technologies suggest the limitations of a bioethical analysis that relies on analytical reasoning and point to a bioethics less dependent on the strictures of philosophy and logical analysis and more closely tied to the human heart and universal experiences of spirit.

Thus, from the regulatory value of human transformation, emerging technologies call for a bioethics connected to the principle of divine love for all creation, as expressed by mystical traditions. From this perspective, the consciousness of fetuses, embryos, animals, ants, tissue, and even planetary bodies and cells makes a difference; even embryonic stem cells may have some form of consciousness, though not the kind of consciousness we typically identify as human.[16] To the mystics of many traditions, everything is God or part of God; to the healer, everything carries consciousness, even if the object is nonhuman, inanimate, or cannot articulate in human language, solve mathematical equations, or elect politicians. At the very least, the nature of consciousness and its evolution deserves consideration, together with rights, liberties, and legal interests, in any approach by future medicine to bioethical norms.

The Bridge of Sentience

Again, while the exact contours of such a new approach cannot yet be precisely mapped, the importance and pervasive nature of consciousness form an important bridge from contemporary bioethics to something new. The focus on consciousness might change, for example, the way that physician-assisted suicide is discussed, since death—from a transformational perspective—carries physical and spiritual connotations; or the way research involving fetuses, anencephalic infants, and animals is regarded, since at present most approaches to measuring moral status in these situations are derived from scientific knowledge or rational approaches.[17]

At the very least, the notion of insentience often ascribed to such aspects of the creation could be revisited. Recognition of sentience potentially extinguishes the fallibility of duality. Such a recognition might, in turn, lead to new perspectives on the notion of ahimsa—nonviolence—as a broader statement of the value of nonmaleficence and have a variety of implications for different bioethical issues. Again, at the center of any such redirection for bioethics are explorations of human consciousness—its reach and grasp and the extent to which it embraces nonphysical realms.

Taking abortion as an example of a bioethical issue that has not been satisfactorily resolved through the rational process, a consciousness of the human energy field may offer useful perspectives. For instance, some healers have had experiences with nonphysical beings, including embryos and parts of embryos—such as the experience of pulling aborted fetuses out of the client's energy field.[18] The healing here includes helping the client "process" the experience in terms of unfinished emotional business between the mother and the fetus. There is also healing for the being that has temporarily approached incarnation through physically dwelling in the mother's womb. By lifting out the energetic remnant of consciousness with love and sending the being to the higher planes for healing and by facilitating unfinished grieving between all beings (including those in physical bodies and those in spirit bodies), the healing connects multiple planes of existence. Healing here takes on a different meaning than committing on an intellectual level to whether the specific surgical procedure at issue (for example, abortion) is ethical or unethical. Healing involves the whole being, including all dissociated parts.

Anecdotal reports of connections between beings in different realms of consciousness challenge conventional care to expand on a variety of levels, whether the question is abortion, physician-assisted suicide, or organ transplantation.[19] Such connections tend to be experienced through energy healing, because healers connect consciousness and energy, sometimes using touch and at other times using simply the awareness of healing and transformation. The experience of this world as multidimensional—as operating simultaneously in several planes— is found in the chakra system and the human energy field, as articulated in chapter 4. It also embodies the wisdom of several world religious traditions. For example, in Tibetan Buddhism, the Medicine Buddha provides a vision of the world in which everything in nature functions as medicine; in indigenous Native American traditions, even rocks and trees and hawks and eagles may have messages for the medicine person. The notion that everything has consciousness lends a different slant to many debates, since energy healing suggests that by "connecting energetically" with the client's biofield, the healer may be able to access material in a way not necessarily available to contemporary medical or psychotherapeutic processes.

As another example of new approaches to bioethics in future medicine, the question of animal consciousness also may benefit from perspectives of energy healing. This issue perhaps rivals contemporary understanding of embryonic consciousness in reflecting conventional medicine's frustration with finding objective criteria to measure the awareness of self. Are animals aware of health, healing, and their own spiritual development in relation to the human realm?

One emerging issue in the arena of animal consciousness is the appropriateness of "species impartiality"—in other words, the question of whether all sentient animal species should be regarded as having "equal" standing. For example, the question goes, if human patients could benefit from transplants of baboon organs, would it be morally acceptable to sacrifice live baboons for fit, human beneficiaries of baboon livers?[20] One answer bioethicists have given to this dilemma is that humans are entitled to "greater respect" because humans differ from animals in at least five important respects: (1) the development of languages in which meanings are understood and communicated, (2) the presence of historical consciousness, (3) the construction of culture involving use of materials manipulated in a symbolic fashion, (4) self-consciousness (awareness of oneself as a self), and (5) the quest for meaning.[21] Therefore—the argument goes—the suggested sacrifice would be morally acceptable.

Such rationally based distinctions, while helpful analytically, are indefensible from the perspective of energy healing. From the perspective of the human energy field (and high sense perception), energetic connections with animals are possible as one aspect of experiencing different levels of nonordinary reality in the higher levels of the field. Some energy healers would experience the soul of a cat, the emotions of a tiger, the awareness of a horse. They would perceive the scintillating energy field of a pet and discern which chakras and levels of the energy field were more or less active (depending on what the pet was experiencing); they would connect kinesthetically with the animal's experience. An analytical distinction concerning equality would be less meaningful than a transformative, experiential attempt to understand and discern the animal's consciousness and experience. Even analytically—based on such an experience—healers likely would challenge the notion that animals lack self-consciousness and the quest for meaning.

The experiential component of connecting one's consciousness with that of an animal reflects the theological debate in many religious traditions as to whether animals, as well as humans, have souls. Although some traditions argue that the soul is unique to humans, the debate suggests that a variety of perspectives exists on the extent to which the animal has a purpose, destiny, inner awareness, and other attributes of a spiritual life. This may be true even though animals do not attend religious worship in the same buildings as humans (except, in some urban settings, in churches commemorating the practices of St. Francis of Assisi). Even on an analytical level, then, healers also likely would challenge the notion that animals do not construct a culture using materials manipulated in a symbolic fashion—witness, for example, the highly complex and symbolic design of the spider's web. Healers would argue that animal consciousness is not readily understood by human instrumentation but that the apparatus of perception may result in new dimensions of understanding.

The dimensions of consciousness that individuals trained in energy healing can experience—whether they are physicians, nurses, acupuncturists, or individuals other than health care professionals—admittedly are subjective, anecdotal, and not verifiable by the tools of contemporary science. But healers would argue that these realms nonetheless are worthy of exploration—through personal journeys of consciousness. By connecting to the animal's energy field kinesthetically, visually, or through auditory high sense perception, the individual may experience the nature and quality of that contact in a way that is radically different than any preconceived mental abstraction. A collective exploration of that experience within the bioethical community may lead to different conclusions regarding animal welfare than even the most carefully constructed theory. Again, such experience might put the suffering of a live (or even deceased) animal in a different light than a simple comparison of the perceived evolution of humans and animals using such rational criteria as, say, the "construction of a culture."

This, perhaps, is one of the ultimate contributions of future medicine: to stimulate a new awareness of health and healing in human transformation so as to accelerate the evolution of human consciousness. By stimulating consciousness in this way, energy healing purports to offer a set of "spiritual technologies": the variety of modes of being aimed at increasing content and flow of psychospiritual energies in the subtle bodies. Thus, while the emergence of new *physical* technologies continually challenges contemporary perspectives on the interface between matter and spirit and what it means to be a human being, correspondingly, energy healing offers to open doorways to the emergence of spiritual technologies that also challenge contemporary notions of heart, health, and soul.

Healing the Shame of Being

The evolution of consciousness contains possibilities for constriction and limitation, as well as for expansion and wholeness. One of the barriers to a fuller comprehension of the implications of emerging material (and spiritual) technologies is the limitation that conventional culture imposes on creative thinking in biomedicine and bioethics by shaming those whose world perspectives challenge existing psychic, as well as scientific, paradigms. Thomas Kuhn notes that those who present new scientific paradigms at first are dismissed, excluded from the mainstream, and marginalized.[22] Kuhn offers the insight that paradigms shift by revolution, not by accretion, since those committed to current paradigms stifle or attempt to smother those whose ideas threaten the foundational order.[23] But this represents more than a denial of new ways to see reality: the systematic exclusion of perspectives opposed to the dominant ideology also imposes a kind of mind control on the culture, a control that enforces conformity and stifles innovation. This mind control is the shame of being.

The shame of being occurs not only through the contours of permissible medical debate but also through the funneling effect of some regulatory action—for example, much historical prosecution of different kinds of healers for the unlicensed practice of medicine and discipline of physicians merely for offering therapies not accepted by conventional medicine (such as homeopathy).[24] These efforts arguably go beyond fraud control, in reflecting a stifling of creative emergence, in stultifying delivery of health care services that appear to oppose dominant paradigms.[25]

The negative bias against those whose perspective threatens the foundational order similarly is reflected in present rules promulgated by some state medical boards that are grappling with regulation of complementary and integrative medical therapies. Some of these medical boards divide complementary and integrative medicine into three categories: "invalidated," "nonvalidated," and "validated."[26] Under "invalidated" are included therapies that "have neither a proven nor any scientific basis for any health benefit." In Kentucky, "invalidated" therapies also include any therapy that:

1. is implausible on a priori grounds (because its implied mechanisms or putative effects contradict well-established laws, principles, or empirical findings in physics, chemistry, or biology);
2. lacks a scientifically acceptable rationale of its own;
3. has insufficient supporting evidence derived from adequately controlled outcome research; and
4. has failed in well-controlled studies done by impartial evaluations and has been unable to rule out competing explanations for why it might seem to work in controlled settings.

The board thus circumscribes the parameters of acceptable reality and determines that practice of a therapy that could be deemed "implausible" within this limited definition could be subject to persecution. Yet as noted, the "implied mechanisms or putative effects" of energy healing—like those of homeopathy—"contradict well established laws, principles, or empirical findings in physics, chemistry, or biology." Under this logic, a physician who incorporates any aspect of energy healing might be subject to discipline, even if no harm was done to the patient and even if the patient benefited. Loss of licensure could result.

This same shame of being also taints both reporting and validation of spiritual experiences by patients (such as the phenomena associated with near-death experiences) and use of spiritual technologies in health care. For example, many patients in the dying process have had the experience of visitations by beings from the "other side," such as departed relatives, ancestors, and spiritual teachers. Typically, caregivers take these experiences in and of themselves as delusional, because scientific medicine provides no "plausible" explanation other than the dying patient's fancy or fantasy (in other words, wish-fulfillment). Indeed, the patient's perception of a deceased relative often is explained as a "manifestation of grief," with no authority of its own.[27] Thus, where the patient, a widow, is experiencing the presence of her husband, conventional wisdom advises the physician to "reassur[e]" her that this "sensation . . . is normal and does not indicate a psychiatric illness, as long as it is not disturbing to her."[28]

Even the mental health care professions have had no difficulty feeding into a culture of negative bias against approaches based on connections between matter and spirit. Some scholars have observed the negative bias in psychiatry against spirituality. For example, in *Inquiries in Bioethics*, Steven G. Post reflects on the use of psychiatric diagnoses to dismiss, marginalize, or shame the use of spiritual technologies. Commenting on the diagnostic category of "negative religious bias" in the DSM-III-R, Post remarks:

> An unnecessary accumulation of religious examples of pathology in the glossary gives the impression that religion is indicative of illness. The examples are presented under "catatonic posturing," "delusion," "delusion of being controlled," "delusion (grandiose)," "hallucination (tactile)," "illogical thinking," "incoherence," "magical thinking," "mood-congruent psychotic features," "mood-incongruent psychotic features," and "poverty of content of speech."[29]

Post observes that the glossary lists "special relationship to a deity" as an example of a "mood-congruent psychotic [feature]."[30] In this way, "suspicion is cast upon persons who feel a proximity to God or the gods."[31]

As Post's analysis suggests, the negative bias against spirituality in psychiatry could make the entire profession of energy healing suspect. After all, healers purport to "channel" universal energy (in other words, *chi*) through their hands or intentionality to help clients heal. They "hear voices" and witness realities that are not evident to those who (in healers' terms) have not stretched their consciousness of the higher levels of the energy field. In having such exclusive experiences (as compared with common, consensus reality), healers thus may tend to feel a "special relationship" to God or the gods, since they are more easily able to access and harness cosmic forces for healing purposes.

Similarly, when the healer's hands grow warm, his or her fingers tingle, or the patient otherwise "obtains the *chi*," the healer and patient know that the healer has accessed a connection to the divine and that healing is present. This again can appear to manifest the awareness of a "special relationship" with the deity. From the limited perspective of fraud control, healers can appear as charlatans or mad persons, with diagnostically categorizable delusions and fantasies. From the perspective of transformation, healers are potentiating human experience of the numinous—and that experience is accessible to all.

Thus, in case 8B, the individual who prays for the safe emergence of a child from the womb could be accused of "magical thinking" if such an individual believed that his or her thoughts, intentionality, and consciousness affected delivery. But from the perspective articulated at the beginning of this chapter, relationships between the living and the preborn also might be important and considered as living and real. One can frame the contradictions between the psychiatric perspective criticized by Post and the healer's perspective through a series of rhetorical questions. Would it be delusional if the individual in case 8B visualized himself as a tiny angel accompanying the homunculus on its journey inside the maternal body and spoke healing prayers to the tiny being, encouraging its assimilation onto the earth plane? Yet would such a thought be any more delusional than praying the Rosary, within the Catholic tradition, and asking Mary to bless the infant? Or would it be more delusional than reciting prayers in a temple or mosque and trusting the process to the divine? Does prayer become labeled as psychopathological merely when articulated in one less-familiar metaphor rather than within the "tenets of an accepted religious tradition"?[32] Are novel modern beliefs more subject to ridicule than those of conventional religions? And how do individuals within medical institutions, committed to scientific rules of evidence, reconcile those principles with the proof of the heart they may adopt in their personal religious practice? Is intuition inherently suspect? Should it be labeled and dismissed as "superstition"? Or is atheism a requirement and correlative of belief in the scientific method?

These provocative questions are aimed to stretch the canvass of bioethical debate. They are not meant to replace one paradigm with another, to substitute one oppressive fundamentalism for another, or to exchange scientific control with religious hegemony. Further, the prospect of delusion, fantasy, and countertransference in the practice of energy healing modalities is acknowledged as real; concern for these shadow aspects of the healer underlies the discussion of fraud, ego, and abuse of spiritual power in chapter 6. Pathology is sometimes pathology. Shadow is not, however, the whole phenomenon. Often "pathology" is only a cultural label for conceptualizations the culture regards as deviant or dangerous and finds threatening.

What the culture requires in extending bioethical metaphors is not a new scientific paradigm nor even a new religious model, but rather psychic boundary-stretching. The mind and heart have to be stretched to incorporate some of the perspectives presented in this book. As chapter 1 suggests, evaluating such matters as nonmaleficence with the same tools that created the concept will not yield any radically new surprises when studying the human condition. In a larger sense, this means that scientific evidence has its place and yet does not control the bioethical debate. For instance, "proof" that Therapeutic Touch "works" will not in itself change consciousness; indeed, as suggested, to require this creates a dualistic, black-and-white, yes-or-no approach to a much more complex phenomenon. Conversation from the intellect, infused with passion from the emotions, does not in itself accelerate the evolution of consciousness. What does change consciousness is an experience of consciousness itself.

The regulatory perspectives of integration and transformation explicitly challenge the mind-set underlying the shame of being and provide antidotes to regulatory perspectives limited to such notions as fraud control. These concepts allow the heart and mind to stretch to new possibilities. But negative bias persists. Post, for example, states that the definition of "magical thinking" reflects possible negative bias against spiritual perspectives and thus permeates (and taints) any effort within psychiatry to understand the spiritual realms. He quotes the DSM-III-R's definition in full:

The person believes that his or her thoughts, words, or actions might, or will in some manner, cause or prevent a specific outcome in some way that defies the normal laws of cause and effect. Example: A man believed that if he said a specific prayer three times each night, his mother's death might be prevented indefinitely: a mother believed that if she had an angry thought, her child would become ill.

Magical thinking may be part of ideas of reference or may reach delusional proportions when the person maintains a firm conviction about the belief despite evidence to the contrary.

   Magical thinking is seen in children, in primitive cultures, and in
Schizophrenic Personality Disorder, Schizophrenia, and Obsessive
Compulsive Disorder.[33]

   Post's critique is instructive: using the logic articulated in the
DSM-III-R (and in any subsequent edition incorporating these views),
"magical thinking" *is* a characteristic of healers and indeed could be
viewed as one of the bases for energy healing. In other words, the application of intentionality and consciousness to healing reflects a belief
that "thoughts, words, or actions might, or will in some manner, cause
or prevent a specific outcome in some way that defies the normal laws
of cause and effect." In fact, part of the definition of energy healing concerns the attempt to use the mind and being to change physical reality.
Since the efficacy of energy healing remains, to date, largely elusive,
this effort could be said to defy normal physical laws as presently
understood. Hence, once again, according to psychiatric convention,
individuals engaging in energy healing are unequivocally delusional.
Even without such increasingly provocative and "irrational" (or "illog-
ical") processes as auditory high sense perception ("hearing voices")
and visual high sense perception (seeing things that "aren't there"), the
label of "magical thinking" condemns energy healing to the unsalvage-
able fringe.

   Yet even apart from energy healing, the practice of talking to God,
and of hearing God internally respond, is an integral part of much religious practice in many traditions. Prayer thus itself invokes a possible
label of delusion. Indeed, Post observes that the DSM's definition of
magical thinking is problematic because it puts *prayer* in the context of
"magical thinking." Prayer violates "what might be generally termed
the 'reality principle' as the empirical tradition of secular psychiatry
defines it."[34] Post also observes that in many traditions, prayers are said
in repetition—which makes them suspect as fetishistic; further, because
the DSM "omits any reference to the possibility of sane prayer," it makes
prayer itself suspect as indicative of psychopathology.[35]

   Post's critique generalizes the attack against energy healing to an
attack against spiritual practice itself. He notes that it is the very nature
of religious belief to include faith despite doubt, including lack of evidence, and that therefore the DSM's definitions are problematic.[36] He
goes on to critique the DSM's association between individuals who pray
and children or "primitive" peoples as "derogatory," in that it infan-

tilizes and ridicules religious persons; Post suggests that the DSM's perspective may be influenced by the fact that according to one formal survey, only 40 percent of psychiatrists professed a belief in God.[37]

Post accuses the DSM-III-R of "insensitivity . . . and tastelessness" when the only example it provides of "catatonic posturing" is the patient who "may stand with arms outstretched as if he were Jesus on the cross."[38] Yet, he observes, many religious traditions advocate use of postures to stimulate consciousness. From a transformational perspective, psychiatry cannot fully assess what psychospiritual benefits might accrue from trance states, including a behavioral "imitation of Christ" at the moment of crucifixion. Such practices are shameful, however, in a paradigm that labels them a priori insane. As suggested, one's predominant personal need and individual philosophy may play a role in the cosmology one adopts professionally: a psychiatrist committed to self-actualization may view "magical thinking" differently than one, for example, operating solely on the level of fraud control or quality assurance. A DSM committed to fraud control would (and clearly does) view such practices as psychopathological.

Post provocatively concludes that in labeling religious belief and practices as psychopathological and suspect, much of the terminology of the DSM may offend the First Amendment's protection for the free exercise of religion.[39] Whether or not prevailing psychiatric models constitute an actual constitutional violation of rights, such models do infringe on the ability of both health care providers and patients to explore territories of consciousness that conventional medicine has tended to stifle or suppress. These models suggest a tendency to label many energy healing practices as dysfunctional, detrimental, and potentially indicative of mental illness. In this way, rather than opening the profession to new ideas and considerations concerning health and healing, conventional psychiatric labels limit human knowledge; they presently thus impose the shame of being.

Healing Relational Cords

One of the emerging spiritual technologies in energy healing that has potential implications for reproductive and other technologies is the notion of healing "relational cords." From the healer's perspective, relational cords are lines of energy that flow between beings; such cords flow between beings whether these beings are living in the physical body, are deceased, or are living in other realms of existence in spiritual bodies.

Relational cords, according to healers, are multifaceted. Barbara Brennan suggests that human beings have at least five major types of relational cords:

1. soul cords to God;
2. cords from past life experiences, on earth and elsewhere in the universe;
3. genetic cords to our birth parents;
4. relationship cords to our birth parents; and
5. relationship cords to other human beings.[40]

Although this typology comes from high sense perception and lacks the kind of scientific validation that would make it more universally acceptable, it does provide a new way of looking at common bioethical issues, including those surrounding reproductive technologies. For example, the notion of healing of relational cords between persons and pre-embryos suggests new frameworks for considering such bioethical issues as counseling mothers regarding multifetal pregnancy reduction. Brennan has suggested that relationship cords develop between the mother and the child prior to incarnation and that the mother's ability to connect and sustain such cords, from the center of her heart chakra, is a factor in her physical ability to achieve pregnancy; on the other hand, a blockage in the heart (due to unhealed emotional wounds) may prevent such a connection.[41] Thus, sidestepping for the moment the legal status of potential beings, new understandings on the level at which the consciousness of such beings *exists* might change psychotherapeutic and medical approaches to these kind of procedures. Some of these possibilities are raised in case 8A.

Similarly, awareness of such relational cords—if they exist—might affect medical practice and health care policy surrounding birthing—incarnation. To date, much debate has focused on the value of safety in the birth process—for example, in legislation and legal rules to allocate roles among physicians, nurse-midwives, and individuals trained to assist in the birth process. A separate question, however, is whether the use of intentionality and consciousness to create a sacred space for the birth process would generate compassion, calm, centeredness, and the equivalent of a temple environment for birth in the modern hospital. If energy fields exist around humans in utero as well as at birth, then there may be merit to the notion of "sending positive, healing energy" to beings as they begin incarnation. This would change procedures in the delivery room—for example, whether and what kind of music is played; who may be in attendance; what happens to the infant immediately after birth (for example, whether it is immediately weighed and put in a cart or left for some time on the mother's heart).

Modern technology doubtless produces a different environment for the incoming soul than childbirth has throughout human history; even if birth has become medically safer, the spiritual experience of birth probably is different than it was a hundred years ago. Certainly the profession of midwifery represents an attempt to reclaim the spiritual components of the birth process and prevent it from being an excessively medicalized experience.

One healer reports:

> One practice in particular, that of anesthetizing mothers to ease their pain, has had repercussions for their babies. In my journeys I have seen that children whose mothers were drugged during labor often came into the world disoriented. In working with one man, I saw in my journey that his soul had floated away like a balloon at the time of his birth. Throughout his life he had experienced a debilitating sense of disorientation.[42]

One can only speculate as to the effect of healing at birth on future crime statistics.

Another healer reports on the effect of prebirth events on human consciousness and the importance of healing those relationships to alleviating present conditions:

> Pedra had smoked her whole life and was suffering from a "smokers' cough." When the healing began, she accessed an emotional reservoir of guilt she had carried since birth, when her twin sister died. Pedra felt "not good enough" and used smoking to fill the hole she felt in her chest. During the healing, Pedra recognized the wound and let go of the feelings. Her field was brighter, more charged, and the heart chakra was balanced. She had dealt with these feelings before in psychotherapy, but energy work helped

charge and balance the chakras and take her more deeply into the emotional experience.

In case 8B, healing began at the prebirth phase: the being was seen as having a decision to make regarding the choice of incarnation or perhaps regarding the amount of struggle necessary to achieve incarnation. This relates to the notion of relational cords between beings on both sides of incarnation: one incarnate, the other about to incarnate. Again, in Bonnie O'Connor's language, the model incorporates relationships between the living and the not-yet-living, with dreams or direct apprehension providing one means of communicating and navigating such relationships.

In fact, the prebirth phase may be viewed as the state of consciousness of the soul in a *bardo* state, somewhat analogous to the postdeath experience discussed in the previous chapter. Healers helping those being born (and those giving birth) might have analogous roles to those suggested in the previous chapter for healers working with the dying. For example, helping to incarnate beings may enable the healer to project warmth, comfort, caring, and other such qualities both to the infant and to the mother and thus to create a spiral of spiritual energy that lifts the incarnating soul out of the bewildering, technological aspects of modern delivery.

Ideally, mother and infant will receive these healing energies. Certainly, the infant could have a different initial experience of human consciousness than in a technological realm alone. It is known that the baby is much more sensitive than adults to inner worlds and to immediate sense-feelings—for example, to the experience of comfort from the mother's heartbeat. According to Brennan, the child's chakras are smaller and less developed than the adult's; during infancy, the child's crown chakra is wide open, connecting to spirit realms, while the root chakra, the earth connection, is a narrow funnel, as the being has not yet grounded the experience of consciousness in the earth plane.[43] Thus, infants, like animals (who also do not have significant mental clutter in the way of receiving spiritual energy), by and large have intact connections to spirit realms and thus are uniquely receptive to the experience of energy healing.[44] This is only one possible extension of the ideas that spiritual technologies might contribute to conventional modes of care and ethical thought.

Conclusion

Energy healing offers a number of possibilities for emerging reproductive and other technologies. While from the perspective of contemporary, conventional care, such possibilities might appear startling or even implausible, the attempt to stretch prevailing models of thought may identify resistances that signify cultural bias or a narrower view of consciousness than adopted by other cultures. To the extent energy healing accelerates awareness of subtle realms and such awareness may be helpful in clinical care, the ideas and experiences presented by energy healing modalities offer the hope of new visions for care, evolvement, and the awareness of health and healing in human transformation.

Conclusion

Integrated Awareness

 The power to bless and the power to curse: the same energy can be used for creation or destruction. *I may be a healer, but I am still on the soul's journey.* Is falling off center not universal? Did Jesus not weep in the garden of Gethsemane, and did he not ask, "Father, why have you forsaken me?" When they spat on him and the crown of thorns dug into his skull, did he not bless them and pray for them and ask God to forgive them? Did he not love them with all his heart and tell the Devil to piss off? Yet when he was scared, did he not sweat blood? Is not the "dark night of the soul" a companion even to mystics and saints?

I look into people's eyes; I see their past lives. This woman, a monk; that child, a scholar; that man, a beggar; that homeless person, a king. Wherever I look, I see the soul. The images and impressions float through my consciousness. I see the heart; it is partly open and needs God's love. I see the third eye, the scope of sight, the breadth of awakening. I see the second chakra, the issues with money, sexuality, and power. I see the cords running from the temples to other realms of consciousness. I see the guides behind them, the guardians, angels, and relatives, companions on the journey.

"And what do you do for a living?" she asked.

He was attending a cocktail party at a museum. The somber, eighteenth-century portraits of dying Christs hung mournfully as he listened to conversation in the presence of iconography. And yet these paintings had graced many dining room tables over the centuries, witness to family crises as well as celebrations. He stood before a statue of Kwan Yin, the Chinese Buddha of compassion. Silently, he offered salutations to the feminine principle of the cosmos, felt her sweet energy penetrate his field. Thoughts came. *There are two ways to visit a museum: one is to look at a statue and examine it, in the objective, scientific sense of Western medicine; the other is to merge with the consciousness that made the statue, that expresses itself through the sculpted.*

"I work with securities," he finally said.

"Emotional?" she asked.

"No. Financial."

Idolatry. My religion admonishes not to worship stone or wood, yet it is the consciousness expressing through the stone and wood that I worship, the same consciousness that peers through my eyes and those of everyone else. He waved at Kwan Yin.

"What do you think of the statue?" he asked the woman.

Without waiting for the woman's response, the statue replied: "*The power of spiritual energy mirrored through the human psyche strikes me as profoundly complicated and misunderstood. Religious doctrines control the minds of many on this plane, yet an openness to energetic perception creates bridges to the fundamental truths behind the doctrines, to the unity conscious-ness behind the labels and identification of a religion, to the felt reality of the Godhead even within objects one culture might proclaim as idols and another might revere.*"

The woman in human form smiled at him. "I like it," she said.

He found himself in two conversations, one verbal to a woman in form and the other telepathic to a woman in spirit. In unity conscious-ness, the two interpenetrated, yet they were separate beings occupying different dimensions of existence.

"Yes," he said, "isn't she lovely?"

The Future of the Future

Future medicine will mean that health care providers and governments internationally collaborate to synthesize technological medicine with different healing systems and traditions from across the globe and to more deeply incorporate spirituality across a range of traditions in the care for human health. Such a synthesis has not yet fully occurred and indeed today is marked by ideological battles in legal, medical and sci-entific, and cultural communities. Nonetheless, with increasing inte-gration of systems of knowledge and cultures, with interpenetration of ancient wisdom and modern know-how, with blending of cultures and viewpoints within the "global village," and with the erosion of biomedical dominance, the advent of future medicine portends a new synthesis in which belief systems of all communities will face challenge and reconciliation.

If disease and health are biopsychically mediated and depend to a significant extent on biofield as well as biochemical interactions, then all of conventional care, from preventive to critical care, may find adaptation in coming to terms with the theories, premises, and tools of energy medicine. Such a revolution in medicine will be based on human perception, not technology; on spirit, not matter; on evolution of the human perceptual apparatus involved in detecting and influencing subtle realities, not on mechanical evolution—on some radical synthesis, evolving new notions of the self.

In heralding the *possibility* of such shifts in thinking, this book departs from traditional ethical analyses—for example, by not performing an analysis of principles such as nonmaleficence as applied to complementary and alternative medicine solely through biomedical perspectives; by taking seriously the proposition that human beings dwell not only within bodies amenable to the normal analytical tools of Western science but also within energetic structures amenable to diagnosis, treatment, study, and intervention through such modalities as acupuncture and traditional oriental medicine, Ayurvedic pulse diagnosis, Tibetan herbal medicine, and nonlocal (distance) healing.

Today, the ethical inquiry—in the health care professions as in law—frequently is reduced to black-and-white, either/or analysis (of whether a profession is ethical/unethical), as therapies are reduced to unidimensional criteria (proven/unproven) and generalized or dismissed away (as effective/dubious, questionable, or worthless). Clinical practice of integrative and energy medicine frequently yields to practical considerations, borne of fear of reprisal for clinical innovation outside accepted paradigmatic boundaries—in other words, to the fear that using one therapy versus another may increase the risk of professional discipline and loss of licensure. Health care providers find themselves persecuted for seemingly casual or innocent activities and for lack of attention to a myriad of hair-splitting rules. Although the purpose of rules governing such behavior is to prevent wrongful conduct, the identification of practices outside conventionally accepted parameters with the concept of consumer fraud persists.[1] Operating from the limited perspective of fraud control, many regulatory structures proceed of their own accord, in an impersonal, almost Kafkaesque manner.

One of the subthemes of this book is the inability of law—as the embodiment of rationality—to deal with human conflict at the deepest level, as well as the inadequacy of the reasoning process as a tool for problem solving when it involves the interface of health care and the soul. As energy healing permeates mainstream thinking, shifts in awareness may require either a whole new set of laws to govern health care or at least a whole new way of thinking about law. For instance, legal rules governing health care approach the human being as solely occupying a physical body. These rules by and large do not conceptualize human consciousness as enfolded within a multilayered auric system of spiritual energy, of which the human body is merely the densest and most readily understood part. Comprehending the energy body may well be an evolutionary leap in human consciousness—and adapting social and regulatory structure to these new insights another.

Returning, for example, to the discussion of safety and efficacy, food and drug law is based on scientific thinking about the human body—in other words, on principles derived from biomedicine. But how does one evaluate "safety and effectiveness" in the auric field? How does one evaluate effects of drugs on the biofield, as well as on the body? How does one evaluate the claims by healers, for example, that radiopaque dyes, injected into the spinal column to diagnose injury, persist in the auric field ten years after a procedure; that chemotherapy "clogs the whole auric field, but especially the liver, with greenish-brown mucus-like energy"; that radiation therapy "frays the structured layers of the field like a burned nylon stocking"; that when an organ is removed, "the etheric organ can still be reconstructed and serve to keep harmony in the auric bodies above the physical body"; or that energy healing can be used to remove anesthesia from the field, thus helping to reduce nausea, postoperative pain, and surgical complications?[2] Finally, what would regulation of such practices look like, coming from the perspective of enlightened, self-actualized beings?

Integration: A Profound Challenge

This book presents multiple levels of meaning and perspective. First, from the perspective of medicine and science, research and evidence are critical to understanding and embracing therapies; one cannot advocate therapies without adequate evidence. From this perspective, ethical decision making and regulatory policy also must be shaped by the available scientific and medical evidence. Yet, as suggested, ethical questions (such as that of consumer access to a drug that has not been approved by the FDA) look different from the perspective of consumer autonomy than they do from the more paternalistic perspective of the state or, possibly, the physician.[3] For example, a patient who is experienced in Reiki healing may consider personal "evidence" of its "efficacy" to be sufficient—though these terms will mean something different to the scientist or the physician. Moreover, legislative recognition often trumps medical recognition: for example, state legislatures can decide to grant citizens access to a specific provider or therapy, even if scientific and medical debate has not concluded in favor of the modality in question.[4]

A second level of meaning and analysis is that of patient care and clinical application. Consumer choices frequently exceed what physicians feel comfortable recommending, providing, or sometimes even discussing with their patients. Further, if the patient has information of known risks and benefits of a particular treatment, yet the physician personally feels the treatment lacks safety and/or efficacy, the physician's sense of his or her obligation to do no harm may conflict with the patient's right of knowing, voluntary, and informed access. Informed consent protects patient choice yet may cause discomfort to the physician who is ideologically opposed to particular forms of therapy (for example, homeopathy).

A third level is that of the therapeutic encounter—what the patient expects and experiences in the crucible of relationship. The placebo effect is said to enhance (or the "nocebo" effect to diminish[5]) the effectiveness of prescription medication.[6] In integrative and energy medicine, the caregiver may be offering therapies that touch on mind/body/emotions/spirit and thus have the potential to enhance this effect, both positively and negatively. Yet the intrusive imposition of legal and ethical rules can constrain the therapeutic encounter and change provider and patient expectations of healing. An example of such distortion involves attempts by physicians and institutions to meet informed-consent requirements through formulaic and bureaucratic consent forms.[7]

A fourth level is that of policy. Public policy ideally is guided by science/evidence on one hand and by patient needs, as expressed in part by market forces, on the other. Practical politics, compromises, and trade-offs, though, often delineate the regulatory framework for consumer access to complementary therapies. For example, turf battles among complementary and alternative medical professions—and not medical standards and science—can dictate the scope of practice for chiropractors, acupuncturists, naturopaths, and other providers in any given state.[8] In similar fashion, judges often evaluate cases involving complementary and alternative medical therapies from the perspective of biomedicine, relying on general medical acceptance to the denigration of the autonomy interest implicated by patient choice of such therapies.[9] Thus, health care policy often is at odds both with medical and scientific criteria and with the stated needs and desires of health care consumers.

Finally, a fifth level is that of the possibility for creative human change, as expressed in the regulatory value of transformation. The possibility for human evolution arises out of the interplay between the various therapies and their effect on the exchange between the psyche and soul of patient and of provider. Evolution here refers to spiritual, not physical, acceleration of the ability for adaptation to the cosmos. As George Vithoulkas puts it, the human being can be understood as a "complex energy unit with the potential for either evolution or degeneration." By "evolution" he means "a greater degree of coherence and informational patterns leading to enhanced capacity for creativity and longevity"; by "degeneration" he means "a greater degree of confusion for these informational patterns within increased tendency for destruction."[10] The more "evolved the human being is, the more organized and coherent" are his or her energy bodies; changes in consciousness "mark the evolutionary process of the human being" and occur as quantum jumps.[11] In the context of this book, therefore, "evolution" refers to the possibility for accelerated emotional and spiritual growth presented by the integration of medicine and spirituality through clinical, research, ethical, legal, and social developments.

The Holy Grail

In the myth of the Fisher King, Parsifal, the young knight who in fact is a holy fool, is instructed to find the Holy Grail and ask, "Whom does the Grail serve?" This question apparently is necessary to release the blessings of the Grail.[12] Parsifal himself forgets to ask the question the first time he arrives in the Grail castle. This is because his mother had told him before he was leaving her not to ask too many questions; underneath his armor, he still is wearing the homespun garment given to him by his mother before he left for his quest.[13] The homespun garment represents all the unconscious material that keeps Parsifal trapped in his childhood, that shackles him to his origins, that prevents him from understanding the world anew.[14] As a myth for social transformation, Parsifal's omission represents the prophetically Kuhnian words of Jesus that one cannot "put new wine in old bottles"—that one cannot grasp a new and revolutionary paradigm through the language and lens of the old paradigm, especially if one is told not to ask too many questions. Parsifal must shed his homespun cloth to claim his knighthood and dignity.

Parsifal's quest is not only for his own maturation but also for all creation: simply by asking the question, "Whom does the Grail serve?" Parsifal will bring healing to the wounded king in the myth, and this will result in a pouring out of the Grail's bounty to all humanity. When, much later in life, Parsifal does reach the Grail castle for the second time and manages to ask the question, the answer that resounds through the castle is astonishingly obvious: the Grail, he learns, serves the Grail King. The myth does not state who or what is meant by the Grail King, and thus the reader is left with paradox, mystery, and metaphor.

According to one interpretation, the answer Parsifal receives symbolizes the "relocation of the center of gravity from the ego to the Self"; such relocation is the "life work" of a human being and "the center of meaning for all human endeavor."[15] The meaning of the Grail is the endpoint of human evolution, the richness of being fully human. Thus:

> The object of life is not happiness, but to serve God or the Grail. All of the Grail quests are to serve God. If one understands this and drops his idiotic notion that the meaning of life is personal happiness, then one will find that elusive quality immediately at hand ... [and] will proceed with the human task of life, the relocation of the center of gravity of the personality to something greater outside itself.[16]

The Grail myth provides an interesting metaphor for this contemplation of future medicine. Whom does health care serve—what is its *ultimate* object and aim (beyond curing an individual patient or a population of patients)? Are medical as well as emotional and spiritual technologies—biomedicine and complementary and alternative medicine—simply tools for physical health, or do they create something deeper than homeostasis, physiological repair, cure of disease, and other current goals of medicine and public health care policy? What is the difference, if any, between a "healthy body" and a "radiant wholeness"—what is meant by health of mind, body, emotions, and spirit? Returning to the notion of self-actualization and evolution of human consciousness, what is the "integration" that defines the goal of integrative health care, and what is the "energy" that defines energy medicine? Such larger questions undergird the subtitle of this book. Legal, regulatory, and ethical rules individually mold, guide, and ideally inspire clinical practice; collectively, they either hinder or nurture the pathway to the awareness of health and human healing.

Ethics Revisited

In ancient times, ethics was regarded as more than a casual inquiry of the mind into questions of right conduct and proper behavior. Rather, the subject of ethics mediated the lives of humans and the gods. By understanding ethics, an individual understood not only the boundaries of karma (action-reaction) and dharma (right conduct) but also the true nature of the universe. For example, in the Indian epic the Mahabharata, knowledge of ethics was so prized as to even confer the boon of raising the dead. In one episode, the king Yudhishtira—the embodiment of dharma—and his four brothers find themselves in a dreadful thirst. One by one, the brothers reach a lake and approach it to drink.[17] Each is warned by a heavenly voice: "You must not drink the water of this lake, not before you have answered certain questions of mine." Each brother in turn fails to heed the voice. As each drinks from the lake, he falls dead. Finally Yudhishtira reaches the lake. The same voice warns him. He sees his dead brothers and begs for their revival. The lake agrees only if Yudhishtira can answer the lake's questions on "ethics." The subject, however, includes not only questions about right and wrong conduct but also questions concerning the human being's highest duty while incarnated on earth.

Q: How is it possible for a man always to have a second
   companion?
A: Steady intelligence serves man as a helpful companion
   always. . . .
Q: What is fleeter than the wind?
A: The mind is fleeter than the wind.
Q: What is more numerous than the grass?
A: The thoughts that arise in the mind of man are more
   numerous. . . .
Q: [What is] the most valuable of all possessions?
A: Knowledge.
Q: The best of all gains?
A: Health.
Q: The best of all kinds of happiness?
A: Contentment.
Q: What is the highest duty in the world?
A: To abstain from injury is the highest of all duties.

Nonmaleficence thus receives an ancient imprimatur as the highest value. Abstaining from injury becomes a universal phenomenon,
generalized beyond the medical realm. But ethics also encompasses
psychology, in that the king's answers reveal a profound understanding of the human psyche. Thus, according to Yudhishtira, contentment
destroys unhappiness; health is the primal gain. In this palimpsest,
ethics also encompasses religion and spirituality, embracing the inner
treasures realized as a result of spiritual practice.

Q: What is it, when renounced, leads to no regret?
A: Wrath, when renounced, leads to no regret. . . .
Q: What is the essential feature of forgiveness?
A: Forgiveness consists in enduring enmity. . . .
Q: Can you tell me what enemy is invincible?
A: Anger.
Q: What disease is incurable?
A: Covetousness is an incurable disease. . . .
Q: What is real ablution?
A: A truth bath consists in washing the mind clean of all
   impurities.

Thus, understanding, tempering, and even transcending the shadow—one's "dark side"—is key in this system to virtue. But ethics is more: it also includes epistemology, tied to the notion of dharma as duty. The dialogue continues:

Q: What is said to be knowledge?
A: True knowledge is the knowledge of divinity. . . .
Q: What is mercy?
A: Mercy means wishing happiness for all. . . .
Q: What is ignorance?
A: True ignorance is not knowing one's duties.

The king's answers ultimately reveal such wisdom that the lake grants him a boon and, in response to the king's request, restores all his brothers to life. The lake also sheds its form and reveals itself to Yudhishtira as the Lord of Dharma, announcing that Yudhishtira already has conquered the kingdom called righteousness. The Lord of Dharma concludes, "Where I am, there will Victory be."

In short, metaphorically, ethics is powerful enough to revive a king's brothers, to create invincible protection and unending victory, and to grant an individual conquest of the kingdom of righteousness. Adhering to ethics is no easy formality, no mere intellectual attainment—such as the passing of a required professional certification exam or the memorization of professional ethics rules. It is rather an achievement of Being. That Yudhishtira has mastered his being, as well as the subject of ethics, is evident not only in his answers, which reveal ultimate truths, but also in his manner of delivering his answers, his humility, his gentleness: "It was a great art which Yudhishtira had mastered, the art of gentleness, the desire not to hurt anyone, not even with his words."[18]

The restoration of ethics to its rightful place as a seminal inquiry embracing a wider circle of concerns than fraud and human chicanery embraces respect for its ancient interpretations and broader implications. This means that bioethics presently is too narrowly defined, based only on biomedicine, and biased by limited social and professional constructs of health; regard for the soul requires deeper consideration. Ethics, rather than serving to impose one set of biases or another on choices involving life, death, and health, can mature into a search for the essential unity behind all health care choices. The nature of this unity is wholeness and embodies transcendental principles of love.

Healing the Energy of Religious Strife

Pragmatically, no single religious path in history has ever united humanity, though different thinkers believed one might. But whether the road was Christianity, Islam, fascism, Marxism, or some other path, the attempt to unify humans under a single ideological banner has usually resulted in doing so at knife's point. The message of love, of unification, of transcendence, of transformation, has turned into a message of death.

Given this history, one might be skeptical of the suggestion that any approach to the problem of existence could solve the tangled cords of human enmity. Nonetheless, if the underlying root of *all* religious paths is spiritual energy, and if that unifying, coherent energy can be perceived from the vantage point of a more enlightened awareness, then perhaps such an awareness has the capacity to heal and transform the divisions that have sowed murder and dissolution among the divine offspring since humanity first crawled out of the primordial sludge.

For example, one suggestion in energy healing is that Mary, Jesus, Buddha, Mohammed, Moses, Zoroaster, and other religious figures throughout human history are living beings—are vibrant spiritual energies that frequent our dimensional reality and can be perceived through high sense perception on the higher levels of the field. These beings, from this perspective, filter perennial truths through a particular language, culture, and/or doctrine but can be accessed by individuals through perception, irrespective of "belief" in any given dogma. If this suggestion has any validity—albeit testable only via consciousness—then some of the tools used by energy healers may allow individuals to tap into any given source of higher wisdom within this larger pantheon of cosmic human caretakers. In other words, the practices of energy healing may provide a portal to other dimensions.

The suggestion of a transcendent cosmic unity underlying all form long has united mystics even when the religious doctrines underlying their mystical paths have divided their priestly counterparts within the same traditions. The possibility that energy healing might provide experiential access to such a transcendental unity may provide a healing crucible to repair the sorrow religious doctrine has sown. In other words, religion keeps us in duality: from a doctrinal point of view, religion X is right, and religion Y is hogwash. From an energetic perspective, love is love—no matter what the form; hate is hate—no matter what the banner. With high sense perception, energetic daggers are what they are no matter what the outward message; rosy arcs of light appear from angelic messengers no matter what spiritual lineage they may represent. Thus, there is no duality; only the form differs, while the underlying unity remains the same. This suggests that one can use energy healing as a tool to assess whether a particular interaction—between humans and humans, between humans and animals or plants, between humans and cosmic spiritual figures—is spiritually potentiated with transformative energies of divine love. To do this would require an embrace of the tools of high sense perception to attune to inner realities and experience the multidimensional. Such an "integration" would be truly "ethical"—in the highest sense of the term, that sense used to describe King Yudhishtira.

Yes, but Is It Ethical?

Living as a multidimensional human is the challenge of evolution:

> It is one thing to look at the ocean; quite another to dive in.
> The wellspring of ethics
> arises from the ocean
> of your own awareness.
> Therefore, first experience your own inner alchemy; and then
>   decide.
> Real gold does not fear even the hottest fire.
> You are that gold. Now dive
> into the crucible
> of possibility.[19]

Being born into Judaism, attending religious studies, becoming fluent in Hebrew and familiar with scripture, and participating in synagogue were integrated with study of hypnotherapy, energy healing, and other modalities; with graduation from an interfaith seminary (while working as a Wall Street lawyer); with the absorption of Catholicism and other spiritual traditions; and with spending time with a meditation teacher from India. This involved holding several contradictions: the paradox of experiencing truth through different religious metaphors; the clash between a demanding professional environment and a spiritual path that included experiences such as lucid dreaming, encounters with figures from *different* spiritual traditions, and undergoing what religious sources call "purification."

A being who accepts truth on multiple levels can transverse the layers of existence. A being who is open can make friends with God; make friends with fellow human beings; make friends with other life forms on this planet, in both physical and nonphysical bodies. This person is a shaman: one who "makes a journey in an altered state of consciousness outside time and space" yet is able to move freely between worlds and bring knowledge back to the present.[20] Shamanism is one of oldest forms of healing and deals with physical illness on the spiritual levels; the shaman helps bring the soul home.[21] For the shaman, "knowledge of the topography of nonordinary reality is crucial to the cure," to retrieving lost parts of the soul from the distant worlds to which they have fled.[22]

While shamans speak of nonordinary realms of consciousness, and Maslow writes of peak experiences, William James describes "saints" as those whose experiences of the numinous "increase the amount of goodness in the world":

> Believing in the sacredness of all human life, they are said to be forerunners leading the way. Because "the world is not yet with them," saints often strike people as preposterous. . . . Saints nevertheless kindle a fire in others, stirring to life otherwise dormant "potentialities of goodness."[23]

Saints thus constitute a "genuinely creative social force" that rescues humans generally from a life of "spiritual stagnancy."[24] Like Maslow, James believes that saintly experience is a natural phenomenon, potentially available to all.[25]

May all who read this book—may all humanity—receive the courage, the wisdom, and the inspiration to continue the work of personal transformation and integration so that together we may complete the mystery cycle of inner revolution, translating this call into a larger evolution for all who share the planet Earth.

Notes

Introduction

1. Michael H. Cohen, *Complementary and Alternative Medicine: Legal Boundaries and Regulatory Perspectives,* 2 (Baltimore: Johns Hopkins University Press, 1998).

2. Cohen 1998, 2.

3. William G. Rothstein, *American Physicians in the Nineteenth Century: From Sects to Science* (Baltimore: Johns Hopkins University Press, 1972).

4. Cohen 1998, 15–23.

5. Ted J. Kaptchuk and David M. Eisenberg, "The Persuasive Appeal of Alternative Medicine," 129 (12) *Ann. Int. Med.*1061 (1998).

6. David M. Eisenberg, R. C. Kessler, C. Foster, F. E. Norlock, D. R. Calkin, and T. L. Delbanco, "Unconventional Medicine in the United States: Prevalence, Costs, and Patterns of Use," 328 *N. Eng. J. Med.* 246, 256 (1993).

7. See Miriam S. Wetzel, David M. Eisenberg, and Ted. J. Kaptchuk, "Courses Involving Complementary and Alternative Medicine in U.S. Medical Schools," 280 *JAMA* 784 (1998); David M. Eisenberg, R. B. Davis, S. L. Ettner, S. Appel, S. Wilkey, Maria Van Rompay, and R. Kessler, "Trends in Alternative Medicine in the United States, 1990–1997: Results of a Follow-up National Survey," 280 *JAMA* 1569 (1998).

8. *Alternative Medicine: Expanding Medical Horizons (A Report to the National Institutes of Health on Alternative Medical Systems and Practices in the United States),* (Sept. 14–16, 1992), xi–xxiii (the "Chantilly Report").

9. Chantilly Report 1992, xi–xxiii.

10. *Nutr. Bus. J.* 3 (Oct./Nov. 1998).

11. See Cohen 1998, 96–101.

12. Minn. Stat. S. 145A.

13. Eisenberg et al.1998.

14. Julie Appleby, "HMOs Take Spiritual Approach: Alternatives to No-Frills Image," *USA Today,* 1A (May 5, 2000).

15. Ted J. Kaptchuk, "Historical/Cultural Perspectives" (paper presented at Complementary and Alternative Medicine: Implications for Clinical Practice and State-of-the-Science Symposia, Harvard Medical School Department of Continuing Education, Mar. 12–15, 2000, Boston, Mass.).

16. *Wilk v. American Medical Association,* 719 F.2d 207 (7th Cir. 1983), *cert. denied,* 467 U.S. 1210 (1984), *on remand,* 671 F. Supp. 1465 (N.D. Ill. 1987), *aff'd,* 895 F.2d 352 (7th Cir. 1990).

17. Phil B. Fontarosa and George D. Lundberg, "Alternative Medicine Meets Science," 280 *JAMA* 1618 (1998).

18. Marcia Angell and Jerome P. Kassirer, "Alternative Medicine: The Risks of Untested and Unregulated Remedies," 339 *N. Eng. J. Med.* 839 (1998).

19. Ted. J. Kaptchuk, "Intentional Ignorance: A History of Blind Assessment and Placebo Controls," 72 *Bull. Hist. Med.* 389 (1998).

20. Wendy A. Weiger, Michael Smith, Heather Boon, Ted J. Kaptchuk, Mary A. Richardson, and David M. Eisenberg, "Advising Patients with Cancer Who Seek Complementary/Alternative/Integrative Medical Therapy: An Evidenced-Based Approach," *Ann. Int. Med.* (submitted 2002), Michael H. Cohen and David M. Eisenberg, "Potential Malpractice Liability Associated with Complementary and Integrative Medical Therapies," 136 *Ann. Int. Med.,* 596–603 (2002).

21. Michael H. Cohen, *Beyond Complementary Medicine: Legal and Ethical Perspectives on Health Care and Human Evolution,* 37–45 (Ann Arbor: University of Michigan Press, 2000); Edzard E. Ernst and Michael H. Cohen, "Informed Consent in Complementary and Alternative Medicine," *Arch. Intern. Med.* 161 (19): 2288–92 (2001).

22. Cohen 2000, 71–87.

23. The group maintains a website at <http://www.integrativemedicine.arizona.edu>.

24. See <http://www.integrativemedicine.arizona.edu>.

25. See <http://www.integrativemedicine.arizona.edu>.

26. Cohen 2000, 80–83.

27. Cohen 2000, 81.

28. Cohen 2000, 81.

29. As one author puts it: "Great healers . . . do not cure by chance but by exact knowledge. Fully understanding the control of life energy, they project a stimulating current into the patient that harmonizes his own flow of life energy. . . . Within the gross vibration of flesh is the fine vibration of cosmic current, the life energy, and penetrating both flesh and life energy is the most subtle vibration, that of consciousness." See Paramahansa Yogananda, *Scientific Healing Affirmations,* 13–14 (Los Angeles: Self-Realization, 1990), quoted in Judith Cornell, *Mandala: Luminous Symbols for Healing,* 29 (Wheaton, Ill.: Quest Books, 1994).

30. The author thanks Malcolm Riley for this distinction.

31. Chantilly Report 1992, 134.

32. Cohen 1998, 39–55.

33. Roger Walsh and Frances Vaughan, "On Transpersonal Definitions," 25 *J. Trans. Psych.* 2 (1993). The website for the Association for Transpersonal Psychology is at <http://www.atpweb.org>.

34. Cohen 2000, 71–73.

35. C. Norman Shealy and Caroline Myss, *The Creation of Health: Merging*

Traditional Medicine with Intuitive Diagnosis (Walpole, N.H.: Stillpoint Publishing, 1988).

36. George Gallup Jr., "Americans More Religious Now than Ten Years Ago, but Less So than in 1950s and 1960s" (Mar. 29, 2001); available at <http://www.gallup.com/poll/releases/pr010329.asp>.

37. Larry Dossey, *Healing Words: The Power of Prayer and the Practice of Medicine* (San Francisco: Harper, 1994); Harold Koenig, *The Healing Power of Faith: Science Explores Medicine's Last Great Frontier*, 24 (New York: Simon and Schuster, 1999).

38. Daniel Callahan, *Pursuing a Peaceful Death*, Hastings Center Report 23 (4), 33, 34 (1993).

39. Indeed, it has been suggested that practice guidelines in complementary and alternative medical therapies may be impractical or infeasible. See Practice and Policy Guidelines Panel, National Institutes of Health Office of Alternative Medicine, "Clinical Practice Guidelines in Complementary and Alternative Medicine: An Analysis of Opportunities and Obstacles," 6 (149) *Arch. Fam. Med.* (Mar./Apr. 1997). Challenges include ambiguity regarding diagnostic and therapeutic definitions, differences in underlying philosophy regarding disease, the inapplicability of conventional guidelines to discussions of imbalance and disharmony in some therapies, and the individualization that characterizes many complementary and alternative medical therapies. See id., 152.

40. James E. Dalen, "'Conventional' and 'Unconventional' Medicine: Can They Be Integrated?" 158 *Arch. Int. Med.* 179 (1998); Wayne B. Jonas, "Alternative Medicine: Learning from the Past, Examining the Present, Advancing to the Future," 280 *JAMA* 1616 (1998).

41. Cohen 1998, 15–23.

42. Thomas Kuhn, *The Structure of Scientific Revolutions* (Chicago: University of Chicago Press, 1970).

43. Callahan 1993, 33, 34.

44. Cohen 1998, 118.

45. Edzard E. Ernst and Michael H. Cohen, "Informed Consent in Complementary and Alternative Medicine," *Arch. Int. Med.* 161 (19): 2288–92 (2001).

46. Rachel Naomi Remen, "Keynote Address" (presented at Complementary and Alternative Medicine: Implications for Clinical Practice and State-of-the-Science Symposia, Harvard Medical School Department of Continuing Education, Mar. 12–15, 2000, Boston, Mass.).

47. 4 *J. Alt. Comp. Med.* 7–8 (1998).

Chapter 1

1. Modified slightly from Karen E. Adams, Michael H. Cohen, David M. Eisenberg, and Albert R. Jonsen, "Ethical Considerations of Complementary and Alternative Medical Therapies in Conventional Medical Settings," *Ann. Int. Med.* (in press, 2002).

2. Modified from the story of the Navarro family [cited Mar. 1, 2000], reported at <http://www.naturalhealthline.com>.

3. Michael H. Cohen, *Beyond Complementary Medicine: Legal and Ethical Perspectives on Health Care and Human Evolution,* 37–39 (Ann Arbor: University of Michigan Press, 2000).

4. Cohen 2000, 39–41.

5. For gingko biloba's effect on circulation, see J. Kleijnen and P. Knipschild, "Gingko Biloba for Cerebral Insufficiency," 34 *Br. J. Clin. Pharm.* 352–58 (1992).

For its effect on Alzheimer's, see P. L. Le Bars, M. M. Katz, N. Berman, T. M. Itil, A. M. Freedman, and A.F. Schatzberg, "A Placebo-Controlled, Double-Blind, Randomized Trial of an Extract of Ginkgo Biloba for Dementia," 278 *JAMA* 1327–32 (1997).

For informed consent with complementary and alternative therapies, see Edzard E. Ernst and Michael H. Cohen, "Informed Consent in Complementary and Alternative Medicine," *Arch. Int. Med.* 161(19): 2288–92. (2001).

6. For example, regarding legal versus ethical standards in the field of psychology, see Patricia Keith-Spiegel and Gerald P. Koocher, *Ethics in Psychology: Professional Standards and Cases,* 6–7 (New York: McGraw-Hill, 1985). The authors argue that ethical standards generally are "higher" than the law, not only because the correspondence between "legal-ethical" and "illegal-ethical" is incongruent but also because ethics committees and other peer-review mechanisms provide controls additional to general criminal and civil law, malpractice complaints, and applicable federal laws and regulations. See id., 5.

7. Cohen 2000, chaps. 4–5.

8. Michael H. Cohen, *Complementary and Alternative Medicine: Legal Boundaries and Regulatory Perspectives,* 29 (Baltimore: Johns Hopkins University Press, 1998).

9. Select Committee on Science and Technology, House of Lords, *United Kingdom Complementary and Alternative Medicine (Sixth Report),* (2000); available at <http://www.publications.parliament.uk/pa/ld199900/ldselect/ldsctech/123/12301.htm>.

10. Cohen 1998, 88–92.

11. American College of Physicians, *Ethics Manual* (4th ed., 1999); available at <http://www.acponline.org/ethics/ethicsman.htm>.

12. American College of Physicians 1999.

13. American College of Physicians 1999.

14. American College of Physicians 1999.

15. American College of Physicians 1999.

16. David L. Sacket, et al., *Evidence-Based Medicine: How to Teach and Practice Evidence-Based Medicine* (New York: Churchill-Livingstone, 2000).

17. George T. Lewith, "The Use and Abuse of Evidence-Based Medicine: An Example from General Practice," in Edzard Ernst, ed., *Complementary Medicine: An Objective Appraisal,* 106–11 (Oxford: Butterworth-Heineman, 1996) (citing studies).

18. Lewith 1996, 110.

19. Lewith 1996, 110.

20. Tom L. Beauchamp and James F. Childress, *Principles of Biomedical Ethics,* 189 (4th ed., New York: Oxford University Press, 1994).

21. Beauchamp and Childress 1994, 38.

22. For nonmaleficence expressed in terms of shielding patients from toxicity, see Adams et al. 2002.

23. David M. Eisenberg, "Advising Patients Who Seek Alternative Medical Therapies," 127 (1) *Ann. Int. Med.* 61 (1997).

24. See Michael H. Cohen, "A Fixed Star in Health Care Reform: The Emerging Paradigm of Holistic Healing," 27 *Ariz. State L.J.* 79, 138–39 (1995).

25. Adams et al. 2002.

26. Adams et al. 2002.

27. See <http://whccamp.hhs.gov/meetings>.

28. Albert R. Jonsen, "Casuistry as Methodology in Clinical Ethics," 12 *Theor. Med.* 298 (Dec. 1991).

29. Beauchamp and Childress 1994, 39.

30. Jay Katz, *The Silent World of Doctor and Patient* (New York: Free Press, 1994).

31. Beauchamp and Childress 1994, 283.

32. Cohen 1995, 138–39.

33. In re *Guess,* 393 S.E.2d 833 (N.C. 1990) (affirming conviction of a licensed physician for administering homeopathic remedies), *cert. denied, Guess v. North Carolina Board of Medical Examiners,* 498 U.S. 1047 (1991), *later proceeding, Guess v. Board of Medical Examiners,* 967 F.2d 998 (4th Cir. 1992); *Rogers v. State Board of Medical Examiners,* 371 So. 2d 1037, 1041 n. 3 (Fla. Dist. Ct. App. 1979), *aff'd,* 387 So. 2d 937 (Fla. 1980).

34. *Plumber v. Department of Health and Human Resources,* 634 So. 2d 1347, 1351 (La. Ct. App. 1994), *cert. denied,* 637 So. 2d 1056 (La. 1994); *United States v. Rutherford,* 438 F. Supp. 1287 (W.D. Okla. 1977), *remanded,* 582 F.2d 1234 (10th Cir. 1978), *rev'd,* 442 U.S. 544 (1979), *on remand,* 616 F.2d 455 (10th Cir. 1980), *cert. denied,* 449 U.S. 937 (1980), *later proceeding,* 806 F.2d 1455 (10th Cir. Okla. 1986).

35. See Cohen 1995, 137–41.

36. Todd Ackerman, "Cancer Treatment for Boy, 4, Sought from Burzynski," *Houston Chronicle* (Feb. 16, 2000).

37. See, e.g., *Hearing of the Oversight and Investigations Subcommittee of the House Commerce Committee on Access to Medical Treatment* (Feb. 29, 1996); available from LEXIS, LEGIS library, CNGTST file.

38. Ackerman 2000.

39. Ackerman 2000.

40. William G. Rothstein, *American Physicians in the Nineteenth Century: From Sects to Science* (Baltimore: Johns Hopkins University Press, 1972).

41. *Pearson v. Shalala,* 164 F.3d 655–60 (D.C. Cir. 1999), *reh'g en banc denied,* 172 F.3d 72.

42. *Pearson v. Shalala,* 655–60.

43. *Pearson v. Shalala*, 655–60.

44. Cohen 1995, 141–42.

45. See David T. Reilly, M. A. Taylor, C. McSharry, and T. Aitchison, "Is Homoeopathy a Placebo Response? Controlled Trial of Homeopathic Potency, with Pollen in Hayfever as a Model," 2 *Lancet* 881–85 (1986).

46. See, e.g., Council on Scientific Affairs, *Alternative Medicine*, report 10-I-96 (Chicago: American Medical Association, 1996). The Federation's new guidelines reflect a change in approach.

47. Beauchamp and Childress 1994, 194–95.

48. For a similar framework, see Michael H. Cohen and David M. Eisenberg, "Potential Physician Malpractice Liability Associated with Complementary and Integrative Medical Therapies," 136 *Ann. Int. Med.* 596–603 (2002).

49. Select Committee on Science and Technology 2000, chap. 4.

50. Wendy A. Weiger, Michael Smith, Heather Boon, Ted J. Kaptchuk, Mary A. Richardson, and David M. Eisenberg, "Advising Patients with Cancer Who Seek Complementary/Alternative/Integrative Medical Therapy: An Evidenced-Based Approach," *Ann. Int. Med.* (submitted, 2002).

51. Edmund de Azevedo Pribitkin and Gregory Boger, "Surgery and Herbal Therapy: Essential Guidelines on Bleeding, Skin Reactions, and Wound Healing," 6 (1) *Comp. Health Practice Rev.* 29–40 (2000).

52. See Select Committee on Science and Technology 2000, chap. 4.

53. See Cohen 1998, 71–87.

54. See Edzard Ernst, "The Ethics of Complementary Medicine," 22 *J. Med. Ethics* 197 (1996); Peter A. Clark, "The Ethics of Alternative Medicine Therapies," 21 (4) *J. Health Pol'y* 447 (2000).

55. See Cohen 1998, 112.

56. Marcia Angell and Jerome P. Kassirer, "Alternative Medicine: The Risks of Untested and Unregulated Remedies," 339 (12) *N. Eng. J. Med.* 839 (1998).

57. See, e.g., Canadian Task Force on the Periodic Health Examination, "The Periodic Health Examination," 121 *CMAJ* 1193—1254 (1979); D. J. Cook, G. H. Guyatt, A. Laupacis, and D. L. Sackett, "Rules of Evidence and Clinical Recommendations on the Use of Antithrombotic Agents," *Chest.* (102): 305S–311S (1992).

58. David Reilly, "Is the Evidence for Homeopathy Reproducible?" 344 *Lancet* 1601 (1994).

59. See, e.g., J. K. McGuire, M. S. Kulkarni, and H. P. Baden, "Fatal Hypermagnesemia in a Child Treated with Megavitamin/Megamineral Therapy," 105 (2) *Pediatrics* E18 (2000); J. A. Bakerink, S. M. Gospe, R. J. Dimand, and M. Eldridge, "Multiple Organ Failure after Ingestion of Pennyroyal Oil from Herbal Tea in Two Infants," 92 (5) *Pediatrics* (1996); E. C. Yu and C. Y. Yeung, "Lead Encephalopathy Due to Herbal Medicine," 100 (11) *Chinese Med. J.* 915–17 (1987).

60. See Richard L. Nahin and Stephen E. Straus, "Research into Complementary and Alternative Medicine: Problems and Potential," 20 (7279) *BMJ* 161–64 (2001).

61. This is the principle underlying the proposed Access to Medical Treatment Act, which would grant patients access to non-FDA-approved therapies provided informed consent and other requirements are met. Access to Medical Treatment Act, H.R. 2019, 104th Cong., 1st Sess.; S. 1035, 104th Cong., 1st Sess. (1995), reintroduced as H.R. 746, 105th Cong., 1st Sess. (Feb. 13, 1997); and S. 578, 105th Cong., 1st Sess. (Apr. 18, 1997). Discussed in Cohen 1998, 78–79.

62. *NIH Consensus Statement 107*, NIH Pub. 15(5) (Nov. 3–5, 1997).

63. See Paul Root Wolpe, "The Maintenance of Professional Authority: Acupuncture and the American Physician," 32 *Soc. Prob.* 409 (June 1985).

64. George A. Ulett, "Acupuncture Treatments for Pain Relief, 245 *JAMA* 768, 769 (1981), quoted in Wolpe 1985, 587–88.

65. Cohen 1998, 6–8 (applying the work of Jan Smuts, *Holism and Evolution* [London: MacMillan, 1926; reprint, Westport, Conn.: Greenwood Press, 1973]).

66. George Vithoulkas describes health on all levels in this way: health in the physical plane is "freedom from pain in the physical body, having attained a state of well-being"; health on the emotional plane is "freedom from passion, having as the result a dynamic state of serenity and calm"; health on the mental-spiritual level is "freedom from selfishness . . . having as a result total unification with Truth." See George Vithoulkas, *A New Model for Health and Disease*, 63–66 (Berkeley: North Atlantic Books, 1991).

67. See, e.g., Elizabeth Lipski, *Digestive Wellness* (2d ed., Los Angeles: Keats Publishing, 2000).

68. Ted J. Kaptchuk, "Editorial," 134 (6) *Ann. Int. Med.* 532 (2001).

69. Richard A Lippin, "Alternative Medicine in the Workplace," 2 (1) *Alt. Therapies* 49 (1996) (citing an unpublished study by Tiffany Field at the Touch Research Institute, University of Miami School of Medicine).

70. See, e.g., Wilhelm Reich, *The Function of the Orgasm* (New York: Farrar, Straus and Giroux, 1986).

71. See, e.g., John C. Pierrakos, *Core Energetics: Developing the Capacity to Love and Heal* (Mendocino: LifeRhythm, 1987).

72. Pierrakos 1987, 91.

73. Larry Dossey, *Healing Words: The Power of Prayer and the Practice of Medicine* (San Francisco: Harper, 1994).

74. Harold Koenig, *The Healing Power of Faith: Science Explores Medicine's Last Great Frontier*, 24 (New York: Simon and Schuster, 1999).

75. See Dossey 1994 (citing studies).

Chapter 2

1. David M. Studdert, David M. Eisenberg, F. H. Miller, D. A. Curto, Ted J. Kaptchuk, and Troy A. Brennan, "Medical Malpractice Implications of Alternative Medicine," 280 *JAMA* 1610, 1612 (1998).

2. Michael H. Cohen, *Beyond Complementary Medicine: Legal and Ethical Per-*

spectives on Health Care and Human Evolution, 27–29 (Ann Arbor: University of Michigan Press, 2000).

3. Cohen 2000, 29–30.

4. Cohen 2000, 47, 51–55; Studdert et al. 1998, 1610–12.

5. Jennifer Barrett, "Wag the Down Dog," *Yoga Journal* 80 (May/June 2000).

6. B. K. S. Iyengar, *Light on Yoga, Appendix II* (rev. ed., New York: Schocken Books, 1976).

7. Barrett 2000.

8. Michael H. Cohen, *Complementary and Alternative Medicine: Legal Boundaries and Regulatory Perspectives,* 109–11 (Baltimore: Johns Hopkins University Press, 1998).

9. Michael H. Cohen and David M. Eisenberg, "Potential Malpractice Liability Associated with Complementary and Integrative Medical Therapies," 136 *Ann. Int. Med.* 596–603 (2002).

10. *Moore v. Baker,* 1991 U.S. Dist. LEXIS 14712 (S.D. Ga., Sept. 5, 1991), *aff'd,* 989 F.2d 1129, 1132 (11th Cir. 1993).

11. David M. Eisenberg, Michael H. Cohen, Andrea Hrbek, John Grayzel, Maria van Rompay, and Richard M. Cooper, "Credentialing Complementary and Alternative Medical Providers," *Ann. Int. Med.* (in press, 2002).

12. Dean Ornish, L. W. Scherwitz, R. S. Doody, D. Kesten, S. M. McLanahan, S. E. Brown, et al., "Effects of Stress Management Training and Dietary Changes in Treating Ischemic Heart Disease," 24 *JAMA* 54 (1983).

13. Cheryl Bender Birch, *Power Yoga,* 180 (New York: Fireside, 1995).

14. *NIH Consensus Statement 107,* NIH Pub. 15(5) (Nov. 3–5, 1997).

15. *Kerman v. Hintz,* 418 N.W.2d 795, 802–3 (Wis. 1988); Cohen 1998, 68.

16. *Tschirhart v. Pethtel,* 233 N.W.2d 93, 94 (Mich. Ct. App. 1975); Cohen 1998, 68.

17. *Stockwell v. Washington State Chiropractic Disciplinary Board,* 359 S.E.2d 87 (Ga. 1987); Cohen 1998, 48.

18. Cohen 2000, 23–26.

19. See Cohen 1998, 87–92.

20. Cohen 1998, 111.

21. Cohen 2000, 55.

22. Colo. Rev. Stat. s. 12–129.5–102(1).

23. N.M. Stat. Ann. s. 61–14A-3(G); Vt. Stat. Ann. tit. 26, s. 3401(1).

24. Cohen 1998, 66–67.

25. Cohen 1998, 67.

26. Cohen 1998, 67.

27. American Chiropractic Association, *Code of Ethics,* Part A (1998).

28. American College of Physicians, *Ethics Manual* (4th ed., 1999); available at <http://www.acponline.org/ethics/ethicsman.htm>.

29. NAFTA Acupuncture and Oriental Medicine Commission, *Model Code of Ethics,* Part A (adopted Jan. 12, 1997). The commission is one organization in a national alliance of institutions involved in legislation and policy for traditional oriental medicine; see <http://www.acuall.org/natl.htm>.

30. American Association of Naturopathic Physicians, Naturopathic Code of Ethics, in *Position Papers and Organizational Documents* (autumn 1999).

31. *The Seattle Statement: Declaration of Principles for People and Organizations Who Use Acupuncture or Oriental Medicine Principles in their Work or Lives* (Olalla, Wash.: Acupuncture Alliance, 1997).

32. American Association of Naturopathic Physicians 1999.

33. Marion Yaglinski, correspondence with author (1994).

34. Yaglinski 1994. Similar provisions are found in the Code of Ethics for the International Association of Reiki Professionals, found at http://www.iarp.org/ethicscode.html>.

35. Yaglinski 1994.

36. Yaglinski 1994.

37. Yaglinski 1994.

38. See <www.healingtouch.net>

39. Yaglinski 1994.

40. See Tom L. Beauchamp and James F. Childress, *Principles of Biomedical Ethics*, 88–90 (4th ed., Oxford: Oxford University Press, 1994) (regarding the ethics of care).

41. *How to Know God: The Yoga Aphorisms of Patanjali*, trans. Swami Prabhavananda and Christopher Isherwood, Pt. 2, v. 29, pp. 140–41 (Hollywood: Vedanata Press, 1981).

42. *How to Know God* 1981, Pt. 1, v. 1, p. 15; id., Pt. 2., v. 28, p. 140.

43. *How to Know God* 1981, Pt. 2, v. 30, p. 141.

44. Iyengar 1976, 31.

45. *How to Know God* 1981, 141.

46. Iyengar 1976, 31.

47. *How to Know God* 1981, 141.

48. Twenty hours of yoga philosophy/ethics/lifestyle presently are required as part of the two-hundred-hour standard suggested by the Yoga Alliance, an affiliation of yogis from different traditions who are involved in a national registry of yoga teachers (Barrett 2000, 86).

49. Iyengar 1976, 31.

50. Iyengar 1976, Pt. 1, v. 3–4, p. 15.

51. J. Bronowski, *Science and Human Values* (New York: Harper and Row, 1956). Biomedicine "is a cultural system in its own right, with its own deeply held belief structures, and faith in specific methods and forms of knowledge." See James M. Perrin, Linda L. Barnes, Gregory A. Plotnikoff, Kenneth Fox, and Sara Pendleton, "Spirituality, Religion, and Pediatrics: Intersecting Worlds of Healing," 106 [suppl.] *Pediatrics* 899–908 (2000) (citing Arthur Kleinman, *Writing at the Margin* [Berkeley: University of California Press, 1995]).

52. Harold Koenig, *The Healing Power of Faith: Science Explores Medicine's Last Great Frontier*, 24 (New York: Simon and Schuster, 1999).

53. Keonig 1999, 24 (citing J. S. Levin, D. B. Larson, and C. M. Puchalski, "Religion and Spirituality in Medicine: Research and Education," 278 *JAMA* 792–93 [1997]).

54. Koenig 1999, 288–89.

Chapter 3

1. Kalu Rinpoche, *The Dharma That Illuminates All Beings Impartially like the Light of the Sun and the Moon*, 55–64 (Albany: State University of New York, 1986).

2. See Sogyal Rinpoche, *Tibetan Book of Living and Dying*, 185–86 (San Francisco: Harper, 1992).

3. This case is based on the experience of Helen Schumann, who "received" the spiritual teachings known as "A Course on Miracles."

4. Michael H. Cohen, *Complementary and Alternative Medicine: Legal Boundaries and Regulatory Perspectives*, 22–23 (Baltimore: Johns Hopkins University Press, 1998)

5. Cohen 1998, 22–23, 56–62, 87–92, 101–6, 112.

6. T. Romeyn Beck, "A Sketch of the Legislative Provision of the Colony and State of New York, Respecting the Practice of Physic and Surgery," 139 *N.Y. J. Med.* (1822), quoted in Cohen 1998, 15.

7. *Dent v. West Virginia*, 129 U.S. 114, 122 (1888).

8. *People v. Steinberg*, 73 N.Y.S.2d 475 (Mag. Ct. 1947).

9. *Stetina v. State*, 513 N.E.2d 1234, 1237 (Ind. Ct. App. 1987).

10. *Rogers v. State Board of Medical Examiners*, 371 So. 2d 1037, 1038 n. 2 (Fla. Dist. Ct. App. 1979), *aff'd*, 387 So. 2d 937 (Fla. 1980).

11. *United States v. Burzynski Cancer Research Institute, et al.*, 819 F.2d 1301, 1313 (5th Cir. 1987).

12. *Board of Medical Examiners v. Burzynski*, 917 S.W.2d 365 (Tex. Ct. App. 1996), *writ of error filed* (May 30, 1996).

13. *United States v. Rutherford*, 438 F. Supp. 1287 (W.D. Okla. 1977), *remanded*, 582 F.2d 1234 (10th Cir. 1978), *rev'd*, 442 U.S. 544 (1979), *on remand*, 616 F.2d 455 (10th Cir. 1980), *cert. denied*, 449 U.S. 937 (1980), *later proceeding*, 806 F.2d 1455 (10th Cir. Okla. 1986).

14. *United States v. Rutherford*, 442 U.S. at 558.

15. Cohen 1998, 15–23.

16. Clayton M. Christensen, Richard Bohmer, and John Kenagy, "Will Disruptive Innovations Cure Health Care?" *Harvard Bus. Rev.* 102–17 (Sept.–Oct. 2000).

17. Cohen 1998, 73–80.

18. Michael H. Cohen, "A Fixed Star in Health Care Reform: The Emerging Paradigm of Holistic Healing," 27 *Ariz. State L.J.* 79–172 (1995).

19. Michael H. Cohen, *Beyond Complementary Medicine: Legal and Ethical Perspectives on Health Care and Human Evolution*, 15–18 (Ann Arbor: University of Michigan Press, 2000).

20. Cohen 1998, 39–40.

21. David M. Eisenberg, Michael H. Cohen, Andrea Hrbek, John Grayzel, Maria van Rompay, and Richard M. Cooper, "Credentialing Complementary and Alternative Medical Providers," *Ann. Int. Med.* (in press, 2002).

22. Cohen 1998, 37.

23. Cohen 1998, 81–82 (citing cases).

24. *People v. Privitera*, 591 P. 919, 927 (Cal. 1979).

25. *Suernam v. Society of the Valley Hospital*, 383 A.2d 143, 146 (N.J. Super. Ct. 1977).

26. Ron Joseph, *Balancing Consumer Protection along the Continuum of Medical Care*, syllabus material for "Complementary and Alternative Medicine: Practical Applications and Evaluations," Stanford Center for Research in Disease Prevention, Stanford University School of Medicine and Center for Alternative Medicine Research and Education, Beth Israel Deaconess Medical Center (Oct. 15–17, 1999).

27. Federation of State Medical Boards, *Report of the Special Committee on Questionable and Deceptive Health Care Practices*, Section I: "Preamble" (1997).

28. Federation 1997, Section IX: "Conclusion." The report also links statistics regarding consumers' visits to complementary and alternative medical providers, with the notion that "up to $100 billion is lost to health care fraud" in the United States annually (id.).

29. Michael H. Cohen, "The Emerging Field of Law and Complementary and Alternative Medicine," 42 (2) *Orange Cty. Lawyer* 30 (2000).

30. Andrew Vickers, "Research Paradigms in Mainstream and Complementary Medicine," in Edzard Ernst, ed., *Complementary Medicine: An Objective Appraisal*, 16 (Oxford: Butterworth-Heineman, 1996).

31. For statutory prohibitions, see Cohen 1998, 24–31; Cohen 2000, 85–87.

For collaboration, see the reports presented at the First International Conference on Tibetan Medicine in Washington, D.C., in 1998; available at <http://www.tibetmedicine.org>.

32. "Standards for Physicians Practicing Integrative and Complementary Medicine," Texas Administrative Code, 22 TAC ss. 200.1–200.3 (1998).

33. Roger Frager, foreword to Abraham H. Maslow, *Motivation and Personality*, xxxiv–xxxviii (3d ed., New York: Addison Wesley Longman, 1987).

34. Abraham H. Maslow, *The Psychology of Science: A Reconnaissance*, 151 (New York: Harper and Row, 1966), quoted in David M. Wulff, *Psychology of Religion: Classic and Contemporary Views*, 602 (New York: John Wiley and Sons, 1991).

35. Wulff 1991, 602 (quoting Maslow).

36. Willis Harman and Christian de Quincey, *The Scientific Exploration of Consciousness: Toward an Adequate Epistemology* (Sausalito, Calif.: Institute of Noetic Sciences, 1994); see also James Lake, "The Future of Psychiatry: Emerging Paradigms and Integrative Approaches in Psychiatric Diagnosis and Treatment," *Frontier Perspectives* (Temple University) 9:1 (2000).

37. M. H. Hall, "A Conversation with Abraham H. Maslow," 35 *Psychology Today* 54–55 (1968), and Abraham H. Maslow, *Toward a Psychology of Being*, iii–iv (2d ed., New York: Van Nostrand, 1968), quoted in Maslow 1987, xxxviii–xxxix.

38. Maslow 1968, iii–iv, quoted in Maslow 1987, xxxix.

39. Maslow 1987, 17–18.

40. Maslow 1987, 28–29.

41. Maslow 1987, 16–22.

42. Maslow 1987, 30.

43. Maslow 1987, 30–31.

44. Robert Thurman, *Inner Revolution: Life, Liberty, and the Pursuit of Real Happiness* (New York: Penguin Putnam, 1998).

45. Maslow 1987, 31.

46. Dean Ornish, *Love and Survival: The Scientific Basis for the Healing Powers of Intimacy* (New York: HarperCollins, 1998).

47. Maslow 1987, 14.

48. Abraham H. Maslow, preface to *Motivation and Personality*, xxi (2d ed.).

49. See Ted J. Kaptchuk and David M. Eisenberg, "Varieties of Healing 1: Medical Pluralism in the United States," 135 *Ann. Int. Med.* 189– 95 (2001).

50. Carl Jung, "Archetypes of the Collective Unconscious," in Violet S. de Laszlo, ed., *The Basic Writings of C. G. Jung,* 34 (New York: Bollingen Foundation, 1959). Jung also stated: "The 'man without a shadow' is statistically the commonest human type, one who imagines he actually is only what he cares to know about himself. Unfortunately neither the so-called religious man nor the man of scientific pretensions forms any exception to this rule" (Carl G. Jung, "On the Nature of the Psyche," in Violet S. de Laszlo, ed., *The Basic Writings of C. G. Jung,* 78 [New York: Bollingen Foundation, 1959]). Jung argued that confrontation with one's own shadow "is an *ethical* problem of the first magnitude" (id.) (original emphasis).

51. Roberto Assagioli, *Psychosynthesis* (New York: Viking Press, 1965), 35.

52. Assagioli 1965, 35.

53. Smith, *History of New York,* 326 (1814), quoted in T. Romeyn Beck, "A Sketch of the Legislative Provision of the Colony and State of New York, Respecting the Practice of Physic and Surgery," *N.Y. J. Med.* 139, 143 (1822).

54. Maslow 1987, 20.

55. In re *Guess,* 393 S.E.2d 833 (N.C. 1990) (affirming conviction of a licensed physician for administering homeopathic remedies), *cert. denied, Guess v. North Carolina Board of Medical Examiners,* 498 U.S. 1047 (1991), *later proceeding, Guess v. Board of Medical Examiners,* 967 F.2d 998 (4th Cir. 1992).

56. Douglas R. Brooks, "The Canons of Siddha Yoga," in Douglas R. Brooks, Swami Durgananda, Paul E. Muller-Ortega, William K. Mahony, Constantina Rhodes Bailly, and S. P. Sabharathnam, *Meditation Revolution: A History and Theology of the Siddha Yoga Lineage,* 288 (South Fallsburg, N.Y.: Agama Press, 1997).

57. See Mathew Fox, *The Coming of the Cosmic Christ: The Healing of Mother Earth and the Birth of a Global Renaissance* (San Francisco: Harper, 1988).

58. Robert Thurman describes this as the creation of an enlightened society composed entirely of buddhas, or illumined beings—a "buddhaverse" (Thurman 1998, 292).

59. Thurman 1998, 26.

60. *Schneider v. Revici,* 817 F.2d 987, 992 (2d Cir. 1987).

61. Hawaii House Bill 428 (Jan. 17, 1997).

62. Maslow 1968, 55.

63. Maslow 1968, 56.

64. Maslow 1968, 56.

65. Phil B. Fontarosa and George D. Lundberg, "Alternative Medicine Meets Science," 280 *JAMA* 1618 (1998).

66. Council on Scientific Affairs, *Alternative Medicine*, Report 10-I-07, 17 (Chicago: American Medical Association, 1996) (citing C. Krauthammer, "The Return of the Primitive," *Time*, 82 [Jan. 20, 1996]).

67. Maslow 1968, 8.

68. Maslow 1968, 4.

69. Maslow 1968, 56.

70. Maslow 1968, 114.

71. Roberto Assagioli distinguishes self-actualization (the "awakening and manifestation of latent potentialities of the human being") from realization of the Self ("the experience and awareness of the synthesizing spiritual Center") (Assagioli 1965, 37). He notes that an individual may achieve self-actualization without developing spiritual attainment; on the other hand, an individual may have genuine spiritual experiences without having an integrated, well-organized personality (id., 38). The author further identifies Self-realization with the central teaching in Vedanta philosophy, *Tat Twan Asi* ("Thou art That") (id., 44–45). Assagioli takes pains to draw these distinctions to conceptualize the difference between "the small ordinary personality, the little 'self' or ego, of which we are normally conscious," and the "absolute . . . truth" represented in the Self; to fail to draw such distinctions can lead to delusion and self-glorification (id., 45).

72. Judith Cornell, *Mandala: Luminous Symbols for Healing*, 2 (Wheaton, Ill.: Quest Books, 1994).

73. Maslow 1968, 110.

74. Thurman 1998, 60.

75. See David Cheek, "Communication with the Critically Ill," 12 (2) *Am. J. Hypnosis* 75 (1969).

76. Sandra Ingerman, *Soul Retrieval: Mending the Fragmented Self* (San Francisco: Harper, 1991).

77. Visions, voices, directions from angels and spirits, and intuitive guidance are common in many religious traditions. For example, in Jewish tradition, one "phenomenon encountered by the disembodied consciousness is the experience of being welcomed into the postmortem realms by previously deceased friends and relatives" (Simcha Paull Raphael, *Jewish Views of the Afterlife*, 290 [Northvale, N.J.: Jason Aronson, 1994]). Visions of the Angel of Death, visions of the presence of God, and a life review also are reported (id., 288–91).

78. For views to the contrary, see <http://jollyroger.com/zz/yreligiond /Christianityhall/cas/47.html>; <http://www.answering-islam.org/Case /case4 .html>; <http://home.earthlink.net/~gbl111/historic.htm>.

79. R. D. Laing, *The Divided Self* (Baltimore: Penguin, 1965); R. D. Laing, *The Politics of Experience and the Bird of Paradise* (New York: Penguin, 1967).

80. Nancy Scheper-Hugher, *Saints, Scholars, and Schizophrenics: Mental Illness in Rural Ireland,* 72 (Berkeley: University of California Press, 1979) (citing Laing 1965; Michel Foucault, *Madness and Civilization* [New York: Mentor, 1967]; and Thomas Szasz, *The Myth of Mental Illness* [New York: Doubleday, 1961]).

81. The therapist who "neither understands nor appreciates the superconscious functions, who ignores or denies the reality of the Self and the possibility of Self-realization . . . may either ridicule the patient's uncertain higher aspirations as mere fancies, or interpret them in a materialistic way, and the patient may be persuaded that he is doing the right thing in trying to harden the shell of his personality, and close it against the insistent knocking of the superconscious Self" (Assagioli 1965, 55).

82. *Secrets of God: Writings of Hildegard of Bingen,* ed. and trans. Sabina Flanagan, 8–9 (Boston: Shambhala Publications 1996).

83. *Secrets of God* 1996, 9.

84. Maslow 1968, 97.

85. Maslow 1968, 97.

86. Gopi Krishna, *Reason and Revelation,* 36–104 (New Delhi: Kundalini Research and Publication Trust, 1979).

87. Gopi Krishna 1979, 120–21.

88. Maslow 1987, 128.

89. Thomas Kuhn, *The Structure of Scientific Revolutions* (Chicago: University of Chicago Press, 1970).

90. Thurman 1998; Douglas R. Brooks, Swami Durgananda, Paul E. Muller-Ortega, William K. Mahony, Constantina Rhodes Bailly, and S. P. Sabharathnam, *Meditation Revolution: A History and Theology of the Siddha Yoga Lineage,* 288 (South Fallsburg, N.Y.: Agama Press, 1997).

91. Gopi Krishna 1979, cover page.

Chapter 4

1. Adapted from Daniel W. Miller, "Past Life Therapist Brought up on Charges in Canada" (letter transmitted to author, May 7, 1996). Defendant, a member of the Canadian Psychological Association, was charged with "the equivalent of witchcraft by her professional organization"—more specifically, with having "committed acts derogatory to the honor and dignity of the profession" by espousing belief in reincarnation and suggesting "past lives therapy," which allegedly contravened scientific principles articulated in the Code of Ethics for Psychologists (id.).

2. Barbara A. Brennan, *Light Emerging: The Journey of Personal Healing,* 75 (New York: Bantam Books, 1993).

3. For evidence-based reviews, see, e.g., Donald P. O'Mathuna, "Evidence-Based Practice and Reviews of Therapeutic Touch," 32:3 *J. Nursing Scholarship* 279 (2000).

For case reports, see, e.g., Eric D. Leskowitz, "Phantom Limb Pain Treated with Therapeutic Touch: A Case Report," 81 *Arch. Phys. Med. Rehab.* 522 (Apr. 2000).

For a thorough compilation of studies on so-called psychic phenomena, see Cindy Crawford and Wayne B. Jonas, "Bibliography of Spiritual Healing, Energy Medicine and Intentionality Research" (paper presented at Science and Spirituality in Healing, Oct. 26–29, 2000, Old Salem, N.C.).

Regarding the application of energy healing in clinical settings, this work has been ongoing for several years at, among other places, Columbia Presbyterian Hospital in New York, under the auspices of Mehmet Oz, a cardiac surgeon. For an early report, see Chip Brown, "The Experiments of Dr. Oz," *New York Times Magazine*, 21 (July 30, 1995).

4. John A. Astin, Elaine Harknes, and Edzard Ernst, "The Efficacy of 'Distant Healing': A Systematic Review of Randomized Trials," 132 (11) *Ann. Int. Med.* 903 (2000).

5. NIH, NCCAM; available at <http://nccam.nih.gov>.

6. NIH, NCCAM, "Exploratory Program Grants for Frontier Medicine Research"; available through <http://www.nccam.nih.gov/>.

7. NIH, NCCAM, "Project Concept Review" (June 12, 2000); available through <http://www.nccam.nih.gov/>.

8. NIH, NCCAM 2000 ("Project").

9. NIH, NCCAM 2000 ("Exploratory").

10. NIH, NCCAM 2000 ("Exploratory").

11. See, e.g., L. Rosa, E. Rosa, L. Sarner, and S. Barrett, "A Close Look at Therapeutic Touch," 279 *JAMA* 1005–10 (1998).

12. David M. Eisenberg, Michael H. Cohen, Andrea Hrbek, John Grayzel, Maria van Rompay, and Richard M. Cooper, "Credentialing Complementary and Alternative Medical Providers," *Ann. Int. Med.* (in press, 2002).

13. Maryland House Bill 1002 (2001). In Maryland, the definition for the practice of massage therapy does not include: "the laying on of hands, consisting of pressure or movement on a fully clothed individual, to specifically affect the electromagnetic energy or energetic field of the human body." *Md. Code Ann.* §§3–5A–011 (g) (2) (iii).

14. Maryland House Bill 1002 (2001).

15. Ted J. Kaptchuk, "History of Vitalism," in Marc S. Micozzi, ed., *Fundamentals of Complementary and Alternative Medicine*, 44 (London: Churchill-Livingstone, 2001). Formulations of vitalism include anima (sensitive soul), vital principle, animal magnetism (Anton Mesmer), psychic force, and subtle energy (id., 44–46). Techniques for harnessing such forces include channeling (contacting noncorporeal realities), mind cure, Christian science, and even their inclusion in chiropractic (innate intelligence), homeopathy (vital energy), naturopathy (vis *medicatrix naturae*—the healing force of nature), and acupuncture (id., 47–50). Kaptchuk argues that "the vital energy has gone psychological" with the creation of modern psychotherapy, with mind-body interventions constituting "a kind of legitimate mesmerism" (id., 51).

16. Massachusetts Board of Registration in Nursing, "Advisory Ruling, Holistic Nursing Practice and Complementary Therapies" (Sept. 10, 1997).

17. Select Committee on Science and Technology, House of Lords, *United Kingdom Complementary and Alternative Medicine (Sixth Report)*, (2000); available

at <http://www.publications.parliament.uk/pa/ld199900/ldselect/ldsctech /123 /12301.htm>.

18. Select Committee on Science and Technology 2000, chap. 6.

19. Select Committee on Science and Technology 2000, chap. 5.

20. Michael H. Cohen, *Beyond Complementary Medicine: Legal and Ethical Perspectives on Health Care and Human Evolution*, 79–80 (Ann Arbor: University of Michigan Press, 2000).

21. *Alternative Medicine: Expanding Medical Horizons (A Report to the National Institutes of Health on Alternative Medical Systems and Practices in the United States)*, (Sept. 14–16, 1992), xlvi, 133–46 (the "Chantilly Report").

22. Chantilly Report 1992, 134.

23. Chantilly Report 1992, 139 (citing Daniel J. Benor, "Healing and a Changing Medical Paradigm," 3 *Frontier Perspectives* 33–40 [1993]).

24. See Michael M. Talbot, *The Holographic Universe* (New York: Harper Perennial Library, 1992) (referencing David Bohm's work).

25. See Philip St. Romain, *Kundalini Energy and Christian Spirituality: A Pathway to Growth and Healing* (New York: Crossroads Publishing, 1991), for a description of awakening through the chakras from an individual steeped in the Christian contemplative tradition.

26. For relation to Kabbalistic teachings, see Will Parfitt, *The Living Qabalah: A Practical and Experiential Guide to Understanding the Tree of Life* (London: Element Books Ltd., 1988).

For relation to the Christian sacraments, see Caroline Myss, *Anatomy of the Spirit* (New York: Harmony Books, 1996).

27. Choa Kok Sui, *Pranic Healing*, 14 (York Beach, Maine: Samuel Weiser, 1990).

28. Barbara A. Brennan, *Hands of Light: A Guide to Healing Through the Human Energy Field* (Bantam Books, 1988), 42–79; Roslyn L. Bruyere, *Wheels of Light: A Study of the Chakras*, 30–44 (Sierra Madre, Calif.: Bon Productions, vol. 1, 1991); Jack Schwartz, *Human Energy Systems: A Way of Good Health*, 14 (New York: Penguin Books, 1980); Kok Sui 1990, 93–116.

29. Brennan 1988, 48.

30. Brennan 1988, 143.

31. Brennan 1988, 71–79.

32. Brennan 1988, 73.

33. Brennan 1988, 89.

34. Swami Ajaya, *Psychotherapy East and West: A Unifying Paradigm*, 247 (Honesdale, Pa.: Himalayan International Institute, 1983).

For chart 10, see Ajaya 1983, 248.

35. Larry Dossey, *Meaning and Medicine: A Doctor's Tales of Breakthrough and Healing* (New York: Bantam Books, 1991).

36. Brennan 1988, 49–53.

37. Valerie Hunt, *Infinite Mind: Science of Human Vibrations of Consciousness* (Malibu: Malibu Publishing Company, 1989); see also Myss 1996.

38. William James, *The Will to Believe and Other Essays in Psychology* (New

York: Dover, 1956) (cited in Andrew R. Fuller, *Psychology and Religion: Eight Points of View*, 31 [London: Rowman and Littlefield Publishers, 1994]).

39. Fuller 1994, 31.

40. Howard Gardner, *Extraordinary Minds: Portraits of Exceptional Individuals and an Examination of Our Extraordinariness* (New York: Basic Books, 1997).

41. William James, "A Pluralistic Universe," in R. B. Perry, ed., *Essays in Radical Empiricism and a Pluralistic Universe*, 266–67 (New York: Dutton, 1971), quoted in Fuller 1994, 26.

42. See William James, *The Varieties of Religious Experience* (New York: New American Library, 1958).

43. For information concerning the film, see <http://www.dolphinsfilm .com>.

44. Charlotte A. Wytias, "Therapeutic Touch in Primary Care," 5 (2) *Nurse Pract. For.* 91, 93 (1994).

45. Wytias 1994.

46. Wytias 1994, 93–94.

47. Wytias 1994, 94.

48. Wytias 1994.

49. Janet F. Quinn and Anthony J. Strelkauskas, "Psychoimmunologic Effects of Therapeutic Touch on Practitioners and Recently Bereaved Practitioners: A Pilot Study," 15 (4) *Adv. Nurs. Sci.* 13, 16 (1993).

50. Beverly Rubik, "Energy Medicine: A Challenge for Science," 40 *Noetic Sci. Rev.* 37 (1993).

51. Institute of Noetic Sciences, *The Heart of Healing: A Multicultural Perspective on Healing*, 127 (Petaluma, Calif.: The Institute of Noetic Sciences, 1993). Premature babies receiving the treatment were found to be calmer and better oxygenated (id.).

52. Wytias 1994, 94.

53. William A. Tiller, "Energy Fields and the Human Body," in John White, ed., *Frontiers of Consciousness: The Meeting Ground Between Inner and Outer Reality*, 230 (New York: Julian Press, 1974).

54. Tiller 1974, 230–31.

55. To the healer, disease may be seen as a combination of external factors— such as germs, malnutrition, toxins, pollutants, too much salami, and so on— and of internal or emotional factors—such as negative emotions, blocked meridians, human energy field depletion and congestion, and chakra malfunctioning (Kok Sui 1990, 16–17).

56. Cohen 2000, 80–87.

57. See Brennan 1988, 76; Kok Sui 1990, 217. Bruyere sees heart disease as a first-chakra disease, a result of "the inappropriate use of red energy" (anger) (Bruyere 1991, 227).

58. Brennan 1988, 71. In each case, healing energy causes the unwinding—or release—of the blockage that caused the malfunction. This is why the client may have a physical or emotional release, such as crying, screaming, laughing uncontrollably, or even vomiting. If, for example, the unwinding involves pro-

cessing, at a deep physical and emotional level, the experience of sexual abuse, the client will not likely float through the unwinding in a state of bliss. Rather, the client will fully feel what has been previously suppressed; the release may emerge in the throat or even in violent shaking along the whole body. In Eastern traditions, such releases while meditating are not unfamiliar; in Sanskrit, the release is known as a *kryia* (Swami Muktananda, *Play of Consciousness,* 24 [New York: SYDA Foundation, 1978]). *Kryias* are "contortions of the body. . . . If anybody were to see these from the outside, they would look very strange and frightening, but the seeker is not afraid" (id.), 24.

59. Brennan 1993.

60. Summarized from Brennan 1993, 187–202.

61. Bruyere 1991, 217. According to Bruyere, cancer patients often have common psychological profiles; they, like their bodies, "us[e] the wrong kind of power for the wrong thing in the wrong place" (id., 1:215).

62. Bruyere 1991, 219–21.

63. Bruyere 1991, 223.

64. Bruyere 1991, 224.

65. Bruyere 1991, 224.

66. Bruyere 1991, 224.

67. Victoria Slater and Denise Rankin-Box, eds., *The Nurses' Handbook of Complementary Therapies,* 28 (New York: Churchill-Livingstone, 1996).

68. Michael H. Cohen, *Complementary and Alternative Medicine: Legal Boundaries and Regulatory Perspectives* (Baltimore: Johns Hopkins University Press, 1998).

69. Cohen 1998, 24–72.

70. See Julie Motz, *Hands of Life* (New York: Bantam Books, 1998).

71. See, e.g., the discussion of the Bhagavad-Gita found at <http://www .dlshq.org/download/gita_vision.htm#_VPID_1>.

72. Robert Thurman has articulated this possibility as a "buddhaverse" (Robert Thurman, *Inner Revolution: Life, Liberty, and the Pursuit of Real Happiness* [New York: Penguin Putnam, 1998]).

73. For licensing practitioners in some form of energy healing, see Cohen 2000, 77–79.

74. Maryland House Bill 1002 (2001).

75. In re *Guess,* 393 S.E.2d 833 (N.C. 1990), *cert. denied, Guess v. North Carolina Board of Medical Examiners,* 498 U.S. 1047 (1991), *later proceeding, Guess v. Board of Medical Examiners,* 967 F.2d 998 (4th Cir. 1992).

76. Slater and Rankin-Box 1996, 28.

77. See, e.g., Bella English, "She Feels Your Pain: As a 'Medical Intuitive,' Rhonda Lenair Reads Clients' Ailments—Even by Phone," *The Boston Globe,* C6 (Aug. 23, 1999).

78. Shafica Karagulla and Dora van Gelder Kunz, *The Chakras and the Human Energy Fields,* 78 (Wheaton, Ill.: The Theosophical Publishing House, 1989).

79. Minn. Stat. Sec. 146A.

80. C. Norman Shealy and Carolyn Myss, *The Creation of Health: Merging Tra-*

ditional Medicine with Intuitive Diagnosis (Walpole, N.H.: Stillpoint Publishing, 1988).

81. Barbara A. Brennan, *Hands of Light: A Guide to Healing through the Human Energy Field,* 151 (New York: Bantam Books, 1988).

82. Robert G. Jahn and Brenda J. Dunne, *Margins of Reality: The Role of Consciousness in the Physical World,* 196 (Orlando, Fla.: Harcourt Brace Javonovich, 1988).

83. David Reilly, "Enhancing Human Healing," 20 (7279) *BMJ* 120, 121 (2001).

84. Brennan 1988, 155.

Chapter 5

1. Wayne R. LaFave and Austin W. Scott, *Criminal Law,* S. 7.15(a), 685 (2d ed., St. Paul: West Publishing Co., 1986).

2. LaFave and Scott 1986.

3. Barry R. Furrow, Thomas L. Greaney, Sandra H. Johnson, and Robert L. Schwartz, *Health Law,* s. 4–33, 148 (St. Paul: West Publishing Co., 1995) (citing cases).

4. See, e.g., *Corey v. City of Dallas,* 352 F. Supp. 977 (N.D. Tex. 1972) (cross-gender massage); *Wes Ward Enterprises, Ltd. v. Allen Andrews,* 355 N.E.2d 131 (Ill. Ct. App. 1976) (clothing); *Pollard v. Cockrell,* 578 F.2d 1002 (5th Cir. 1978) (clothing).

5. See, e.g., *Florida v. Bales,* 343 So.2d 9 (Fla. 1977) (stating that "there is no federal constitutional impediment to the enactment of legislation embodying an irrebuttable presumption that the massage of a person by a member of the opposite sex is inconsistent with the public health, safety, or welfare").

6. "The scope of the definition of massage is so broad that any human contact more intimate than a handshake falls within its proscription, and any place where such contact occurs (other than the residence or office of the person treated and other than a State-licensed hospital, a State-licensed nursing home or similar State-licensed institution) is a massage institute requiring a city license. . . . It is thus apparent that in order to bar vice under the guise of regulating massage, the City Council has involved every profession in which one human being touches another." *New York State Soc'y of Medical Masseurs, Inc. v. City of New York,* 345 N.Y.S.2d 866 (S.Ct., Special Term, 1973).

7. See, e.g., *People v. Jaramillo,* 30 P.2e 427 (Cal. App. Ct., 1934) (defendant, who had given tuberculosis patient several massage treatments, then asked her to have sexual intercourse with him for the sake of her health); *Slakter v. DeBuono,* 694 N.Y.S.2d 496 (N.Y. App. Div., 1999) (patient testified that licensed psychiatrist kissed her goodbye on the lips, gave her neck and shoulder massages, lifted her shirt over her head, and unhooked her brassiere; psychiatrist admitted to hugging and massaging patient and conceded his conduct was inappropriate to the therapeutic relationship).

8. David M. Eisenberg, *Encounters with Qi*, 26 (New York: Penguin Books, 1987).

9. Patricia Keith-Spiegel and Gerald P. Koocher, *Ethics in Psychology: Professional Standards and Cases*, 253 (New York: McGraw-Hill, 1985).

10. Maryland House Bill 1002 (2001).

11. Risk Management Foundation of the Harvard Medical Institutions, *100 Questions About Health Care Risk Management*, 43 (Cambridge: Risk Management Foundation of the Harvard Medical Institutions, 1996).

12. Risk Management Foundation 1996.

13. Keith-Spiegel and Koocher 1985, 253.

14. Euripides, "The Bacchae," in David Grene and Richmond Lattimore, eds., *Euripides V: The Complete Greek Tragedies* (Chicago: University of Chicago Press, 1959).

15. Euripides 1959, 220.

16. Swami Muktananda, *Play of Consciousness*, 90–95, 98–99 (New York: SYDA Foundation, 1978).

17. Keith-Spiegel and Koocher 1985, 253.

18. Keith-Spiegel and Koocher 1985, 253.

19. Keith-Spiegel and Koocher 1985, 253.

20. Keith-Spiegel and Koocher 1985, 256.

21. Rachel Naomi Remen, *Kitchen Table Wisdom: Stories That Heal*, 49–50 (New York: Riverhead Books, 1996).

22. American College of Physicians, *Ethics Manual* (4th ed., 1999); available at <http://www.acponline.org/ethics/ethicsman.htm>.

23. American Chiropractic Association, *Code of Ethics*, Addendum (1998).

24. R. Davidhizar and J. N. Giger, "When Touch Is Not the Best Approach," 6 (3) *J. Clin. Nurs.* 203 (1997).

25. Keith-Spiegel and Koocher 1985, 261.

26. Barbara A. Brennan, *Light Emerging: The Journey of Personal Healing*, fig. 14–1 (New York: Bantam Books, 1993).

27. Barbara A. Brennan, *Hands of Light: A Guide to Healing Through the Human Energy Field* (New York: Bantam Books, 1988), fig. 11–2, 105.

28. Choa Kok Sui, *Pranic Healing*, 251 (York Beach, Maine: Samuel Weiser, 1990).

29. Krieger 1987, 77.

30. For the description as a natural state of expanded awareness, see Shafica Karagulla, *Breakthrough to Creativity: Your Higher Sense Perception* (Los Angeles: De Vorss, 1967).

For the description as heightened intuitive capacity, see, e.g., Anthony Fejfar, "A Road Less Traveled: Critical Realist Foundational Consciousness in Lawyering and Legal Education," 26 *Gonz. L. Rev.* 327, 332 (1990–91), which contrasts "synthetic relational intuitive understanding" with abstract or formal analytic understanding; and Joseph Goldstein, *The Experience of Insight: A Simple and Direct Guide to Buddhist Meditation*, 135 (Boston, Mass.: Shambhala Publications, 1987), which describes the experience of relating "without the boundaries of an image . . . [or] through the veil of concept."

For the description as using nonordinary states of consciousness to access information, see Todd Pressman, "The Therapeutic Potential of Non-ordinary States of Consciousness, as Explored in the Work of Stanislav Grof," 32 *J. Humanist Psych.* 8, 24 (winter 1993); see also W. Cowling, "Unitary Knowing in Nursing Practice," 6 (4) *Nurs. Sci. Q.* 201 (1993).

31. See, e.g., Michael Harner, *The Way of the Shaman* (New York: Harper and Row, 1990). Shamanistic cultures use the concept of "nonordinary reality" to explain subtle sense perception. The shaman is able to access nonordinary reality to restore missing parts of the client. For the shaman, both worlds—the ordinary and the nonordinary—are equally valid, and the shaman moves easily between the two.

32. Trance "is the state in which learning and openness to change are most likely to occur. It does not refer to an induced somnolent state . . . [but to] a natural state experienced by everyone" (Sidney Rosen, *My Voice Will Go with You: The Teachings of Milton H. Erickson*, 26 [New York: W. W. Norton and Co., 1982]). According to Rosen, daydreaming is the most familiar trance state, and other trance states occur during meditation, prayer, and exercise (such as jogging): "In these situations, a person is aware of the vividness of inner mental and sensory experiences, and external stimuli, such as sounds and movements, assume lesser importance" (id., 26–27).

33. For management, see Weston H. Agor, *Intuitive Management: Integrating Left and Right Brain Management Skills* (1984).

For philosophy, see, e.g., Henri Bergson, *The Creative Mind*, (New York: Carol Publishing Group, 1997) (reprinted).

34. Kok Sui 1990, 31.

35. Gopi Krishna, *Kundalini for the New Age: Selected Writings of Gopi Krishna*, ed. Gene Keffer, 94 (New York, Bantam Books, 1988).

36. In Eastern literature, subtle sight has been referred to as the opening of the "third eye," or the brow chakra. There are many scriptural references. For example, in the Bhagavad-Gita, when Arjuna, the charioteer, asks the Lord to reveal His cosmic form, the Lord replies, "But you are not able to see Me with your own eyes. I give to you a divine eye, behold My majestic power." Luke 11:34 states, "If therefore thine eye be single, thy whole body shall be full of light." In ancient Egypt, the eye of Horus symbolized the open brow chakra. In the United States, we have the remarkable image above the pyramid on the back of the dollar bill.

In his book *The Doors of Perception* (New York: Harper, 1954), Aldous Huxley remarks that if the "doors of perception" were opened, everything would be infinitely cleansed. Huxley was referring to his extraordinary perceptions after taking mescalin. Through the drug, Huxley entered the shaman's or healer's world of nonordinary reality. For most contemporary healers, subtle sense perception does not rely on the use of any stimulant.

37. See, e.g., Karagulla 1967; Leonard Laskow, *Healing With Love: A Breakthrough Mind/Body Medical Program for Healing Yourself and Others* (Mill Valley, Calif.: Wholeness Press, 1992).

38. See Lee Sannella, *The Kundalini Experience* (Lower Lake, Calif.: Integral

340 • Notes to Pages 191–201

Publishing, 1992), which chronicles case histories, summarizing signs and symptoms and relating awakening to psychological and spiritual transformation; Philip St. Romain, *Kundalini Energy and Christian Spirituality*, 19–23 (New York: Crossroads Publishing, 1991).

39. Brennan 1988, 50.

40. Robert S. DeRopp, *The Master Game: Pathways to Higher Consciousness beyond the Drug Experience*, 180, 183 (New York: Bantam Doubleday Dell Publishing Group, 1968).

41. DeRopp 1968, 183.

42. Concluding a discussion of the possible neurobiological basis for the placebo effect, researchers noted: "By the time we've reached a model that truly can account for all the things . . . it is no longer 'just' a neurobiological model. . . . It's something that integrates, that blurs what we consider to be the self 'inside' and the self 'outside.' And when a way of thinking like that is established, we won't be just doing neurobiology. We will be doing something new, something integrative that we can't yet fully imagine" (Stephen Kosslyn, quoted in Anne Harrington, "Placebo: Conversations at the Disciplinary Borders," in Anne Harrington, ed., *The Placebo Effect: An Interdisciplinary Exploration*, 249 [Cambridge: Harvard University Press, 1997]). The placebo is defined as "any therapy prescribed knowingly or unknowingly by a healer, or used by laymen, for its therapeutic effect on a symptom or disease, but which actually is ineffective or not specifically effective for the symptom or disorder being treated" (Arthur K. Shapiro and Elaine Shapiro, "The Placebo: Is It Much Ado about Nothing?" in Anne Harrington, ed., *The Placebo Effect: An Interdisciplinary Exploration*, 12 [Cambridge: Harvard University Press, 1997]).

43. The division of the healing process into effects of the self-healing process of the human body, nonspecific effects, and specific effects is artificial; nonspecific factors such as the doctor's white coat, the color of the medication, informed consent, and the expectations of provider and patient interact with specific factors (Jos Kleijnen and Anton J. M. de Craen, "The Importance of the Placebo Effect: A Proposal for Further Research," in Edzard Ernst, ed., *Complementary Medicine: An Objective Appraisal*, 36 [Oxford: Butterworth-Heineman, 1996]).

44. Brennan 1988, 201–50.

45. Brennan 1988, 40, 139.

46. See Cheryl Bender Birch, *Power Yoga*, 19–20 (New York: Fireside, 1995) 19–20; Swami Muktananda, *Play of Consciousness*, 32–33 (New York: SYDA Foundation, 1978).

47. Douglas R. Brooks, Swami Durgananda, Paul E. Muller-Ortega, William K. Mahony, Constantina Rhodes Bailly, and S. P. Sabharathnam, *Meditation Revolution: A History and Theology of the Siddha Yoga Lineage*, 502–3 (South Fallsburg, N.Y.: Agama Press, 1997) (citing sources).

48. Julie Motz, *Hands of Life* (New York: Bantam Books, 1998).

49. See, e.g., Swami Muktanada, *Kundalini Stavah* (Ganeshpuri, India: SYDA Foundation, 1980).

50. Ken Wilber has created one typology in his book *No Boundary* (Boston: Shambhala Publications, 1999). Carlos Warter creates a somewhat different typology in *Who Do You Think You Are? The Healing Power of Your Sacred Self,* 103 (New York: Bantam Books, 1998). Warter postulates a "healing pyramid." At its base is "earth medicine" (technology), consisting of allopathic, alternative, and integrative healing modalities; next comes "mind medicine" (awareness), representing self-empowerment and responsibility; next is "heart medicine" (heart consciousness), consisting of love, forgiveness, and understanding; then comes "sacred self medicine" (integrity; complete oneness), consisting of essential identity; and finally, "divine medicine," the uninterrupted awareness of "God as Love" (id., 103). Warter views the pyramidic shape as embodying a union of earth and space: "We see the energy of heaven streaming into the apex of love, while gravity grounds us securely on the earth" (id., 104). In this sense, his model resembles the chakra system, with the heart region serving as gateway between heaven and earth, cosmic and personal, infinite and finite, divine and human.

51. George Vithoulkas, *A New Model for Health and Disease,* 74–87 (Berkeley: North Atlantic Books, 1991).

52. Vithoulkas 1991.

53. See, e.g., Hilde Bruch, *Learning Psychotherapy: Rationale and Ground Rules* (Cambridge: Harvard University Press, 1974).

54. Brennan 1988, 230.

55. Brennan 1988.

56. Brennan 1988, 199.

57. Mark 1:26.

58. Brennan 1988, 201–50.

59. Ashley Montagu, *Touching: The Human Significance of the Skin,* 1 (2d ed., New York: Harper and Row, 1978).

60. Montagu 1978, 315–16. He adds: "The raw sensation of touch as stimulus is vitally necessary for the physical survival of the physical organism. In that sense it may be postulated that the need for tactile stimulation must be added to the repertoire of basic needs in all vertebrates, if not in all invertebrates as well. . . . As we have seen . . . different cultures vary in both the manner in which they express the need for tactile stimulation and the manner in which they satisfy it. But the need is universal and is everywhere the same, though the form of its satisfaction may vary according to time and place" (id., 317).

Chapter 6

1. Benedict M. Ashley and Kevin D. O'Rourke, *Healthcare Ethics: A Theological Analysis,* 10 (St. Louis: The Catholic Health Association of the United States 2d ed. 1994).

2. See, e.g., NY CLS Penal § 165.35 ("A person is guilty of fortune telling when, for a fee or compensation which he directly or indirectly solicits or

receives, he claims or pretends to tell fortunes, or holds himself out as being able, by claimed or pretended use of occult powers, to answer questions or give advice on personal matters or to exorcise, influence or affect evil spirits or curses; except that this section does not apply to a person who engages in the aforedescribed conduct as part of a show or exhibition solely for the purpose of entertainment or amusement. Fortune telling is a class B misdemeanor"); Mass. Ann. Laws ch. 140, § 185I ("No person shall tell fortunes for money unless a license therefore has been issued by the local licensing authority. Said license shall be granted only to applicants who have resided continuously in the city or town in which the license is sought for at least twelve months immediately preceding the date of the application. No such license shall be transferred or assigned. Unless otherwise established in a town by town meeting action and in a city by city council action, and in a town with no town meeting by town council action, by adoption of appropriate by-laws and ordinances to set such fees, the fee for each license granted under this section shall be two dollars, but in no event shall any such fee be greater than fifty dollars. Whoever tells fortunes for money unless licensed under this section shall be punished by a fine of not more than one hundred dollars"); N.C. Gen. Stat. § 14–401.5 ("It shall be unlawful for any person to practice the arts of phrenology, palmistry, clairvoyance, fortune telling and other crafts of a similar kind in the counties named herein. Any person violating any provision of this section shall be guilty of a Class 2 misdemeanor. This section shall not prohibit the amateur practice of phrenology, palmistry, fortune telling or clairvoyance in connection with school or church socials, provided such socials are held in school or church buildings").

3. Matthew 17:1–2.

4. Matthew 10:1.

5. "Through . . . advanced practices . . . accomplished practitioners can bring their lives to an extraordinary and triumphant end. As they die, they enable their body to be reabsorbed back into the light essence of the elements that created it, and consequently their material body dissolves into light and then disappears completely. This process is known as the 'rainbow body' or 'body of light,' because the dissolution is often accompanied by spontaneous manifestations of light and rainbows" (Sogyal Rinpoche, *The Tibetan Book of Living and Dying*, 167–68 [San Francisco: Harper, 1992]).

6. See *Tarasoff v. Regents of the University of California*, 551 P.2d 334 (Cal. 1976) (holding that a therapist treating a mentally ill patient owes a duty of reasonable care to warn threatened persons against a foreseeable danger created by the patient's condition).

7. Joseph Campbell, *The Hero with a Thousand Faces*, 3 (2d ed., Princeton: Princeton University Press, 1968).

8. Howard Brody, *The Healer's Power*, 20 (New Haven: Yale University Press, 1992).

9. Brody 1992, 30. Brody draws material from Samuel Shem's novel about an intern's life in a modern hospital, an institution Shem ironically calls *The*

House of God (New York: Dell, 1978). According to Brody, in the novel, "the interns are placed in a fundamentally inhumane situation without any power over their destinies. Their patients are really their fellow victims; but to feel this kinship fully would be to admit in a terribly painful way both their own powerlessness in their own vulnerability to aging and death. Their only way (they think) to avoid feeling victimized and helpless is to avoid identifying with the patients, to see the patients instead as their tormentors and then to unleash their angry humor at the patients" (Brody 1992, 25).

10. Brody 1992, 30–31.

11. Brody 1992, 30.

12. Carl G. Jung, "On the Nature of the Psyche" in Violet S. de Laszlo, ed., *The Basic Writings of C. G. Jung*, 78 (New York: The Modern Library, 1959).

13. Carl G. Jung, "Archetypes of the Collective Unconscious, " in Violet S. de Laszlo, ed., *The Basic Writings of C. G. Jung*, 315 (New York: The Modern Library, 1959).

14. Jung 1959 ("Archetypes"), 316.

15. Jung 1959 ("Archetypes"), 305.

16. Robert Bly, *A Little Book on the Human Shadow*, 7 (New York: Harper-Collins, 1988).

17. Bly 1988, 26.

18. See Ted Kaptchuk, "Varieties of Medical Pluralism," 135 (3) *Ann. Int. Med.* 189–95 (2001).

19. Rinpoche 1992, 120.

20. Bly 1988, 53.

21. Brody 1992, 36, 42, 65.

22. Brennan 1988, 104–6.

23. Brennan 1988, 104–6.

24. Brennan 1988, 104–6.

25. The story may be apocryphal, but it is described in Trevor Ravenscroft, *Spear of Destiny* (York Beach, Maine: Samuel Weiser, 1987).

26. *Mahabharata*, trans. Smt. Kamala Subramaniam (Bombay: Siddhi Printers, 1995).

27. Elaine Pagels, *The Origin of Satan*, 14 (New York: Vintage Books, 1995).

28. Revelations 13:13–14.

29. Exodus 7:8–12.

30. Bly 1988, 53.

31. John C. Pierrakos, *Core Energetics: Developing the Capacity to Love and Heal*, 148–55 (Mendocino: LifeRhythm, 1987).

32. Brody 1992, 263. He also argues that this would make a "litany of rules and rights" unnecessary (id.). From another perspective, Brody calls explicitly for greater conversation about "virtue" in bioethics. Such discussion means that "one is no longer occupied solely with discrete problems and resolutions but also with 'practices' as organized, evolving forms of human excellence and with the internal standards that inform such practices" (id., 253). Brody observes that the list of "humanistic qualities" identified by the American

Board of Internal Medicine (which includes integrity, respect, and compassion) if taken seriously "would call for a wholesale housecleaning in many traditional residency programs" (id., 254–55).

33. I Corinthians 12:7–10.

34. I Corinthians 3:18, 21; 8:1–2.

35. I Corinthians 13:13.

36. II Corinthians 12:7.

37. Detailed legal analyses of some of the risks and potential practice pitfalls engendered by the various layers of the so-called Stark statutes and regulations can be found at <http://www.kutakrock.com> or in briefing papers published by Emord and Associates, available through the law firm's Website, at <http://www.emord.com>.

38. Patricia Keith-Spiegel and Gerald P. Koocher, *Ethics in Psychology: Professional Standards and Cases*, 29 (New York: McGraw-Hill, 1985).

39. Barbara A. Brennan, *Hands of Light: A Guide to Healing through the Human Energy Field*, 75 (New York: Bantam Books, 1998); Brennan, 1993, Fig. 15–12.

40. See, e.g., R. D. Laing, *The Politics of Experience and the Bird of Paradise* (New York: Penguin, 1967).

41. Another explanation as to why some individuals and not others develop highly refined high sense perception is that such acute sensitivities develop in individuals who are forced, as a result of family dynamics, to develop "hyper-vigilance." That is, because of the perception of imminent infliction of physical or emotional distress, such individuals learn to monitor the subtle behavioral cues in family members that will signal a threatening situation; simultaneously, they learn to "leave their bodies" and gain information from nonordinary realms of reality about potential dangers. These realms also provide a haven—a place of safety—when the physical world is dangerous; healers thus acquire a highly developed ability to soothe themselves through contact with such realms. This may help explain some of the early psychopathology underlying the development of intuitive abilities, but as William James observed, mystical experiences should be explored in their own right, and not dismissed as psychopathology.

42. See, e.g., Darrel Irving, *Serpent of Fire: A Modern View of Kundalini* (York Beach, Maine: Samuel Weiser, 1995).

43. Roslyn Bruyere, *Wheels of Light: A Study of the Chakras*, 1:163 (Sierra Madre, Calif.: Bon Productions, 1991).

44. Brihadaranyaka, in Swami Prabhavananda and Frederick Manchester, trans., *The Upanishads: Breath of the Eternal*, 131 (Hollywood: Vedanta Press, 1975).

45. Roberto Assagioli, *Psychosynthesis*, 98 (New York: Viking Press, 1971).

46. Assagioli 1971, 98–99.

47. Barbara Carston, "If No One Has Linked You to a Prayer Chain, Count Your Blessings: People with Problems Can Find Their Names and Woes Aired on Well-Meaning Web Sites," *Wall Street Journal*, A1, column 4 (Mar. 7, 2001).

48. Frieda Fromm-Reichmann, *Principles of Intensive Psychotherapy*, 34 (Chicago: University of Chicago Press, 1960). Fromm-Reichmann defines

"mature love" as "the state of interpersonal relatedness in which one is as concerned with the growth, maturation, welfare, and happiness of the beloved person as one is with one's own," a capacity that "presupposes the development of a healthy and stable self-respect" (id.). She equates self-realization with self-actualization, referring to "a person's use of his talents, skills and powers . . . to reach out for and to find fulfilment of his needs for satisfaction and security, as far as they can be attained without interfering with the law or the needs of his fellow-men" (id., 34–35).

49. Fromm-Reichman 1960, 36. The author adds that it would be easy for the therapist "to feel flattered by the patients' trust and dependence rather than to remain alert to the fact that their insecurity, hence overdependence, is part of the disturbance for which they seek treatment."

50. Fromm-Reichman 1960, 41.

51. Fromm-Reichman 1960, 42.

52. Keith-Spiegel and Koocher 1985, 41–43.

53. Deuteronomy 18:11; Leviticus 20:27; Isaiah 8:19; and 1 Samuel 28:7, quoted in Simcha Paull Raphael, *Jewish Views of the Afterlife*, 50–51 (Northvale, N.J.: Jason Aronson, 1994). The term *baalat eishet ob* literally means "a woman who has mastery over a ghost" (id.).

54. Brody 1992, 266.

55. Brody 1992, 263–64.

56. Keith-Spiegel and Koocher 1985, 46.

Chapter 7

1. Tom L. Beauchamp and James F. Childress, *Principles of Biomedical Ethics*, 37, 47–100 (4th ed., New York: Oxford University Press, 1994).

2. Beauchamp and Childress 1994, 44–46.

3. Beauchamp and Childress 1994, 47.

4. Bonnie Blair O'Connor, *Healing Traditions: Alternative Medicine and the Health Professions*, 184–85 (Philadelphia: University of Pennsylvania Press, 1995).

5. O'Connor 1995, 184.

6. Michael H. Cohen, *Beyond Complementary Medicine: Legal and Ethical Perspectives on Health Care and Human Evolution*, 159 (Ann Arbor: University of Michigan Press, 2000).

7. "That is why it is called Babel, because the Lord there made a babble of the language of all the world" (Genesis 11:5–9).

8. See, e.g., Richard Dixon, *On the Difference between Physician-Assisted Suicide and Active Euthanasia*, Hastings Center Report 28 (5), 25–29 (1998).

9. Sogyal Rinpoche, *The Tibetan Book of Living and Dying*, 185 (San Francisco: Harper, 1992).

10. American Academy of Pediatrics, "Palliative Care for Children," 106 *Pediatrics* 351–57 (2000).

11. Rinpoche 1992, 186.

12. Rinpoche 1992, 209.

13. Rinpoche 1992.

14. See also Cohen 2000, 71–87.

15. American College of Physicians, *Ethics Manual* (4th ed.); available at <http://www.acponline.org/ethics/ethicsman.htm>.

16. Margaret Pabst Battin, *The Least Worst Death: Essays in Bioethics on the End of Life*, 93 (New York: Oxford University Press, 1994).

17. Daniel Callahan, *Pursuing a Peaceful Death*, Hastings Center Report 23 (4), 33, 34 (1993).

18. Brennan 1988, 67.

19. Brennan 1988, 69.

20. Brennan 1988.

21. A similar description of separation and disintegration of the lower energy bodies at death is given by Shafica Karagulla and Dora van Gelder Kunz, *The Chakras and the Human Energy Fields*, 38 (Wheaton, Ill.: The Theosophical Publishing House, 1989).

22. Simcha Paull Raphael, *Jewish Views of the Afterlife* (Northvale, N.J.: Jason Aronson, 1994).

23. Raphael 1994, 56 (citing Genesis 2:7; Leviticus 21:11; and Numbers 6:6).

24. Raphael 1994, 121–40, 132.

25. Raphael 1994, 286–98.

26. Raphael 1994, 295–96 (citing Lama Lodru, *Bardo Teachings: The Tibetan Way of Death and Rebirth*, 3 [Boulder, Colo.: Karma Dawa Tashi, 1979]).

27. Berakhot 8a, quoted in Raphael 1994, 286.

28. Raphael 1994, 370.

29. Raphael 1994, 372–80.

30. Raphael 1994, 379.

31. Raphael 1994, 385.

32. Raphael 1994, 385.

33. Raphael 1994, 386.

34. Raphael 1994, 393–94.

35. Louis Ginzberg, ed., *Legends of the Jews*, trans. Henrietta Szold, 1:57–58 (Philadelphia: Jewish Publication Society, 1967–69), quoted in Raphael 1994, 393–94 (also citing original sources).

36. For stories of prebirth consciousness, see <http://www.spiritweb.org /Spirit/prebirth-communication-danna.html>.

37. Barbara Brennan, *Light Emerging: The Journey of Personal Healing*, 75–76 (New York: Bantam Books, 1993).

38. Susan Renkel, R.N., personal communication (May 3, 1995).

39. Chris Griscom, *Feminine Fusion: The Power to Transform Strength with Sensitivity, Logic with Intuition, and Sexuality with Spirituality*, 109 (New York: Fireside, 1991).

40. Griscom 1991, 109–10.

41. Raphael 1994, 386.

42. Raphael 1994, 384.

43. Raphael 1994, 385–86.

44. Brennan 1988, 68.

45. Brennan 1988.

46. Brennan 1988, 69.

47. Zohar I, 218b, quoted in Raphael 1994, 378.

48. Raphael 1994, 378 (citing Ken Wilber, "Death, Rebirth and Meditation," in Gary Doore, ed., *What Survives: Contemporary Explanations of Life After Death* (Los Angeles: J. P. Tarcher, 1990, 179–84); see also Stanislov Grof and Christina Grof, *Beyond Death: The Gates of Consciousness* (New York: Thames and Hudson, 1980).

49. Raphael 1994, 378–79.

50. Brennan 1988, 68.

51. See Brennan 1988, 219.

52. Raphael 1994, 375.

53. William James, *The Varieties of Religious Experience*, 34 (New York: New American Library, 1958), quoted in Andrew R. Fuller, *Psychology and Religion: Eight Points of View*, 11 (London: Rowman and Littlefield Publishers, 1994).

54. James 1958, 58–61, quoted in Fuller 1994, 15.

55. See, e.g., Cohen 2000, 129–31.

56. Swami Kripananda, *Jnaneshwar's Gita: A Rendering of the Jnaneshwari*, 160–63 (Albany, SUNY Press, 1989) (rendering Bhagavad-Gita, chap. 11, v. 25–30).

57. Kripananda 1989, 18 (rendering Bhagavad-Gita, chap. 1, v. 11–12).

58. Kripananda 1989, 174 (rendering Bhagavad-Gita, chap. 11, v. 55).

Chapter 8

1. "Report of the Ethics Committee of the American Fertility Society," 53 (6) *J. Am. Fertility Soc.* 345–55 (1990), quoted in *Davis v. Davis*, 842 S.W.2d 588, 5940596 (Tenn. 1992).

2. The quotation is from William Walters, "Selective Termination in Multiple Pregnancy," 152 *Med. J. Australia* 451, 452 (May 7, 1990).

3. Bonnie Blair O'Connor, *Healing Traditions: Alternative Medicine and the Health Professions*, 185 (Philadelphia: University of Pennsylvania Press, 1995).

4. *Roe v. Wade*, 410 U.S. 113 (1973).

5. *Planned Parenthood of Southeast Pennsylvania v. Casey*, 505 U.S. 83 (1992).

6. *Davis v. Davis*, 842 S.W.2d 588 (Tenn. 1992).

7. *Davis v. Davis*, 842 S.W.2d 594–96.

8. See, e.g., Dena S. Davis, "Informed Consent for Stem Cell Research Using Frozen Embryos," *Lahey Clinic Medical Ethics Newsletter* 4 (spring 2001).

9. CNN, "NIH Seeks More Stem Cell Research," (July 18, 2001); available at <http://europe.cnn.com/2001/HEALTH/07/18/stem.cell/>.

10. Barbara A. Brennan, *Hands of Light: A Guide to Healing through the Human*

Energy Field 219–30 (New York: Bantam Books, 1998).

11. See Michael H. Cohen, *Beyond Complementary Medicine: Legal and Ethical Perspectives on Health Care and Human Evolution,* 159–66 (Ann Arbor: University of Michigan Press, 2000).

12. Diane Beeson, "Social and Ethical Challenges of Prenatal Diagnosis," *Lahey Clinic Medical Ethics Newsletter* 1 (winter 2001).

13. Beeson 2001.

14. See the discussion of relationship cords, infra.

15. Ellen M. McGee and Gerald Q. Maguire, "Implantable Brain Chips: Ethical and Policy Issues," *Lahey Clinic Medical Ethics Newsletter* 2 (winter 2000).

16. The United Kingdom's previous approval of use of embryos up to fourteen days old for very narrowly defined research purposes has been widened to embrace a variety of other potential research and development uses. See Susan Mayor, "House of Lords Supports Human Embryonic Stem Cell Research," 27 (322) *BMJ* 189 (2001).

17. See, e.g., Robert J. Levine, *Ethics and Regulation of Clinical Research,* 313 (2d ed., New Haven: Yale University Press, 1986).

18. Cohen 2000, 160.

19. See Julie Motz, *Hands of Life* (New York: Bantam Books, 1998).

20. Stephen G. Post, *Inquiries in Bioethics,* 173 (Washington, D.C.: Georgetown University Press, 1993).

21. Post 1993, 166.

22. Thomas Kuhn, *The Structure of Scientific Revolutions* (Chicago: University of Chicago Press, 1970).

23. Kuhn 1970.

24. See Michael H. Cohen, *Complementary and Alternative Medicine: Legal Boundaries and Regulatory Perspectives,* 29–31 (Baltimore: Johns Hopkins University Press, 1998).

25. See Cohen 2000, 87–95.

26. See, e.g., the Kentucky Board of Medical Licensure, *Board Policy Statement on Complementary and Alternative Medical Therapies* (1999).

27. David Casarett, Jean Kutner, and Janet Abrahm, "Life After Death: A Practical Approach to Grief and Bereavement," 134 (3) *Ann. Int. Med.* 208–15 (2001).

28. Casarett, Kutner, and Abrahm 2001.

29. Post 1993, 57.

30. Post 1993, 57.

31. Post 1993, 57.

32. See Cohen 2000, 186, n. 30; D.C. Code s. 2–3301.4(d)(1).

33. *Diagnostic and Statistical Manual of Mental Disorders* (Third Edition-Revised) (Washington, D.C.: American Psychiatric Association, 1987), quoted in Post 1993, 57.

34. Post 1993, 58.

35. Post 1993, 58.

36. Post 1993, 58.

37. Post 1993, 59 (citing American Psychiatric Association Task Force, *Report*

10: *Psychiatrists' Viewpoints on Religion and Their Services to Religious Institutions and the Ministry* [Washington, D.C.: American Psychiatric Association, 1975]).

38. Post 1993, 59.

39. Post 1993, 75.

40. Barbara Brennan, *Light Emerging: The Journey of Personal Healing*, 184 (New York: Bantam Books, 1993).

41. Barbara Brennan, lecture (July 21, 2001, Boston, Mass.).

42. Sandra Ingerman, *Soul Retrieval: Mending the Fragmented Self*, 90 (San Francisco: Harper, 1991).

43. Brennan 1988, 63–65.

44. Brennan 1988, 63–65.

Conclusion

1. Michael H. Cohen, *Complementary and Alternative Medicine: Legal Boundaries and Regulatory Perspectives*, 112 (Baltimore: Johns Hopkins University Press, 1998).

2. Barbara A. Brennan, *Hands of Light: A Guide to Healing through the Human Energy Field*, 142–43 (New York: Bantam Books, 1998).

3. Cohen 1998, 112.

4. David M. Eisenberg, Michael H. Cohen, Andrea Hrbek, John Grayzel, Maria van Rompay, and Richard M. Cooper, "Credentialing Complementary and Alternative Medical Providers," *Ann. Int. Med.* (in press, 2002).

5. Robert A. Hahn, "A Socialcultural Model of Illness and Healing," in *Placebo: Theory, Research, and Mechanisms*, ed. Leonard White, Bernard Tursky, and Gary E. Schwartz, 167–95 (New York: The Guilford Press, 1985).

6. Recently, this has been questioned. See Asbjorn Hrobjartsson and Peter C. Gotzsche, "Is the Placebo Powerless? An Analysis of Clinical Trials Comparing Placebo with No Treatment," 344 (21) *N. Eng. J. Med.* 1594–1602 (2001).

7. See Jay Katz, *The Silent World of Doctor and Patient* (New York: Free Press, 1994).

8. Cohen 1998, 54–55.

9. Cohen 1998, 22–23.

10. George Vithoulkas, *A New Model for Health and Disease*, 90 (Berkeley: North Atlantic Books, 1991).

11. Vithoulkas 1991.

12. Robert A. Johnson, *He: Understanding Masculine Psychology*, 45 (New York: Harper and Row, 1989).

13. Johnson 1989, 45–46, 51–52.

14. Johnson 1989, 51–52.

15. Johnson 1989, 78.

16. Johnson 1989, 79, 82.

17. *Mahabharata*, trans. Kamala Subramaniam, 241–50 (Bombay: Siddh Printers, 1995).

18. Mahabharata 1995, 224.

19. Michael H. Cohen, answer to the question, "When Is It Ethical to Offer Patients Complementary and Alternative Therapies?" (Philadelphia: University of Pennsylvania School of Medicine, conference, 1999).

20. Sandra Ingerman, *Soul Retrieval: Mending the Fragmented Self*, 1 (San Francisco: Harper, 1991).

21. Ingerman 1991, 3–17.

22. Ingerman 1991, 21.

23. William James, *The Varieties of Religious Experience*, 277 (New York: New American Library, 1958), quoted in Andrew R. Fuller, *Psychology and Religion: Eight Points of View*, 22 (London: Rowman and Littlefield Publishers, 1994).

24. James 1958, quoted in Fuller 1994.

25. James 1958, quoted in Fuller 1994.

Index